Location
and
Space-Economy

THE REGIONAL SCIENCE STUDIES SERIES
edited by Walter Isard

Location
and
Space-Economy

A General Theory Relating to Industrial Location,
Market Areas, Land Use, Trade,
and Urban Structure

WALTER ISARD

 The M.I.T. Press
Massachusetts Institute of Technology
Cambridge, Massachusetts, and London, England

Second printing, June 1960
Third printing, November 1962
Fourth printing, September 1965
Fifth printing, October 1967
Sixth printing, June 1968
First MIT Press paperback printing, April 1972

ISBN 262 09001 5 (hardcover)

ISBN 262 59005 0 (paperback)

Library of Congress Catalog Card Number: 56-11026

Printed in the United States of America

To
Alvin H. Hansen
and
Abbott P. Usher

Preface

Over the historical record, the process of social development and economic growth has been for the most part cumulative though at times seemingly erratic. On occasion it has been recessive. Some of its stages have been forced to start at their origins more than once. Moreover, these stages have started independently at diverse places on the earth at different times. Together with the manifold cultural, political, social, and economic forces which have evolved this fact has led, over the centuries, to marked regional differentiations and to tremendous disparities in the welfare of the peoples of the several regions of the world.

Such a record of man's adaptation to, and interaction with, his physical environment suggests that a comprehensive theory of society or economy should embrace both time and space dimensions. It should be able to unravel the dynamic interplay of forces not only currently but also over the long past. Its propositions should be testable against the background of historic development in the several regions of the world and concomitantly should offer explanation of this development. Its hypotheses should encompass the influence of past events and intermingling of forces upon existing economic and social structure and conditions. Ideally, its conceptual framework should enable one to anticipate the course of future development, given certain premises and judgments.

Unhappily, the state of the social science disciplines leaves very much to be desired in the way of achieving such a comprehensive theory. The dynamic frameworks of these disciplines, frameworks which are designed to catch the effect of what some characterize as the "time variable," are rather crude and even at times naive. Still more so are their spatial and regional frameworks.

It is the basic objective of this volume to improve the spatial and regional frameworks of the social science disciplines, particularly of economics, through the development of a more adequate general theory of location and space-economy. As a matter of course, we must work within the setting of dynamic techniques and frameworks currently available. Since these are inadequate, a chief limitation of this volume is its inability to cope satisfactorily with the development process over time.

Another limitation is imposed by the inherent weaknesses of general theories. General theories have a widespread reputation for being sterile in terms of concrete social problems and related policy recommendations. As one critic has put it, we "are all too apt, seizing upon the conditions of a particular period of time *and extent of space* and applying the simplifying processes of selection and emphasis to which economic theorizing seems all too prone, to come forth with a system of universalized 'laws,' a system which is perhaps not implausible at its time *and place* of origin, but which, as it becomes increasingly concerned about the consistency of its internal logic, turns in upon itself, and grows more and more remote from reality."[1]

Admittedly the general theory of location and space-economy evolved in this volume is of little direct utility for handling specific problems of reality. That it should be of immediate relevance was not the author's intention. But as one proceeds to the materials to be contained in a second volume,[2] where less general and more useful theoretical frameworks are developed, he may perceive how the general principles and constructs derived in this volume are of use in furnishing penetrating insights into the operation of economic processes in the real world. Also, they facilitate the choice of those structural relations subject to empirical estimation which are the more significant ones for analytic purposes. At least the author has found the general statement of conditions of equilibrium extremely helpful as a background against which various location and spatial doctrines could be contrasted and

[1] John H. Williams, "An Economist's Confessions," *The American Economic Review*, XLII, March 1952, pp. 6–7. The words in italics have been inserted by the author.

Significant, however, is Professor Williams' willingness to attribute some significance to Keynes' remark that without theory we are "lost in the woods" (*ibid.*, p. 23).

[2] For some details on the contents of this second volume, see pp. x–xi.

subsequently ordered and evaluated according to content. This eased the process of digestion, enabling the author to achieve for himself an improved and less confusing reformulation of ideas. It also provided a sharper conception of the manifold spatial processes at play and the manner in which individual ones are related to each other and to the array as a whole.

Still another serious limitation of the analysis is to be noted. A presentation of conditions of equilibrium in a theoretical system may seem to imply a tendency toward the attainment of a state of equilibrium in the real world. But in a full historic sense, actual economic life never does realize a state of equilibrium. There are always changes impinging upon the economy. The process of adjustment is constantly in operation. Witness, for example, the adaptation of population to environment. There has never been a complete adjustment which might be said to characterize an optimum or equilibrium spatial distribution of population.

As Usher has neatly put it,

"Classical and neo-classical theory rest upon a concept of equilibrium that becomes a source of serious difficulty in historical analysis. It is implied that disturbances of the socio-economic equilibrium are small in magnitude and quickly corrected by adaptive changes. Such disturbances do exist, and market processes have developed that deal with some measure of adequacy with these minor disturbances of the equilibrium. But these are not the only disturbances that occur in the socio-economic world. The world economy is beset by other disturbances, whose magnitude is of such an order that adjustments require several generations. . ." [3]

"The most dangerous of all transfers of the equilibrium concept appears when the ideal of stability is represented as a characteristic of long-run conditions. All the data of history show that the empirical phenomena are dynamic, and that for the world economy as a whole secular change is positive; in some periods, the rates of growth are not large; in particular regions contraction may occur over substantial periods of time. Whether it be growth, or cumulative change that may be classed as progress, secular change cannot be described as a condition of equilibrium." [4]

Despite the disrupting effects of technological advance and other dynamic phenomena and the consequent failure to attain equilibrium in the secular sense,[5] there is still value in equilibrium analysis. It is

[3] Abbott P. Usher, "The Pattern of the World Economy," unpublished essay, pp. 10–11.

[4] *Ibid.*, p. 17. These statements were written in the 1930's, and should be modified somewhat in view of subsequent developments in equilibrium analysis.

[5] Usher's thesis is of broader content. Its more extensive ramifications are worth noting here. In Usher's words:

"The broad elements of differentiation among societies in their various historical worlds rest on differences in the maturity of settlement of the various

thought pertinent and worthwhile by some who conceive of the socio-economic system as a body tending toward a moving equilibrium and by others who find in equilibrium analysis categories of reference with which the extent of disequilibrium can be measured. Most important, equilibrium analysis is valuable because it enables one to grasp better the laws of change and the workings of a system. In doing so, it necessarily casts light upon the long-run interaction of diverse forces and can yield valuable insights for historical trend projection in any concrete situation.[6]

As the reader will quickly perceive, the first and third chapters of this volume were designed for a book which would encompass a broader field than is actually covered. The initial plan was to devote a considerable part of this volume to regional analysis. However, as the structure of the manuscript took form, it became advisable, in view of the quantity of materials to be developed, to present the materials in two volumes. During the next years therefore a companion volume will be prepared which will treat the principles of regional science and general regional theory. (The impatient reader may glean some of the contents of this second volume from the articles cited below.[7]) Together these two volumes will form a unit, to which the first and third chapters of this first completed volume relate.

---

regions, differences in culture, differences in technical knowledge, differences in the material resources of the region. Much theoretical discussion presumes that the first three classes of differences will be progressively equalized by the diffusion of population, culture, and technical skills. Some even presume that differentiation of material resources becomes less and less important as technical knowledge progresses. . ."

"There is nothing in the historical record to warrant the presumption that the elements of difference have diminished significantly in intensity. Changes of great importance have occurred, but it would not be difficult to defend the proposition that the world of effective contacts at the present time is more highly differentiated than the world as known to the Romans of the Augustan age, or the world of the third century A.D." (*Ibid.*, p. 4.)

". . . it must be evident that the discovery of means of utilizing new materials merely sets new limits to the scarcities that dominate our social life. The unbalanced and unequal distribution of material resources must always leave us with a world pattern of unequal and unbalanced distribution of the resources of primary importance to social life. Regional differentiation will remain important however much the specific patterns of distribution may be changed by new discoveries and new technologies." (*Ibid.*, pp 7–8)

[6] For example, concentration upon substitution among transport inputs along the lines of classical and neoclassical equilibrium analysis to be discussed in a subsequent chapter yields a framework for partially explaining not only the current locational pattern of the iron and steel industry but also the changing historical pattern over the last two centuries.

[7] The author's writings, which contain materials to be incorporated and further

The writing of this volume was begun some ten years ago. Consequently, certain materials may seem a bit dated. In particular, Chap. 2, which was largely completed by 1947, points up an imbalance in the Anglo-Saxon literature which during recent years has been somewhat corrected. Nonetheless, the earlier statements have not been qualified or tempered. The sharp criticism and emphasis of these statements are retained in order not to lose whatever potency and vigor the argument as first developed may have contained.

In the light of this partial correction of the imbalance in the Anglo-Saxon literature, I have changed my terminology, for which I must apologize. In previous writings the movement of a unit weight of a particular commodity over a unit of distance was defined as a *distance input*. Such a movement could also have been defined as a *transport input*. This latter term would have been more in keeping with the existing usage of words. However, given the neglect by economic theorists of the distance variable and role of space, it was decided in these early writings to use the term distance inputs. This was judged desirable in order to make as *explicit* as possible the significance of transport costs and the distance factor in shaping economic phenomena.

---

expanded in this volume, are in chronological order of development: "Interregional and Regional Input-Output Analysis: A Model of a Space-Economy," *Review of Economics and Statistics*, Vol. 33 (November 1951), pp. 318–328; "Regional and National Product Projections and Their Interrelations" (with G. Freutel), *Long-Range Economic Projection*, National Bureau of Economic Research, Studies in Income and Wealth, Vol. 16, Princeton University Press, Princeton, 1954, pp. 427–471; "Some Empirical Results and Problems of Regional Input-Output Analysis," in Leontief *et al.*, *Studies in the Structure of the American Economy*, Oxford University Press, New York, 1953, pp. 116–181; "Some Emerging Concepts and Techniques for Regional Analysis," *Zeitschrift für die Gesamte Staatswissenschaft*, Vol. 109 (1953), pp. 240–250; "Regional Commodity Balances and Interregional Commodity Flows," *Papers and Proceedings of the American Economic Association*, Vol. 43 (May 1953), pp. 167–180; "The Impact of Steel upon the Greater New York-Philadelphia Industrial Region: A Study in Agglomeration Projection" (with R. E. Kuenne), *Review of Economics and Statistics*, Vol. 35 (November 1953), pp. 289–301; "Location Theory and Trade Theory: Short-run Analysis," *Quarterly Journal of Economics*, Vol. 68 (May 1954), pp. 305–320; "Economic Structural Interrelations of Metropolitan Regions" (with R. Kavesh), *American Journal of Sociology*, Vol. 60 (September 1954), pp. 152–162; "Industrial Complex Analysis and Regional Development with Particular Reference to Puerto Rico" (with T. Vietorisz), Abstract in *Papers and Proceedings of the Regional Science Association*, Vol. 1 (1955); "The Value of the Regional Approach in Economic Analysis," *Regional Income*, National Bureau of Economic Research, Studies in Income and Wealth, Vol. 21, Princeton University Press, Princeton, 1956; "Regional Science, The Concept of Region, and Regional Structure," *Papers and Proceedings of the Regional Science Association*, Vol. 2 (1956), pp. 13–26; and an extensive manuscript on tools and techniques of regional analysis to be published by Resources for the Future, Inc.

Now that economists are more aware of the space axis and the spatial aspects of their subject matter, it seems appropriate to employ the more customary terminology of *transport inputs*, particularly in order to facilitate interdisciplinary exchange of knowledge, ideas, and techniques of analysis in the broad field of regional and area studies.

I am indebted to a host of individuals, each of whom has contributed in one way or other to the writing and preparation of this volume. The major influence of one of the two outstanding economists and personalities to whom this book is dedicated is immediately apparent in the first few sentences of the Preface. Professor Abbott P. Usher has been a constant source of inspiration. His ever-present encouragement and guidance and his vast fund of knowledge, which was always generously made available, have been invaluable in the development of ideas.

An equally strong influence stems from the teachings and writings of Professor Alvin H. Hansen. The tremendous stimulation derived from discussions with Professor Hansen, especially in the formative stages of this study, cleared the way of obstacles which often beset an attempt at general theorizing. His persistent urgings to make bold and creative attacks upon problems have added immeasurably to the contents of the volume.

My wife has given freely of her time and patience in the preparation of this volume. She has assisted not only in the presentation of ideas but also in their logical derivation.

Many others—former teachers, graduate students, and associates— have been helpful in diverse ways. At the risk of failing to mention all who deserve such mention, I gratefully acknowledge the help of Joseph Airov, Martin J. Beckmann, John F. Bell, Edward H. Chamberlin, Edgar Dunn, Guy Freutel, Gottfried von Haberler, Seymour E. Harris, Edgar M. Hoover, Robert Kavesh, John Kimber, Robert E. Kuenne, Sven Laursen, Wassily W. Leontief, Fritz Machlup, Russell Mack, Leon Moses, C. Reinold Noyes, Merton J. Peck, Winfield Riefler, Paul A. Samuelson, Eugene Schooler, Benjamin Stevens, Edward L. Ullman, and Thomas Vietorisz.

Gerald A. P. Carrothers has rendered invaluable service in the construction of the figures; and Richard Pfister, in the development of the index. I am indebted to Alexia Hanitsch and Gabrielle Fuchs for competent secretarial assistance.

The Harvard University Press, the Yale University Press, Richard D. Irwin, Inc., the Addison-Wesley Publishing Company, Inc., and the editors of the *Quarterly Journal of Economics, Econometrica*, and *Metroeconomica* have kindly granted permission to use previously published materials in direct or amended form. Chapters 2, 4, 9, and parts of Chap. 5 are largely drawn from articles appearing in the November 1949, May 1951, February 1954, and August 1951 issues, respectively, of the *Quarterly Journal of Economics*. Some materials from these articles also appear in other chapters of this book. Chapter 10 is a splicing of two articles, one of which appeared in *Econometrica*, Vol. 20, No. 3, July 1952, and the other in *Metroeconomica*, Vol. 5, No. 1, April 1953.

I am grateful to the Social Science Research Council for a post-doctoral fellowship which enabled me to initiate the development of this general theory. The writing of the final chapters, the construction of the index, and the completion of this book has been facilitated by a grant from Resources for the Future, Inc.

WALTER ISARD

Cambridge, Massachusetts
September, 1956

Contents

CONTENTS

List of Figures

Chapter 1

Introduction:
Posing the Location
and Regional Problem

In this chapter, we wish to paint broadly the location and regional problem, especially for the reader unacquainted with the literature and with little training sympathetic to and appreciative of the spatial nature of social phenomena. We shall cast the discussion against a background which traces the evolution of an area and shall raise certain key questions. In a final section, we shall consider several possible approaches to the analysis of the location and regional problem.[1]

1. SOME BASIC DEVELOPMENT PROCESSES

Broadly speaking, economic evolution stems from the action of technologic man upon the elements of his physical environment. On the whole, these elements are passive, most of them changing imperceptibly over human time. However, certain changes in environmental features, such as soil erosion or silt agglomeration at mouths of rivers, do in our time accumulate to a critical point and then provoke wholesale economic and social adjustments. These relatively few instances are the exceptions to the statement that the dynamic force in economic development lies in the activities of man almost to the point of exclusion. His reaction with his environment, his constant modification of the restraints and scarcities which it imposes, and his incessant

---

[1] The reader is reminded that this chapter serves as an introduction not only to this volume but also to a future volume on the principles of regional science and general regional theory.

1

construction of techniques which revalue resources and cause certain natural features to be less restrictive and others more spell economic and social change and progress.

Hence, it is not inappropriate to begin with a framework in which natural resources, physical configuration, and the matrix of technological conditions are given. We may imagine an area at the start isolated from other areas because of the friction of physical distance. Upon this area of varying topography and uneven resource content settlement takes place.

One or several individuals or family units may be presumed to begin the occupation. The selection of a site for initial habitation and cultivation of crops will depend on a host of factors. These include the existing vegetation and the difficulties of clearing, transport resources, climate, topography, type of soil and nature of drainage, the available tools and techniques, defense considerations and the cultural inheritance of the individuals and family units which in any given instance sharply defines existing knowledge and organizational experience and, thus, the horizon of possibilities. But also, in at least some respects, the selection may be arbitrary and indeterminate in terms of any *ex ante* rational framework. This selection may be subject to the whims and fancies of the first inhabitants and perhaps to a particular series of historical events. And, because of the play of the economic "irrational," the first site of settlement may be later abandoned for another not bristling with so many hazards and rigors.

Once a fairly stable adjustment with the environment is attained, the process of development is more subject to predictive analysis though capricious elements remain in the picture exerting influence to varying degrees. As more individuals and family units come to inhabit the area, presumably they will settle in close vicinity to the first. The "gregarious instinct," as early social psychologists were prone to term it, or, more accurately, previously acquired behavior patterns would tend to foster nucleation. It is not to be denied that where individuals have diverse cultural backgrounds there may be clash and dispersal rather than agglomeration, or that idiosyncratic elements of individual personalities may dominate those which are socially and culturally determined and thereby induce an unpredictable spatial pattern of settlement, though in all likelihood a more unstable one. However, economic forces or, more specifically, increasing returns from co-operation in combating the elements when population numbers are small, operate strongly to encourage nucleation. In a sense these economic forces are already imbedded in an existent culture, having previously conditioned the emergence of particular culture traits and complexes and previously influenced the dominant interests and focal values and attitudes to which a given cultural pattern is oriented.

In any case, sooner or later a population cluster does precipitate. What is its internal structure? What principles govern its spatial configuration and, in particular, the spatial configuration of its economic activities?

For a society which engages predominantly in agricultural activities, the conceptual framework developed by von Thünen and his followers is illuminating. In a uniformly fertile plain of considerable extent, which is undifferentiated in its physical features and isolated from the rest of the world and which contains a single population cluster at some distance from its periphery, cultivation of diverse crops and production of other farm commodities will tend to take place in concentric zones around the cluster as center. To each zone there will correspond a particular agricultural product or combination of products. The demand for the various products by the given population, the effort involved in transporting a unit of each of the several products over any unit of distance, the intensity and associated cost at which a unit of area can yield each product or combination of products, and the resulting prices or barter ratios are among the various factors determining in which zone each product will be produced. The relaxation of the uniformity assumptions and the introduction of realities such as differentiation in soil, climate, and topography and a finite number of transport routes in general irregularly placed engender serious distortions of the concentric pattern. An enclave of land devoted to grazing may appear in a wheat-growing zone simply because the topography of the enclave precludes any other activity. In an area stretching along a transport route, cultivation of land may be much more intense than in an area closer to the population cluster but untapped by transport media and may yield entirely different crops. In short, any physical semblance of zonal arrangement may be completely absent. However, in terms of time-cost distance and in terms of other concepts which would give explicit recognition to areal differentiation with respect to significant variables, the concentric zonal arrangement would remain undisturbed, as will be indicated in a later chapter.

This conception of competitive equilibrium in land use is at least partially refutable, however, because of its static nature. As already mentioned, society is in a constant state of disequilibrium, continually striving toward a condition of perfect adjustment but just as persistently being jarred off its course by forces of change. A population nucleus and its associated hinterland are no less a dynamic organism.

The nucleus typically grows in size from an initial small compact mass reflecting the centripetal drive of increasing returns to a larger and larger but less and less compressed body, at times even sprawling seemingly chaotic and without coherence. The centrifugal effects of diminishing returns from increasing intensity in the use of land and the mounting diseconomies and congestion from multiplying numbers become manifest in the growing extent of the spatial spread. At the peripheries of each of the zones of cultivation, the process entails transition from one type of land use to another. But does the transition take place smoothly and orderly or abruptly and haphazardly? Unquestionably, cultural values and institutions condition the nature

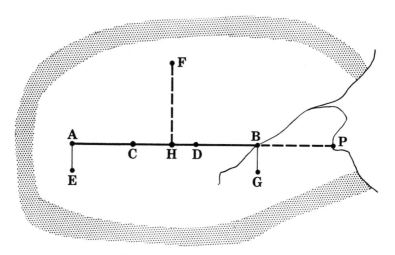

Fɪɢ. 1.　A hypothetical region.

of the transition. But just as certainly economic forces are at work pressing forward the succession of uses to which a given piece of land is subject and intensifying its exploitation. But how? Unfortunately, little is known and can be said about this dynamic process.

　　Imagine before the nucleus and its hinterland have reached massive proportions that a new item appears in the food basket of the inhabitants of the city which we shall designate as point A (Fig. 1). Fish are found to abound in a stream some days' journey from A. Owing to previously acquired inclinations or to initially favourable reactions and a non-resisting set of social attitudes and institutions, this new commodity is cumulatively accepted by the populace. A small colony of settlers is established at point B contiguous to the stream. (See Fig. 1.) Since, in terms of the best known transportation means,

B is located at a distance of several days' journey from A, still smaller colonies are established at C and D, primarily to facilitate the process of transportation and exchange between A and B through servicing the porters and their carriage animals.

The phenomenon of geographic specialization *among separated areas* unevenly endowed with resources appears in full flush. Geographic specialization *per se* is not a new phenomenon as it has already been present on a local level. Because of economies of scale, individuals, of necessity residing at different points in city A, have come to specialize in particular activities. The specialization in the cultivation of land differently situated with respect to the center of A has already been alluded to. In both these forms of local specialization, transport considerations are of fundamental importance. Likewise, the critical significance of transport cannot be denied for geographic specialization among separated areas. For imagine that the intervening distance between A and B were to be gradually lengthened. Transport costs would gradually mount and reach a point where they would become intolerable. Trade and specialization between A and B would gradually diminish and ultimately cease. Or, imagine the opposite. A and B are gradually brought into apposition. Interareal exchange and specialization become more pronounced as the resistance of intervening distance declines.

The critical significance of transport considerations is indirect as well as direct. The process of zone formation is not unique to A. Only a fraction of the food requirements of the populace of B will, in general, be procured in exchange for fish. Transport costs on certain commodities may be prohibitive and may compel the cultivation or production of these commodities in the immediate hinterland of B. A zonal spatial design, distorted by peculiarities of topography, soil characteristics, and a host of other factors, emerges around B as the focus. Clearly, the number of commodities for which transport costs will be judged by consumers at B as prohibitive, the number of persons engaged in fishing, the width of the zones, and the intensity of land use about B are interrelated and dependent, too, upon distance from A. The greater the intervening distance, in general, the smaller the trade between A and B, the fewer who ply at fishing, and the higher the degree of self-sufficiency at B. But the effect upon the spatial pattern of cultivation at B is not subject to easy perception. It is evident, too, that because the magnitude of the exchange of agricultural products for fish is related to intervening distance, the amount of agricultural product required of A's hinterland and hence its zonal pattern and associated intensity of land use will also be affected by intervening distance. This distance will also affect the amount of servicing activities provided by C and D, and consequently the character of their hinterlands, which will be of more limited extent than those of A and B.

As trade develops pure barter arrangements may be presumed to be displaced by the introduction of a medium of exchange and money prices. We do not purport to treat at length here or elsewhere the culture complex embodying price and monetary mechanisms, broadly conceived. However, like all sets of associated culture traits, it comprises behavior forms which have evolved consciously or unconsciously as part of an effort to achieve directly or indirectly a more effective adjustment to a given environment. And as do all culture traits and sets of interrelated culture traits, price and monetary mechanisms condition the changes in cultural forms, complexes, and patterns which transpire as a society evolves. It is invalid, then, to take the position that price and monetary phenomena are merely surface manifestations and reflections of the more nearly basic and underlying relations and interactions of man with his physical environment. Price systems and monetary institutions are in modern society an indispensable set of cultural tools, which are inextricably interwoven into the fabric of man's culture and which strongly shape the evolving organizational form and nature of man's economic and social activities. It is equally invalid to assign a secondary role to the geographic distribution of resources, topography and spatial position, and other characteristics of environment as some trade and economic theorists are inclined to do. It is all too clear from the above remarks that trade, relative and absolute spatial position, and the geographic pattern of resources are fundamentally interrelated. Our basic position, which we shall reiterate again and again, is that location and trade are as the two sides of the same coin. The forces determining one simultaneously determine the other. To understand and anticipate the interaction of these forces, a knowledge of resources, position, topography, and other environmental characteristics and a knowledge of price, exchange control and monetary mechanisms, and other cultural institutions and behavior complexes and patterns are each indispensable.

Into this relatively simple frame of general interdependence, another element of change may be injected. Iron ore is discovered. Previously acquired experience or successful experimentation with iron products leads to the exploitation of the iron ore deposits. Deposits, qualitatively and quantitatively adequate, are found to exist at points E, F, and G. Since charcoal derived from timber is required for smelting the ore, the use of coal being infeasible for one reason or another, and since timber may be assumed to be ubiquitous in this early stage of development, iron will tend to be produced at E and G. Working of ore close to markets, scattered over an area according to the scatter of markets, is characteristic at this stage, provided local timber resources and supplies of water and water power suffice. This pattern minimizes total transport costs on raw materials and finished products. Necessarily, new transport routes emerge, interconnecting E and A, and G and B.

The iron manufacture sparks an incipient industrialization. The character of this industrialization is markedly different from that observable in modern industrialized societies. The agricultural stratum serves as the base to which the structure of industry is oriented. The agricultural stratum provides the market for industrial products, the raw materials where they are agricultural, and the labor for the factories. This labor frequently is available only seasonally or secondarily as female labor and thereby immobile. Additionally, the agricultural stratum furnishes the food and drink for the worker, which frequently exceeds the weight of the raw materials used by the worker combined with the weight of the finished product attributed to his effort. This condition dictates orientation to points of food supply. Hence, the industrial pattern becomes tied to and reflects the underlying agricultural stratum, as do the patterns of tertiary and secondary activities for related reasons.

Deviations, however, do crop up as when indispensable but immobile and highly localized mineral resources must be tapped. More important in fostering deviations, and in nurturing a cumulatively mounting emancipation of the industrial stratum from the agricultural, is the increasing productivity stemming from improvements in technology. Technological advance revalues resources not only by broadening the horizon of materials subject to transformation and by multiplying production possibilities but also by altering the strategy of diverse spatial patterns of activities, of mineral deposits, and of transportation routes through changing rates of output. As the laborer works up greater quantities of raw materials which yield larger amounts of finished products, while simultaneously his consumption of food and drink at most rises at a considerably smaller rate, the pull of the agricultural stratum is attenuated and in time loses its dominance. Relocation at sites of mineral reserves and at new critical nodes takes place. Industry severs its geographic bonds to agriculture and, concomitantly, partially binds agriculture.

As an instance, posit with the passage of decades the discovery of an excellent bed of coking coal in the vicinity of F and the acquisition of crude blast furnace techniques. Compared to the weight of food and drink of the worker and of iron ore smelted per weight unit of manufactured iron, the weight of coal required is so prodigious as to dictate location of blast furnaces at the coal site. Major industrialization ensues at F oriented to coal resources and iron manufacture. A host of iron and steel fabricating activities, of heavy fuel-consuming processes, of ancillary by-product, input-product, and service functions, as well as the allied subsidiary operations indirectly induced or required to support the flow generated by the basic activities develops in juxtaposition, each activity in its peculiar way attuned to the major transport and agglomeration economies at F. The rise of F signifies drastic changes in the pattern of transport routes and commodity movements, and the emerging steam-steel complex makes feasible more modern transport facilities. A superior type of facility, more suited to large-scale movement of heavy industrial goods, may be presumed to be constructed to connect F with the old established transport route AB at H. The crossroads position of H, its centrality as well as the probable imbalance of traffic and thus unutilized transport capacity in certain directions, hastens the advent and growth of new enterprises at H.

Realignment of agriculture is necessitated. Zone formation proceeds about F and H while the configurations of cultivation around the old foci repattern themselves to the changing geographic structure of industrial and household demands. More commercialization of agriculture and greater exchange of the products of the farm for those of the factory take place. Dependence of agriculture upon industry mounts, and the associated problems of agricultural prices, output, and income emerge and grow in complexity.

The rise of F and H spells relative and perhaps even absolute decline of E and G, and C and D. At these fading cities, workers are displaced at their iron-manufacture and transport-servicing trades. Owing to established modes of behavior and institutions and the occupational and geographic immobilities attached thereto, the workers of these cities form a pool of cheap, downgraded labor upon which parasitic industry may draw. Elsewhere, socially sanctioned agricultural practices deeply rooted in folkways and community structure may resist change. A resulting inadequate income or material content of living may impel elements of the agricultural population to offer their services at bargain rates, thereby attracting industry that has no strong inclination to locate at any particular site. Additionally, at F and H where heavy basic industry, mining, and transport can utilize effectively the labor of the chief breadwinner only, the reserve of surplus women and child labor nurtures the growth of otherwise footloose industry. This growth of footloose activities at F and H, however, is not independent of the growth of such activities as well as basic industry and agriculture elsewhere. It takes place within a system of activities interdependent spatially and industrially, and only against such a system as background can it be fully understood.

2. SOME FUNDAMENTAL QUESTIONS

This general descriptive analysis of the evolutionary course of an hypothetical area could be carried forward and developed extensively. To proceed thus, however, would not point up as forcefully as we should like: (1) certain fundamental location and regional problems; and (2) the need for the general type of theoretical analysis with which this book is concerned. We now wish to focus upon these problems and this need by posing a number of key questions which, at the same time, maintain the emphasis on the spatial order.

For example, as the area industrializes, at what point does it abandon the phase of isolation and commence trading with the outside world? Which sites develop as major and minor ports? In what commodities will the area trade? If our hypothetical area has developed late relative to other regions of the world, it may at the beginning of trade export agricultural and mineral commodities in exchange for manufactures. If so, does its general composition of imports and exports change toward export of manufactures and import of raw materials, food, and specialized machinery and equipment as newer areas are brought into the orbit of world trade? How does the transition from one import-export pattern to another proceed? If, because of the conjunction of various natural factors, cultural forces and historical incidents, P emerges as a dominant port, what types of industry develop at P and how much of each?

With further economic development, a diversified transport network evolves. Internal waterway and highway projects are pushed to completion; pipelines are laid. But what is an optimum mix and spatial pattern of the diverse transport facilities? In what ways is such a mix or pattern conditioned by the character of industrial traffic generated and the nature of intercommunity and intracommunity population movement? Should any government subsidy be forthcoming? If so, how should it be distributed among the several facilities and the several areas and between current and capital expense?

As industrialization proceeds, problems of relocation arise. In the initial stages of heavy manufacturing, textiles may have been drawn to F because of the location there of excellent coal deposits and of a reserve of women and child labor available at relatively low rates. With time a heavy concentration of textiles may have developed at F, reflecting, partially, the attraction of a pool of skilled labor and, partially, historical inertia. But, as the force of innovation presses the spatial structure of the economy and its parts into ever new configurations, the strategy of existing textile sites alters. The reserve of low-cost labor at these textile sites may have become depleted; what was once low-cost labor may have been converted into high-cost labor owing to the continued use of obsolete equipment and processes. Elsewhere, cheap and abundant labor incident to "cultural lag" and creeping industrialization and urbanization may make available savings which warrant geographic shift despite heavy costs of relocation. Resisting, however, is the force of historical inertia, a force intimately associated with the cultural variable. A critical point may exist at which this force is overcome. But exactly how does this point vary with the institutional environment? Furthermore, if relocation is expedient, what would be an optimum localization pattern of textiles? What distribution among regions? How large the factory? To what extent can a textile factory serve as a focal point for employment in an esthetically designed "new town"? How do creative minds generate ideas which modify accepted ideals and values which in turn form the scaffolding within which decisions are made by consumers, and political, social, and business leaders? How do these creative minds condition the manner in which the spatial structure yields to stresses and strains?

The problem of adjustment to change in the relative strength of the several location factors may be raised again in connection with iron and steel location. Foreign ores become accessible while concomitantly improvement in smelting and rolling techniques and utilization of a swelling supply of scrap reduce the quantity of coal spent per ton of steel. Should a major integrated iron and steel works be established contiguous to the port P? Or should the manufacture of steel at P be limited to the operation of scrap furnaces only? At what point will the pull of the market and scrap supplies at A be sufficient to draw some steel capacity to A? Does the relative decline of steel at F also imply absolute decline? Furthermore, how do competitive ethics and practices and institutional pricing arrangements, whether f.o.b., basing point, or some other, affect the process of locational adaptation? Finally, do impending new techniques, continuous casting for example, spell complete decentralization for the far future?

Intimately associated with the historic shiftings of iron and steel location are the dynamic processes of the urban-metropolitan complexes at P, F, H, and A. Clearly, the magnitude of each complex is linked to its content of such basic economic activity as iron and steel. Spatial realignment of such activity is tantamount to reshuffling of the ranks of cities. But exactly how does employment in any particular basic activity or combination of basic activities generate employment in non-basic activities? Why does the ratio of non-basic to basic vary from city to city, and in what way is it related to the input structure and gravitational impulse of a particular basic activity? Can a meaningful dynamic structure of an urban-metropolitan complex be constructed and depicted in terms of interactivity relations?

Additionally, spatial physiognomy of the urban-metropolitan region is a primary concern. Intensity of land use is a function of, among other factors, distance from the core. At the core the pyramiding of activities attains a maximum maximorum. With movement away along radials in all directions the intensity of land use diminishes, but differentially in the various directions. Moreover, the rate at which this intensity falls in any direction changes with distance. In addition, after a point along many of the radials, the intensity reaches a relative minimum, reverses its trend by creeping upward, and attains a relative maximum, only to decline again and perhaps to repeat this undulatory performance. Along a few of the radials, generally the strategic ones along which the rate of decline from the core is among the least for all radials, relative maxima for the entire metropolitan region are realized. These latter represent subfoci from which, for some distance at least, intensity falls off in all directions. The strategic radials also exercise a degree of dominance to the extent that, in directions perpendicular to their course, intensity decreases.

In short, an urban-metropolitan region comes to comprise an hierarchy of strategic nodal sites, classifiable by order and degree of dominance. This multinucleated body is, viewed from another angle, a network of transport interconnections and hence of interstitial areas each subject to hierarchical order. What is the nature of the ecological process that gives rise to this dynamic organism? How do (1) the cost relations of the numerous economic activities, (2) the spatial and product preferences of consumers, of familial and various associational units, and (3) the friction of distance interact? How does progress in the state of transport technology, which in turn is conditioned by the preferences and ideals of these units, impel change and rearrangement of centers and population nuclei? On a more concrete level, what determines the use to which any given piece of land is put?

Which types of retail, wholesale, cultural, governmental and adminis- trative, industrial, and service activities tend to appear in the core and in each of the several types of subcenters and satellite cities in the various phases of urban-metropolitan growth? In what form does specialization among the several metropolitan regions emerge? Are there forces which pervade the intrametropolitan and intermetropolitan structures which yield stability in the size distribution of sites and cities as a whole, even though there is constant reshuffling of the ranks of individual members of any meaningfully defined population of sites and cities? Do such forces deny the concept of an optimum-size city?

For our hypothetical region these questions become more crucial with time. Impending innovations, such as aircraft and atomic energy with destructive as well as constructive potential, compel a recasting of national and regional values. The inherited cultural ideals and productivity sanctioning and extolling the cosmopolitan life in peace- time must be weighed against the suddenly increased risks, whether calculated or imagined, of vulnerability when a state of war exists or portends. Policy questions concerning urban decentralization arise. Intelligent answers to these questions, however, require foresight on the probable "normal" effects of these innovations. To such effects we first turn.

Environmental barriers deflect the path of growth of any community, metropolitan area, or regional unit. Physical features, however, have critical value as barriers only with respect to a given or assumed state of technology, and in particular of transport technology. With the advent of aircraft, what aspects of topography lose significance as obstacles to the movement of people, ideas, and goods? Which acquire new importance? Will any new trade routes and major realignment of trade patterns develop? Will the strategy of sites for trading activities be altered, with a consequent relative decline of P? Will the emphasis on air traffic in international trade provoke the rise of new centers more suitably geared to such traffic? To what extent will aircraft find widespread use in industry and foster increased productivity and new location patterns? How will metropolitan structures be affected both indirectly through increased effective demand for a myriad of service activities made possible by greater productivity and directly through increased population mobility inherent in the use of family aircraft? What should be the position of aircraft in a diversified transport system, and to what degree and in what manner should air transport be subsidized?

The harnessing of atomic energy poses somewhat similar questions. Will nuclear power be competitive with conventionally produced power? If not, will a given society deem justifiable the allocation of a disproportionate share of costs to the military to encourage active participation by private enterprise in the production of nuclear power and in the atomic energy industry in general, and hence to build up and maintain skills and capacity for the production and effective utilization of fissionable materials? Does competitive or cheap nuclear power augur for our hypothetical area the emancipation of heavy industry from coal belts, the dissolution of industrial concentrations, and a wide and more even spread of economic activities? Or will such nuclear power alter the significance of merely one of many location factors and in doing so modify location patterns to a small degree only, even to the extent of fostering increased industrial concentration rather than diffusion or dispersion? Will a host of new processes and industries develop concomitantly to yield indirect effects of revolutionary proportions? Which, if any, of the existing industrial sectors, including the public utilities, are likely to become obsolete in whole or in part? What may be the impact of nuclear power upon other regions of the world deficient in fuel and power resources, upon trading relations with these regions, and thus indirectly upon the structure of our hypothetical space-economy?

Tentative answers to these and many other questions are required for an intelligent approach to urban-metropolitan and industrial decentralization. A program of decentralization must be geared to the anticipated future geographic, economic, and social organization of metropolitan regions, not just to current demands. Decentralization policy is partially "deviational" policy, a policy designed to accelerate certain tendencies and strengthen the effectiveness of certain forces, not all necessarily centrifugal, in accordance with certain values judged to be in the interest of the commonweal. It therefore involves insight into processes indicated in the above paragraphs, which are subject to a fair amount of objective analysis. It also involves evaluation of the impact of innovation upon the psychology of the individual and social groups and requires some estimate of how imagined or impending military applications of such innovations as aircraft and atomic energy ultimately affect individual and group space preferences. These questions, like a host of others of similar stamp, are subject to considerably less objective analysis.

Identification of meaningful sectors of the metropolitan region which should be dissected from the urban mass and located elsewhere, whether in the periphery or in more distant districts, is not unlike some of the age-old problems of regional resource use and conservation. A meaningful sector is not necessarily, and perhaps only infrequently, a wedge of activities contiguous in space. It is a complex of activities where association leads to definite agglomeration economies, but where, subject to certain restraints, presence of these activities within a Greater Metropolitan Region in any of many possible patterns of scatter and concentration may more often than not satisfy the spatial associational requirement. Hence, contiguity in physical space is only one of several constraining factors each of which is critical in the determination of some of the several combinations of activities which comprise meaningful sectors for decentralization purposes. Other restraints bear upon such matters as the volume and time-pattern of demand for transportation and diverse utility services, the structure of labor requirements by occupation and other characteristics, and the interrelations of activities in terms of stages of production, by-product use, and input-output functions. Yet, given a knowledge of the types of restraints operative and even detailed information about the nature of some, how evaluate the net interaction of different groups of them under different sets of circumstances in order to identify and effectively to carve out sectors from the metropolitan region?

Correlatively, how achieve a satisfactory geographic balance in our hypothetical region if the pattern of activity is adjudged too concentrated and vulnerable in certain sections, for example, along the industrial band which stretches from A to H and H to F? Put otherwise, how plan the long-run utilization and conservation of resources in the entire region, weighing the economic desirability of each development design against its military, political, and other virtues and limitations. Guiding new growth along certain channels and in specific parts of the region is one expedient for achieving a redistribution of activity. Some costly relocation of other activities may be justifiable. More significant, an entire set of activities located within an industrial band may be subject to decentralization as an integral unit, when decentralization of the activities individually would be, from an economic standpoint, highly irrational because: (1) they feed inputs into each other and utilize each other's by-products, (2) together they can maintain the high quality transport service which each requires, (3) together their labor forces form a substantial pool of diversified skills, the existence of which is a *sine qua non* for each, (4) together their combined demand for diverse urban and professional services is of such a magnitude as to insure efficient performance at relatively low cost, and (5) their combined labor force constitutes a market for consumer products of such a scale as to restrict the cost of living and hence money wages to moderate, if not low, bounds. To ascertain each of these sets of activities where the force of historical inertia binds location to original or old sites of development, where *relocation in the small* is precluded but where *relocation in the large* can be economically sanctioned is, to reiterate, a difficult problem. To attack this problem, and, more generally, to formulate effective governmental policy for decentralization and for the long-run planning of resource development to achieve an optimum geographic distribution of activities, requires full utilization of all the existing skills of social scientists. And, more important, it requires continued and, if possible, accelerated progress in the social sciences in the fashioning of new tools and techniques for analyzing the interdependence of the various sectors of the space-economy, and hence the net effects of certain specified changes.

3. POSSIBLE THEORETICAL APPROACHES [2]

Having posed a host of key questions, we must confess to an inability to provide even partial answers. Our intention, as stated earlier, is to point up the need for the general type of theoretical and empirical analysis with which the remainder of this book is concerned. What follows is a modest attempt to depict and understand some of the basic spatial interrelations which underlie the location of economic activities and regional development.

Various approaches were possible in undertaking this assignment. Several are recorded in the event that future students of location and regional development may find them of some use. One obvious approach toward a more general theory would involve amassing new and reinterpreting existing historical material—to a very limited extent along the lines of Roscher, Schäffle, Ritschl, Weber, and Engländer—to a very significant extent along the paths explored by Dean and Usher. (The von Thünen framework for agricultural location would be of critical value here for understanding initial stages of development.) Unquestionably, historical generalizations, more comprehensive and at the same time more incisive than those we now possess, can be achieved in the study of the past and current spatial and regional structure of the world economy and its various sectors.

A second approach might begin with the pure abstractions of Lösch. These are presented at some length in the following chapter. Cannot one further pursue these abstractions with profit as Lösch does to some extent? Imagine one relaxes the assumption of uniform population scatter, an assumption which is inconsistent with the derived

---

[2] This section is written primarily for the research worker. It assumes a knowledge of the works and approaches of the several individuals cited. The contributions of these individuals are at best only partially recorded in the following chapters.

results which yield cities and towns of diverse sizes. Further, one can introduce geographic inequalities in endowment of resources of all kinds, differences in consumers' space preferences, a finite number of transport routes reflecting high fixed costs and economies of scale, and a number of other restraints which permit a closer correspondence to actual conditions. Could not a more meaningful system of nets and hierarchy of sites be depicted? Since the character, magnitude, and direction of trade among all sites are functionally related to the nature of the postulates underlying one's abstractions, would not a more realistic trade pattern be yielded? Furthermore, the Löschian framework, which has most relevance for market-oriented processes and service functions which use ubiquitous raw materials or none at all, may be extended to incorporate agricultural activities. About each population cluster, whatever its size, zones of cultivation tend to develop à la Thünen though within a complex web of interrelations about which some remarks will be made in the following paragraphs.

Another approach might rather build upon Thünen's model with extensions at later stages to encompass the significant elements of Löschian and Weberian theory. Imagine two isolated city regions, each region comprising the central city and its surrounding hinterland devoted to agriculture and forestry. With the development of transport technology we may suppose that resistance imposed on movement by topographic obstacles and by the sheer friction of distance is gradually reduced. This change, as well as growth in population numbers, will induce an increase in the consumption of various agricultural and forest products and perhaps also in the types of products available. A new equilibrium arrangement of expanded zones will, after a sufficient lapse of time, be established for each city region although, as we have already indicated, little is known about the dynamic process of transition from one equilibrium pattern to another, a process which is intimately linked with cultural values and institutional modes of behavior. In time, and under the assumption that resources are uniformly and equally distributed among the city regions, the hinterlands of these two isolated city regions may have expanded to such a degree that their outer boundaries become tangent or coincide along a certain stretch. Nonetheless, the hinterlands do not overlap and still can be rigorously defined. However, the symmetrical concentric zonal arrangement about each city is disturbed although in a systematic, identifiable manner. The introduction of a third, a fourth, and finally an nth city region merely adds to the complexity of the resulting design. It does not entail any overlapping of hinterlands or any less rigor in their demarcation using standard Thünen principles, to be discussed in a later chapter.

The schema of a space-economy composed of many city-regions with some hinterlands bordering on each other for limited stretches, *and without interregional trade,* is subject to considerable improvement. Recognition of relations which Ohlin and Lösch have emphasized— namely, the force of concentration of production imbedded in economies of scale and the force of scatter of production engendered by the cost of transportation—immediately lays the basis for trade. Returning for the moment to the fiction of two city-regions, we may recognize that not all commodities produced are agricultural and forest, that some commodities are services to be performed at central places, and that others are associated with market-oriented production processes which currently we may postulate use only ubiquitous raw materials. Each of the commodities belonging in these latter two sets may be classified as to the size of market area most economical for its production. Some may be produced and distributed most efficiently when one factory serves both city-regions. These commodities may be classified as supraregional and national. Others may be produced and distributed most efficiently when two factories operate, one located in each city, each serving consumers in its corresponding city-region. These may be classified as regional. Still others may be most efficiently produced and distributed when they are produced in many factories, symmetrically located within the combined area of the city-regions. The commodities these factories produce may be considered subregional; and since their sites of production to a large extent lie outside the core of the two main cities, they give rise to new central function sites. As these sites come to represent population nuclei, effective demand for agricultural products gives rise to zone formations at each of them.

In sum, superimposing a Löschian framework upon a Thünen arrangement leads to an hierarchical pattern of sites within each city-region and generates interregional as well as increased intraregional trade. Confining attention to only two city-regions raises the basic question: Which of the two serves as the site for producing supraregional and national commodities, or does a new intermediate city emerge as the site for producing such commodities? Historical evidence would seem to favor the hypothesis that one of the two existing cities usurp national commodity production. This tends to spell relative decline for the other. The latter tends, as a consequence, to expand its output of agricultural products (and hence its hinterland) in order to provide the wherewithal to purchase supplies of national commodities from the former. This condition in turn entails relative contraction of the agricultural supply hinterland of the former and specialization among the city-regions. However, it should be borne in mind that there may be decided transport advantage to an intermediate location and that, where there are a sufficient number of national commodities, a major shift to an intermediate location may take place. This shift may involve either a simultaneous relocation of many producers or a gradual transition whereby a one-by-one sequence of relocations is experienced.

To pursue this interesting two city-region schema in greater detail is outside the scope of this book. More relevant, but still beyond our defined bounds, would be a multicity-region construct, resulting again from both population growth and advance in transport technology. Here, more determinacy is likely to be present. The city-region central to all is, from the transport standpoint, the ideal location for national commodity production. It tends to specialize in these commodities while on balance the remaining city-regions tend to specialize in agriculture; necessarily this specialization involves zonal adaptations. At the same time, there may be subnational commodities which are also supraregional. The existence of such commodities generates a still greater hierarchical arrangement of city-regions.

Hitherto, the postulate that resources are uniformly and equally distributed among city-regions has been maintained. Let this postulate be relaxed; let us return to the simple two city-region schema where both regions are initially isolated from the rest of the world and from one another. In time, as there is advance in transport technology and increase in population numbers, trade may well take place before the hinterlands have expanded so as to be contiguous with one another over some stretch. There may be partial or even complete specialization in the production of various agricultural products, each city-region supplying to the other crops for whose production it is most suited by reason of its resources. Upon this improved Thünen arrangement, which should also be expanded to embrace many city-regions, a Löschian framework may be superimposed to inject into the analysis service activities and ubiquitous raw-material-using, market-oriented production processes. Once again, a hierarchical arrangement of cities and towns evolves, with consequent major alterations in zonal patterns. A more realistic portrayal of a space-economy results.

However, the analysis of the space-economy can be further improved. Relaxing the assumption of uniform and equal resource distribution allows one to take into account basic production processes (for example, steel, aluminum, and chemicals) which use raw materials which are localized in varying degrees (for example, coal, ores, and hydropower). Here the Weberian type of analysis can be added to the derived Thünen-Löschian model. Consideration of transport costs (as they are related to weight loss, relative weights, relative positions, and rate structure), of labor costs and other costs, and of agglomeration and deglomeration economies is required. New sites of production and cities may emerge, to be added to the Thünen-Löschian hierarchy; and of the existing cities, some may grow while others decline. The spatial pattern of agricultural production and of service and market-oriented activities based on ubiquitous raw materials will concomitantly undergo change, particularly where strong local multiplier effects are associated with basic industry (reflecting partially agglomeration effects).[3]

In short, the development of a combined Thünen-Löschian-Weberian framework along channels suggested above and elsewhere in this book represents another approach toward achieving a general theory of location and space-economy and toward a more thorough understanding of the interrelations of the space-economy.[4]

A fourth approach might proceed through entirely different channels. Imagine there exists only one non-agricultural, non-service production

---

[3] To be specific, imagine that in the Thünen-Löschian framework a steel plant, using localized ore and coal, is introduced. Since steel production on the whole tends to be transport-oriented, the steel plant may or may not be located in an existing city. If the point of minimum transport cost for steel production does not coincide with or lie close to an existing city, a new city tends to arise especially since steel production is an agglomeration-inducing type of activity. It is easily seen how service and agricultural activities in city-regions close by are directly affected, and more remote city-regions are indirectly affected. Likewise, that there are important direct and indirect repercussions when the optimal transport point for steel production coincides with an existing city is easily perceived.

[4] The above approach takes into account a steady advance in the state of transport technology and a gradual reduction in resistances to and costs of movement. A variant of this approach would start at the other extreme. Transport costs are assumed zero. A corresponding spatial pattern of economic activities is derived. By degrees, transport costs are permitted to rise, approaching more and more the levels of reality. For a while, at least, inequalities of human and natural resources become more and more critical. The previous spatial pattern related to consumer and social group space preferences increasingly takes on an economic hue. An hierarchy of sites, of trade routes, and of flow phenomena in general develops, as well as zone formations and industrial agglomerations at strategic mineral and nodal sites. Ultimately, as transport costs rise to exorbitant levels, the hierarchy disappears, as does interregional trade, and the hypothetical isolated city-regions of Thünen are attained.

In this Thünen-Löschian-Weberian approach and its variant, the effects of tariff barriers, exchange rate and balance of payments considerations, central banking

process which involves only a single stage. Its location will be associated with a population cluster. Either it is a market-oriented operation and, hence, drawn to an agricultural and related service population nucleus, or it is an operation which is tied to a raw material source and which, hence, binds a population cluster composed of the families of its labor force and of the labor force of allied service activities. Associated, too, with the latter population cluster will be a farming population, but one which does not need to be in the immediate environs owing to the possibility of engaging in long-distance (interregional) trade.

Consider an advance in technology which permits the production of the identical product at lower cost, but by a two-stage process. Both stages may be carried on at a market site or at a raw material site. But also the production process may be split geographically, the earlier stage being linked to the raw material site, the later stage to the market. Another type of long-distance (interregional) flow phenomenon may be observed, namely, the movement of semifinished manufactures in exchange for finished products. History records that in time such a flow phenomenon appears as a region develops. But what are the conditions that the process be split geographically and, hence, that such a flow phenomenon exists? Are these conditions similar to the conditions for long-distance (interregional) trade in finished products? Cannot the conditions for both these types of flow phenomenon be expressed in terms of common concepts and principles?

Permit the economy to become still more complex. Technological advance compels, through making possible significant cost savings, the shift to a three-stage, to a four-stage, and finally to an n-stage production process. Again, what are the conditions that the process be split geographically and among more than two sites when more than one raw material is utilized? The statement of these conditions should involve merely a further generalization of a common set of principles.

Pursue the generalization further. Allow the production by a single-stage process of another industrial commodity. What determines the location of such production? In addition to the factors which were relevant for the first industrial commodity, linkage relations between the two industrial commodities must be considered. Location at a

---

and monetary institutions, obstacles to immigration and labor mobility, and various other political and social frictions and policies should be investigated to obtain a still better understanding of the space-economy of reality and in particular of international trade.

site of one of the raw materials utilized in the manufacture of the
first industrial commodity, at any intermediate point at which a
stage in such manufacture may have become situated as well as at
the market, at a site of a raw material consumed in the production
of the second industrial commodity, or at other relevant intermediate
points must be investigated.   The appearance of agglomeration
economies may alter the spatial configuration simply derived by superimposing upon the location pattern of the first, the location pattern
of the second industrial commodity which would have obtained in
the absence of production of the first. As already intimated, additive
procedures are insufficient. But how evaluate the effect of agglomeration? What are the principles which relate these forces to others?

   In response to successive technological advances, the production
of the second industrial commodity is performed in two stages, three
stages, and finally n stages. Should not the identical principles apply
to the spatial affinities of one or more stages of one production process
as to one or more stages of the other? Further introduce more industrial commodities each produced in one or more stages. Can these
principles be as extensively generalized? Moreover, since these principles relate the location of any one stage of a production process to
the location of the next stage or the consumer (industrial or household), should not these same principles simultaneously govern flow
phenomena in the postulated model and, hence, all trade?

   Why consider industrial commodities singly? Slicing the economy
by individual industrial commodities represents an extreme of industrial disaggregation. For certain purposes a more aggregative analysis
in terms of groups may be more useful. For example, a somewhat
less disaggregated classification such as a fine Leontief-type breakdown may be more expedient for purposes of operation. At the other
extreme, the highly aggregative Colin Clark classification of primary,
secondary, and tertiary, or a fourfold classification of heavy industry,
light industry, agriculture, and trade and services may be more
appropriate in other instances. Could not the previously derived
principles be restated to be valid for groups, the nature of the reformulation being dependent upon the degree and manner of aggrega-
tion? Could these principles be extended, though at best only partially,
to encompass the effects upon the spatial industrial pattern of different
types of pricing policies and institutional business ties, different geographic patterns of income distribution, different kinds of space
preferences of individual household consumers and diverse types of
aggregates of household consumers, and like factors?

   The framework may even be extended to consider interrelations of large regions. We have alluded to long-distance trade as interregional. Recognizing that an hierarchy of regions exists, we may conceive at the start of this long-distance (interregional) trade as taking place among the smaller regions of one large major region, but not as occurring beyond the bounds of a large major region. Thus, it is possible to have a construct of several large major regions, each initially isolated from the other, but each experiencing its own variety of internal development which is subject, however, to explanation in terms of a common set of general principles.

Of the several large regions, consider two neighboring ones. One may possess, relative to existing technology, abundant mineral resources and niggardly amounts of agricultural resources. In the other, the opposite situation may obtain. (It is clear that, *ceteris paribus*, in one region the character of development will be more industrial in the other more agricultural.) Let there be progress in transport techniques such that the geographic barriers to commodity movement are reduced sufficiently to permit intercourse. The pattern of geographic specialization in each large region changes. Industry shifts from one region to the other with concomitant increases in productivity, gross output, and degree of specialization. Trade internal to each large region likewise changes, and an hierarchical order of trade relations develops. As further transport advances permit the introduction of a third, fourth, and finally an nth large region into the circle of inter-relations, further changes ensue, each functionally dependent upon the state of transport technology and level of transport costs. To understand the resulting spatial phenomena, notwithstanding their complexity, could not the same common set of general principles, somewhat adapted and extended here and there, be invoked? Does not the introduction of hierarchical relations merely add complexity to the statement of these principles, and not basic change?

With the raising of these questions the discussion of the fourth type of approach to a general theory of location and space-economy is concluded. The recently developed approaches of Vining, who places emphasis on the search for distributional stability characteristics among spatial flow phenomena, and of Koopmans and others, whose primary attack is upon the transportation problem, are other fruitful ones. Several other approaches associated with the older location literature will be discussed at length in the following chapter. Still another approach, a variant of the fourth, might start with individual persons rather than with individual production processes. The spatial preference of each person, both as a consuming unit and as an income-earning unit, would be considered. Aggregating individuals to form meaningful social and economic groups would introduce group space preferences, which in turn would affect the geographic association of employment opportunities, and thus industrial location and trade. Optimal spatial patterns from the standpoint of a group are not necessarily consistent with an optimal position for each individual. Conflicts may arise which involve some of the hitherto unsolved problems of welfare economics. In this manner the variant of the fourth approach might proceed.

Before this chapter is brought to a close, a few words might be said about the author's approach. In a real sense it is eclectic, drawing upon various elements of the works of others. It aims at developing in this volume principles for a general theory through reducing to common simple terms the basic elements of the various location theories, beginning first with Weberian dogma. It does not purport to present in detail and evaluate various location theories nor to weave the fabric of a complete and realistic space-economy. Rather, with a full recognition of the deficiencies and non-operational character of our general location principles, it seeks to bring the separate location theories into one general doctrine, to the extent possible; and to fuse the resulting doctrine, where this can be done, with existing production, price, and trade theory. This is sought in order to develop a superior set of tools and conceptual framework for the theoretical and empirical type of regional analysis which will be attempted in a second volume and which, together with the general location analysis, aims at increasing the understanding of the structure and changing character of spatial phenomena.

Chapter 2

Some General Theories
of Location and Space-Economy[1]

1. THE ANGLO-SAXON BIAS

The difficulties of the problem depend chiefly on variations in the area of space, and the period of time over which the market in question extends; the influence of time being more fundamental than that of space.[2]

Thus spoke Marshall, in line with Anglo-Saxon tradition, and in the half-century to follow Anglo-Saxon economists were to hearken to his cry. Theoreticians of today are chiefly preoccupied with introducing the time element in full into their analyses, and the literature abounds with models of a dynamic nature. Yet who can deny the spatial aspect of economic development: that all economic processes exist in space, as well as over time? Realistically, both time and space must be vital considerations in any theory of economy. Unfortunately, however, aside from those of the monopolistic competition

---

[1] As already indicated in the Preface, the basic material for this chapter was written in 1947 and published in 1949. At that time we emphasized an imbalance of the Anglo-Saxon literature. Since then this imbalance has been partially corrected, in particular in the works of Enke, Samuelson, Koopmans, Beckmann, and Fox which will be cited in a later chapter. Nevertheless, the statements are left unqualified in order to retain the forcefulness of the argument as first developed.

It should be noted that this chapter is not intended as a survey of all location theory but only of general location theory up to 1947. It therefore fails to treat many of the contributions to partial location theory of such individuals as Thünen, Launhardt, Engländer, Palander, and Hoover.

[2] Alfred Marshall, *Principles of Economics*, 8th ed., London, 1936, Book V, Chap. xv, Sect. 1.

school of thought, particularly Chamberlin,[3] the architects of our finest theoretical structures have intensified the prejudice exhibited by Marshall. They continue to abstract from the element of space, and in so doing they are approaching a position of great imbalance.[4]

Let us consider, as an example, modern general equilibrium theory. The latest contributors have concentrated their efforts on attacking the problem of time to the exclusion of that of space. Hicks,[5] Mosak,[6] Lange,[7] and Samuelson,[8] to name a few, have all treated an economy in which all factors and producers, commodities and consumers are, in effect, congregated at one point. Hicks, to be sure, begins by formulating the problem in a manner pregnant with spatial implications:

> It turns out, on investigation, that most of the problems of several variables, with which economic theory has to concern itself, are problems of interrelations of markets. Thus, the more complex problems of international trade involve the interrelations of the markets for imports and exports with the capital market. . . .
>
> . . . The method of General Equilibrium, which these writers (Walras, Pareto, and Wicksell) elaborated, was especially designed to exhibit the economic system as a whole, in the form of a complex pattern of interrelations of markets. Our work is bound to be in their tradition, and to be a continuation of theirs.[9]

But actually he confines himself to a wonderland of no spatial dimen-

[3] E. H. Chamberlin, *The Theory of Monopolistic Competition*, Cambridge, Mass., 1933; and Chamberlin's doctoral dissertation deposited under the same title in the Harvard University library, 1927. In his doctoral dissertation Chamberlin treats the space factor somewhat more thoroughly and more as an integral part of his theory. See also S. Enke, "Space and Value," *Quarterly Journal of Economics*, Vol. LVI (August 1942), pp. 627–37.

[4] Outside of the field of monopolistic competition there have been scattered treatments by Anglo-Saxon theorists of certain aspects of space as an economic factor. For example, F. A. Fetter has treated space in "The Economic Law of Market Areas," *Quarterly Journal of Economics*, Vol. XXXVIII (May 1924), p. 525; treatises on international trade have attributed some importance to spatial resistances; rent theorists have been forced to recognize, however inadequately, the existence of space in the separation of immobile natural resources and markets; and so forth. But in these latter instances only passing attention has been given to this vital consideration.

[5] J. R. Hicks, *Value and Capital*, Oxford, 1939.

[6] Jacob L. Mosak, *General Equilibrium Theory in International Trade*, Cowles Commission Monograph No. 7, Bloomington, Ind., 1944.

[7] Oscar Lange, *Price Flexibility and Employment*, Cowles Commission Monograph No. 8, Bloomington, Ind., 1944.

[8] Paul A. Samuelson, *Foundations of Economic Analysis*, Cambridge, Mass., 1947.

[9] Hicks, *op. cit.*, p. 2. The words in parentheses are added.

sions. Apparently he assumes markets to be perfect, one price ruling throughout each of them. Or, otherwise expressed, transport costs and other costs involved in movement within a "market" are assumed to be zero. In this sense the factor of space is repudiated, everything within the economy is in effect compressed to a point, and all spatial resistance disappears.[10]

The approach to unreality which is inherent in such a treatment is best illustrated by Mosak's work, *General Equilibrium Theory in International Trade,* which is excellent in other respects. Although Mosak expands Hicks's analysis to embrace an international economy, spatially speaking he is still dwelling within a dimensionless habitat. His study of the effects of international exchange, of unilateral payments, and of impediments to international trade,[11] can be interpreted as treating an anomalous field: *a one-point world, which somehow or other is conceived as divided into* n *parts, representing* n *nations, between which trade and trade barriers exist.*[12]

We may now consider the relations of general equilibrium theory to the general theory of location and space-economy envisaged in this book. We conceive the general theory of location and space-economy to be one which comprehends the economy in its totality. Not only

[10] The explanation may partly lie in Hicks's rejection of monopolistic competition theory generally in favor of perfect competition on the ground that the former introduces elements of indeterminacy, whereas his preference is for determinate solutions (*op. cit.,* pp. 83–85). It is clear that Hicks fails to reveal an appreciation of the spatial aspect of monopolistic competition theory and of the extent to which determinate solutions are obtained in monopolistic competition analysis through its consideration of the space factor.

Professor Schumpeter has pointed out to me in conversation that one might maintain that transport cost is implicitly contained in production cost, and that the Hicksian analysis is thus sufficiently comprehensive. My point is this: production theory, having gone beyond the mere statement that the producer maximizes his profits (in which statement all production costs are implicitly treated), from a methodological standpoint cannot justifiably treat certain production costs explicitly and other important ones implicitly in order to avoid the obstacles to analysis which the latter present. For a balanced treatment, the particular effects of transport and spatial costs in separating producers from each other must be considered. They are too vital to be sidestepped through implicit treatment, as Hicks and others may be interpreted as having done.

[11] Transport costs are not explicitly treated. The analysis of their effects, it is maintained, follows similar lines to that of the effects of import and export taxes (Mosak, *op. cit.,* pp. 64–65).

[12] At this stage in the development of theory, it is as unjustifiable and inadequate to lump transport costs into one category along with all trade resistances in the theory of trade as it is to treat them as implicit production costs in the theory of production.

Although these indictments are levelled specifically at Mosak, they apply to others as well.

are the mutual relations and interdependence of all economic elements, both in the aggregate and atomistically, of fundamental importance; but the spatial as well as the temporal (dynamic) character of the interrelated economic processes must enter the picture. Seen in this perspective, Hicksian general equilibrium analysis is but a very special case of a general theory of location and space-economy which concerns itself with the local distribution of factors and resources as well as with local variations in prices and, thus, with the immobilities and spatial inelasticities of factors and goods.

In the sections to follow, the contributions of several authors who have pioneered in this field will be restated and critically evaluated. It will not be surprising to find that these authors have come under the influence of German thought.[13] The classical school and their followers were too prone to overlook the local differences within the English economy. England's dominant international position and the dynamic aspects of her industrial development further helped to cloud their vision. It was in international trade theory that the spatial structure of the domestic economy was most explicitly assumed away or relegated to the background. This step facilitated a macroscopic process analysis (though quite elementary) of international trade which seemed so urgent to the classical school.

On the other hand, the reaction of German thought to classical teachings, which precipitated the rise of the German historical school, ploughed the ground for contributions in the field of "Raumwirtschaft." In the study of the stages of economic development, the spatial structure of economic processes was necessarily a primary concern. And, with the impress of the Lausanne school of thought upon German economics, it was almost inevitable that attempts would be made at a fusion of space with general equilibrium analysis.

2. SOME EARLY ATTEMPTS AT GENERAL THEORY

The first attempt to construct a general location theory is to be attributed to Alfred Weber in his Chap. VII, "Manufacturing Industry Within the Economic System."[14] It is true that the father of location theorists, von Thünen, who was far in advance of his time, did progress

[13] In his various writings Chamberlin, who has not come under German influence, does treat spatial position explicitly, but only as one of the leading manifestations of the broader category of "product differentiation." From his analysis emerges explicitly the need for applying the techniques of monopolistic competition in handling the space-economy of reality. However, his works cannot be classified as general location theory.

[14] *Über den Standort der Industrien,* Tübingen, 1909; English translation with introduction and notes by Carl J. Friedrich, *Alfred Weber's Theory of the Location of Industries,* Chicago, 1929.

somewhat toward a general locational analysis. It may have been that his interests and experiences in the operation of his estate 'Gut Tellow' served to restrict the generality of his abstract thinking. Nonetheless, the seeds for developing the basic methodology in analysis of specific as well as general location problems can be found in Thünen's work.[15] The science of economics has suffered from the relative neglect of his methods during the nineteenth and early twentieth centuries.

Launhardt, the other major predecessor of Weber, also failed to achieve sufficient generality in his analysis. In fact Launhardt's studies of industrial location and market areas[16] treated a narrower set of circumstances than were encompassed in Thünen's isolated state.

Weber's attempt at general locational analysis was undoubtedly greatly influenced by the writings of Roscher and Schäffle.[17] Weber pursued an essentially evolutionary approach. He tried to develop the general basis upon which any given historical system orients itself or, in other words, a theory of the transformation of locational structures.

His method is to inquire into the forces that come into operation

---

The material in the rest of Weber's book does not concern general location. It deals with what is usually conceived of as Weberian location theory, namely, an industrial location theory under the special conditions that: (1) the location and the size of the places of consumption are fixed; (2) the location of the material deposits is given; (3) the geographic cost pattern of labor is given, and at any one point labor is unlimited in supply at constant cost.

Weber's other important contribution ("Industrielle Standortslehre: Allgemeine und kapitalistische Theorie des Standortes," *Grundriss der Sozialökonomik*, Part VI, 2nd rev. ed., Tübingen, 1923) merely touches the field of general location theory.

[15] Johann Heinrich von Thünen, *Der isolierte Staat in Beziehung auf Landwirtschaft und Nationalökonomie*, Hamburg, 1826. See also the interesting article by Bertil Ohlin, "Some Aspects of the Theory of Rent: von Thünen vs. Ricardo," *Economics, Sociology and the Modern World: Essays in Honor of T. N. Carver*, Cambridge, Mass., 1935.

[16] See, in particular, "Die Bestimmung des zweckmässigsten Standortes einer gewerblichen Anlage," *Zeitschrift des Vereins deutscher Ingenieure*, Vol. XXVI, No. 3, Berlin, 1882, and *Mathematische Begründung der Volkswirtschaftslehre*, Leipzig, 1885, Part III.

[17] Wilhelm Roscher, "Studien über die Naturgesetze, welche den zweckmässigen Standort der Industriezweige bestimmen," *Ansichten der Volkswirtschaft aus dem geschichtlichen Standpunkte*, 3rd ed., 1878; A. Schäffle, *Das gesellschaftliche System der menschlichen Wirtschaft*, 3rd ed., Tübingen, 1873. Both were of the German historical school and were primarily concerned with discovering whether or not there were any natural laws or regularities in the evolving locational structures of economies. Their contribution rests in their collection of historical facts and in their presentation of an abundance of conflicting ideas.

when a people occupy an undeveloped country and establish an isolated economic system. At first an agricultural stratum forms to produce the necessary means of subsistence. As indicated in the preceding chapter, the settled area with its agricultural population serves then as the geographical foundation for all other strata. It determines in the first instance the loci (places) of consumption for the second stratum, namely, the primary industrial stratum, which produces for the agricultural stratum. In turn, the primary industrial stratum serves as the loci of consumption for the third stratum, namely, the secondary industrial stratum. This third stratum actually consists of numerous substrata, each of which is oriented to and is smaller than the preceding one, the first substratum being the only one directly oriented to the primary industrial stratum. These three strata form the core of the economic system. The mass of local tradesmen and functionaries, engaged in the process of circulation and in performing personal services, strengthens proportionally the different parts of this system.

A fourth stratum, the central organizing stratum, is essentially independent of any of the three preceding ones. It consists of officials and businessmen with general organizing and managing functions, members of the liberal professions, and persons living off accumulated wealth. Their pattern of locations within the economic system, if not arbitrary, is determined not by economic forces but by others. A fifth stratum, the central dependent stratum, is formed and tied to the central organizing stratum in the same way as is the secondary industrial to the primary industrial stratum.

The locational structures of these five strata are interrelated with forces playing back and forth among them. For example, though the agricultural stratum appears on the scene first, the formation of cities incident to industrial development induces rearrangements of the agricultural structure to conform more closely to the pattern of concentric zones as conceived by von Thünen.

This is as far as Weber goes. Despite the later writings of Engländer,[18] which elaborate and develop the evolutionary approach

[18] Oskar Engländer, "Kritisches und Positives zu einer allgemeinen reinen Lehre vom Standort," *Zeitschrift für Volkswirtschaft und Sozialpolitik,* Neue Folge, Vol. V, Nos. 7–9 (1926). With Engländer the problem is to investigate first the spatial form of primary production, i.e., of a land and forest economy, where all households are self-sufficient. Next, specialized products are assumed to be cultivated on land of particular quality, and the consequent changes in the spatial structure of the economy are observed. In turn, agricultural industries, mining, manufacturing, and other economic elements and complicating factors are successively introduced and the resulting spatial realignments of economic activities

in other ways, and of Ritschl,[19] too, no essential advance in this technique of general analysis is made. The technique is currently inadequate; it does not present any general, heuristic principle by means of which one can order the spatial complexities involved in the total location of economic activities. It merely records the interrelations of the various strata and some of the reactions of one stratum upon another. For any given stratum, or combination of strata, it fails to get at the rule or rules governing structure and provides no common denominator in terms of which all the forces stemming from the various interrelations can be expressed and evaluated and by means of which a net effect could perhaps be deduced.[20] This is the task of a general theory of location and space-economy.

Nonetheless, the evolutionary approach is very useful. It not only furnishes a convenient and meaningful breakdown for studying historical sequences of locational structures and for classifying historical facts but also will be very suggestive for pursuing dynamic analysis, once an improved general static theory has been achieved.[21]

---

noted. Ultimately, according to Engländer, an approximation to the picture of a modern economy is realized.

[19] Hans Ritschl, "Reine und historische Dynamik des Standortes der Erzeugungszweige," *Schmollers Jahrbuch*, Vol. LI (1927), pp. 813–70. Ritschl, recognizing that the location picture is historically relative, follows Weber's classification of strata and traces in detail their development during the periods of village, city, territorial, national, and world economy.

Also see R. G. Hawtrey, *The Economic Problem*, New York, 1925, Chaps. VII and IX, in which to some extent he adopts the approach of Engländer and Ritschl.

[20] This is clearly indicated in Ritschl's work. After describing in detail, in a section on pure dynamics, the various possible effects of changes in ten or more major locational elements, he is unable to find a method for combining their effects. (*Op. cit.*, pp. 853–56.)

[21] In the order of treatment of subject matter, the work of E. M. Hoover, *Location Theory and the Shoe and Leather Industries*, Cambridge, Mass., 1937, somewhat resembles the evolutionary approach. But Hoover's analysis is definitely partial, though in a broad setting. Through carefully drawing up a set of assumptions and relaxing them one by one, he is able to proceed from an analysis of extractive industries to a treatment of manufacturing, first under simple conditions and then under more complex ones. He emphasizes the major specific forces at work and does not pay too much attention to general interrelations, especially when they can be stated only in broad terms. In this way he is able to synthesize the various theoretical contributions of his predecessors that are of practical value and, by employing illustrative empirical material, is able to stick close to reality. From the standpoint of balance and sound judgment Hoover's writings are the best. See also his *Location of Economic Activity*, New York, 1948.

Other major works in English on location theory are by A. P. Usher (*A Dynamic Analysis of the Location of Economic Activity*, unpublished) and by W. H. Dean, Jr. (*The Theory of the Geographic Location of Economic Activities*, doctoral

3. PREDÖHL'S CONCEPTION

Shortly after the appearance of Weber's book, Bortkiewicz[22] and Schumpeter[23] recognized the need of a general equilibrium analysis to supplement partial locational theories.[24] Considerably later Engländer[25] came to appreciate in full the implications of a general theory of location. The pure theory of location, according to Engländer, is the general theory of "local conditionality" within an economy. Any given entrepreneur, in choosing the site at which to produce or render services, considers the various supply prices existing in the various localities for the inputs that he might possibly employ. At the same time he considers the various prices which might be obtained in the various localities for his product or services. When finally he does locate at a site, he influences in turn the prices of various inputs and outputs. Through being so interrelated, the pattern of local price differences and the location of economic activities are simultaneously determined by a general theory of "local conditionality."[26]

---

dissertation, Harvard University, 1938: Selections published by Edward Brothers, Inc., Ann Arbor, Mich., 1938). Usher and Dean, too, follow a partial approach both in their static analyses and in their dynamics where they rely upon extensive use of historical material. Their interests are in "the broader aspects of the developing geographic patterns of population density" and in "the relations of these patterns to localized resources and to the significance that regional resources possess under the technological conditions of each historical period." (Usher, *op. cit.*, p. 2.) They study: (1) topography as a vital and partially independent factor in the pattern of settlement; (2) the impact of transport innovation particularly as it relates to the accessibility of resource deposits to the primary regions of the world; (3) nodality and industrial agglomeration; (4) externally-conditioned labor and the controlling role of energy resources; (5) the historical patterns of urban settlements; and (6) other related subjects. These studies are in a sense interwoven, but at best only loosely. The result is a set of highly valuable partial analyses, and not a finely spun general framework.

[22] *Deutsche Literaturzeitung*, Vol. XXXI (1910), pp. 1717–24.

[23] *Jahrbuch für Gesetzgebung, Verwaltung und Volkswirtschaft*, Vol. XXXIV, No. 3 (1910), pp. 444–47.

[24] V. Furlan ["Die Standortsprobleme in der Volks- und Weltwirtschaftslehre," *Weltwirtschaftliches Archiv*, Vol. II (1913), pp. 1–34] makes a somewhat abortive attempt at general locational analysis. The complicated interrelations of various economic factors as well as the "spatial transformation of goods" are fully recognized; but the contributions to knowledge are essentially along the lines of developing overly simplified models of markets, domestic and international, more specifically of determining points of collection and distribution of goods and of export and import, and the related paths of commerce.

[25] *Op. cit.*

[26] Further: (1) by classifying raw materials and factors of production, whether mobile or immobile, as place-free (available everywhere under the same condi-

32   LOCATION AND SPACE–ECONOMY

Somewhat earlier (1925) than Engländer's publications there appeared an article, "Das Standortsproblem in der Wirtschaftstheorie,"[27] by Andreas Predöhl, which utilized a principle by means of which a general equilibrium approach could be systematically applied to location analysis. This was none other than the familiar substitution principle, already well established in general equilibrium theory.

Although Predöhl did visualize new horizons in the extended use of this principle, he unfortunately tried to remain within the scope of traditional thought. He purported to deduce a general location theory as a special case of the existing general economic theory, as a logical and inherent element of it. The general economic theory to which he alluded was the theory of interdependent prices and quantities, of general equilibrium as expounded successively by Walras, Pareto, and Cassel. He wished to investigate how far the location problem is a price problem; location theory, a price theory. In other words, to what extent does the local distribution of production lie inside the economic relationship of interdependent prices?[28]

Predöhl contends that the problem of the local distribution of economic activity is synonymous with the problem of the distribution of determined groups (bundles) of productive factors (he groups productive factors under the categories of land, labor, and capital) since every economic activity uses a grouping of factors. The distribution of determined groups of productive factors in turn is a special case of the distribution of productive factors in general.[29] To Predöhl,

tions), conditionally place-bound (available at all or some places under unequal conditions), and unconditionally place-bound (present at one site), and (2) by conceiving immobile goods as goods of infinite weight which enter into production with infinite weight-loss, Engländer brings together the specific location theories of industry and agriculture within the confines of his pure location theory, not as distinct compartments, but as internally related sectors.

Elsewhere, too, Engländer has attacked a broad range of location problems, but only through elucidation of simplified, isolated cases. See his *Theorie des Güterverkehrs und der Frachtsätze*, Jena 1924, and "Standort" in *Handwörterbuch der Staatswissenschaften*, 4th rev. ed., Jena 1926, Vol. VII.

[27] *Weltwirtschaftliches Archiv*, Vol. XXI (1925), pp. 294–331. A briefer article in English, "The Theory of Location in its Relation to General Economics," appeared in the *Journal of Political Economy*, Vol. XXXVI (1928), pp. 371–90. A much more recent statement in German which was available only after the following paragraphs were written is contained in his book, *Aussenwirtschaft: Weltwirtschaft, Handelspolitik und Währungspolitik*, Göttingen, 1949. Also see Predöhl's reply to Engländer's criticism, "Zur Frage einer allgemein Standortstheorie," *Zeitschrift für Volkswirtschaft und Sozialpolitik*, Vol. V, Nos. 10–12 (1927), pp. 756–63.

[28] "Das Standortsprobleme . . ." *Op. cit.*, pp. 295–97.

[29] As will be shown later, this statement is very weak, if not untenable.

general interdependence theory explains the distribution of productive factors in general by means of the principle of substitution. Therefore general location theory is deducible from the application of the principle of substitution to the employment of the several groups of productive factors.[30]

Predöhl in his reasoning overestimates the scope of Walrasian-Casselian general equilibrium analysis. On the whole he seems to be under the impression that this analysis implicitly embraces the space element in its entirety. However, as indicated previously, modern as well as earlier general equilibrium analyses, with minor exceptions, concern a one-point world. The element of transport cost is generally abstracted; factors and products possess perfect mobility. In essence there is no spatial distribution of factors; the relevant problem is the distribution of factors among the various types of production. In reality, then, the situation is the reverse of what Predöhl has conceived although several times he appears to realize the truth of the matter. As we have pointed out, Walrasian-Casselian general equilibrium analysis is but a special case of a general location theory.[31]

Nevertheless, the tools shaped by general equilibrium theory are useful, as Predöhl discovered. Starting with the familiar case of Thünen's isolated state,[32] Predöhl assumes all locations fixed except that of one enterprise. A shift of this enterprise toward the periphery implies that capital and labor outlays (including transport outlays) are substituted for land-use outlays. The reverse takes place in a shift toward the central consumption point. Application of the principle of substitution will yield the site of minimum cost so far as these two all-inclusive groups of expenditures are concerned. However, within these two all-inclusive groups, there are other substitution points. For example, within the former group, there is a substitution point between transport outlays and *local* capital and labor outlays (such as is involved in determining whether or not to process a product

---

[30] *Op. cit.*, pp. 299–303.

[31] However, see Predöhl's reaction to these statements in his recent article "Von der Standortslehre zur Raumwirtschaftslehre," *Jahrbuch für Sozialwissenschaft*, Band 2, Heft 1, pp. 97–102.

[32] The features of Thünen's familiar model are: a uniform plain with equal fertility and possibilities for agricultural production at all points, at the center of which lies a city possessing potential transport facilities of similar character in all directions (i.e., transport costs proportional to weight and distance). Production aligns itself around the city in rings in accordance with the price and transport cost of each particular product cultivated. Predöhl adopts at the start an expanded version of Thünen where all conditions for all production, whether agricultural or industrial, are uniform throughout the plain (*ibid.*, p. 299).

in order to reduce its weight or bulk); and within the category of transport outlay, there may be a substitution point involved in allocating a given portion between transporting a raw material lying at the periphery and transporting a raw material lying near the consumption center. In this manner innumerable interdependent points of substitution arise which determine the location of any individual enterprise. This proposition, states Predöhl, can be extended by means of general equilibrium analysis to cover the location of all economic activities.[33]

Inequalities in local resource patterns, land, labor, capital, and transport do not invalidate the operation of the substitution principle. They present various technical possibilities for production which are different from those that would exist in Thünen's homogeneous plain; but essentially these new production possibilities, like the old, can be expressed in terms of economic values and, thus, fall within the scope of substitution operations. Similarly, economic values can be imputed to various historical-political forces, though here many more difficulties and arbitrary elements creep in. Recognizing these various limitations (for example, in accounting for the locus of consumption of the rentier classes), Predöhl does, however, maintain that the locationally relevant substitution points, thus logically deduced, are applicable in general.[34]

It is to be expected that Predöhl in this first attempt at substitution analysis would be unable to resolve all the difficulties that beset his path. His argument is particularly weak when he becomes specific and illustrates substitution operations—a step which he avoids as much as possible. For example, he utilizes a vague concept, namely, a land-use unit, and speaks of rent outlays at different sites as being proportional to the quantities of land-use units at those sites. Land more distant from a city and yielding less rent therefore relates to fewer technical units of land use than does land less distant which yields greater rent. Engländer easily demonstrated that this proposition is false: that two pieces of land unequally distant from a city can

<hr/>

[33] "Der Standort der Produktion bzw. Produktionsstufe ist also bestimmt durch ein System von Substitutionspunkten, das derart gegliedert ist, dass die Gruppen einer übergeordneten Kombination untergeordnete Kombination in sich enthalten. Übertragen wir diese Lösung auf sämtliche Produktionen, dann können wir unter Zuspitzung eines allgemeinen Casselschen Satzes auf unser besonderes Problem sagen: Wenn das Preisverhältnis in dieser Weise für jeden einzelnen Betrieb die standortlich relevanten Substitutionspunkte bestimmt, sind offenbar durch dasselbe für die gesamte Gesellschaft die zu verwendenden Mengen in Verhältnis zueinander, mithin die Standorte bestimmt." *Ibid.*, pp. 306–7.

[34] *Ibid.*, pp. 308–11.

be of the exact same quality and be utilized to the same degree, and yet yield different rents.[35]

Further, Predöhl tends to convert all spatial and quality differences into differences in quantities of use units. Immobile labor, situated at diverse places and of different qualities, can be converted into amounts of labor-use units and thus made comparable. And so with all types of resources.[36] In this way all geographic differences in land, labor, and capital can be summed up into use units of land, labor, and capital at any given point. This reasoning lies behind Predöhl's argument that the distribution among various economic activities of determined groups of productive factors (each group at any point of time having a unique spatial position) is a special case of the distribution among various economic activities of productive factors in general in terms of a one-point society.

It is not necessary to carry the argument to such an extreme, if not untenable, position. It is appropriate now to suggest certain revisions and extensions to be developed in subsequent chapters in order to strengthen the basis for a widespread use of the substitution principle in location analysis.

First one ought to distinguish between two types of substitutions: (1) that between transport inputs; and (2) that between outlays, between revenues, and between outlays and revenues. If there is any sense at all to location economics, it is because there are certain regularities in the variations of costs and prices over space. These regularities arise primarily because transport cost is some function of distance. If this were not so, if transport costs were completely irregular and their changes unpredictable—for example, if transport costs on a certain item were positive for a distance of 100 miles and negative for a distance of 101 miles—there would be little sense in searching for a general economics of plant locations. The spatial pattern of industrial concentrations, of consuming centers, and of the production of raw materials would be quite arbitrary from the economic standpoint.

Since it is the distance factor that is the heart of locational analysis, there is every reason to speak of transport inputs (a concept to be defined later), wherein distance and weight are the two basic factors, and of transport rates as prices of these inputs. Location theorists unfortunately have shied away from such a concept. However, it

[35] "Kritisches und Positives . . . ," *op. cit.*, pp. 499–500. See Predöhl's weak reply, ("Zur Frage . . . ," *op. cit.*, pp. 758–60). Also see his later and stronger reply ("Von der Standortslehre . . . ," *op. cit.*, pp. 100–101).

[36] "The Theory of Location . . . ," *op. cit.*, pp. 380–81.

brings into bold relief the basic aspects of spatial analysis without the necessity of tagging each unit of land, labor, and capital with a set of absolute spatial co-ordinates or of converting them into common units, if, indeed, this can be done. The problem of production becomes a problem of choosing the right combination of the various types of capital, labor, land, and transport inputs. In the case of transport-oriented industries and transport-oriented sets of economic activities, how the essential location analysis reduces to a consideration of substitution between transport inputs will be demonstrated.

The selection of the correct substitution points between transport inputs is easy to visualize although in practice it may be difficult to effect because of the complicated nature of transport rate structures. However, selection of the correct substitution point between a transport input and a labor input, or between the two groups, transport inputs and labor inputs, cannot be so satisfactorily handled. That here the choice of the optimum location requires an outright comparison of outlays on the various kinds of labor, or of total labor outlays and total transport outlays, or of total labor outlays and total interest outlays, and so forth will be indicated. Substitution analysis in terms of outlays and revenues must supplement substitution analysis in terms of transport inputs in order to achieve a proper locational methodology.

By this approach, Predöhl's original conception can be made more digestible and broadened into a general equilibrium theory of space-economy, which includes as special cases various types of location theories as well as actual modern general equilibrium theory.[37]

[37] It is interesting to note that Predöhl and others have rightly pointed out that Weber's industrial location theory is chiefly based on technical empirical knowledge. Transport costs are reduced to weight and distance, i.e., to technical factors; varying raw material prices and other elements are reduced in similar fashion. Technical concepts such as locational weight, material index, coefficient of labor, Formkoeffizient, and others are the critical measures. The point of transport orientation is merely the point of minimum transportation in terms of *ton-kilometers*. Essentially Weber abstracts from most economic interrelations and reactions. Only under severe limitations is Weberian doctrine generally applicable.

However these criticisms do not detract from the merits of Weber's contribution. Formal theory, in and of itself, is highly unsatisfactory, too general and, accordingly, too sterile. As Predöhl emphasizes, it needs to be supplemented by concrete information; abstract and vague values must be replaced by exact, quantitative data. In other words, supplementary explanations are required, even if they are obtained in such a manner as to limit their general validity. It is in fulfilling this need that Weber's work is of great significance. If the general theory of location constructed upon the principle of substitution is to be of pragmatic value, to it must be added empirical location theory and statistical investigation which seeks out regular movements in major economic variables, even though

4. WEIGMANN'S FORMULATIONS

In this section a summary of the contributions of Hans Weigmann,[38] which have received but slight attention in the literature is presented. Weigmann's writings on general location theory are very difficult to comprehend, because of both his vague style and the complexity of the basic concepts. These concepts do not lend themselves to a general synthesis as do those of other contributors. Nonetheless, they seem to disclose some of the more promising channels of exploration for further theoretical development.

Weigmann attempts to formulate the foundations for a *realistic* economic theory which embraces the spatial structure of economic processes, the spatial extent and bonds of markets, and the spatial interrelations of all economic quantities.

The first principle that Weigmann establishes is that a theory of space-economy embraces a theory of limited competition. Actually all factors and goods, regardless of setting, face immobilities of varying extent in all directions; and, in accordance with the nature of the obstacles to movement, whether they be economic, social, political, or cultural, markets are restricted in scope. The competition which any good or factor can offer to other goods and factors at different locations is incomplete. The existence of physical space implies immobility,

---

this means eliminating the numerous special factors which affect each individual situation. Weber's theory of industrial location is just such a supplementary, empirical theory (it excludes economic details which he considers relatively unimportant, and thus in great part hypothesizes that the set of technical substitution points approximately parallels the set of economic substitution points). But ultimately all such empirical technical functional observations must be translated into economic terms.

Indeed, it is only by utilizing chiefly the Weberian approach with supplementary economic data that I have found it meaningful to analyze the locational structure of the iron and steel industry. See my "Some Locational Factors in the Iron and Steel Industry since the Early Nineteenth Century," *Journal of Political Economy*, Vol. LVI (June 1948); and (with W. Capron) "The Future Locational Pattern of Iron and Steel Production in the United States," *Journal of Political Economy*, Vol. LVII (April 1949). Also see E. Niederhauser, "Die Standortstheorie Alfred Webers," *Staatswissenschaftliche Studien*, Vol. XIV (Weinfelden, 1944).

[38] "Ideen zu einer Theorie der Raumwirtschaft," *Weltwirtschaftliches Archiv*, Vol. XXXIV (1931), pp. 1–40; and "Standortstheorie und Raumwirtschaft" in *Joh. Heinr. von Thünen zum 150 Geburtstag*, ed. by W. Seedorf and H. Jurgen, Rostock, Carl Hinstorffs, 1933, pp. 137–57. To trace the development of Weigmann's thought the reader is also referred to the following of his works: *Kritischer Beitrag zur Theorie des internationalen Handels*, G. Fischer, Jena, 1926, and *Politische Raumsordnung*, Hanseatische Verlagsanstalt, Hamburg, 1935.

limited competition, and spatial inelasticity (or negative spatial elasticity). Thus the generally accepted principle of pure competition is not applicable to the analysis of spatial economic processes.[39]

A second basic principle concerns the question of form. In place of customary linear causal analysis, Weigmann favors the approach of general equilibrium theory in the employment of Gestalt analysis. He observes the space-economy as a whole in its full array of spatial markets. In that sense he aims at presenting a realistic functional picture of the "form-full" of economic life, wherein the various elements are weighted in accord with their importance. Having adopted this methodology, he confronts the primary problem of determining the basic form (Grundgestalt) of economic phenomena, i.e., the Gestalt core. This basic form should then provide an heuristic principle to help master and order systematically the "form wealth" of real economic life, or in other words, the countless spatial forms of moving economic processes.[40]

At this point Weigmann differentiates between statics (mobility or competition as potential energy) and dynamics. Since he purports to describe the space-economy in its realistic setting, he is compelled to complicate his problem manifoldly by introducing the time element and by assigning time co-ordinates to his various markets and processes. Weigmann poses the perplexing problem of dynamics as follows: to choose that time period which would yield in the resulting spatial array of markets a competition field (a broad market area in time and space) which could be valid as the basic form.[41] He resolves the problem by formulating a concept quite difficult to comprehend, the concept of "relative maximum." It states that as an increasing amount of physical space (therefore spatial resistance) is to be overcome in movement by an economic object, the time period necessary for such movement increases until it reaches a maximum—a maximum in the sense that given still more time a further spatial movement would be improbable because of the overpowering force of the countless obstacles. There,

---

[39] "Ideen zu . . . ," op. cit., pp. 6–9. These points are also developed by Chamberlin in his doctoral dissertation of 1927, op. cit., especially pp. 105–09, 167–84; and in The Theory of Monopolistic Competition, 1933, passim. In the latter, a portion of the earlier analysis devoted to two-dimensional space was simplified to one dimension and removed from Chapter 5 to Appendix C.

[40] Ibid., pp. 9–12.

[41] ". . . welches Konkurrenzgebiet ist essentiell im Sinne des Gestaltganzen, wenn beliebiger Absteckung der Zeitgrenzen eine Fülle räumliche variierender Flächen entsteht? Oder anders ausgedrückt: welcher Zeitraum ist zu wählen, damit ein mit diesem Zeitmass gegebenes Konkurrenzfeld als Grundgestalt gelten kann?" Ibid., p. 14.

where the time period reaches its maximum, competition ends and the competition field becomes bounded. In other words, the force of competition does not have the power to span a distance greater than the radius (or axis) of its field, irrespective of the time factor for all practical purposes. This principle contains the definition of basic form. The basic form is depicted as that unit of space (corresponding to a market region or competition field) of the relatively greatest time-weight, hence, of the relatively greatest stability and permanence.[42]

Having exposed the tremendous magnitude of the task of formulating a theory of space-economy, Weigmann stops for breath. How to locate the basic form? How to represent as an empirical Gestalt unit the multitude of interlaced, mutually related individual markets, market strata, and market densities? From here on our author can only offer fruitful suggestions and preliminary observations for conquering the manifold difficulties which appear. First we have the classification of markets according to structure. Each individual commodity market including its labor, capital, and land orientation possesses a particular structure which offers a certain resistance to change. Some change frequently, others slowly. Some are active, others highly inactive. By definition those markets of a relatively permanent nature, of persistent inactivity, are grouped together as the essential ones, as the basic form; their combined structure determines the basic structure of the Gestalt whole, of the space-economy under question. On the other hand, the rapidly changing markets are considered as accidental or secondary; their movements are characterized as minor modifications of the Gestalt form, and these movements are to a certain extent conditioned by the already determined basic form, by the core of markets of greatest continuity. Fundamental organic change of the Gestalt picture of the space-economy, therefore, implies only change within this relatively immutable core of persistent markets.[43]

[42] ". . . und führen angesichts des Vorhandenseins eines relativen Maximums zeitkostender Bewegung innerhalb jedes Gestaltganzen zu einem Bilde sich bündelnder und überschneidender Konkurrenzfelder als den akzidentiellen und peripheren Erscheinungsformen einer zentralen Grundgestalt. Der Begriff des relativen Maximums besagt dabei folgendes: Die Konkurrenz wird gradweise beschränkt und als dort aufhörend bedacht, wo die zahlreichen hemmenden Faktoren den sukzessiv steigenden Zeitaufwand der Bewegung zu einem Maximum hinführen, bei dem unter den konkret gegebenen Umständen die weitere Bewegung unwahrscheinlich wird oder auf lange Sicht nicht mehr die Kraft besitzt, mit Ansicht auf anhaltenden Erfolg Spannungsunterschiede aufzugleichen. Die Grundgestalt ist also die Raumeinheit des relative grössten Zeitgewichtes; die Dauer des Bestandes gibt ihr den Charakter der essentiellen Form." Ibid., pp. 14–15.

[43] Ibid., pp. 16–19.

Our task is further illuminated by reference to the structures of the specific markets for land, labor, and capital goods. Weigmann maintains that the markets for the productive factors of labor and land are primary constituencies of the basic form. Movements in all commodity markets course back to these two, whether directly or indirectly, through semifinished products and various stages of production. And in these markets for labor and land, which offer great resistance to change, are focused the facts of scarcity within the economy.

The land market is portrayed as a spatially-connected area of supplied land services. Actually each individual piece of land is distinct and immobilized by nature, so that its supply area has no spatial extent. But for practical purposes Weigmann conceives of a Gestalt whole (space-economy) already in existence. This whole exerts an hypothetical aggregate demand which, in turn, defines the boundaries of the land market, the peripheral area being considered as marginal land. The supply of land in general is not perfectly inelastic, spatially speaking. Change in the land market ensues (1) from additions or subtractions at the fringe to the land under cultivation, i.e., an expansion or contraction of the space base of the economy, and (2) from variations in the intensity of use and in the methods of cultivation and organization of each individual land unit.[44]

The size and nature of the hypothetical demand mentioned above is obviously related to the labor market. The labor market, in contrast to the market for land, is much less rigid and invariable; for that reason the conception and description of it are theoretically and empirically much more difficult. There are many forms of labor immobility and inelasticity. Weigmann makes a beginning at analysis by explaining one, namely migration mobility. To delimit the labor market accordingly, one must recognize the various time stages of migration (e.g., seasonal, cyclical, and secular) and their spatial forms. In line with familiar Weberian technique, the long-run labor base is presented as a continually moving, organic process whereby labor, step-by-step through varying intervals of time, gradually moves from farms or rural communities to giant metropolitan centers via town and urban clusters of increasing size.[45] This ever structural

[44] *Ibid.*, pp. 20–23.

[45] Weber ("Industrielle Standortslehre . . . ," *op. cit.*, pp. 74–84) distinguishes two stages of modern capitalistic development: (1) bound (gebundene) capitalism and (2) free capitalism. In the former, which characterizes the sixteenth to the eighteenth centuries, labor is historically fixed, locationally immobile. In the latter, which characterizes the present times, labor becomes mobile, released from

movement within the labor base is designated as one of the essential dynamic aspects of modern space-economies.[46]

With respect to markets for capital goods, Weigmann offers a few suggestions. First we must distinguish capital in substance from capital in title. The former obviously has far more limited mobility. Second, capital goods (a concept which in its broadest formulation includes all commodities) must be classified according to the extent to which they become bound up in production. At one end of the scale would be "combination-free" capital goods; at the other end would be capital goods permanently tied to a given production combination. The spatial elasticities and markets of the several divisions of capital goods would vary accordingly. Unfortunately, present day terminology regarding capital (e.g., fixed and circulating) is unsuited for depicting its spatial elasticity; nor has theory recognized the influence of spatial elasticity upon the various other elasticity forms of capital.

The formulation of the problem of a theory of space-economy thus is more comprehensive than that of traditional location theory. The latter has chiefly treated capital as a "combination free" factor in its long-run agglomerative setting but has given little attention to the mobility of existing equipment, to the short-run adaptability of capital goods. In fact, for an empirical theory, there are even strong grounds for considering the mobility of a given combination of various productive factors as a whole, rather than of their constituent parts—a phase of the problem which location theory has rarely posed.[47] Furthermore, location theory has frequently been of restricted scope in that it has often sought the ideal location of a given firm, others assumed in equilibrium.

Thus Weigmann sketches his picture of the space-economy as a rhythmic-moving Gestalt whole with a core composed of the markets for land, labor, and capital goods and of numerous other markets superimposed upon these, overlapping and irregularly intersecting each other and at times extending into other space-economies.[48] His

---

its historical bonds. The economies of concentration and large-scale organization can come into operation and can offer incentives for huge masses of labor to agglomerate at given points. On the other hand, these forces are offset by the community attachments (home feeling) of the individual laborer, by his lack of perspective and initiative, and by the consequent increase in rent at the points of agglomeration. The net result is the step-by-step migration already mentioned.

[46] "Ideen zu . . . ," op. cit., pp. 23–27.

[47] Ibid., pp. 27–32.

[48] In the Thünen Festschrift (op. cit.) Weigmann commences with existing location theory (the Engländer and Predöhl versions) and approaches a theory of

presentation lacks clarity and frequently one is forced to construe an imaginary model in order to follow the argument. Nevertheless, one obtains penetrating insight into the subtle spatial relations of economic life and is given an original as well as a challenging view of the immense magnitude of the assignment.

5. Palander's Criticisms and Lösch's General System

In Sect. 3 a development of the framework of a general (static) theory of location and space-economy in terms of the substitution principle has been suggested. However, it has been customary in general equilibrium analysis to present the relations of a given one-point economic order by means of a system of mathematical equations. Should a solution for this system of equations exist, the merit of the presentation is generally regarded as considerably enhanced. Can a solvable system of equations be evolved for a space-economy?

Tord Palander, in the first major work on location theory to originate outside of Germany, addressed himself to this question.[49] He considered insuperable the difficulties encountered by the general approach in representing or even closely approximating reality.

First, states Palander, writing in 1935, the Walras-Pareto-Cassel general equilibrium theory in its present form is meaningful for a locational analysis only of an economic district wherein transport costs are zero, capital and labor perfectly mobile, and technical conditions of production uniform throughout—in other words, where the district in question can be compressed into a point market. To be sure, he continues, a somewhat closer approximation to reality can be obtained by withdrawing one by one the simplifying assumptions given above. For example, there might be introduced into the simplified model the following series of complications: freight costs on product based on distance and weight, transport costs for mobile production factors, equal real wages throughout the district, consumption as dependent upon location choice, and so forth. Even so, contends Palander, this procedure would not take us far, for in respects other than the neglect of local differences in demand and supply of factors and commodities, the deviations of a general equilibrium theory from

space-economy ("total localization") in part through the extension of Predöhl's substitution principle to include "quantity elasticity." Quantity elasticity is synonymous with a broad definition of elasticity of supply, one that embraces, among others, spatial elasticity. In this way Weigmann brings out the logical bond of location theory and general price theory.

[49] *Beiträge zur Standortstheorie,* Almqvist & Wiksells Boktryckeri-A.-B., Uppsala, 1935, Chaps. X and XI.

reality are severe. Interdependence theory has as an underlying premise the principle of pure competition. Yet, in no sense at all, can the traditional interpretation of this premise hold when we introduce space and thus transport costs into the analysis. If the various places in a region under consideration are treated as different markets (corresponding in this way to the varying local prices resulting from transport costs between these places), then the necessary condition of a large number of buyers and sellers for each commodity and factor at each market, cannot be fulfilled. If the region itself is viewed as one market, one could interpret the different prices ruling for a given commodity at the various places within the region (1) as signifying non-uniformity of product, or better yet, (2) as signifying a uniform product in a persistently imperfect market where individuals are in monopoly situations in accordance with the advantages of their respective positions. Neither case could be regarded as pure competition.[50]

If one now discards the premise of pure competition, he must necessarily forsake certain supplementary simple principles which have served as scaffolding for general equilibrium theory, namely, that the price of a commodity equals average cost (the latter including a normal profit) and that the price of a factor equals the value of its marginal product.[51]

Further censure of general equilibrium analysis follows from its limitation to static conditions, a widely recognized limitation which does not need to be discussed here.[52] Palander insists on the necessity of depicting the economic development process. His conscience thus compels him to forego Walrasian economics in favor of the Launhardt-Weber tradition. His energies are confined to analyzing the economic starting point, the adaptations of enterprise during a time period, the movement of factors during the same period, and the concomitant changes of technique, institutions, and consumer base.[53]

August Lösch, however, has not accepted these views. In his monumental work, *Die räumliche Ordnung der Wirtschaft*,[54] he goes

[50] *Ibid.*, pp. 273–77.

[51] *Ibid.*, pp. 277–78.

[52] However, see the work of Samuelson which relates the comparative statical behavior of a general equilibrium system to its dynamical stability properties (*op. cit.*, Part II).

[53] Palander, *op. cit.*, pp. 278–85.

[54] G. Fischer, Jena, 1st ed. 1940, 2nd ed. 1944. All page references are to the second edition. Part of the material of this book is available in English in the article "The Nature of Economic Regions," *Southern Economic Journal*, Vol. V (July 1938), pp. 71–78, and in a review article by W. F. Stolper, *American Eco-*

beyond partial analysis and the mere recognition of the complex spatial interrelations of economic factors. He presents succinctly, through a set of elementary equations, a highly simplified static model of a space-economy operating *under conditions of monopolistic competition.* To appreciate fully this model, one must understand Lösch's concept of the market, by means of which space is introduced into the problem and which represents his other major contribution to location theory. What is the market area? How is it bounded? These questions are fundamental.

Lösch postulates the following: a broad, homogeneous plain with uniform transport features in all directions and with an even scatter of industrial raw materials in sufficient quantity for production; a uniform distribution of agricultural population with a uniform set of tastes and preferences, each homestead at the start being self-sufficient; technical knowledge disseminated throughout the plain and production opportunities available to all. In all other respects, too, extra-economic forces are excluded. If in this situation an individual finds it profitable (owing to the economies of large-scale production as opposed to the handicap of transport cost) to produce a commodity over and above the needs of his homestead, his market area would assume a circular form. However, if one farmer finds it profitable to produce over and above his needs, so will others, and the force of competition, by eliminating all excess profits, not only will contract the market area of the original producer but also will transform the circular shape of the market area into a hexagon. The hexagon is the ideal economic form of market area, it is maintained. Firstly, a net of hexagonal market forms will exhaust (completely cover) any area under consideration, whereas circular ones will leave empty unutilized corners, as is readily seen from a graphic presentation. Secondly, of all the regular polygons (hexagon, square, and triangle) which will exhaust a given area, the hexagon deviates least from the circle form and, in consequence, minimizes the transport expenditures in supplying a given demand or, expressed differently, maximizes the demand of the population of a given area.[55]

For each commodity, then, the plain is dissected into a honeycomb

nomic Review, Vol. XXXIII (September 1943), pp. 626–36. Also see Lösch's article, "Beiträge zur Standortstheorie," *Schmollers Jahrbuch,* Vol. LXII (1938), pp. 329–35.

Since the writing of this and other chapters, Lösch's basic work has become available in an English translation: *The Economics of Location,* Yale University Press, New Haven, 1954.

[55] *Die räumliche Ordnung . . . , op. cit.,* pp. 70–78.

(a net of hexagons) of market areas. Lösch next groups these honeycombs according to the size of their respective market units. And, in a manner consistent with the established criterion of minimum transport effort, he orders the resulting nets about a common, central production point to obtain his system of nets.[56]

We are now in a position to reproduce Lösch's attempt at a general equilibrium scheme. At the start Lösch attacks the problem of the location of the production of industrial goods alone. The same hypotheses which were basic to the above determination of market areas are retained for the general analysis. Table I presents the symbols of spatial arrangement. The position in the plain of each production place of each commodity is designated by a set of x, y co-ordinates; the boundary of the market area of each production place is described by a set of equations, each equation being represented by a corresponding Greek symbol in Table I.

Lösch puts forth the following, as either given or unknown:

A. Given:

$d^m = f^m(\pi)$ individual demand for good m

$\pi_q{}^m = \phi^m(D_q)$ the factory price $\}$ of the good m at place q as a function of the total demand

$k_q{}^m = \chi^m(D_q)$ the average production cost $\big[D_q{}^m = \psi(f^m, x_q{}^m y_q{}^m, \alpha_q{}^m \beta_q{}^m \cdots \epsilon_q{}^m, \sigma, \sigma_q{}^m \cdots).$

$S_q{}^m = D_q{}^m(\pi_q{}^m - k_q{}^m)$ the profit on product m at place q

σ = rural population per square kilometer

$\sigma_q{}^m$ = population of the city $p_q{}^m$

r = freight rate

m = number of products

G = total surface area

B. To be sought:

		Number of unknowns
1. $\pi_q{}^m$	= factory price of the good m at location $p_q{}^m$	n
2. G^m	= market area of the location $p_q{}^m$ in square kilometers	n
3. q^m	= the number of towns which produce good m	m
4. $x_q{}^m, y_q{}^m$	= co-ordinates of the location $p_q{}^m$	$2n$
5. $\alpha_q{}^m, \beta_q{}^m \cdots \epsilon_q{}^m$	= equations of the boundaries of the market area of $p_q{}^m$	N

Total: $4n + m + N$

Corresponding to the list of unknowns, Lösch presents in Table II a set of equilibrium conditions. The first condition for equilibrium

[56] *Ibid.*, pp. 79–90.

LOCATION AND SPACE–ECONOMY

TABLE I. SYMBOLS OF SPATIAL ARRANGEMENT

Product Number	Production Places		Market Boundaries	
	Position	Number	Abbreviations of their equations	Number
1	$p_1^1(x_1^1 y_1^1); p_2^1 \cdots p_a^1$	a	$\alpha_1^1, \beta_1^1 \cdots \epsilon_1^1; \alpha_2^1, \beta_2^1 \cdots$	A
2	$p_1^2(x_1^2 y_1^2); p_2^2 \cdots p_b^2$	b	$\alpha_1^2, \beta_1^2 \cdots \eta_1^2; \alpha_2^2, \beta_2^2 \cdots$	B
.	.	.	.	.
.	.	.	.	.
.	.	.	.	.
m	$p_1^m(x_1^m y_1^m); p_2^m \cdots p_q^m$	q	$\alpha_1^m, \beta_1^m, \cdots \rho_1^m; \alpha_2^m, \beta_2^m \cdots$	Q
m	(total)	n	(total)	N

$$= a + b + \cdots + q \qquad\qquad = \frac{A + B + \cdots + Q}{2}$$

which must be fulfilled is that each producer occupy a spatial position which maximizes his profits; as a result he will not find it desirable to change his location either in the x or y direction.

Second, the whole plain under consideration must be exhausted by the various market areas for any particular good. Third, no abnormal profit may exist; the cost of each commodity produced at any factory must equal its factory price. Fourth, the changes in average price and average cost ensuing from an infinitesimal change in the size of any producer's market area must be equal. This follows from the assumption of free entry into any line of production and from the negatively sloping demand curve confronting each producer. In other words, a Chamberlinian tangency solution results which guarantees that the size of each producer's market area must be the minimum economically possible. This condition together with the second and third insures a maximum number of independent producers.

The fifth condition requires that any consumer on any boundary line be indifferent as to the possible production sources from which he can obtain a given commodity at the same minimum delivered price.

Since, *in toto*, the number of fulfilling equations of Table II equals the number of unknowns, the system of spatial economy is determinate; the unknowns can be derived.[57]

[57] *Ibid.*, pp. 63–68. Tables I and II and the lists of given and unknown conditions are for the most part literal translations.

TABLE II. EQUILIBRIUM SYSTEM I

Condition	Fulfilling Equations	Number of Equations
1. Maximum profits (so far as 2–4 allow)	$\dfrac{\partial S_q{}^m}{\partial x_q{}^m} = 0;\ \dfrac{\partial S_q{}^m}{\partial y_q{}^m} = 0$	$2n$
2. Total area utilized	$G_1{}^m + G_2{}^m + \cdots + G_q{}^m = G$	m
3. No abnormal profits	$\phi_q{}^m(D_q) = \chi^m(D_q)$	n
4. Area as small as possible	$\dfrac{\partial \pi_q{}^m}{\partial G_q{}^m} = \dfrac{\partial k_q{}^m}{\partial G_q{}^m}.$	n
5. Indifference lines as boundaries	For any point $x,\ y$ on boundary equation α: $\pi_q{}^m + r_q{}^m \sqrt{(x - x_q{}^m)^2 + (y - y_q{}^m)^2} = \pi_{q-1}{}^m + r_{q-1}{}^m \sqrt{(x - x_{q-1}{}^m)^2 + (y - y_{q-1}{}^m)^2}$	N

Maximum number of producers

In a manner analogous to the above, states Lösch, the location of the production of agricultural goods can be analyzed. In a similar manner, too, the reverse propositions, which concern the conditions for the best location of industrial and agricultural places in their capacity as consumption centers, can be attacked. Unfortunately, however, the optimal location for production does not necessarily coincide with the optimal location for consumption; and Lösch fails to develop the necessary additional sets of equations.

This is the way in which Lösch spins his web of general equilibrium. Although his approach minimizes the elements of interdependence and does not comprehend the space-economy as a whole but as consisting of several major sectors, and, although it has other severe limitations,[58] we have here for the first time an attempt to encompass general spatial relations in a set of equations. And through eschewing the assumption of pure competition and postulating monopolistic competition in its stead, Lösch goes far toward meeting Palander's objections to spatial general equilibrium analysis.

One need not, however, proceed, as does Lösch, in deriving a set of equations. Lösch assigns a set of spatial co-ordinates to each producer and consumer. This step permits, in a sense, a geographic description of a space-economy. But his presentation would become exceedingly complex if one were to relax the simple uniformity assumptions which are basic to his model—if one were to allow inequality in raw material, labor, and capital resources, an uneven and discontinuous distribution

[58] Some of the more significant criticisms of Lösch's scheme may be noted:

1. Lösch's model is not a true general equilibrium system since his commodity and factor markets are not interrelated via utility and production functions in the complex manner which typifies a Walrasian system. E.g., the model is based on the assumption that the price of a commodity is a simple function of its demand, an assumption which is open to serious objection.

2. A simple count of equations and unknowns does not necessarily prove the existence of an equilibrium.

3. His treatment of boundary equations as single unknowns is also subject to major criticism. A conception of a continuous field of price gradients would be much superior.

4. It may be claimed that Lösch's model has both too many unknowns and too many equations. If conditions are assumed which lead to the formation of a honeycomb of regular hexagonal market areas for any given commodity, then once the location of one producer of that commodity is fixed and once the equation of one of his six boundary lines is known, the location of all other producers of that commodity and the equation of all other boundary lines are known and determined.

5. His system is built implicitly upon an hexagonal net of market areas whose derivation and construction involve inconsistencies some of which will be noted later in this book.

of population, and all other types of local differences. To introduce inequality in the spatial pattern of inputs alone is a very difficult task.

From a *functional* standpoint—one that is relevant to the incessant struggle within the economy as a whole, as well as within its various parts, to obtain the correct set of substitution points with respect to inputs, outputs, outlays, and revenues—Lösch's model is anemic. It is much more meaningful to design a set of equations depicting general equilibrium in terms of input-output relations and price-cost relations, including therein transport inputs (and if possible local price-cost variations) in order to give explicit recognition to the factor of space. This latter model, constructed without reference to absolute spatial co-ordinates, would be much more able to cope with further possible theoretical developments, for example, with the structural, dynamic developments visualized by Weigmann; although, to be sure, any spatial description of the order of Lösch is desirable if it does not impose restrictions upon the basic operations of the model.[59]

With respect to input-output relations, the Leontief technique, within the severe limits to substitution imposed by its assumptions, offers a powerful tool of analysis.[60] It will be seen in a second volume that one can give an increasing amount of play to spatial substitution operations (1) through rearranging the activities included in the structural matrix and bill of goods sector in order to incorporate locational shifts of basic industries (and the associated local multiplier effects) resulting from substitution between transport inputs and between various outlays (including transport outlays) and revenues; (2) through detailing interindustry flow tables by decomposing the nation into regions and establishing an hierarchy of regions; and (3) through introducing resource limitations and other non-linearities by employing an iterative approach, by changing relevant coefficients, and by other devices. Such a modified model can thus reflect, to a large extent, the interactivity relationships of the space-economy.

Apropos of price-cost relations, it cannot be too strongly emphasized that the theories of space-economy and of monopolistic competition (broadly conceived[61]) are inextricably bound together. The note-

[59] For other relevant criticism of Lösch, see W. F. Stolper, *op. cit.* and Hans Ritschl, "Aufgabe und Methode der Standortslehre," *Weltwirtschaftliches Archiv,* Vol. LIII (1941), pp. 115–25.

[60] W. W. Leontief, *The Structure of American Economy, 1919–1939,* New York, 1951; and W. W. Leontief *et al., Studies in the Structure of the American Economy,* New York, 1953.

[61] To include oligopoly with or without product differentiation. See E. H. Chamberlin, "Some Final Comments," *The Review of Economics and Statistics,* Vol. XXXI (May 1949), pp. 123–4.

worthy contribution of Chamberlin in developing techniques for spatial analysis has not been treated specifically since it has been largely digested by Lösch and Palander. Progress along Chamberlinian lines, however, is a *sine qua non* for developing further the theory of the space-economy in its welfare aspects[62] which, however, are beyond the scope of this book. Triffin has already built upon Chamberlin's structure, setting the monopolistic competition techniques in a general equilibrium framework.[63] Triffin's interdependence analysis, in many places explicitly cloaked in substitution terms, is not unlike Predöhl's substitution technique (although, to be sure, Triffin hardly thinks in terms of spatial or location relations). In this sense, then, a generalized theory of monopolistic competition, broadly defined and including the physical production (input-output) problem in its spatial setting, can be conceived as synonymous with our general theory of location and space-economy.

6. OHLIN'S VIEW OF TRADE AND LOCATION THEORY

One final matter should be discussed, namely, the interrelation of trade theory and the general theory of location and space-economy. In 1911 Weber pointed out that classical trade theory ignored entirely the transport cost involved in traversing space.[64] He particularly criticized the classicists for overlooking the large portion of internationally distributed industry which is transport-oriented and which seeks the minimum transport cost point with respect to raw materials and markets, and for attributing to international division of labor and capital the international distribution of transport-oriented industry.

Furlan, Engländer, Ritschl, Weigmann, and others have stressed

[62] For most situations of the space-economy, it is quite meaningless to apply the norms of pure competition. Also see Chamberlin, *Theory of Monopolistic Competition*, Cambridge, Mass., 3rd ed., 1938, pp. 208–13.

[63] R. Triffin, *Monopolistic Competition and General Equilibrium Theory*, Cambridge, Mass., 1940. Although the monopolistic competition of Chamberlin seems to be more than a particular equilibrium theory (certainly it is at least a quite broad particular equilibrium theory for it embraces the problems both of *individual* equilibrium and of *equilibrium* for an elastically defined *group*), nonetheless it is not a general equilibrium theory in the full meaning of the term (see Triffin, pp. 8–9, 54, 67, and elsewhere). Triffin's contribution consists of extending the scope of monopolistic competition to encompass the complex net of competitive interrelationships throughout the entire economic collectivity. In doing this, Triffin discards the concepts both of an industry, and of a group of firms. Rather, he emphasizes the individual firm (or more strictly, the maximizing unit) and the various coefficients of interdependence between any given firm and each of all the other firms in the economy, both with respect to factors and to products.

[64] "Die Standortslehre und die Handelspolitik," *Archiv für Sozialwissenschaft und Sozialpolitik*, Vol. XXXII (May 1911), pp. 667–88.

the interrelation of trade and location theories, but not until the appearance of Ohlin's *Interregional and International Trade*[65] do we have a serious attempt to integrate the two. As one of his objectives Ohlin purports:

"to demonstrate that the theory of international trade is only part of a general localization theory, wherein the space aspects of pricing are taken into full account, and to frame certain fundamentals of such a theory as a background for a theory of international trade, wherein the influence of local differences in the supply of factors of production and transportation costs within each country is duly considered."[66]

Ohlin plants his objectives within the framework of a mutual-interdependence theory of pricing, the latter to be expanded to enfold the multitude of markets and local price variations which ensue from the varying spatial immobilities and indivisibilities of goods and factors. Thus his general localization theory would determine simultaneously prices, markets, location of industry, commerce and agriculture, spatial distribution of factors and commodities, and other economic magnitudes.

It would seem logical that Ohlin should first develop a general localization theory. Then, by focusing upon certain forms of immobilities of factors and goods (consideration of other relations set aside for the time being) he could develop at length his theory of interregional and international trade as a special case. Unfortunately, Ohlin adopts an entirely different procedure and as a consequence has to employ a nearly unique casuistry. Parts I and II of his book are devoted to the theory of interregional trade and a simplified version of international trade, respectively. These parts, however, are constructed upon an unrealistic set of hypotheses. The region is defined as that area within which there is perfect mobility of factors. Between regions factors are considered perfectly immobile. And all impediments to movement of commodities are assumed away. In Part III he attempts to approach reality through the successive introduction of the following: (1) interregional costs of transfer of commodities; (2) interregional factor movements; (3) interior costs of transfer and factor movement; (4) local differences in labor and capital supply. The inclusion of the last two items represents an effort to subject the theory of interregional trade to a broadening process and thus convert it into a general localization theory.

[65] Cambridge, Mass., 1933. Some of his other relevant works are: *Handelns teori*, Stockholm, 1924, and "Some Aspects of the Theory of Rent: von Thünen vs. Ricardo," *op. cit.*

[66] *Op. cit.*, p. vii.

Ohlin at most achieves a weak (and only verbal) general localization theory. He does not attain the total systematic analysis which characterizes his interregional trade theory. His treatment of locational forces (Chaps. X–XII, inclusive) is quite sketchy and flimsy. At the start, a modified version of Thünen's isolated state is applied to industrial production within a district, "the frontiers of which are not described." Ohlin imagines at first that his district possesses "uniform transport features" throughout its area and that within it the factors of labor and capital are perfectly mobile. At the center lies a strategic natural resource, perhaps coal or iron ore deposits. The surrounding zones of cultivation of various agricultural products, rent of land, and prices of commodities can be determined only through a mutual-interdependence system. Next, the general approach on the whole is abandoned in favor of a step-by-step analysis commencing in typical Weberian style. The localization of manufacturing, of raw material production, of consumers' markets, local differences in transport resources and facilities, economies of large-scale operation and concentration, local differences in capital and labor supply are successively considered. In the end, however, Ohlin returns to a general interdependence setting in depicting the relations of the various economic forces.

This singular approach has turned out to be misleading to many. One sympathetic critic maintains that Ohlin does not successfully bridge the gap between interregional trade theory and general localization theory, and thus does not achieve a unified theory; for the district whose total localization is supposed to be explained by a general theory does not necessarily have to possess the same mobility characteristics as the region, which is the unit of study for interregional trade.[67] To the extent that the exposition of the total analysis for the district is deficient (and of this there is no question), the gap is not bridged, but the district itself can be conceived as boundless or, more realistically, as synonymous with the world (which Ohlin does not explicitly do). A satisfactory, exhaustive, total analysis for the district would then describe all economic relations within the world and explain all manner of trade. One could then deduce interregional trade analysis (no

[67] Tord Palander, op. cit., pp. 266–67. Elsewhere (pp. 262–64) Palander summarizes Ohlin's earlier study, Handelns teori. Here an attempt is made to extend interregional trade to a theory of interlocal trade (thus accounting for local differences in factor supply) through subdividing the region (within which perfect mobility of factors reigns) until the subregions become identical with the localities themselves. Obviously this technique is inadequate; it assumes away the location problem, for at the start the basis of interregional trade is presumed to be the different relative scarcities of productive factors among regions.

matter on what basis the region and subregions are delineated) by singling out from among the complex of relations those of relevance.[68]

However, it is not necessary at all to view trade theory as narrowly as Ohlin does. It is true that international trade theory historically and as it exists in such standard works as Viner's[69] and Haberler's[70] does tend to correspond to Ohlin's conception of it. It is still subject to Weber's criticism: it does not incorporate transport-oriented industry into its analytical framework and is thus inadequate for determining policy. Nonetheless, one can view trade theory and the general theory of location and space-economy as synonymous. For (1) location cannot be explained unless at the same time trade is accounted for and (2) trade cannot be explained without the simultaneous determination of locations. Once we recognize this it is futile to argue whether trade theory is or is not a special form of general location theory.[71] As we shall see later, an improved location-trade doctrine can be achieved through synthesis of the better elements of existing trade and location theories.

7. CLOSING REMARKS

In summary, the general theory of location and space-economy is conceived as embracing the total spatial array of economic activities, with attention paid to the geographic distribution of inputs and outputs and the geographic variations in prices and costs. Modern general equilibrium theory is a special case of this theory, in which transport costs are taken as zero and all inputs and outputs are viewed as perfectly mobile; international trade theory, as narrowly conceived by Ohlin, is also a special case of this theory. One proceeds from the latter to the former by assuming a given locational structure of economic activities, by erecting appropriate barriers within the world economy to correspond to the boundaries of nations, and so forth.

[68] Lösch ("Beiträge zur Standortstheorie," *op. cit.,* p. 331) has also charged Ohlin with lacking a clear answer to the location problem within his regions, and with a failure to perceive labor distribution as a result of economic activity between men, not between regions. The latter accusation falls, however, with the definition of the district as the world, or as an area greater in extent than, and inclusive of, the region.

On the other hand, one may perhaps with some justification raise objections to the liberal and generous interpretation given herein to Ohlin's reasoning.

[69] *Studies in the Theory of International Trade,* New York, 1937.

[70] *The Theory of International Trade,* London, 1936.

[71] Thus Viner's cynical remark about Ohlin's dictum that the theory of international trade is nothing but international location theory is really unnecessary and indicates either Viner's confusion or his failure to appreciate the scope of location theory (*op. cit.,* p. 468 note).

However, it is important to bear in mind that the distinction between trade theory and the general theory of location and space-economy is one of definition only. Trade theory can be broadly conceived as synonymous with the general theory of location and space-economy. And in a sense, too, because of the monopoly elements which are almost invariably present in spatial relations, a broadly defined general theory of monopolistic competition can be conceived as identical with the general theory of location and space-economy.

The substitution principle provides one of the best analytical tools for developing this general theory. However, Predöhl's use of this tool must be modified and extended to embrace various substitution relations between transport inputs, and between various types of outlays and revenues. The formulation of these relations in terms of a system of mathematical equations ought first to embrace the concept of transport inputs and later, if possible, Lösch's sets of spatial co-ordinates.

The evolutionary approach of Weber and others, and especially the writings of Weigmann, who conceives the space-economy as a rhythmic-moving Gestalt whole with a basic structural core of land and labor markets, should be very helpful in suggesting lines along which this general theory may be nurtured to embody dynamic relations.

Chapter 3

Some Empirical Regularities
of the Space-Economy

Before the development of appropriate concepts is undertaken, it is pertinent to examine some of the currently available empirical material and observations on the space-economy. This should establish whether or not there are in fact significant regularities associated with variation in the distance factor. If there are, these empirical regularities should furnish a valuable background against which concepts and techniques may be silhouetted. Concomitantly they should afford insights into the ways in which new concepts and techniques should be fashioned. A comprehensive canvass and processing of available material is not intended, since this is beyond the scope of the book. Rather we wish to benefit from what a preliminary and cursory examination reveals.

Historically, the empirical rank-size rule for cities, noted by Auerbach, Lotka, Gibrat, Singer,[1] and others, has spurred on the search for related empirical regularities over space. The rank-size rule which is claimed to have widespread validity is given by the equation:

$$(1) \qquad r \cdot P^q = K$$

[1] F. Auerbach, "Das Gesetz der Bevölkerungskonzentration," *Petermanns Mitteilungen,* Vol. 59 (February 1913), pp. 74–76, and Chart 14; A. J. Lotka, *Elements of Physical Biology,* Baltimore, 1925, pp. 306–7; R. Gibrat, *Les Inégalités Économiques,* Paris, 1931, pp. 250–52, 280; H. W. Singer, "The 'Courbe des Populations.' A Parallel to Pareto's Law," *Economic Journal,* Vol. XLVI (June 1936), pp. 254–63.

where q and K are constants for the given group of cities, r stands for the rank of a particular city in population, and P its population. For example, according to the 1940 census data on metropolitan districts for the United States, in which instance q is approximately equal to

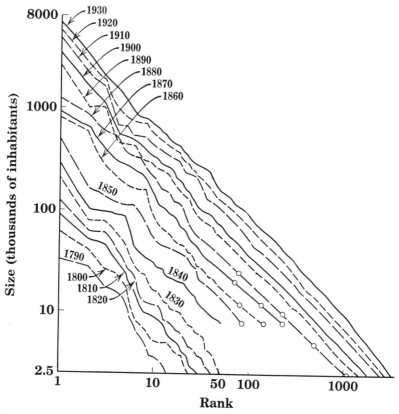

Fig. 2. Communities of 2500 or more inhabitants, ranked in decreasing order of population size. U. S. A. 1790–1930. (Source, G. K. Zipf, *Human Behavior and the Principle of Least Effort*, Addison-Wesley, Cambridge, Mass., 1949.)

unity, the population of the New York metropolitan area was 11,690,520. This roughly sets the value for K since the New York area ranks first. And in line with the rank-size rule the Boston metropolitan area which ranked fifth ($r = 5$) had a population of 2,350,514, approximately one-fifth of K. In logarithmic terms the above equation is:

$$\log r = -q \log P + C$$

which, just as does the equation representing Pareto's "law" of income distribution, yields a straight line on double logarithmic paper.

The best presentation of the empirical findings on rank and size of cities is given by Zipf.[2] In Fig. 2 he has plotted the relevant decennial data for the United States over the period 1790–1930, logarithmic scales being used on both the horizontal and vertical axes.[3] The closest approximation to a linear distribution, as is implied by Eq. 1, seems to be reached in year 1930. The distributions for earlier years seem to diverge increasingly from a linear form. It should also be noted that the distributions for metropolitan districts of the United States for years 1940[4] and 1950[5] each show roughly as close an approximation to a straight line as do the distributions in Fig. 2 since 1900.

How much validity and universality should be attributed to this rank-size rule is, at this stage, a matter of individual opinion and judgment.[6] However, it cannot be denied that, to a limited extent at least, there is some basis for the formulation of hypotheses and additional exploration. If further research corroborates the belief that these and other distributions exhibit a statistical regularity over various time periods and diverse parts of the world, expectation that there are regularities associated with the distance variable would not be unjustified. For, according to one possible line of reasoning, modern cities have become increasingly centers of numerous market-oriented activities, each activity tending to have a defined sales area. Since the size of a city is positively associated with the number of activities which locate within it and since economies of scale and other factors

[2] G. K. Zipf, *National Unity and Disunity*, The Principia Press, Bloomington, Ind., 1941; and *Human Behavior and the Principle of Least Effort*, Addison-Wesley Press, Cambridge, Mass., 1949, Chaps. 9 and 10.

[3] The encircled points are estimates of Zipf. For full particulars on the processing of the data, see *National Unity and Disunity*, pp. 41–43. It should be observed that early census data are particularly faulty.

[4] G. K. Zipf, *Human Behavior . . . , op. cit.*, p. 375.

[5] See Figs. 1 and 2 in Rutledge Vining, "A Description of Certain Spatial Aspects of an Economic System," *Economic Development and Cultural Change*, Vol. III (January 1955), pp. 147–195.

[6] See the interesting statistical analysis in G. R. Allen, "The 'Courbe des Populations': A Further Analysis," *Bulletin of the Oxford University Institute of Statistics*, Vol. 16 (May and June 1954). This analysis lends considerable support to the rank-size rule.

Additionally, Zipf has plotted relevant rank-size data on cities for Canada, 1881–1931, for Germany, 1875–1939, for France, 1886–1936, for India, 1911 and 1921, and for other areas. In general, he concludes that the data conform to a rectilinear pattern (logarithmic scales). However, as in the case of the United States in 1840 and of the Austro-Hungarian empire in 1910, the conformity is not always good; this fact is interpreted by Zipf as an indication of some inherent political, economic, or social instability within the system. (Zipf, *Human Behavior . . . , op. cit.*, Chap. 10.)

preclude the presence of each activity in each city, cities of different sizes emerge. Further, one can expect the longer (and a larger volume of) population and commodity flows to be generally associated with the larger cities which have been fortunate in usurping those functions wherein economies of scale are marked and with which the larger market areas are linked. Still more, economies of scale have varying significance for different commodities and activities; when they are most dominant, the commodity produced (or service rendered) tends to be national, being supplied to all market points from one location. Hence, that city which captures the largest amount of these "national market area activities" and which concomitantly engages in all other activities whose market areas are of lesser geographic scope tends to be largest in size. It tends to be a terminal point of the longest average population and commodity flows and of the largest volume of such flows, *ceteris paribus*. And that city which captures the next largest amount of these national activities, while at the same time being a center of all "non-national" activities, would tend to be second in size and to rank second in average length (and volume) of population and commodity flows, *ceteris paribus*. And in like fashion the third, fourth . . . *n*th largest city would tend to rank third, fourth . . . *n*th in average length (and volume) of flows, *ceteris paribus*, the progression of activities from those with national markets to those with major regional markets to those with minor regional markets . . . to those with only local markets being duly taken into account.[7] As a consequence, a statistically regular hierarchy of average length and volume of flows emerges. Thus regularity of flows over distance and regularity in the spatial patterning of cities can come to be associated with a statistically regular hierarchy of cities, *ceteris paribus*.[8]

The *ceteris paribus* clause, however, excludes so many differentials (such as in the geographic distribution of mineral resources) that the above argument not only is open to serious qualification but even may be subject to major restatement. Nonetheless, there is some basis, as

---

[7] For development of this classification of markets see A. Lösch, *Die räumliche Ordnung der Wirtschaft*, 2nd ed., G. Fischer, Jena, 1944, pp. 70–79, 307–16; W. Christaller, *Die zentralen Orte in Süddeutschland*, G. Fischer, Jena, 1935; E. Ullman, "A Theory of Location for Cities," *American Journal of Sociology*, Vol. XLVI (May 1941), pp. 853–64; and W. Isard, "Some Empirical Results and Problems of Regional Input-Output Analysis," in W. Leontief, *et al.*, *Studies in the Structure of the American Economy*, New York, 1953, pp. 148–81.

[8] In this regard also see E. M. Hoover, "The Concept of a System of Cities: A Comment on Rutledge Vining's Paper," *Economic Development and Cultural Change*, Vol. III (January 1955), pp. 196–98.

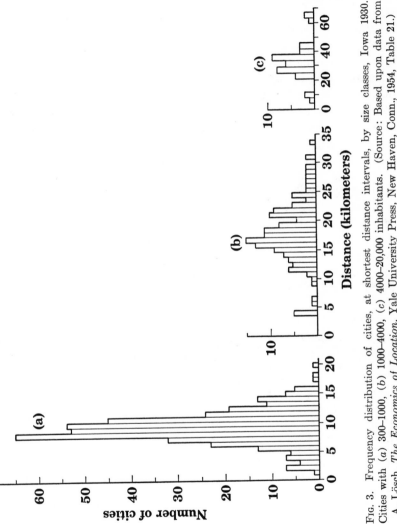

FIG. 3. Frequency distribution of cities, at shortest distance intervals, by size classes, Iowa 1930. Cities with (*a*) 300–1000, (*b*) 1000–4000, (*c*) 4000–20,000 inhabitants. (Source: Based upon data from A. Lösch, *The Economics of Location*, Yale University Press, New Haven, Conn., 1954, Table 21.)

Lösch would maintain, for searching for statistical regularities of commodity and population flows over distance and regularities in the spatial patterning of cities—the more so if one attributes, as Zipf does, statistical regularity to the rank-size findings on cities.

Among others, Christaller and Lösch have studied the spatial patterning of cities, recognizing the numerous resource inequalities which tend to distort regularities inherent in the resistance of distance, *per se.* Figure 3 is one of the better illustrations of spatial regularity in city patterning. The data which it presents are consistent with the reasoning in the above two paragraphs and with the central place theories of Christaller and Lösch. They indicate that as one proceeds from smaller to larger class sizes of cities, the distance separating cities of like class size increases, although with considerable variation about any average.[9]

Zipf, as have many others, has intuitively associated city size with market area complex. He has searched for simple rectilinear, and presumably stable, interactions over distance, although the logic connecting his statistical findings on the one hand and his Forces of Unification and Diversification and principle of least effort on the other is not at all clear. In Figs. 4 to 7 some of his findings are presented.

Figure 4 refers to railway-express shipments (less than carload lots). Since the data are recorded for shipments between pairs of cities with different populations and since there is a presumption that tonnage of shipment will vary directly with the number of originating and terminating units (individuals), Zipf employs a $P_1 \cdot P_2$ element.

---

[9] Christaller's study of settlements in South Germany (*op. cit.*), most of which provide services (or central functions) for the surrounding population, also indicates that settlements of a typical size tend to be spaced regularly. According to his interpretation of the data, not only do the populations of the several sizes of typical settlements tend to bear a regular relation to each other but also the distances separating any pair of settlements of like size tend to increase by the $\sqrt{3}$ as one proceeds from a settlement of a given size to the settlement of next higher size. Thus market hamlets are found to be spaced roughly 7 kilometers apart, township centers 12 kilometers, county seats 21 kilometers, district cities 36 kilometers, small state capitals 62 kilometers, provincial head cities 108 kilometers, and regional capital cities 186 kilometers. For a full theoretical explanation of Christaller's findings, see Lösch, *op. cit.*, pp. 70–97; and for an objective evaluation, see Ullman, *op. cit.*

Lösch has accumulated additional empirical evidence on settlement patterns as well as evidence on a host of other significant relationships involving the distance factor, such as the spatial distributions of various non-agricultural activities, the sizes and shapes of market areas, the variations of prices, wages, and interest with distance from strategic geographic points of reference or over space or both.

(P_1 and P_2 represent the populations of any given pair of cities.) Accordingly, weight of shipments between any pair of cities and the corresponding $P_1 P_2/D$ factor for the given pair of cities (times $1/10^7$) are plotted in Fig. 4, where D represents distance. If one accepts

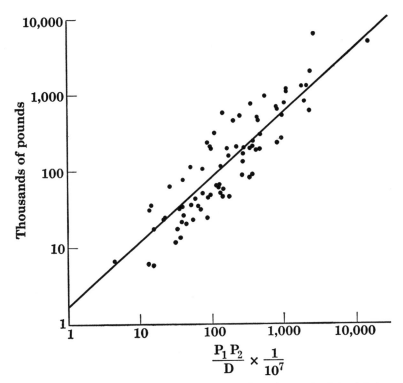

Fig. 4. Railway express. Movement by weight (less than carload lots) between 13 arbitrary cities in the U. S. A., May 1939. (Source: G. K. Zipf, *Human Behavior and the Principle of Least Effort*, Addison-Wesley, Cambridge, Mass., 1949.)

Zipf's $P_1 \cdot P_2$ element, then the linear tendency of the data portrayed by Fig. 4 indicates a definite inverse relationship between tonnage of railway express and distance, as is indeed demonstrated by other data.[10]

Figures 5 and 6 refer respectively to telephone messages and bus-passenger movements. Again Zipf introduces, for the same reason as in Fig. 4, a $P_1 \cdot P_2$ element. If one accepts this element, the charts indicate that the numbers of both telephone messages and bus pas-

[10] Zipf, *Human Behavior . . . , op. cit.*, p. 402, Fig. 9–20(a).

sengers definitely fall off in linear fashion as the distance between any
pair of cities increases.[11]

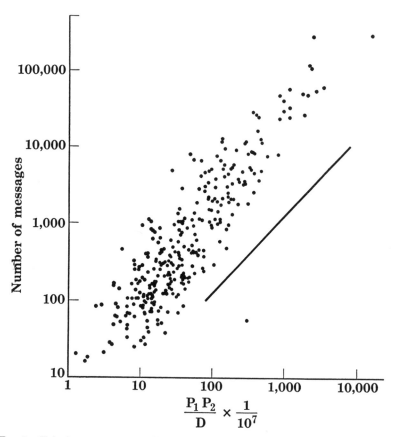

Fig. 5. Telephone messages. Number of messages interchanged between 311
arbitrary pairs of cities in the U. S. A., 1940. (The line has a slope of 1.00.)
(Source: G. K. Zipf, *Human Behavior and the Principle of Least Effort,*
Addison-Wesley, Cambridge, Mass., 1949.)

[11] That number of messages falls off with distance is directly depicted in Zipf,
ibid., p. 402, Fig. 9–20(b).

Among others, Zipf presents the following interesting distributions (although
at times their rectilinearity is questionable): on railway passengers, airway passengers, and the P_1P_2/D factor; on number of different news items in *The
Chicago Tribune,* number of obituaries in *The New York Times,* average circulation per day of *The New York Times,* and the P_1P_2/D factor; on charge
accounts of Jordan Marsh Co., Boston, in 96 cities and a P/D factor; on length
and number of one-way trips for both trucks and passenger cars; and on number
of marriage licenses issued and distance separating applicants. For full details

Figure 7 refers to some limited data processed by Stouffer on internal migration within Cleveland.[12]   These data as they are chartered by

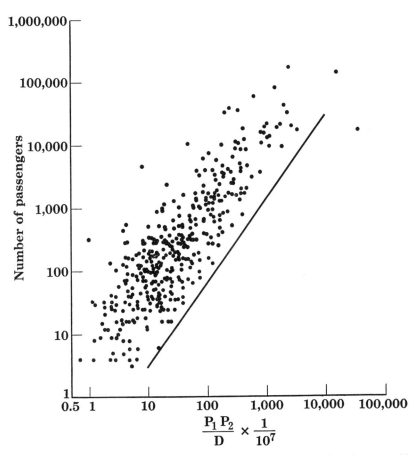

FIG. 6. Bus passengers. Movement of persons by highway bus between 29 arbitrary cities in the U. S. A. during intervals in 1933 and 1934. (The line has a slope of 1.25.) (Source: G. K. Zipf, *Human Behavior and the Principle of Least Effort*, Addison-Wesley, Cambridge, Mass., 1949.)

Zipf clearly suggest that the number of families moving between separated areas varies inversely with distance, and in general the data

---

on the nature of his samples and on the particular points of time to which they refer see Zipf, *Human Behavior* . . . , *op. cit.*, pp. 386–414.

[12] S. A. Stouffer, "Intervening Opportunities: A Theory Relating Mobility and Distance," *American Sociological Review*, Vol. 5 (December 1940), pp. 845–67.

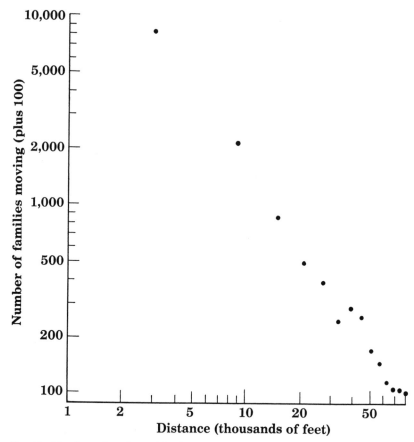

Fig. 7. Family migration. Number of families (plus 100) moving varying distances within or between separated areas in Cleveland, 1933–1935. (Source: G. K. Zipf, *Human Behavior and the Principle of Least Effort*, Addison-Wesley, Cambridge, Mass. 1949. Adapted from the data of S. A. Stouffer.)

are consistent with the reasoning and limited empirical findings of Ravenstein[13] and others.[14]

[13] E. G. Ravenstein, "The Laws of Migration," *Journal of the Royal Statistical Society*, Vol. 48 (June 1885), pp. 167–227, and Vol. 52 (June 1889), pp. 241–301.

Ravenstein was perhaps first to classify migrants in terms of distance spanned and to show comprehensively with statistical material that the extent of migration into a given center of absorption from any given point, in general, varies inversely with the distance separating the two.

Stouffer has attempted to generalize the relationship between migration and distance. His hypothesis "assumes that there is no necessary relationship between mobility and distance. . . . It proposes that *the number of persons going a given distance is directly proportional to the number of opportunities at that distance*

Stewart has also been inspired to search for empirical regularities associated with the distance variable in connection with his study of social physics.[15] Following Newtonian physics, Stewart has formulated new concepts to observe vital aspects of the space-economy. Stewart advances the thesis: (1) that the *demographic* (gravitational) *force* F of attraction between two groups of N_1 and N_2 average Americans separated by r distance is given by $F = N_1 N_2/r^2$, where F acts along the line joining the two groups;[16] (2) that accordingly their *demographic energy* by virtue of this force field is given by $E = GN_1 N_2/r$, where G is a constant; (3) that the *potential* which

---

and inversely proportional to the number of intervening opportunities" (*op. cit.*, p. 846).

Mathematically $\Delta y/\Delta s = a\Delta x/x\Delta s$, where Δy equals the number of persons moving from an origin to a circular band of width Δs; x equals the number of intervening opportunities, i.e., the cumulated number of opportunities between the origin and distance s; and Δx equals the number of opportunities within the band of width Δs. Data on residential mobility in Cleveland, on net interstate migration for the United States in 1930, and on intercounty migration in Sweden between 1921 and 1930 tend to substantiate this hypothesis, an hypothesis which conceivably can be further generalized to cover to some extent movement of commodities as well as persons. See also M. L. Bright and D. S. Thomas, "Interstate Migration and Intervening Opportunities," *American Sociological Review,* Vol. 6 (December 1941), pp. 773–83; and E. C. Isbell, "Internal Migration in Sweden and Intervening Opportunities," *American Sociological Review,* Vol. 9 (December 1944), pp. 627–39.

[14] See Stuart C. Dodd, "The Interactance Hypothesis: A Gravity Model Fitting Physical Masses and Human Groups," *American Sociological Review,* Vol. 15 (April 1950), pp. 245–256. For a very interesting set of empirical tests of the Zipf and Stouffer hypotheses as they relate to migration, refer to T. R. Anderson, "Intermetropolitan Migration," *American Sociological Review,* Vol. 20 (June 1955), pp. 287–91.

[15] J. Q. Stewart, "Empirical Mathematical Rules Concerning the Distribution and Equilibrium of Population," *Geographical Review,* Vol. XXXVII (July 1947), pp. 461–85; "Demographic Gravitation: Evidence and Applications," *Sociometry,* Vol. XI (February–May 1948), pp. 31–58; "Potential of Population and its Relationship to Marketing," *Theory in Marketing,* ed. by R. Cox and W. Alderson, Chicago, 1950, pp. 19–40; "The Development of Social Physics," *American Journal of Physics,* Vol. 18 (May 1950), pp. 239–53; and other studies cited in these four articles.

[16] Stewart reduces the gravitational constant to unity by a suitable choice of other units. The molecular mass of the "average American" is taken as unity, thus permitting this simple formulation. Later, Stewart relaxes this assumption. The reader is referred to any standard college physics textbook for explanation of the concepts and equations used in this paragraph.

It should be noted that Stewart's concept of demographic force is translatable into Reilly's law of retail gravitation (W. J. Reilly, "Methods for the Study of Retail Relationships," *University of Texas Bulletin,* No. 2944, November 1929).

the group of N_1 individuals produces at the point where the second group is located is given by $V_2 = GN_1/r$; and (4) that the *potential at any point* produced by the entire population of any given terrain is given by $V = \int \frac{1}{r} DdS$, where D is the density of population over the infinitesimal element of area dS, the integration being extended to all areas of the plane where D is not zero. The potential at any point, according to Stewart, may also be taken as an inverted measure of the proximity of the point to people in general.[17]

Stewart has computed population potentials for various areas of the world for different periods of time.[18] Since population is reported not for infinitesimal elements of area but rather for comparatively large units of area, only approximations to potentials can be achieved. In Fig. 8 are depicted equipotential contour lines for the United States in 1940.[19] It is extremely interesting to observe that east of the Sierras there is, in all directions, a continuous fall in potential with increase in distance from New York City, the major peak of the country, except that all other cities are local peaks on the general downhill slope.[20]

Working with approximate averages of potential for rural areas in a sequence of 28 states from Texas to Maine[21] and using double log

[17] "Demographic Gravitation . . .," *op. cit.,* pp. 32–36.

[18] See "Empirical Mathematical Rules . . . ," *op. cit.,* pp. 476–79; "Potential of Population . . . ," *op. cit.,* p. 22; and "The Development of Social Physics," *op. cit.,* p. 250.

[19] "Potential of Population . . .," *op. cit.,* p. 22. In this article Stewart does not indicate the number of areas in which he divided the United States. Obviously the larger the number of areas, and hence control points, the more precise the computed potentials, and the more likely that local peaks corresponding to cities will appear. See "Empirical Mathematical Rules . . . ," *op. cit.,* pp. 473–82, for a discussion of some of the problems in computing potentials.

In the construction of Fig. 8, Stewart weighted population in the Deep South by a factor of 0.8; in the main sequence of 28 states from Maine to Texas by unity; and in the Far West by 2. For his reasoning on this step, see "Potential of Population . . . ," *op. cit.,* pp. 29–30. However, it should be noted that if population is unweighted, a similar contour map results except that the potentials in the Far West are of considerably smaller value. See his "unweighted" map in "Concerning Social Physics," *Scientific American,* Vol. 178 (May 1948), p. 22.

[20] This statement, of course, might require qualification if a finer-grained map were constructed. Nonetheless, the resulting configuration of contours and its relation to the distance variable would still be impressive. And it is very likely that all of the contour lines in non-urban parts would close around New York City.

According to Stewart, the major structure of United States' potentials has not altered much since 1840 when New York City was already the principal peak.

[21] Observations are confined to these 28 states because these states exhibit a con-

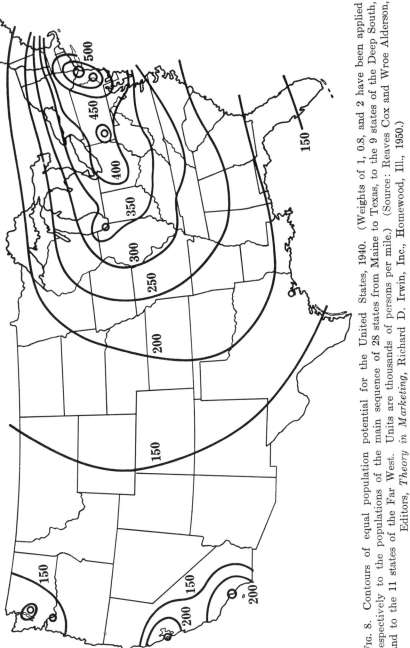

Fig. 8. Contours of equal population potential for the United States, 1940. (Weights of 1, 0.8, and 2 have been applied respectively to the populations of the main sequence of 28 states from Maine to Texas, to the 9 states of the Deep South, and to the 11 states of the Far West. Units are thousands of persons per mile.) (Source: Reaves Cox and Wroe Alderson, Editors, *Theory in Marketing*, Richard D. Irwin, Inc., Homewood, Ill., 1950.)

paper, Stewart claims to obtain fairly good linear relations by plotting the data on potential for these areas against the data on each of the following: (1) density of rural population; (2) density of rural non-farm population; (3) rents of rural non-farm dwelling units; (4) value of farmland per acre; (5) rural road mileage per square mile; and (6) railroad mileage per square mile. In each case, as potential rises from area to area (the potential, in essence, measures the influence upon any particular area of people at a distance), each of these items tends to increase. Other still more interesting associations which Stewart notes and judges to be linear (logarithmic scales) are those: (1) between potential and number of wage-earners in manufacturing for 253 rural counties;[22] (2) between demographic energy (a concept related to distance) and income for various states (a) in the main sequence of 28 states, (b) in 11 western states, and (c) in 9 southern states; and (3) between potential produced at New York City by the populations of various branch Federal Reserve districts and the daily flow of bank checks for October 1948, into New York City from these districts when grouped according to the above three classes of states.[23]

Human ecologists—McKenzie,[24] Hawley,[25] Bogue,[26] and others—have also closely studied spatial phenomena and the impact of distance upon the interrelations of human beings in adapting to environment. Of these, Bogue has most explicitly considered the distance variable within the framework of metropolitan regional analysis. Figure 9 depicts some of his summary findings in a forceful manner. As Bogue has neatly stated:

"On the average, as the distance from the metropolis increases, the number of persons per square mile of land decreases. With increasing distance, each square mile of land area supports steadily decreasing average amounts of retail trade, services, wholesale trade, and manufacturing activities. This finding is noteworthy for the following reasons: first, it is a statement of a set of conditions which applies to the entire land area of the United States. . . .

---

siderable degree of statistical homogeneity, a homogeneity which has already been noted to be different from that of the 11 western states and from that of the 9 southern states.

[22] Stewart uses counties (in the main sequence of 28 states) which contain zero or only relatively small urban populations in order to avoid the local distortion of potentials that is produced by the influence of nearby cities.

[23] "Demographic Gravitation . . . ," *op. cit.*, pp. 39–51; and "Potential of Population . . . ," *op. cit.*, pp. 27–30

[24] R. D. McKenzie, *The Metropolitan Community*, New York, 1933.

[25] A. H. Hawley, *Human Ecology*, New York, 1950.

[26] D. J. Bogue, *The Structure of the Metropolitan Community*, University of Michigan, Ann Arbor, 1949.

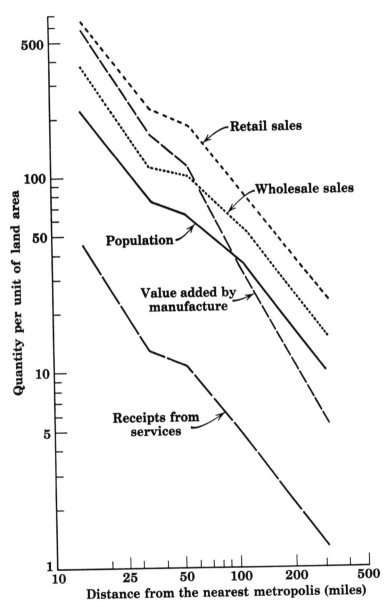

Fɪɢ. 9. Population per square mile and dollar value of selected sustenance activities per 1/100 sq mile of hinterland, by distance outward from the nearest metropolis: for 67 metropolitan communities in the U. S. A., 1939–1940.

"Second, the distance pattern encompasses the entire area which has been called the 'hinterland.' The effect of distance from the metropolis does not cease to exist at the suburb, but continues throughout all distances. . . .

"Third, the distance patterns for the suburban and for the most distant zones are shown here to be only different aspects of the same phenomenon. There is a fairly constant rate of change between relative decreases in land occupancy and relative increases in distance."[27]

It should also be noted that in general these regularities with distance hold for each size class of metropolitan region, though with different rates of change. Likewise, on a per capita basis, retail sales, receipts from services, wholesale sales, and value added by manufacture each manifests a fairly regular pattern with distance from the nearest metropolis, for all metropolitan regions, for metropolitan regions broken down by size classes, and for various types of sectors of metropolitan regions. In addition Bogue finds many other related regularities with distance.[28]

To complete this brief survey of empirical material, we wish to re-examine more carefully data on tonnage of commodity flows over distance, both on an intranational and international basis. Fortunately, data for the United States have recently become available, recording for each of 261 I.C.C. commodity classes and for each of five consolidated groups of these classes state-to-state Class I railroad shipments as well as the average short-line haul per ton (in miles) for commodities in each class. These data are probably the most comprehensive commodity-flow data currently available.[29]

As is to be expected, the friction of distance is of different significance for the diverse commodities. Certain flows, such as those of cement, are extremely sensitive to the distance variable; others, such as those of oranges and grapefruit, extremely insensitive. For our purposes, it is sufficient to chart the data on total commodity flows. Doing this tends to average out the particular sets of resource, market, transport rate, and other relations peculiar to any given commodity flow and to isolate more effectively the general impact of the distance variable.

---

[27] Bogue, op. cit., p. 31.

[28] Also, see the supporting material in C. Clark "Urban Population Densities," Journal of the Royal Statistical Society, Vol. CXIV, Part IV (1951), pp. 490–96.

[29] The I.C.C. data are derived from a continuous representative 1 per cent sample of the carload waybill terminations of Class I railroads only. For our purposes the data can be used with confidence. Errors from omissions because of the disclosure rule, from rebilling, from double billing of rail-water-rail movements, etc. are minor. For full details on shortcomings of the sample see the introductory note of Interstate Commerce Commission, Carload Waybill Analyses, 1949, Washington, D.C., 1950–1951.

In Figs. 10 and 11 are plotted the data on tonnage of total com-modities moving over various distances, by 25-mile zones and 100-mile zones respectively.[30] The impact of the distance variable is unques-

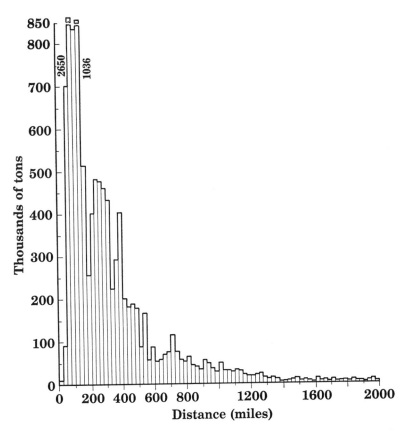

FIG. 10. U. S. A. Class I railroad shipments. Tonnage of all commodities, by distance shipped (25-mile zones), 1949. Bar chart.

tioned, whether the data are recorded by 25-mile zones, or by the larger 100-mile zones in order to smooth out some of the irregular-

[30] The assistance of Mr. Merton J. Peck in preparing the data for Figs. 10–14 is gratefully acknowledged.
    The reader is also referred to the excellent set of charts, independently derived, in Vining *op. cit.*, and in R. Vining, "Delimitation of Economic Areas: Statistical Conceptions in the Study of the Spatial Structure of an Economic System," *Journal of the American Statistical Association*, Vol. 48 (March 1953), pp. 44–64; and to Edward L. Ullman, *Maps of State-to-State Freight Movement for 13 States of the United States in 1948*, mimeographed.

ities.[31]   Also, to examine whether or not any linear relation is present, using double log paper, the data for the mile zones lying between 75 and 1400 miles are graphed as a set of points in Fig. 12.[32]   A straight

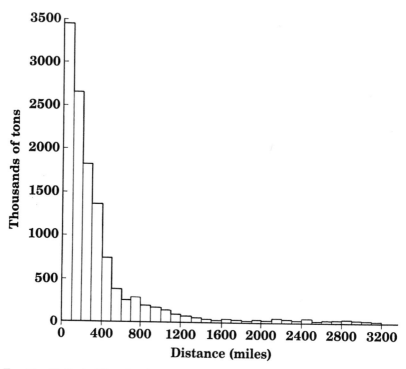

FIG. 11.   U. S. A. Class I railroad shipments.   Tonnage of all commodities, by distance shipped (100-mile zones), 1949.   Bar chart.

[31] Also it is interesting to note that each of the four significant I.C.C. major groups of commodities—products of forests, products of agriculture, products of mines, and manufactures and miscellaneous—show shipments falling off fairly regularly with distance, though less regularly than the aggregate for all commodities.   Shipments of products of mines fall off most precipitously; those of products of agriculture least.   Shipments of the fifth, and by far the least significant of the I.C.C. major groups, namely, animals and products, evidence no real tendency to fall off with distance.

[32] In Fig. 12 the tonnage data for the extreme zones are not plotted.   For the zones falling between 0 and 75 miles they have little significance since rail transport over relatively short distances is infeasible for so many commodities.   For zones falling beyond 1400 miles, the tonnage of shipments is very small and the data not only become less reliable but also reflect shipments of commodities under special conditions.   However, the reader may still care to plot the data for the extreme zones (see Fig. 10).

line has been drawn in freehand. *A priori*, the data seem to conform well to a linear pattern.

On an international level, there is, unfortunately, a paucity of comprehensive physical shipment data. However, one set of reliable and

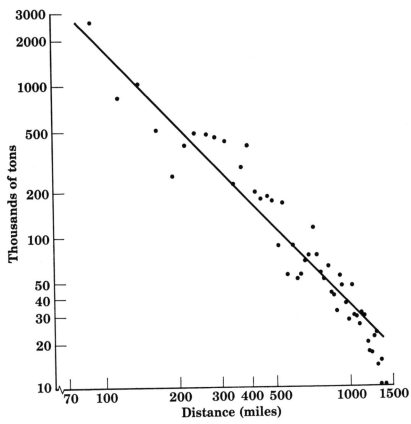

FIG. 12. U. S. A. Class I railroad shipments. Tonnage of all commodities, by distance shipped (25-mile zones), 1949. Point chart.

relevant data has been developed during the 1920's by the German National Bureau of Statistics.[33] The world is divided into 23 areas and the total flow of goods via water in tons from any given area to itself and each of the other 22 is indicated for years 1913, 1924, and

[33] "Der Güterverkehr der Weltschiffahrt," *Vierteljahrshefte zur Statistik des Deutschen Reichs*, Ergänzungsheft zu Heft 1928, I, vom Statistichen Reichsamt, Berlin, 1928. For sources and adequacy of data, see the first page of this monograph.

1925. Upon the data for 1925, Figs. 13 and 14 are based; in these the distance between any two areas is taken as the distance between the two ports, each of which was the most important port in its area in 1925.[34]

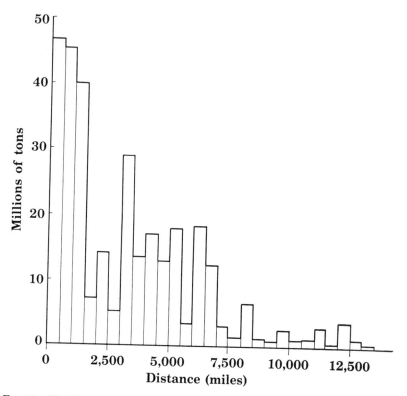

FIG. 13. World ocean-going freight. Tonnage, by distance shipped (500-mile zones), 1925.

[34] The 23 areas and the corresponding ports of origin and destination are: Baltic countries and Scandinavia (Stockholm); Germany (Hamburg); Great Britain and Ireland (London); Holland and Belgium (Antwerp); France (Cherbourg, and for trade through the Mediterranean, Marseilles); Spain and Portugal (Lisbon); Italy (Genoa); Eastern Mediterranean countries and Turkey (Alexandria); countries on the Black Sea (Odessa); North Africa excluding Egypt (Algiers): West Africa (Lagos); South Africa (Durban); East Africa (Zanzibar); Arabia, Persia, and British India (Bombay); Indo-China, the East Indies, and the Philippines (Singapore); Eastern Asia including Asiatic Russia (Yokohama); Australia, New Zealand, and Oceania (Sydney); West Coast of Canada and the United States (San Francisco); East Coast of Canada and the United States (New York); Mexico, Central America, and West Indies (Havana); Brazil and

Once again the significance of the distance variable is demonstrated.[35] This is so whether one observes the configuration by the 500-mile zones of Fig. 13 or the more regular configuration by 2000-mile zones of Fig. 14. The latter, based upon more aggregative data, tends to conceal the significance for international trade of the uneven world pattern of resources and of the particular cultural and political institutions which have evolved in the individual nations participating in international trade.[36]

In conclusion, it must be recognized that significant regularities are associated with variation in the distance factor. However, considerable caution and circumspection must be exercised in

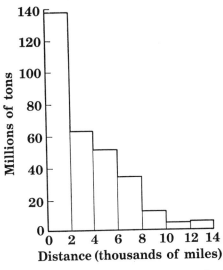

FIG. 14. World ocean-going freight. Tonnage, by distance shipped (2000-mile zones), 1925.

attributing significance to particular sets of data and related findings which have been presented here and elsewhere. In a number of cases

Northern South America (Rio de Janeiro); remainder of the East Coast of South America (Buenos Aires); and West Coast of South America (Antofagasta).

In selecting the chief port in each area and in deriving the distances between ports the author had to use his best judgment in several instances. Other individuals may have made different choices. Also, inaccuracy creeps in because not all traffic moves by the shortest navigable routes as is assumed here. But adjustment for these factors would affect Figs. 13 and 14 only in a minor way.

A more serious shortcoming is that international trade *within* any given area was excluded because we had no knowledge of the distances over which such trade moved. As a result the volume of shipment over distances falling within the smaller distance zones is considerably underestimated in Figs. 13 and 14.

Shortest navigable distances between ports in nautical miles were obtained or estimated from U.S. Navy Department, Hydrographic Office, *Table of Distances Between Ports*, Washington, D.C., 1942.

35 Also see Lösch, *op. cit.*, pp. 305–07.

36 The manner in which the data are aggregated, of course, influences the smoothness with which tonnage falls off with distance when the aggregated data are charted. When the data are aggregated by 1500-mile zones, tonnage for the second zone is considerably less than for the third. However, by 2500- and 3000-mile zones, the "falling-off-effect" is regular as it is by 2000-mile zones.

the data are inadequate; and the statistical processing and techniques are suspect or deficient or both. Nonetheless, after an over-all view of the empirical material, it is undeniable that the friction of distance manifests itself in a number of important ways and markedly conditions the structure and functioning of critical sectors of the social system. The impact of transport, both direct and indirect, is crucial. In at least certain major analyses of the economy the spatial framework cannot be ignored.

Chapter 4

Transport Inputs and
Related Spatial Concepts

1. GENERAL INTRODUCTORY REMARKS

Having presented some of the more important statistical findings on spatial relations and having established that there are significant regularities associated with variation in the distance factor, we are now in a position to develop appropriate concepts for theoretical analysis. This is not to deny the usefulness of the approach of the astronomer Stewart who advocates the methods of Tycho Brahe and Kepler, namely, accumulating extensive observations and condensing the voluminous data into concise empirical rules before formulating a general theory. Such has been the point of departure, in business cycle analysis, of the National Bureau of Economic Research. Nonetheless, it is also valuable at this stage, given the extensive material already amassed, to formulate operational and functional concepts for a general theory of space-economy which could facilitate systematic and large-scale observation and possibly abet the extraction of more empirical rules from the data.[1]

As before we must recognize the obvious fact that economic activity takes place in a time-space continuum. In general, to minimize effort

[1] For a thorough discussion of the methodological issues involved see T. C. Koopmans, "Measurement without Theory," *Review of Economic Statistics*, Vol. XXIX (August 1947), pp. 161–72; and R. Vining and T. C. Koopmans, "Methodological Issues in Quantitative Economics," *idem*, Vol. XXXI (May 1949), pp. 77–94.

or factor services in producing a given social output or to maximize social output with a given amount of effort and factor services, is not to choose a path of action with respect to the time axis alone, or to the space axis alone, but rather with respect to both axes.

Aside from personal preferences and acquired interpersonal behavior forms, there are, as mentioned above, at least two major sets of economic factors which press society into a spatial framework: one, deglomeration forces, including the operation of the law of diminishing returns; the other, inequality of resource endowment.[2] Viewed in terms of a young developing economy, the transition and growth of a population nucleation from a village into a town, in general, involves spatial extension of the agricultural hinterland. Obviously, despite the greater transport effort or cost that may be incurred in marketing the output of the new, more distant land brought under cultivation, the *net* return from the application of intramarginal doses of capital and labor to that new land is usually greater than that from the application of additional doses to old, less distant land. And obviously too, spatial bonds must be established with other geographic points if this nucleation is to consume mineral or other products not available locally. In terms of the existing economy of the United States, it is inconceivable for these reasons that the entire population be herded about New York City, and perhaps a few additional focal points,[3] notwithstanding the sharpening of the New York peak implicit in Stewart's[4] application of physical analogues to demographic study.[5]

---

[2] Space can also be introduced through assumption as it is by Lösch (*Die räumliche Ordnung der Wirtschaft*, Jena, 1944, Chaps. 8 and 9). All economic resources as well as completely self-sufficient homesteads can be postulated to be uniformly distributed over any given plain. Spatial relations, however, do not become important until specialization and trade ensue.

[3] Even herding of population is inconsistent with a spaceless one-point economy.

[4] "Empirical Mathematical Rules . . . ," *op. cit.*, pp. 480–81. Diminishing returns and inequality of resources in a sense set in motion centrifugal forces which balance the tendency toward centripetal shift along the lines of force in a field toward the peak of potential.

[5] Our interpretation of the factors at play seems to be at variance with Zipf's. Zipf offers a theoretical explanation of the spatial arrangement of the economy as well as of other processes of human ecology in terms of two major forces: the Force of Diversification and the Force of Unification. The Force of Diversification reflects the economy of moving "the population to the immediate sources of raw materials in order to save the work of transporting the materials to the persons . . ." and operates "to split the population into a larger n number of small, widely scattered and largely autarchical communities . . ." The Force of Unification, on the other hand, reflects the economy of saving the work of transporting finished products to each consumer and "operates in the opposite direction of moving the materials to the population, with the result that all production and

It is proposed to express some of the complex spatial relations of an economy in terms of a simple common concept of transport inputs. We define a transport input as the movement of a unit of weight over a unit distance; e.g., we may speak of pound-miles, ton-kilometers, etc.[6] In an indirect sense, transport inputs correspond to the exertions of effort and other factor services required to overcome resistance encountered in movement through space where friction is present. In a space-economy we obviously wish to minimize these, *ceteris paribus*.

It is imperative to think in terms of some such concept as transport inputs if one is to comprehend fully the significance of space in actuality. One cannot ignore transport cost and merely concentrate upon

---

consumption will take place in one big city where the entire population . . . will live" (*op. cit.,* p. 352). Only in terms of the functioning of both forces can the actual location of population be understood, according to Zipf.

Though in its present form there may be considerable value to Zipf's theoretical framework for a general study of human behavior, it needs to be substantially revised and extended for an analysis of the space-economy. Though his framework rightly points out the essential factor of minimizing transport effort in terms of probable distributions of raw materials in general, it should in addition encompass the vital consideration of agglomeration (and deglomeration) economies which consist of the economies (and diseconomies) of scale within the plant, the economies (and diseconomies) of localization, and urbanization economies (and diseconomies). On the one hand, agglomeration economies partially nullify the Force of Diversification acting toward scattered production and autarchical communities when a small "diversity of raw materials is used, with an increased likelihood of finding them in a restricted area" (*op. cit.,* p. 365). On the other hand, deglomeration economies prevent the economy from virtually collapsing to a point as implied by the Force of Unification when the "diversity of needed raw materials increases, with the decreasing probability of finding them in a single spot" (*op. cit.,* p. 365).

Also, Zipf's framework tends to minimize the major roles played by certain industries in our economy—such as iron and steel, aluminum, and glass—whose chief raw materials are highly localized in a relatively few places. The location forces operating on these industries in terms of both factor immobilities and transport costs on raw materials and products tend to lead to large population nuclei at places other than Zipf's least-work center which would be the point at which the sum of all "least-work distances to every person on the terrain" is at a minimum. Nor need all innovations which increase the diversity of materials increase the Force of Unification as Zipf maintains. For, by revaluing the attributes and resources of certain areas, as atomic energy has recently done, a major innovation can introduce more "dispersion" from a least-work center.

[6] Just as we frequently use the general term, man-hours, when we speak of social aggregates and specify man-hours of particular types of labor—skilled, unskilled, etc.—when we speak of the production process of a particular firm, so with transport inputs we shall speak of ton-miles when we think in terms of aggregates and specify ton-miles of particular commodities when we deal with an individual line of production.

the labor, raw material, and other costs which compose transport cost; nor can one ignore transport inputs and merely concentrate upon the labor, capital, and other inputs which, as we shall presently show, compose transport inputs if he is to understand the full array of dynamic spatial phenomena.[7]

(To avoid confusion with earlier writings of mine, it should be noted again that the term *transport inputs* is being substituted for the term *distance inputs* which has been previously used. As mentioned in the preface, distance inputs is inferior to transport inputs as a term when considered with respect to the everyday usage of words; and also distance inputs is misleading to non-economists who use the term transport inputs with a correct spatial perspective. It is felt that the non-spatial bias of traditional economic theory has by now been sufficiently overcome to justify the employment in this book of the superior term, transport inputs.)

[7] A highly simplified example may be illuminating at this point. Assume that a society's iron manufacture has advanced to the stage where it requires 300 lb of coal, 200 lb of ore, and 10 hours of direct labor to produce 100 lb of iron (we ignore other raw material and factor requirements). Transportation of coal and ore is required if production is at the market site, A; of coal and the finished product if production is at the ore site, B; and of ore and the finished product if production is at the coal site, C. Allow 20 labor-hours to transport the necessary coal and ore to produce 100 lb of iron at A, 10 labor-hours to transport the necessary coal per 100 lb of iron to B and 100 lb of finished product from B to A, and 7 labor-hours to transport the necessary ore per 100 lb of iron to C and 100 lb of finished product from C to A. (We postulate that the services of land and capital goods required in the above transportation are negligible.) Therefore we have:

For production at A: $30h + 2r + 3c \to i$
For production at B: $20h + 2r + 3c \to i$
For production at C: $17h + 2r + 3c \to i$

where $h = 1$ labor-hour, $r = 100$ lb of ore, $c = 100$ lb of coal, and $i = 100$ lb of iron delivered at A.

This formulation, following traditional lines, points out the need for minimizing the amount of labor inputs. But it conceals the real issue which is to minimize the effort at overcoming spatial resistances, in a sense, to economize on distances to be traversed with appropriate weighting for the type and amount of traffic in any direction. The presentation of alternatives should be:

For production at A: $20d + 10h + 2r + 3c \to i$
For production at B: $10d + 10h + 2r + 3c \to i$
For production at C: $7d + 10h + 2r + 3c \to i$

where $d = $ a transport input so defined as to require 1 hour of effort.

This presentation does emphasize explicitly that it is transport inputs or effort at overcoming space resistance which is to be minimized. It does not leave implicit the real problem which, if left implicit, becomes quickly concealed as soon as we treat a modern economy with complex stages of production.

2. Transport Inputs Contrasted with Capital Inputs

Before certain operational uses of transport inputs are demonstrated, this and related concepts should be developed more fully.

It is instructive to contrast transport inputs and capital[8] inputs. Neither can be considered an ultimate factor of production. Both in a sense are derived even if the analyst (à la Knight) must go back to the beginnings of time to justify this view.[9] As capital goods, and thus services of capital goods, transport inputs stem from direct labor inputs with or without direct land inputs (as, for example, the services of land underlying the roadbed upon which a railway is constructed), with or without the services of capital goods (as, for example, that of rail equipment), and with or without other transport inputs (as, for example, the transport inputs required in bringing coal to the locomotive). Ultimately, they can be traced back to direct labor and land inputs only.

The same motive lies behind decisions respecting the use of capital inputs and the use of transport inputs. The motive in the traditional sense is to maximize profit. Methods requiring the use of capital goods or the increased use of capital goods are adopted when they are found to be more productive, given any initial amount of labor-hours and other inputs to be expended. Or these methods may enable the production of goods otherwise unobtainable and at an expenditure of effort which society is willing to make. Likewise with transport inputs. When in a simple economy a farmer with a given amount of capital and other resources chooses to apply his efforts at cultivating new land on the periphery of the hinterland of a growing town rather than at cultivating intensively a more limited quantity of old land near the town, in general he anticipates reaping greater returns despite the fact that he applies less of his available labor to cultivation and more to marketing his harvest. In effect he substitutes transport inputs (indirect labor inputs) for direct labor inputs. He finds it profitable[10]

---

[8] In using the word *capital*, we are thinking in real terms and chiefly of capital goods. Controversy over the definition of capital is not desired. The argument that follows holds, except perhaps for minor revisions, regardless of the particular definition of real capital adopted.

[9] And even if he must contrast capital with unskilled labor and virgin soil. Among others, see F. Knight, "The Theory of Investment Once More: Mr. Boulding and the Austrians," *Quarterly Journal of Economics*, Vol. 50 (November 1935), pp. 45–50; and K. Wicksell, *Lectures on Political Economy*, New York, 1934, Vol. I, Part II, especially pp. 145–46, 149–51, 185–86.

[10] It should be emphasized that just as every investment for a longer period (made possible by the accumulation of additional capital) will not necessarily

to do so in the same way that in using a plough that he has built, he finds it profitable to substitute services of capital goods (indirect labor inputs) for direct labor inputs.[11] Also, when the United States public over the years has chosen to consume coffee and at an increasing rate rather than to consume more of domestically produced commodities, there has resulted an increase in the spatial extent of the United States economy. This resembles the increase in the time extent of production which took place when society decided to mine and refine uranium ore (as well as produce the requisite equipment) partly with labor drawn from unmechanized agriculture.[12]

Many economists think of methods using the services of capital goods as roundabout methods which increase the time extent of production, or to be more precise, the time period of investment.[13] We need not judge the validity of such reasoning.[14] If one accepts it, one can draw a parallel with respect to the use of transport inputs. Methods which use transport inputs are also roundabout, and they tend to increase the spatial extent of production.

Further, if one adheres to Hayek's theory of capital and discards the concept of an *average* investment period, to account for a greater use of capital "it is sufficient to say that the investment period of some

---

yield a larger product, so every increase in the use of transport inputs and in the spatial extent of society will not necessarily be desirable. Only those spatial lengthenings of production which are profitable will be adopted. Compare F. von Hayek, *The Pure Theory of Capital,* London, 1941, p. 60.

[11] For a discussion of relations between direct and indirect labor which is designed to elucidate certain capital aspects of production but which to a large extent is also applicable to spatial aspects, see O. Lange, "The Place of Interest in the Theory of Production," *Review of Economic Studies,* Vol. III (June 1936), pp. 159–70.

[12] In the sense that both capital and transport inputs are derived, society withdraws certain resources from immediate direct application in order to exploit, or exploit more efficiently, other potential resources. And these potential resources, as they are drawn into the production process, need not be immediately consumed, but may be employed to exploit still other potential resources and thus to increase further the time and space extent of production. In this way the process of capital and spatial growth of the economy can be cumulative.

[13] As Hayek has pointed out, the concept of a single or average period of production may be not only a confusing but also a meaningless abstraction. One must think in terms of periods for which particular factors are invested. "The Mythology of Capital," *Quarterly Journal of Economics,* Vol. 50 (February 1936), pp. 199–205.

[14] J. B. Clark, Knight, Nurkse, Smithies, and others have attacked it. For bibliography on this controversy, see N. Kaldor, "Annual Survey of Economic Theory: The Recent Controversy on the Theory of Capital," *Econometrica,* Vol. 5 (July 1937), and *Readings in the Theory of Income Distribution,* Blakiston, Philadelphia, 1946, pp. 694–99.

factors has been lengthened while those of all others have remained unchanged; or that the investment periods of a greater quantity of factors have been lengthened than the quantity of factors whose investment periods have been shortened by an equal amount; or that the investment period of a given quantity of factors has been lengthened by more than the investment period of another equal amount has been shortened."[15] In parallel fashion, we need not speak of an *average* spatial extent of production, which concept if meaningful could pose serious problems in measurement. But when more transport inputs are utilized, and profitably so, we can assume that the spatial extent of production *in general* is increased: (1) that the spatial dimension of some production lines is lengthened (as, for example, through the extension of marketing and purchasing areas); (2) that the spatial dimensions of certain production lines are lengthened while those of others are shortened by an equal amount, but that the former group is of greater quantitative significance; or (3) that of two equally important groups of production lines, the increase in the spatial dimension of those lengthened is greater than the decrease of those shortened.[16]

Connected with the roundaboutness of capitalistic production one frequently finds the concept of time preference over which has raged a controversy that I do not wish to discuss.[17] However, I do wish to

[15] "The Mythology of Capital," *op. cit.*, p. 206. Also see F. Machlup, "Professor Knight and the 'Period of Production,'" *Journal of Political Economy*, Vol. 43 (October 1935), pp. 584–93.

[16] To correspond to Knight's contention that increase in the use of capital does not necessarily entail an increase in the period of production [see F. Knight, "Professor Hayek and the Theory of Investment," *Economic Journal*, Vol. 45 (March 1935), pp. 79–81], it is difficult to visualize how a profitable absorption of additional transport inputs might shorten the spatial extent of production *in general*.

I am inclined to reject Knight's views that all capital is normally conceptually perpetual, that its replacement has to be taken for granted as a technological detail, that, in consequence there is no production process of determinate length other than zero or "all history," and that, in the only sense of timing in terms of which economic analysis is possible, *production and consumption are simultaneous*. (Hayek, "Mythology of Capital," *op. cit.*, p. 202.) It certainly would be meaningless to use the Knightian emphasis for the development of space concepts. It would negate the very existence of a space-economy. There could be no space separating production and consumption. And so forth.

[17] For various points of view, see, among others, E. von Böhm-Bawerk, *The Positive Theory of Capital*, 1891, Book V; I. Fisher, *The Theory of Interest*, New York, 1939, especially Chap. XX; F. Knight, "Professor Fisher's Interest Theory: A Case in Point," *Journal of Political Economy*, Vol. 39 (April 1931), pp. 176–212; and F. von Hayek, *Pure Theory of Capital*, London, 1941, Chaps. 17 and 18, and Appendix I.

emphasize that, if one thinks in terms of time preference, there is strong justification for thinking in terms of space preference.[18] Psychologists and sociologists, whether speaking of a gregarious instinct or of acquired behavior patterns or of both, have emphasized the social nature of man and his propensity to associate with groups of various sorts.[19] One can reason that such a propensity, acquired or instinctive, is a manifestation of a positive space preference. In the extreme, unreal case, where there are ubiquitous resources, no diminishing returns on land, and no congestion problem that sets in motion dispersive forces, people would aggregate in one or many herds of different sizes—a phenomenon which is biologically valid.[20] To induce them to separate, there would have to be an incentive. In the real world the incentive for non-herd existence, *economically speaking*, is greater productivity obtainable through (1) capitalizing deglomeration economies (such as postponing the operation of the laws of diminishing returns) and (2) exploiting the uneven geographic distribution of resources. This incentive (it can be maintained) is analogous to that which induces people to defer present consumption of commodities for the possession of a greater amount at a later date.

It should be stressed that not all individuals need have a positive space preference. There are hermits. They exhibit negative space preference, being willing in general to accept a lower productivity (a lower standard of living) in order to be spatially apart from society. They resemble those well-to-do individuals who fear and exaggerate the insecurities of the future, who have a negative rate of time preference, and who would be willing to accept if necessary a negative interest rate.

Less extreme is the introvert whose need for social contact is not intense. He possesses a mild space preference. He is easily *induced* to lead a fairly isolated life, though in actuality he may not do so. Not so with the extrovert. His need for social interchange is acute; his space preference markedly high. He parallels the sailor, child,

[18] For this expression I am indebted to Dr. E. M. Hoover.

[19] Refer, among others, to W. McDougall, *An Introduction to Social Psychology*, Boston, 1926, pp. 87–90, 175–78, 303–8, 456–60; L. L. Bernard, *Instinct, A Study in Social Psychology*, New York, 1924, especially pp. 357–59, 369–72; K. Young, *Source Book for Social Psychology*, New York, 1927, Chaps. I–IV; and W. F. Ogburn and M. F. Nimkoff, *Sociology*, Cambridge, Mass., 1940, Part IV.

[20] See W. Trotter, *Instincts of the Herd in Peace and War*, London, 1916; and W. C. Allee, *The Social Life of Animals*, New York, 1938. Small herds (cities), and not necessarily one huge herd (city), may be sufficient to satisfy the social needs of man.

savage, and spendthrift whose positive rate of time preference is likewise towering.[21]

On balance it does seem that, despite the many serious qualifications one must make in generalizing about such psychological principles as time preference and space preference and despite the recent centrifugal tendencies in population movement (which we will discuss briefly below), individuals in society, in general, do manifest a positive space preference just as they seem to manifest a positive time preference.

Associated with time preference has been the procedure of discounting over time. The present value of a future product is equal to its expected future price discounted by the prevailing rate of interest. The return to an input is equated to its discounted marginal productivity. And so forth. The usefulness of this procedure is obvious. But there is also a discounting over space, which enables one to compare values of two or more goods, yields, or inputs spatially separated and differently distant from any particular geographic point of reference. The rate of discount in space is of course the transport rate. Though economists have never spoken explicitly of spatial discounting, nonetheless they have performed the operation.[22] In doing so, they have most frequently been considering a one-point market served by a surface producing area (as we find in farming). In such a case the farther the site of production from the market the more the market price is discounted to yield the net price on the output of that site. However, far more complex situations, involving all types of possible purchasing areas and selling areas for the relevant inputs and outputs, have been handled by location analysts.[23] The

[21] The reader who is interested in constructing other parallels may refer to the various possible types of time preference cited by Fisher (*op. cit.*) and Böhm-Bawerk (*op. cit.*).

Just as we can have different rates of time preference for various commodities (e.g. see Hayek, *The Pure Theory of Capital*, op. cit., pp. 241–42) we can conceive of different space preferences with respect to various social activities. And certainly the state of technology, the geographic environment, and the cultural milieu affect the nature of one's space preference. Compare the age of the automobile with the age of the horsecar.

[22] As an instance, Alfred Marshall states: "If in any industry, whether agricultural or not, two producers have equal facilities in all respects, except that one has a more convenient situation than the other, and can buy or sell in the same markets with less cost of carriage, the differential advantage which his situation gives him is the aggregate of the excess charges for cost of carriage to which his rival is put. And we may suppose that other advantages of situation, such for instance as the near access to a labour market specially adapted to his trade, can be translated in like manner into money values." (*Principles of Economics*, Book V, Chap. XI, Sect. 1.)

[23] We cite a few works: O. Engländer, *Theorie des Güterverkehrs und der*

explicit use of spatial discounting can clear the ground for a more *functional* analysis of the factor of *situs* in economic activities.

3. TRANSPORT RATE: THE PRICE OF A TRANSPORT INPUT

In speaking of an input, one also thinks in terms of the price of, or the return to, that input. What determines its reward? What determines interest, rent, wages, profits, or in Knightian terms the annual rate of return in perpetuity? What is the return or price corresponding to a transport input? The last question can be partly answered with a simple supply and demand approach conventionally used to answer the first two questions.

If, from the standpoint of society, we think of a transport input as equivalent to the movement of a ton of any commodity over 1 mile and if, for the moment, we put aside the complicated transport structures of reality, then the price of a transport input is the transport rate. From the standpoint of suppliers, at higher and higher transport rates, there will be a tendency for more and more transport inputs to be furnished. More and more direct labor and land services and services of capital and capital goods will flow into the area of transport inputs. The supply curve for transport inputs is positively inclined (where transport rate is measured along the vertical axis and quantity along the horizontal). On the other hand, the demand curve for transport inputs, as can be expected, is negatively inclined. It may be claimed that such a demand curve reflects the marginal productivity corresponding to various quantities of transport inputs. It would then be anticipated, given a state of technology, tastes, and resources, that as the spatial extent of production is continually lengthened through the application of more and more transport inputs,[24] the additional product associated with each successive lengthening, after a point, tends to fall off.[25]

Frachtsätze, Jena, 1924; T. Palander, *Beiträge zur Standortstheorie*, Upsala, 1935, especially Chaps. VII and XII; E. M. Hoover, *Location Theory and the Shoe and Leather Industries*, Cambridge, Mass., 1937; and A. Lösch, *op. cit.*

As Professor Haberler has suggested, transport costs may be compared with storage costs: the former, in moving from one point in space to another; the latter, from one point in time to another in the future.

[24] Of course, for many lines of production the spatial extent, like the time period of investment, increases by only large jumps.

[25] It seems trivial to argue whether or not physical output is to be attributed to the use of transport inputs and whether or not a marginal physical product can be assigned to the use of an additional dose of transport inputs. The farmer who does use an additional dose of transport inputs, when he finds it profitable to shift his farming operations to a location somewhat more distant from his

It is instructive to examine somewhat more thoroughly the effect of a change in the price of a transport input. Suppose an advance in the state of transport technology pushes the supply curve of transport inputs to the right and results in a lower price. From the viewpoint of industrial production there will be both a scale and a substitution effect. Historically we find that reduced transport rates have tended (1) to transform a scattered, ubiquitous pattern of production into an increasingly concentrated one, and (2) to effect progressive differentiation and selection between sites with superior and inferior resources and trade routes.[26] The resulting increase in geographic specialization and in the spatial extent of production in general is, in essence, a *substitution* of transport inputs for various other inputs (particularly for those inputs at inferior sites) as well as a substitution of inputs in general at the favored sites for inputs in general at the disfavored sites. As to the *scale* effect, the tremendous increases in output engendered by the cheapening of transport inputs are too well known to require discussion.

Also with respect to consumer behavior, there are scale and substitution effects. With a fall in the time and money cost of population movement (as realized with the development of the street and electric railway, the automobile, bus, and aircraft), a person in general can maintain a given level of social contact (or space preference) and at the same time consume more of other products. He can,

---

market point, does realize an addition to total product, *ceteris paribus.* Also, in the case where a firm decides to exploit a deposit of richer ore which, however, is more removed from the point of smelting, there corresponds to the increase in transport inputs (whether large or small) an increase in physical product, *ceteris paribus.*

Some may contend that in both cases the addition to total product is not the result of the additional use of transport inputs *per se* but rather a result of a more efficient combination of land, labor, and capital services. Others may insist that just as a (marginal) productivity is attributed to capital, even though capital inputs (e.g. the services of capital equipment) are not productive *per se* but merely allow the services of labor to be more productive, so should a (marginal) productivity be assigned to transport inputs.

From our standpoint, the significant point is the association, whether one interprets it causally or merely statistically, of greater physical product with increased use of transport inputs, *ceteris paribus.* This explains in part the demand for transport inputs and, for obvious reasons, a demand schedule which indicates that, at a lower and lower price for transport inputs, there will be a tendency for more and more of transport inputs to be purchased.

[26] See W. H. Dean, Jr., *The Theory of the Geographic Location of Economic Activities,* Ann Arbor, Mich., 1938, especially Chap. 3; E. M. Hoover, *op. cit.,* Chap. 3; and H. Ritschl, "Reine und historische Dynamik des Standortes der Erzeugungszweige," *Schmollers Jahrbuch,* Vol. 51 (1927), pp. 813–70.

at the given level of social contact, enjoy more of the amenities of life that come from living in a less congested area away from the compact urban mass. This *scale* effect which obviously requires a greater consumption of transport inputs partly accounts for the process of dispersion of urban population[27] and the settlement of peripheral metropolitan areas that has taken place during the last half-century.[28] But this development is also partly due to the operation of the *substitution* effect. Consumption of transport inputs has been substituted for the consumption of other commodities and services. Expenditures on travel, whether intraurban or other, appear to have absorbed an increasing proportion of the consumer's budget.

Hitherto we have spoken of a single transport rate as the price of a transport input. However, in modern society there is a multitude of rates which vary with length of haul, nature of haul, type of commodity, degree of competition, character of topography, etc. Similarly, although we speak of a single prevailing interest rate as the price of capital, there is a multitude of interest rates varying according to the nature of the risk, length of the loan, type of region, etc.[29] It is to be expected that in the operation of a complex, institutionalized society there will be all types of transport rates and discriminations in the application of these rates. But this does not invalidate thinking in general terms of *the* transport rate as a hypothetical, representative one, one that reflects the general movement of the multitude of actual transport rates. The basic analysis is essentially unaffected by such a fiction.[30]

[27] All income classes have, in general, been affected. At one extreme the lowest income groups have gradually moved out of the worst slums into somewhat better districts, generally somewhat younger, less congested, and farther from the core of the city. At the other extreme the highest income groups, who though on higher planes of living do not necessarily possess different space preferences, in general have vacated by degrees their existing residences to construct new ones more removed, although some individuals have moved closer to the core. For further material see H. Hoyt, *The Structure and Growth of Residential Neighborhoods in American Cities* (Federal Housing Administration), Washington, 1939; and U.S. National Resources Committee, *Our Cities*, Washington, 1937.

[28] Also, the mobility and flexibility of rural population has been increased. Living apart from one's fellow creatures, as is involved in many rural occupations, may require sacrifice of social contact for increased productivity. Reduced time and money cost of movement allows greater social intercourse for a given productivity. It may also induce the individual with a given space preference to exploit resources which hitherto lay idle because of the social isolation involved.

[29] Refer to Fisher, *op. cit.*, Chap. IX.

[30] It should be borne in mind that the determination of the transport rate and spatial extent of production is not independent of the interest rate (and vice versa). Since an increase in the potential availability of transport inputs in a

4. TRANSPORT INPUTS AND THE CLASSIFICATION OF FACTORS

A few words should be said about how transport inputs fit into the various classifications of productive agents or the conceptual classifications presented as substitutes. One might venture the hypothesis that historically, had there been a certain social class which owned all transport facilities and performed all transport services, the Classicals might well have thought of transport as a fourth factor of production and have been more conscious of distance and the spatial aspect of production. Such was not the case, and in any event a classification based on socio-economic groups could not have much meaning today.

Perhaps the most salient feature of a transport input is its momentary character. A transport input is realized at a given time from the performance of various services. There can be no stock of transport inputs. There can only be a stock of services which can be used to yield transport inputs. A particular individual engaged solely in transporting goods represents a stock of potential labor services. It would be wrong to conceive of him as also a stock of potential transport inputs since in the future his services need not be employed at rendering transport inputs.

Or take a piece of equipment, a locomotive. It should not be considered a stock of transport inputs. Rather it represents a stock of services of a particular capital good, which services when combined with labor and other services simultaneously yield transport inputs. This, too, is merely another way of saying that a transport input is an indirect input.

From the standpoint of orienting transport inputs within the framework of other types of inputs, it seems best to utilize the approach of Walras,[31] which has been well developed by Knight.[32] There the fundamental dichotomy is between resources or capital (as broadly conceived by Knight) and services. There is nothing of a resource or capital nature in the concept of a transport input. Rather it is in the nature of a service and has the same time dimension as the service of

---

modern society involves an increase in capital investment in transport equipment and facilities, the conditions under which capital is available do influence the nature of the supply curve of transport inputs and, hence, the price of a transport input and the structure of the space-economy. In this way, too, land values and differential rents from superior situations are affected by the interest rate.

[31] L. Walras, *Éléments d'économie politique pure*, Lausanne, 1926, pp. 175–84.

[32] F. Knight, "The Ricardian Theory of Production and Distribution," *Canadian Journal of Economics and Political Science*, Vol. I (May 1935), pp. 3–25; and "Capital and Interest," *Encyclopaedia Britannica*, Vol. IV, 1946, pp. 799–801. Also see the approach of I. Fisher (*op. cit.*, Chap. I).

a given person, piece of land, or capital good, though to be sure there are stocks which correspond to these latter services. It flows indirectly from given resources and capital and competes with and substitutes for all other types of inputs (services) in the production process.

Nonetheless, one can utilize the Marshallian approach, if one follows a *functional* analysis. In a production process there are requirements for labor at a given place, capital at a given place, land services, organizing ability, and finally transport inputs, i.e., the composite of services needed to move raw materials, equipment, labor, and finished product to the appropriate places. Expressed differently, the transport function (defined in the broadest sense possible) can be singled out as a vital aspect of production, as vital perhaps as the functions of labor, capital, land, and the entrepreneur. The inputs corresponding to the transport function we have called transport inputs, and by paying attention to this function and its associated inputs we are able to describe the spatial aspects of the economy. But one need not necessarily think of the transport function as another factor of production. The important thing is to recognize the role that transport inputs do play in production and consumption processes.

Chapter 5

The Locational Equilibrium of the Firm: Transport — Orientation

1. SOME DEFINITIONAL AND CLASSIFICATIONAL REMARKS

The theoretical, conceptual, and empirical materials of the previous chapters form a background against which we shall re-examine, restate in part, and attempt to extend existing location theories. In doing so we shall have as a prime objective the synthesizing of partial location theories into a more general theory which yields any given specific location theory capable of being spelled out in detail when the appropriate set of conditions are postulated.

In this chapter we shall confine ourselves to the locational equilibrium of the firm[1] when the problem of transport-orientation obtains. The utility of the concept of transport inputs in the determination of the firm's geographical position will be demonstrated. Also, this concept will enable us to fuse much of traditional Weberian locational doctrine and modern production theory. At the same time certain difficulties which have confronted location theorists for a long time will be resolved.

[1] For simplicity's sake we shall speak of a firm as consisting of one or more plants operating at one and only one site and of a producer as managing one and only one firm. There is no logical difficulty in extending the analysis to enterprises which operate plants spatially separated, whether these plants correspond to the same or different stages of production. However, one must then consider transport inputs within the enterprise and consequently the analysis becomes more complex.

91

However, it is advisable, first, clearly to define the problem of this chapter and to stress the various levels of abstraction at which locational analysis is possible. This is necessary in order to avoid criticism similar to some which has been directed at Weber but which has failed to appreciate that the interpretation and significance of the Weberian doctrine are different for each of these levels.[2] It is possible, of course, to establish different classifications of levels at which inquiry can be conducted. Although the reader may prefer to adopt another classification, it is satisfactory for our purposes to set up the following one which distinguishes among at least four levels of inquiry:

1. For the small, individual producer who has a negligible influence upon prices (with the exception of the price of his own product), the locus of consumption, the supply costs and sources of factors, transport rates, agglomeration economies, and other locational variables;

2. For the small or large producer who does influence these variables;

3. For an industry as a whole or for a group of producers who form a meaningful aggregate for analysis because they are homogeneous with respect to certain characteristics, or because, though heterogeneous, they complement each other;[3]

4. For a regional or world economy (where general analysis should account for the determination of values for all possible location variables).

In this chapter we shall confine ourselves chiefly to the first level. However, it should be emphasized that the accepted dualism in location theory—viz., a Thünen type of analysis for the agricultural sphere, a Weberian schema for the industrial sector—and the opposition to incorporating these two models into one general framework totters once we recognize these levels of inquiry. The Thünen school confines itself to an aggregative analysis. Its problem is the distribution of agricultural production over a given region. It assumes away any problems of location for the individual producer by assigning to him

[2] A systematic presentation and refutation (in many respects, valid) of these criticisms is found in E. Niederhauser, "Die Standortstheorie Alfred Webers," *Staatswissenschaftliche Studien,* Vol. XIV (Weinfelden, 1944).

[3] Chamberlin has pointed out the limitations of the group concept for analyzing substitution effects among the products of individual firms (*The Theory of Monopolistic Competition,* Cambridge, Mass., 1933, especially pp. 103–4) and has particularly criticized the industry in this respect. See his "Product Heterogeneity and Public Policy," *Papers and Proceedings of the American Economic Association,* Vol. XL (May 1950), pp. 85–92; and "Monopolistic Competition Revisited," *Economica,* November 1951. Our industry or group of firms, however, may be conceived in terms of similar techniques of production, or inputs, or in terms of a set of external economies achieved by agglomeration of similar or dissimilar lines of production.

a fixed location, an infinite immobility. The Weberian school, on the other hand, is primarily concerned with the locational problem of an individual firm which produces a given product. True, the Weberian doctrine frequently shifts to aggregative analysis when it considers agglomeration economies, the various economic strata of society, and the like. But in this type of aggregative analysis the Weberian school explicitly avoids the problem of the efficient spatial distribution, both qualitative and quantitative, of the various types of industrial production over a given region. Thus, the Thünen and Weberian schools have carved out for themselves separate, non-overlapping areas of inquiry. In real life, of course, this clear-cut line of demarcation in locational decisions disappears. No agricultural producer is perfectly immobile; he quite frequently does consider changing location. Accordingly, the Thünen scheme is insufficient for explaining such an agriculturalist's decision. Analysis on the individual level is also required. On the other hand, the Weberian dogma is grossly inadequate for the over-all regional type of industrial planning which has been undertaken in the last decade or two by international, national, and regional authorities. The Thünen methodology can be of great service here. The task ahead is thus to conduct analysis at each level of inquiry and ultimately to fuse the results into one comprehensive framework.[4] This task I can hope to accomplish only partially in this and subsequent chapters.

It is also desirable at this point to consider the categories of commodities (embracing factor services) which have grown out of Weber's doctrines. Commodities have been classified according to mobility, dispensability, geographic occurrence, and weight loss. We frequently encounter in the literature[5] commodities described in terms of the first three of these characteristics and thus falling into one of the following categories:

1. Indispensable, single-source, immobile commodities
2. Indispensable, single-source, mobile commodities
3. Indispensable, many-source, immobile commodities
4. Indispensable, many-source, mobile commodities
5. Dispensable, single-source, immobile commodities
6. Dispensable, single-source, mobile commodities
7. Dispensable, many-source, immobile commodities
8. Dispensable, many-source, mobile commodities

This classification may be useful for certain purposes. From our

[4] Compare O. Engländer, "Kritisches und Positives zu einer allgemeinen reinen Lehre vom Standort," *Zeitschrift für Volkswirtschaft und Sozialpolitik*, Neue Folge, Vol. V (1926), pp. 475–79.
[5] See, for example, Dean (Selections) *op. cit.*, pp. 8–12.

viewpoint, however, these various categories can be reduced to a series of relations which involve substitution, *both in the large and small.* Category 8 is the most general. Here, three explicit types of substitution possibilities exist: (1) substitution between transport inputs and between various outlays and revenues associated with the use of any of several different commodities or combinations of commodities in the production process, (2) substitution associated with the use of any of several sources of any one commodity, (3) substitution associated with the various places to which a commodity can be transported. The fourth characteristic which Weber underscored, namely, weight loss or the degree to which the weight of a good does enter into the weight of the finished product, also lends itself to a substitution analysis which emphasizes the desirability of various places as the site of production according to transport expense.

Categories 1 to 7 can be viewed as special cases of category 8, each limiting in some respect the range of substitution. Thus, when a commodity is technically indispensable for a given production process (though from the social-aggregative standpoint, no commodity is indispensable), substitution between the transport inputs and outlays associated with the location of the given commodity and those associated with the location of a potential substitute commodity is non-existent. When only one deposit or locality exists as a source of a commodity (as is rare from a world-economic standpoint), then the substitution problem connected with diverse sources disappears. Finally, when a commodity is perfectly immobile, no substitution problem arises in connection with production at places other than sources (or points of consumption) of this commodity. Although, to maintain a formal, complete substitution framework we may, as Engländer has done, eschew from our analysis the attribute of mobility by considering immobile commodities to be goods of infinite weight entailing infinite weight loss in production (or consumption).[6]

No matter what scheme of classification is selected, the whole production process, as Predöhl indicated, may be conceived as a complex substitution problem in space, involving such spatial substitutions in the large and small as implied by the above classification

---

[6] A strategic and rare labor skill available at only one locality might in the short run be an instance of a service falling in category 1. Category 2 would embrace those raw materials which Weber considers in the early part of his book; however, as soon as he introduces replacement deposits, the goods which he treats come to fall in category 4. Categories 3 and 4 have been treated by Palander and Hoover in their supply and market area analyses, and to some extent at least, categories 5 to 8 in their more generalized analyses.

as well as those substitutions ordinarily conceived in the production theory (and consumption theory) of a one-point economy.[7]

2. TRANSPORT-ORIENTED EQUILIBRIUM UNDER SIMPLIFIED CONDITIONS

We commence the analysis of the locational equilibrium of the firm under the simplifying assumptions that: (1) its productive activities do not affect the locus of consumption, transport rates, prices of raw materials, labor and other factors and products, and agglomeration economies and other locational variables; and (2) its actions do not provoke retaliatory measures by other producers.

Assume a point C whereat are concentrated all consumers of the product of an individual firm. Also let point M_1 be the only source of a raw material indispensable for the production of the good. Other

---

[7] Palander's criticisms of Predöhl's principle of substitution are in the main unwarranted—or at least are unjustified in view of modern developments in production theory. (See Tord Palander, *Beiträge zur Standortstheorie*, Uppsala, 1935, pp. 254–61.) Palander has first of all underestimated the fruitfulness of decomposing the whole production problem into a set of substitution problems between the various possible pairs of spatially-defined inputs and outputs—as well as into a set of substitution problems between various pairs of groups of these spatially-defined inputs and outputs. Clearly, Predöhl had in mind the substitution problems between groups of commodities (commodities as defined in our broad sense) and those between possible subgroups when he concludes: "Der Standort der Produktion bzw. Produktionsstufe ist also bestimmt durch ein System von Substitutionspunkten, das derart gegliedert ist, dass die Gruppen einer übergeordneten Kombination untergeordnete Kombination in sich enthalten" ("Das Standortsproblem in der Wirtschaftstheorie," *Weltwirtschaftliches Archiv*, Band XXI, 1925, pp. 306–7). Such substitution analysis between groups, subgroups, and pairs of commodities has been developed by Hicks and others and has been generally considered to be feasible and of value.

Secondly, Palander's point that such problems as scale of plant are excluded from substitution analysis is also no longer valid. For, through admitting discontinuities in the technical transformation function, as can be done, variations in scale can easily be treated, being viewed as sudden large and jumpy increases in plant, equipment, and the like. This fact, too, overrides Palander's objection to substitution analysis for its restriction to cases of continuous variation and its failure to treat such important discontinuous variations as are involved in shifts to labor locations (a problem which will be fully discussed at a later point).

Thirdly, there are not two distinct substitution problems as Palander maintains, one between the various factors where scale, location, and prices are given, and the other where technique (the proportion of factors) and scale are fixed, but where production is free to adjust to the spatial variations in the prices of factors and products. Fundamentally decisions in both of these categories are interrelated and are contained within the over-all substitution problem of the individual firm. Further, on a simple two-dimensional diagram, changes in prices and other locational variables can be treated together with changes in the proportion of factors.

productive factors are taken to be ubiquitous, available everywhere in the correct amounts and at the same price.[8] If the raw material

FIG. 15. A locational line.

at M_1 were immobile, such as ore deposits, then the productive activity (mining) would be at M_1, price and profit conditions permitting. Here, however, we assume that the indispensable raw material is mobile, and, further, that a straight line railway connects points M_1 and C. See Fig. 15. Where will the firm locate?

Before we attempt to answer this question it is wise to make clear our use of the terms *transformation function* and *transformation line*. We conceive the transformation function to embrace the numerous technical substitution relations between any pair of outputs, any input and any output, and any pair of inputs. As indicated in the preceding chapter, transport inputs are viewed as any other set of inputs in the transformation-production process. They substitute for other inputs and products.

In the rest of this section and in Sect. 3, we reformulate the Weberian transport orientation doctrine. In this doctrine, the weights of various raw materials and the market demand are assumed to be constant. Therefore, variation in the transport input variables reduces to variation in the distances over which the raw materials and finished product must move. *Hence, a transformation relation between any two transport inputs reduces to a consistent set of variations in two distance variables. In what follows we shall view the relevant consistent sets of variation in two distance variables as a transformation line between these two distance variables, although the transformation line rigorously speaking has reference to variation in the corresponding transport inputs.* The reader, however, need not accept this procedure. He can deny transformation relations between distance variables, and proceed, as in Sect. 4, to state the Weberian dogma in terms of transformation relations between the variable transport inputs. The basic analysis and conclusions, however, remain unchanged.

Returning to the problem of Fig. 15, we observe that in our simple case we have two distance variables, (1) distance from point C and (2) distance from point M_1. When we plot these two variables on Fig. 16 we obtain a straight transformation line with a slope of -1. Of course it is possible to select a location involving unnecessary

[8] This implies that none of the inputs and outputs of the transformation function changes as we move production from site to site except those which will be associated below with the distance variables.

transportation, i.e., a point not on line M_1C, or in other words, a set of distances from points C and M_1 lying above and to the right of line VW in Fig. 16. But since we assume that the producer minimizes costs, he will not select a location involving unnecessary distance, just as he will not employ unnecessary labor.[9]

Let us complicate our case. Production now requires a second raw material present at only one source, M_2. If this good is both indispensable and immobile, the site of production, if production is at all feasible, will coincide with this source. Where this second good is mobile, for each possible (realistic) distance from

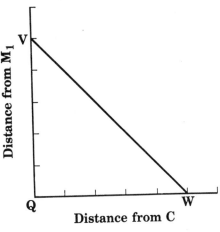

Fig. 16. A transformation line for the line case.

M_2, there exists a transformation line between the variables, distance from C and distance from M_1; and for each possible (realistic) distance from M_1 there exists a transformation line between the variables, distance from C and distance from M_2; and finally, for each possible (realistic) distance from C there exists a transformation line between the variables, distance from M_1 and distance from M_2. The exact nature of all the transformation lines will, of course, depend upon the relative positions of M_1, M_2, and C. Take an example where the distances between C and M_2, C and M_1, and M_2 and M_1 are 8, 5, and 7 units respectively (Fig. 17). For any value, let us say 3 units, of the variable distance from C, we obtain a transformation line representing the different possible sets of the variables, distance from M_1 and distance from M_2, given by arc TS, the locus of points constructed with a radius of 3 units from point C. The transformation line turns out to be convex to the origin Q (Fig. 18). Obviously this transformation line contains no sets of variables represented by points outside the triangle CM_1M_2 of Fig. 17. That would be covering unnecessary distance.

[9] However, as we shall see later, when discriminatory transport rates nullify the distance principle and cause the cost between two termini to be less than that between an intermediate point and one of the termini, it is quite possible for an entrepreneur to choose a location involving unnecessary distance in the transformation sense.

Our problem becomes still more complicated when we introduce additional indispensable but mobile raw materials, each obtainable

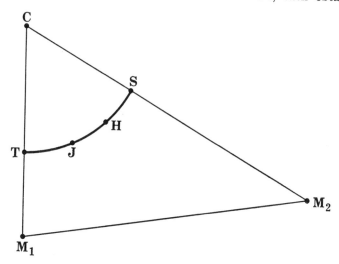

Fig. 17.   A locational triangle.

at an only source.   Let M_3 represent the sole source of a third indispensable but mobile raw material.   Let M_3 be 7 units distant from C

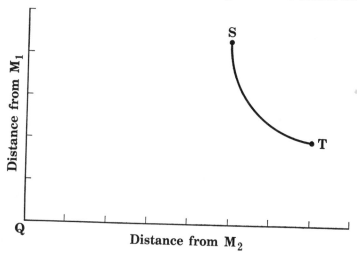

Fig. 18.   A transformation line for the triangle case.

and 2 units from M_2.   See Fig. 19.   Here we must pose the substitution question somewhat differently.   Ordinarily we would hold constant all inputs and outputs but two and observe the substitution relations between these two. Here, if we assign fixed values to the variables, distance from M_1 and distance from M_2, say RM_1 and RM_2, respectively, and values which also permit a location at point R within the polygon of Fig. 19, then necessarily the values of the other two variables, distance from C and distance from M_3, are determined, being RC and RM_3, respectively. No substitution problem arises. The situation would resemble one emerging under the ordinary non-spatial conception of the production problem, where we examine the substitu-

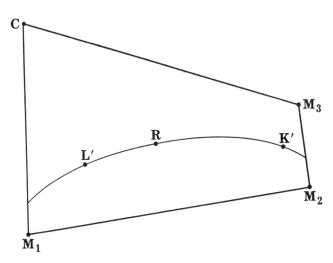

FIG. 19. A four-sided locational polygon.

tion relations between two factors, each for technical reasons bearing a fixed relationship to another factor in the given basket of commodities. There would be no possibility of substitution.

However, a real substitution problem does exist in the case of our polygon of Fig. 19. The entrepreneur is concerned with minimizing transport expense. He will move to a new position if, for example, the shorter distance from C lessens his transport expense by more than the amount which the increased distance from M_3 adds to his transport expense, the summed expenses of transporting the fixed quantities of raw materials from M_1 and M_2 remaining constant. Hence, given the sum to be expended on transport to consumption place and from all raw material sources but two, what are the technical substitution relations between the distance variables from these two points? Thus in this formulation all distances are variables, although the values of all but the relevant two are restrained by a total cost condition and although all distances are subject to the obvious condition that they be measured to a common point, the production point. If, for example, as in Fig. 19, we assume that transport cost is proportional to distance and that equal weights of raw materials from sources M_1 and M_2 are required[10] (simple hypotheses which we later discard), we can

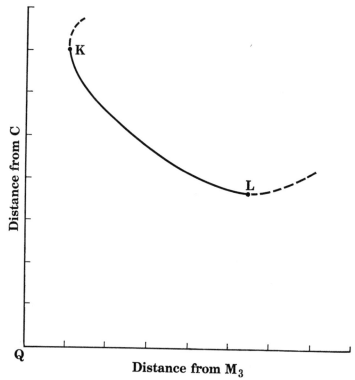

Fig. 20. A transformation line for a four-sided polygon.

indicate the locus of possible sites by an elliptical curve at any point on which the sum of distance from M_1 and distance from M_2, and thus the amount expended on transport from M_1 and M_2, is constant. From this curve we obtain the transformation line of Fig. 20, which represents the possible sets of values for the variables, distance from

[10] Obviously in reality the weights of raw materials to be transported from various sources are of different magnitude, and the transport tariffs vary from raw material to raw material as well as for longer and shorter distances. But, given any set of real information, we can construct theoretically and the entrepreneur can calculate empirically a curve of constant transport costs to or from all points but two.

C and distance from M_3.[11]   Similarly, we can obtain a transformation line for these same two variables if a different total amount is to be expended on transporting the fixed quantities of raw materials from M_1 and M_2 respectively.   And likewise we can obtain transformation lines for any two of the possible distance variables, given the sum to be spent on transport of given amounts of raw materials and product from other sources or to the consumption place.   This same procedure can be extended to the cases where we have 4, 5, 6, ..., n raw materials and consumption places.[12]

Thus far we have tacitly assumed that transport facilities of uniform cost character radiate in all directions from all points and thus cover the entire plane under consideration.   We drop this assumption, and for the time being adopt a less abstract one.   Within any locational polygon transport facilities of uniform cost character are taken to connect a finite number of points with all or some of the corners of that polygon.   For simplicity we assume that: (1) on arc TS of Fig. 17 only points T, J, H, and S can be considered as possible production sites because of the limited transport facilities; and (2) these points are connected by straight transport lines to each corner of the triangle. We have at once injected discontinuity into our spatial model.   Given the parametric value of 3 units for the variable distance from C, the corresponding transformation line for the two variables, distance from M_1 and distance from M_2, degenerates into a series of points which can be connected by straight lines with different slopes and which we shall continue to call a transformation line.   See Fig. 21.

Paralleling an established procedure in production analysis, we now desire information about the prices or costs of every pair of variables.

[11] It should be noted that beyond both points K and L the transformation line of Fig. 20 turns back on itself; both variables increase as we move respectively to the right of K' and to the left of L' on the elliptical curve of Fig. 19.   Theoretically such movement involves unnecessary distance and would not happen; realistically, as we shall see, this can occur.

[12] It should be reiterated that the substitutions are subject to a spatial restraint. The values assigned to the distances of the production site from the several raw material sources and from the consumption place(s) must be spatially (geometrically) consistent.   A change in one of the two distance variables in general not only involves a change in the second distance variable under consideration but almost invariably necessitates changes in the parametric values of at least some of the other distances.   Here then we cannot speak of a "fixed basket" of goods. And in order to obtain a meaningful substitution relation between the two variable distances in question we need to nullify the effects of changes in the other distances by imposing a total cost restraint upon the transport of all items over these other distances.

With these prices and costs we can derive the price-ratio lines (à la Hicks) which together with the technical relations depicted by the various transformation lines allow us to determine a partial locational equilibrium position.

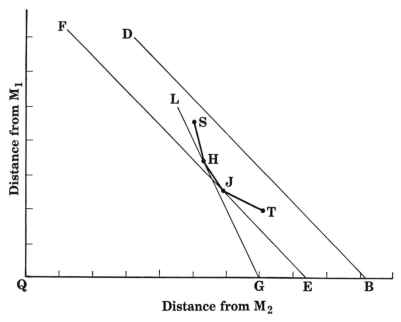

Fig. 21. Locational equilibrium: discontinuous transformation line.

Before we can identify the costs associated with the two variables, distance from M_1 and distance from M_2, we must know: (1) the weight of each of the raw materials to be transported; and (2) the transport rate(s). For the locational problem depicted in Fig. 17, assume that 1 ton of the first raw material must be transported from source M_1, that 1 ton of the second raw material must be transported from source M_2, and that the transport rate on these commodities is the same and is proportional to distance. As a consequence, the transport charge per unit of distance which is associated with each distance variable is identical. It then follows that the various price-ratio lines for these two distance variables must be straight and must have a slope of -1. Two such lines are EF and BD of Fig. 21.

The transformation line of Fig. 21 and the derived price-ratio lines yield point J as a partial equilibrium position. This follows since J is that realistic point on the transformation line TS which lies on the lowest possible price-ratio (iso-outlay) line. This lowest line is EF.

Note that at J the following conditions are satisfied: (1) to the right of J the price-ratio line is steeper than the transformation line; and (2) to the left of J the same price-ratio line is less steep than the transformation line.[13]

However, what if we allow the distance from C to vary? Taking as fixed the distance from M_2 consistent with location at point J, we can construct a transformation line for the variables, distance from M_1 and distance from C. And, knowing the transport rate structure, which for the present we shall take to be the simple one described above, we can construct price-ratio lines and determine the partial equilibrium position for these two variables. Presumably, this new (and better) partial equilibrium position will be consistent for a value of the variable distance from C different from that assumed in the preceding paragraph and in Fig. 21. As a consequence, the transformation line between the variables, distance from M_1 and distance from M_2, changes, and therefore it may be necessary to find a new partial equilibrium position with respect to these two variables. And so this process continues. We finally reach a "full" equilibrium position when the three partial equilibrium positions with respect to (1) distance from C and distance from M_1, (2) distance from C and distance from M_2, and (3) distance from M_1 and distance from M_2 coincide. Here there will be no tendency to alter any of the values

[13] When the variables, distance from M_1 and distance from M_2 (or more strictly speaking the corresponding two transport input variables), are considered as commodities r and s (and as commodities are expressed as negative quantities since they correspond to inputs) and when the graphical solution is approached from an origin from which positive quantities of these commodities are measured, the stated inequalities have to be reversed. And in mathematical terms, we have: (1) to the left of the partial equilibrium point, $p_r/p_s > - \Delta y_s / \Delta y_r$; and (2) to the right of the partial equilibrium point, $p_r/p_s < - \Delta y_s / \Delta y_r$, where Δy_r and Δy_s are finite changes in the quantities of the commodities r and s when one moves from the partial equilibrium point to a point representing the next possible site of production in the relevant direction along arc TS, and p_r and p_s are respectively the transport charges per unit distance on the raw materials from M_1 and M_2 required for the production of a unit of output.

In this situation, where a transformation line consists of only a finite number of points, twin partial solutions may be possible for any pair of distance variables. This possibility will occur if the slope of the price-ratio line is the same as that of the segment connecting two consecutive points of the transformation line, each of which lies on the lowest of the price-ratio lines which course through points of the transformation line. A certain degree of indeterminacy is thus introduced into the over-all solution. But this indeterminacy is not a major consideration in view of the analysis to come. The reader can easily restate the graphic and mathematical conditions for a twin solution.

Also see Samuelson, *op. cit.*, pp. 70–74 for a treatment of discontinuities in the production function.

of the variables. Each partial equilibrium position must satisfy the two conditions stated above.[14]

Although we have dealt with only a triangle of raw material sources and consumption place, this procedure is applicable to any polygon of such sources and place. In the case of a four- or more-sided polygon, we do not hold constant all distance variables but two, but only the total transport expenditure upon these other distance variables. We then find the partial equilibrium position with respect to these two variables. When there are n distance variables, there are of course $\frac{1}{2}n(n-1)$ partial equilibrium points. At a full equilibrium position all of these coincide.

3. TRANSPORT-ORIENTED EQUILIBRIUM WITH REALISTIC RATE STRUCTURES

Having described locational equilibrium under extremely simple conditions, we commence now to introduce various real complexities, especially those dealing with transport rate structure and costs.

We abandon the postulate that equal weights of raw materials or product are transported from the various sources and to the consumption place. Our price-ratio lines need no longer cut the horizontal and vertical axes symmetrically; they can cut these axes at any angle depending upon the relative weights of the raw materials moved. Suppose, for example, that the production of $1\frac{1}{2}$ tons of final product requires 1 ton of the first raw material (from M_1) and 2 tons of second raw material (from M_2). Retaining a pure weight and distance basis for computing the transport cost schedule, we obtain a new series of price-ratio lines with different slope. Of this new series line GL in Fig. 21 is the relevant one for the circumstances represented there. Point H rather than point J becomes the partial equilibrium position for the two variables, distance from M_1 and distance from M_2. Similarly, the other partial equilibrium points and the final equilibrium position will be altered by the change in relative weights.[15]

[14] Except for qualifications relating to twin solutions noted in footnote 13.

We also have assumed in our simple case that the dynamic postulates implied by our iterative procedure do not lead to an oscillatory situation.

[15] Save in one respect the problems of this paragraph resemble Weber's: fixed points indicate the consumption place and raw material sources, unequal weights are transported from the several sources to the production site and from there to the consumption place, and transport tariffs are based solely on weight and distance. His analysis, though later qualified (*op. cit.*, pp. 82–83 and elsewhere) assumes a uniform transport system completely flexible, i.e., uniform transport facilities radiating from all points in all directions. His is a case of continuous variation of all distance variables. Ours, thus far, is one of simple discontinuous variation.

Of still greater moment is the relaxation of our assumption that transport rates are proportional to distance, an assumption which is valid only for areas where primitive transport mechanisms still operate. In industrialized areas modern transport media require large overhead expenditures and incur many costs and offer many services (especially terminal) which are unrelated to the distance covered in a given shipment. Typically, tariff per distance unit or zone is steep for the first zone and falls abruptly from the first to the second zone and considerably less abruptly between each succeeding zone (or set of zones) and the one after. Tariff structures are graduated, rates being less than proportional to distance.[16]

One can best demonstrate the significance of typical modern rate structures for the spatial equilibrium of the firm by constructing appropriate price-ratio lines or iso-outlay lines. We utilize the 1945 standard maximum first class rates on freight shipments prescribed by the I.C.C. for railroads operating in the Eastern Territory.[17] On the basis of 2 short tons of raw material from source M_2 and 1 ton from source M_1 per ton product, we have constructed, in Fig. 22, price-ratio or iso-outlay lines corresponding to outlays of $24.00, $26.40, and $30.00.[18]

Several characteristics of these iso-outlay lines are important to note. First, in effect, they are not lines but a series of rectangles and squares which have been blacked in. These rectangles and squares border each other or are connected by dashed lines. This particular form of iso-outlay line results from the zonal character of the rate structure. For example, the rate for a shipment of a given weight is the same for all distances 40 miles or less but greater than 35 miles. Hence, if we consider two shipments of different goods and weights, we find that total cost of these shipments will not vary for any combination of distances for these two shipments which can be represented by a point lying within a square (such as square A of Fig. 22) which is bounded on two sides by two 40-mile lines and on

16 For further details, see E. M. Hoover, *The Location of Economic Activity*, New York, 1948, Chaps. 2–4.

17 As published in *I.C.C. Docket* 15879 Appendix E and as given in *The Freight Traffic Red Book,* New York, 1945, pp. 1194–95 in the column Appendix E under Eastern Class Rates.

18 Along each axis of Fig. 22 we measure mileage from the respective source and also cost of transporting over the different distances the amounts of raw materials required per ton of output. The $30.00 line, for example, shows the various combinations of values for distance from M_1 and distance from M_2 which would occasion a total transport outlay on the raw materials from M_1 and M_2 of $30.00 per ton of product.

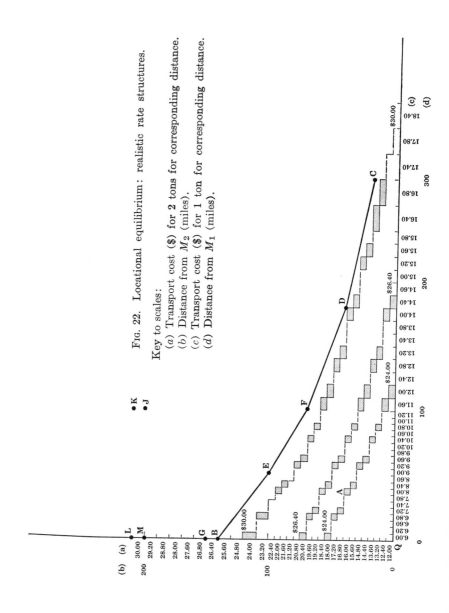

Fig. 22. Locational equilibrium: realistic rate structures.

Key to scales:

(*a*) Transport cost (**$**) for **2** tons for corresponding distance.
(*b*) Distance from M_2 (miles).
(*c*) Transport cost (**$**) for **1** ton for corresponding distance.
(*d*) Distance from M_1 (miles).

the other two sides by two lines approaching the limit of 35 miles. Thus the producer may have some leeway in choosing a rational location and may select a site which compels him to traverse "unnecessary distance" (in terms of the minimum quantities hypothesized in the transformation function) without increasing his costs.[19]

Second, because the rate structure is graduated, the iso-outlay lines tend to be convex to origin Q, as in Fig. 22. This fact has significant implications. Frequently, price-ratio or iso-outlay lines are taken to be straight or concave to the origin. One then obtains a unique stable solution that involves quantities of both inputs, when, as is usually the case, the transformation curve is convex to the origin from which positive quantities of inputs are measured. If both the transformation line and iso-outlay line are irregularly convex to the origin, particularly if the latter is more convex than the former, as it may well be with modern rate structures, then the equilibrium point is likely to be an "end" point, that is, a realistic point on one of the ends of the transformation line and one which also may correspond to a corner of the locational polygon. The equilibrium point always is an end point in the case where the locational polygon collapses to a line, e.g., where there is only one raw material used in the production process.[20]

Further, the likelihood of an end point solution is considerably increased by the fact that modern rate structures call for a relatively large increment in shipping charges from the zero (i.e., not shipping at all) to the first zone and relatively small increment for any other two successive zones. For example, on the horizontal scale of Fig. 22 transport cost for 1 ton of the raw material from M_1 rises $6.00 if one decides to ship 1 mile instead of zero miles, but rises only 20 cents if one decides to ship 6 miles instead of 5. As a result price-ratio or iso-outlay lines have "tails" on both ends. Our $30.00 and $26.40 lines have respectively the vertical stretches LM and BG as tails on the left.[21] Their tails on the right (horizontal stretches) are not shown

[19] Such a minor degree of indeterminacy also appears with respect to the quantities of other factor inputs employed when these inputs are sold in lot quantities which are not divisible, as where the services of a machine are rented by the month. The analysis is not seriously qualified, even though the typical mathematical solution implies unique amounts of inputs.

[20] In this case, the transformation line is a straight line or consists of a number of realistic points lying on a straight line. Compare Dean, op. cit., pp. 17–18. Also see the Appendix to this chapter for some discussion of the simple line case.

[21] In the case of our $30.00 line, a decision not to ship the raw material from M_1 at all instead of to ship it to a point within 5 miles permits a saving of $6.00 or allows the movement of the raw material from source M_2 over an additional 90 miles without increasing transport cost. Thus, the tail LM.

in Fig. 22, above, since they extend beyond the limits of the diagram.

In Fig. 22 we have constructed the transformation line, $BEFDC$. Point B corresponds to the source of M_1; it represents a zero value for the variable distance from M_1. At point D the usual equilibrium conditions are satisfied since to the left of D the arithmetic slope of the iso-outlay line ($30.00) is less than that of the transformation line, and, to the right of D, the arithmetic slope of the former exceeds that of the latter. However, D is only a relative minimum transport cost point. Only in contrast to the points in its own neighborhood does it represent the most desirable combination of values for the distance variables. End point B, lying on the tail GB, is still more desirable for it falls on the $26.40 iso-outlay line not on the $30.00 one. In the given situation and for this pair of values for the distance variables, B represents the position of stable equilibrium.

Thus, our technique clearly demonstrates the strategy of locating at corners of the locational polygon, given modern transport rate structures.[22] It is consistent with the emphasis that Palander, Hoover, and others[23] have given to such location and the minor importance they have attached to locations intermediate between raw material sources and market centers. It implies that the individual producer must not be content with an equilibrium position arrived at by the usual substitution operations conceived in production theory, but must compare the spatial equilibrium so obtained with each possible relative minimum transport cost position which corresponds to a zero value for one of the distance variables.[24]

We pause to consider a significant aspect of our technique. One of the most devastating shortcomings of the Weberian model has been its inability to encompass realistic transport rate structures less than

---

[22] In situations where neither one raw material nor the market is dominant (in Weber's sense) so that locational polygons are meaningful constructs, it should not be inferred that relative minimum points will never exist at corners of these polygons unless there is a large initial increment followed by relatively small increments in the rate structure. Palander (op. cit., pp. 314–16) has demonstrated that relative minima may occur at corners of polygons when a tariff structure mildly graduated from beginning to end is in vogue. However, the advantage of corner location is generally not so pronounced with such a structure.

[23] Palander, op. cit., pp. 198–99, 330–33; Hoover, op. cit., pp. 52–57; and B. Ohlin, Interregional and International Trade, Cambridge, Mass., 1933, pp. 185–202.

[24] Making this comparison is not so difficult as might appear. When any distance variable is assigned a zero value, the values of the other distance variables are uniquely determined. Thus the producer need only calculate the total transport cost for each corner of his locational polygon and for whatever relative minimum cost points (in the usual case, only one) which may be determined through spatial substitution within the locational polygon.

proportional to distance. Weber proposed to take account of such rate structures by using fictitious distances. Distances should not be stated in their geographic length, but in proportion to the decreasing rate scale. In general the longer the distance, the more it should be shortened for geometrical analysis.[25] Bortkiewicz early showed that such a procedure is inconsistent with the construction of a locational polygon.[26] For, how can we know how much to shorten the distance of any corner of the locational polygon from the given site of production and thus be able to calculate the relative distances between the various corners of the locational polygon until the actual location of the production site is determined; whilst on the other hand the very location of the production site is dependent upon the relative distances between the various corners of the locational polygon?

It is just this Weberian dilemma that our present technique cuts through. We need not speak of fictitious distances nor are we bound to a geometrical technique applicable only to situations where rates are proportional to distance.[27] Further, our technique brings out the critical importance of terminal and loading charges which the Weberian analysis essentially sidesteps.

[25] We quote Weber: ". . . Die sinkenden Staffelungen der Sätze mit wachsender Entfernung machen dabei keine Schwierigkeiten . . . . Man hat sich zu sagen, dass kartenmässige Entfernungen bei Vorhandensein solcher Staffelungen nicht mit ihrer tatsächlichen Länge in die Rechnung einzustellen sind, sondern unter Reduktion derselben entsprechend den sinkenden Staffeln. Wird also, wie beim deutschen Stückguttarif der allgemeinen Klasse, für 50 Kilometer ein Satz von 11 Pfg., für die nächsten 150 km einer von 10, für weitere 100 km von 9 Pfg. usw. berechnet, so ist dabei eine Strecke von 100 km nicht mit ihrer vollen Länge, sondern mit $50 + (50 - 50/11)$ km, also mit 95,4 km einzustellen . . ." (*op. cit.*, pp. 43–44).

[26] L. Von Bortkiewicz, "Eine geometrische Fundierung der Lehre vom Standort der Industrien," *Archiv für Sozialwissenschaft und Sozialpolitik*, Vol. XXX (1910), pp. 769–71. On this point Niederhauser's defense of Weber (*op. cit.*, pp. 173–75) is not convincing.

[27] In one sense Weber should not be criticized too severely for failing to realize the inconsistency in his geometrical construction. At the time of his writing the German rate structure (although not the French, British, United States, and Belgian, among others) was proportional to distance, save for small consignments and a few bulky goods, and was quite uniform (refer to M. Colson, *Transports et Tarifs*, 3rd ed., 1907); and Weber, as he frequently stated, was preoccupied with conditions of the German economy. On the other hand, Weber was explicitly attempting to erect a pure theoretical model applicable to all times and all regions.

We should mention that when the transport rate structure is not proportional to weight, it is perfectly admissible, though we do not do so, to make adjustments as Weber does (*op. cit.*, pp. 44–46). A rate per ton-mile greater than normal for a given good, whatever the reason, implies an "ideal" weight greater than actual; a rate below normal implies an "ideal" weight less than actual.

Returning to the main thread of the argument, we find it also possible to account for the effects of breaks in transport routes, which characteristically occur at transport junctions where the direction of movement has to be changed, where the shipment has to be unloaded and reloaded onto another transport medium or system, or where another scale of transport charges becomes effective, and so forth. To pass over such breaks entails sudden large increments in transport cost, whether due to switching, to loading, or to other charges. Industry often locates at such breaks in order to avoid these large increments. This is borne out by Fig. 23. Here we assume a break in a given transport route 100 miles from each of the two sources M_1 and M_2. Along each axis is measured the cost of transporting over various distances the amount of raw material from the respective source which is required to produce 1 ton of finished product. If there were no break in the transport route we would have a cost scale along each axis similar to that on Fig. 22. But a break does exist, and to pass over it involves an added cost of 50 cents per ton of raw material from M_2 and 60 cents per ton of raw material from M_1. Accordingly we have added another scale (the outer one) of transport charges for various distances along each axis after the hundred-mile mark. At point F, the graphic position of the break, the raw materials can be assembled from both sources M_1 and M_2 without either one's bearing the added expense of passing over the break. The total transport cost is \$33.60, and we have constructed the iso-outlay line of \$33.60.[28] We have also inscribed a transformation line $GFJEH$. If no break existed, the equilibrium point would be G where the transformation line would meet the tail end of the iso-outlay line of \$32.80. But because there is a break, which necessitates additional transport

[28] In constructing this iso-outlay line we have assumed that to reach points other than the break itself one of the raw materials must pass over the break. Obviously the other must travel less than 100 miles in this case since the line goes through the break itself and since we have taken it to be regular in its course.

For the case where both materials traverse distances greater than 100 miles to any place where they are assembled, we need to know for each potential site whether both pass over the break or, if only one does so, which one. However, complications arise as soon as we introduce alternative routes from raw material sources to any potential site, or to alternative transshipment points varying in distance from each source, or to both. Then the iso-outlay lines tend to be highly irregular and tend to criss-cross one another. We can avoid considerable irregularity by excluding from the analysis certain potential sites which are known to be inferior for any number of reasons—such perhaps as those involving unnecessary distance. Or, alternatively, we can derive the best equilibrium position for each transshipment point or route or both and then compare these sites and select the optimum one.

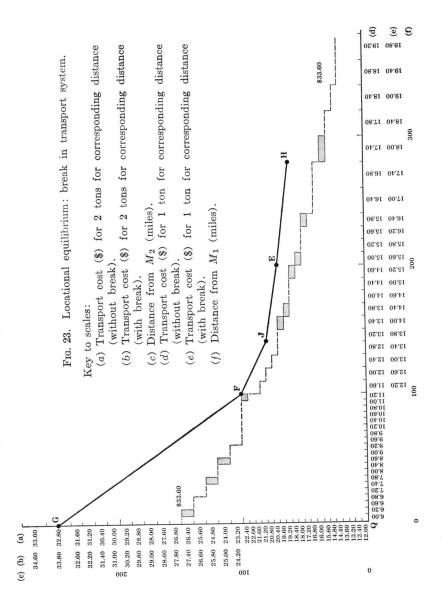

Fig. 23. Locational equilibrium: break in transport system.

Key to scales:

(a) Transport cost ($) for 2 tons for corresponding distance (without break).

(b) Transport cost ($) for 2 tons for corresponding distance (with break).

(c) Distance from M_2 (miles).

(d) Transport cost ($) for 1 ton for corresponding distance (without break).

(e) Transport cost ($) for 1 ton for corresponding distance (with break).

(f) Distance from M_1 (miles).

expense, G lies on the tail end of an iso-outlay line of $33.80. Point F, which satisfies the equilibrium conditions when both distance variables have positive values, lies on the iso-outlay line of $33.60. It is the preferred position.

There are numerous other deviations from a pure weight and distance rate structure. Most of these can be encompassed by a set of iso-outlay lines. When different ton-mile rates apply to different commodities—whether because one is more bulky than the other, more valuable, more fragile or perishable, more difficult to handle, closer to the stage of finished product, better able to bear a high transport charge, etc.—one can account for these differences in rate structure by adjusting the transport scale on the appropriate axis. Different rates are frequently set for different directions of movement because one is uphill and the other downhill, because one encounters more severe topographical obstacles, because one bears a greater volume of traffic, because greater speeds are attainable in one direction, etc. By changing the transport cost scales on the respective axes one can incorporate these rate differences into the analysis so long as the direction of movement of each raw material and finished product remains the same for all realistic points on the transformation line. If this condition does not hold, then for the movement of any particular good it is necessary to use several different transport cost scales along the axis relevant for such movement. And, accordingly, in constructing any iso-outlay line on which a given realistic point on the transformation line lies, we must use, for each raw material and finished product, that transport cost scale which is relevant for the direction in which the good moves to reach the realistic site under consideration.

Again, if different types of transport facilities are used in any one journey or if alternative types of transport facilities are available for reaching the various possible production sites, we must construct several transport cost scales along the relevant axis or axes and use the appropriate one in deriving the iso-outlay line upon which a given realistic point on the transformation line lies.[29] It is also necessary to adjust the transport cost scales when various types of import and export duties, or special levies or transport expenses, are incurred at different points along a given route. Where there are alternative routes with various special charges and duties along them, alternative transport cost scales must be set up.[30]

[29] See Palander, *op. cit.*, pp. 333–58, for a full discussion of substitution possibilities between various types of transport media and between cheaper and dearer facilities.

[30] It should also be mentioned that eccentricities in transport rate structures

4. TRANSPORT-ORIENTED EQUILIBRIUM FURTHER EXTENDED

The analysis of the preceding sections has emphasized distance as a variable. This initial emphasis has been pursued partly to counteract the traditional bias toward consideration of spatial relations. For a complete analysis of transport-orientation, however, change in more variables than merely distance must be examined. Clearly, the amounts of the raw materials used may vary with the location of the plant, particularly if alternative sources of different quality are exploitable. Also, in any true transport-orientation problem the variations from site to site in other costs such as labor and power must not be assumed away. They must be explicitly introduced as possible deviational forces, even though they turn out to be dominated by variations in transport outlay. To comprehend better the interaction of these variables, a transport-orientation framework less restrictive than the one already developed (which has reference to variations in distances alone) is desired. Further, a more general framework is imperative, as will be seen below, in order to establish connections among the several types of location theories and to uncover principles common to all. Moreover, such a framework would facilitate the fusion of location theory and production theory.

We now propose to employ the concept of transport inputs as defined in Chap. 4. To repeat: a transport input represents the movement of a unit weight over a unit distance. It may be expressed in such terms as a hundredweight-kilometer and a ton-mile. We therefore encounter transport inputs in the shipment of any raw material to the production site and in the shipment of the finished product from the production

---

which run counter to transport cost as a monotonically increasing function of distance are reflected in eccentricities of iso-outlay lines. For example, the historically important practice in the United States of levying a smaller total charge for movement between two nodal termini served by two or more competing railways than for movement between one of these termini and an intermediate point or between two intermediate points on one of the alternative routes causes the iso-outlay lines to criss-cross. If, for instance, the raw material from M_2 could be moved from its source, a terminal, to another terminal 210 miles distant on a special rate, then point K in Fig. 22, which may represent a combination of values of 210 miles for distance from M_2 and 100 miles for distance from M_1, would lie on a lower iso-outlay line than point J. Obviously such eccentricity enhances the attraction of terminal sites, particularly when these sites are raw material sources or consumption places. As a consequence, a commodity may travel an unnecessary distance, that is, to a site lying outside the locational polygon. Similarly this occurs when back hauls and roundabout hauls take place because of the rigidities of the transport net, especially in water and water-rail transport.

site to the market. Since the distance variable as well as the weight variable is encompassed by the concept of transport inputs, all the relations among distance variables discussed above may be translated into relations among transport inputs. To demonstrate this, reconsider

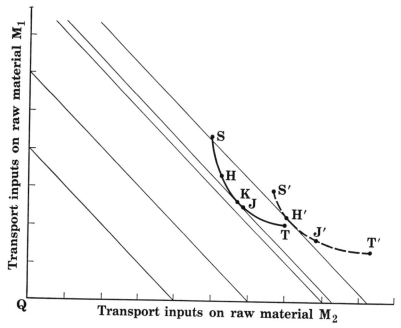

FIG. 24. Shift of transformation curve and equilibrium site with change in weights.

the minimum transport cost solution for the locational triangle of Fig. 17.

In the problem associated with Fig. 17 we substitute for the three distance variables (distance from M_1, distance from M_2, and distance from C) three new variables, namely: (1) transport inputs on the raw material from source M_1; (2) transport inputs on the raw material from source M_2; and (3) transport inputs on the product to the market. Relations among these new variables can be presented in terms of meaningful transformation lines. For the situation where we consider as a possible production site each point along arc TS of Fig. 17, we obtain a transformation line between transport inputs on the raw material from M_1 (which we shall henceforth designate transport inputs on raw material M_1) and transport inputs on the raw material from M_2 (which we shall designate transport inputs on raw material M_2). This transformation line, $SHJT$, plotted in Fig. 24

resembles the transformation line of Fig. 18. The only difference between the two charts thus far is that in one case distance variables, in the other transport inputs, are measured along the axes.

It should be noted that the transformation line is drawn as a continuous curve. Although in reality it should be a finite number of points, as in Fig. 21, we present it as a curve in order to facilitate the analysis and the synthesis of transport-orientation theory and production theory. The latter in its more familiar form utilizes curves rather than a finite number of points and continuous production functions rather than discontinuous ones.

If transport rates are proportional to distance and if they are the same for both raw materials, then the relevant set of price-ratio lines are straight lines which cut both axes symmetrically. The prices involved are the rates per ton-mile transportation of the two raw materials. In this case the prices are different from those in the situation depicted in Fig. 21. There each price was the cost of moving 1 mile the weight (tonnage) of a given raw material required per weight unit (1 ton) of the product. Hence, when the weight requirements of raw materials were altered, so were the slopes of the price-ratio lines, the transformation line expressed in terms of the distance variables remaining unchanged. Here in the situation depicted in Fig. 24, the prices are rates on the movement of a weight unit over a unit of distance (e.g. rates per ton-mile). When weight requirements of raw materials change, the price-ratio lines remain the same. The requirements of transport inputs, however, change. A new transformation line between transport inputs becomes relevant. For example, suppose we assume as previously that the production of $1\frac{1}{2}$ tons of finished product requires 1 ton of the raw material from M_1 and 2 tons of the raw material from M_2. These new weight relations yield, for the locational figure of Fig. 17, a transformation line $S'H'J'T'$ between transport inputs on raw material M_1 and transport inputs on raw material M_2. See Fig. 24. The point S' on the dashed transformation line refers to the identical geographic location as does S; H as does H'; J as J'; and T as T'. However, although the transformation line rather than the price-ratio line shifts in this new formulation, the equilibrium point of location is unaffected. Before the change in weight relations, both the old and the new formulation of the problem yielded a location at or in the vicinity of J in Fig. 17.[31]

[31] When the transformation line is a series of points, as in Fig. 21, the partial equilibrium point is at J. When the transformation line is assumed continuous, as in Fig. 24, the partial equilibrium point is somewhat to the left of J in the direction of H at the point K where the transformation line is tangent to a price-ratio line.

After the change in weight relations, both formulations yield a location at H in Fig. 17.

As indicated, the new formulation of the problem in terms of transport inputs is superior to the first one in several respects. However, in at least one basic respect it is inferior to a formulation in terms of distance variables. In the first formulation, shifts of the transformation line can take place only when the distance variable from C assumes another value or when new sources of raw materials are utilized with a consequent alteration of the locational triangle. In the new formulation, shifts of the transformation line can take place as well when weight relations change. Hence, in the new formulation it becomes impossible to identify the cause of a shift from mere observation of the transformation lines and to know whether or not a change of location (geographic position) is entailed. The new formulation hence loses the spatial perspective which the first formulation permits. (Since the new formulation is much more in line with orthodox economic analysis, this is consistent with the weak spatial perspective of orthodox economic thinking.) To reiterate, it is for this reason that the less elegant formulation in terms of distance variables has been presented first for emphasis.

Returning to the problem of partial locational equilibrium which is achieved when the geographic point of production lies *within* the locational triangle and corresponds to the point on the transformation line which lies on the lowest price-ratio line (and hence incurs least total transport cost), we note two necessary conditions. One, *the first order condition,* is that the geographic point of production correspond to a point of tangency between a price-ratio line and the transformation line. This signifies, in general, that the rate of substitution at the margin, or the marginal rate of substitution, between any two transport inputs be equal to the reciprocal of their prices (the corresponding transport rates). Two, *the second order (or stability) condition,* is that at the point of tangency the transformation line be more convex to the origin than the price-ratio line. Since in Fig. 24 the transformation lines $SHJT$ and $S'H'J'T'$ are convex throughout, whereas the price-ratio lines are straight, this stability condition is fulfilled at any point which may prove to be a point of tangency. The convexity of the transformation lines to the origin signifies a *diminishing marginal rate of substitution* between the two transport inputs. It should be noted that at both points K and H', these two necessary conditions are satisfied. Since throughout its course each transformation line is convex to the origin, no other points of tangency occur, and K and H' each represents the partial locational equilibrium position for its particular situation.

As before, a "full" equilibrium position is attained when the three partial equilibrium positions with respect to the three pairs of variables [here: (1) transport inputs on product and transport inputs on raw material M_1; (2) transport inputs on product and transport inputs on raw material M_2; and (3) transport inputs on raw material M_1 and transport inputs on raw material M_2] coincide.

Just as we have converted the locational triangle problem of Figs. 19 and 20 into a problem of substitution among transport inputs, so we can convert the other locational problems depicted in the previous sections. The set of possible sites of production in the locational line case (see Figs. 15 and 16) can be presented in terms of a transformation line for two transport input variables rather than for two distance variables. In the case of the four-sided polygon (see Figs. 19 and 20), transformation lines for pairs of transport inputs substitute for transformation lines for pairs of distance variables. Along the axes of a diagram similar to Fig. 20, we measure transport inputs rather than distances. Again, in the identification of the path of substitution between any pair of transport input variables, the same restraint obtains as in the formulation with distance variables: the sum of transport costs associated with all other variables (here, transport inputs) must remain constant. Once again, the over-all location equilibrium involves the positional coincidence of more than one partial equilibrium between pairs of variables.[32]

When we inject realistic rate structures and discontinuities in the transformation function, we can (though we need not) construct for a locational triangle problem figures somewhat comparable to Figs. 22 and 23. The scales along the axes, however, would be different. Scale b of the figure corresponding to Fig. 22 and scale c of the figure corresponding to Fig. 23 would measure transport inputs on raw material M_2 in ton-mile units, and would be numerically twice as large as the existing scale. Scale d of the figure corresponding to Fig. 22 and scale f of the figure corresponding to Fig. 23 would measure transport inputs on raw material M_1 in ton-mile units and would be numerically the same as the existing scale. The other scales would be transport cost scales as in Figs. 22 and 23, respectively, but would be designated somewhat differently. The transformation lines would correspond respectively to the transformation lines of Figs. 22 and 23, but would of course refer to transport inputs rather than distance variables. The equilibrium analysis and statement of equilibrium conditions would essentially parallel that presented for Figs. 22 and 23.

[32] See Chap. 10 for a full statement.

Before this chapter is brought to a close stress should be placed on this important point. The two necessary (the first- and second-order) conditions, as stated above for a partial locational equilibrium, when generalized to consider for any transport-orientation problem substitution among any pair of transport inputs, are no different from those formulated by Allen, Hicks, and other production theorists when the problem of substitution between two inputs or factors of production is posed.[33] At an equilibrium point, in Hicks' words, the "price-ratio between any two factors (*inputs*) must equal their marginal rate of substitution," and for "the substitution of one factor (*input*) for another, 'diminishing marginal rate of substitution'" must hold.[34]

Even when the transformation line is taken as a finite number of points, the necessary conditions for transport-oriented equilibrium are essentially the same as those stated by Samuelson for a firm given a discontinuous production function.[35] Further, when realistic rate (transport price) structures are introduced, the necessary conditions again resemble those which can be derived from Samuelson's statements.

Thus, it is along these lines that by using the concept of transport inputs[36] we are able to fuse much traditional (Weberian) doctrine

[33] R. G. D. Allen, *Mathematical Analysis for Economists,* New York, 1939, Chaps. XIV and XIX; and J. R. Hicks, *Value and Capital,* Oxford, 1939, Chap. VI.

[34] *Ibid.,* pp. 86–87. Italics are mine.

[35] Samuelson, *op. cit.,* Chaps. III and IV.

[36] In order to illustrate the general applicability of the concept of transport inputs, let us refer to a transport-oriented production process such as iron and steel. The United States Steel Corporation recently constructed 1.8 million tons of steel capacity immediately below Trenton for serving the Eastern seaboard market centering around New York City with steel produced from Venezuelan ore. Of the suitable waterfront sites, this was probably the closest to New York City. In choosing a site at Trenton rather than one farther from the market but closer to coal, the corporation substituted transport inputs on coal from the coal source for transport inputs on product to the market. Considering, first, the possible combinations of quantities of these two transport inputs, given the quantity of transport inputs on ore from Cerro Bolivar, Venezuela, which for practical purposes remains constant for all Middle Atlantic seaboard points, and second, considering the quantities of coal and scrap that might be used per ton steel, the ton-mile transport charges on these items, and as a consequence the significantly higher price of a transport input on product to the market than of a transport input on coal from the coal source—one can easily portray the Trenton site as the point of locational equilibrium in the given situation. In making this statement we also consider variation in the quantity of transport inputs on ore from Cerro Bolivar, for the given requirement of ore per ton steel. A meaningful larger quantity of this input would involve an inland location which, in view of the significant cost of transshipment to rail and of the geography of ore, coal, and market sites, would not be an over-all locational equilibrium

on transport-orientation and production theory for the firm, thereby extending both.[37] Restatement of the problem of transport-orientation in terms of substitutions among transport inputs automatically establishes a point of connection with other substitutions among the diverse inputs (and outputs) of a firm and, hence, allows improvement in any statement on transport-orientation. At the same time, inclusion of transport inputs in the transformation function of the firm adds a spatial dimension to production theory and allows this theory to embrace the situation of transport-orientation.[38]

APPENDIX TO CHAPTER 5

TRANSPORT INPUTS AND SOME FORMULATIONS OF THE TRANSPORT-ORIENTATION PROBLEM

In this chapter, the general transport-orientation problem has been essentially restated. In Chap. 10 the transport-orientation problem is presented in more rigorous mathematical terms. Nevertheless, it may be helpful to some readers to translate some of the more familiar formulations of the transport-orientation problem into substitution relations among transport inputs in a way which is simple and direct.

We may begin with the line case already alluded to at the beginning of Sect. 2 of this chapter. Suppose 1 ton of raw material from source M_1 is required to produce 1 ton of product which is consumed at point C. Let C be connected by a straight line railway to M_1. See Fig. 15. It then follows that the various combinations of the variables, transport inputs on raw material M_1 and transport inputs on product, corresponding to the innumerable efficient locations possible along line CM_1 are given by a transformation line with a slope of -1. Such a transformation line is given by Fig. 16 when we appropriately measure along the axes transport inputs rather than distances.

If we now posit that transport rates on both product and raw material are identical and proportional to weight and distance, we obtain a set of price-ratio lines whose slopes are also -1. When we superimpose such a set of lines upon Fig. 16, we find that the transformation line and one and only

---

point when translated into the relevant sets of transformation and iso-outlay lines. Neither would a location in the Southern Atlantic seaboard, which would involve a smaller quantity of this input. See, in this connection, W. Isard and J. Cumberland, "New England as a Possible Location for an Integrated Iron and Steel Works," *Economic Geography,* Vol. 26 (October 1950), pp. 245–59.

[37] This fusion is more rigorously demonstrated in Chap. 10.

[38] It is perhaps unnecessary to reiterate the point in the final paragraph of Chap. 4, namely, that the extension of production theory to include transport inputs as another set of inputs does not commit a person to the acceptance of the transport function as another factor of production, if he is not inclined to do so.

one of the set of price-ratio lines coincide completely. This fact signifies that each of the innumerable possible locations along line CM_1 incurs the same total transport cost. The locational equilibrium problem is therefore indeterminate, as Weber noted. Any point on the transformation line corresponds to as good a site of production as any other.

Determinacy is immediately introduced if an ubiquity which enters into the weight of the product plus a pure material from source M_1 are required for production. In this instance, the relevant transformation line will fall off less rapidly than the transformation line of Fig. 16. When price-ratio lines with slope of -1 are superimposed upon this new transformation line, the point of the transformation line which lies on the lowest price-ratio line will correspond to an end-point solution, specifically to location at the market, as Weber indicated.

Determinacy can also be introduced if we assume that the raw material is weight-losing and that, as a consequence, more than a ton of raw material is required per ton product. In this case the new transformation line falls off more rapidly than the transformation line of Fig. 16. When price-ratio lines of slope -1 are superimposed, that combination of transport inputs on raw material and finished product which corresponds to location at M_1 lies on the lowest price-ratio line.

Most of the indeterminacy of the first case is eliminated if graduated (Staffel) transport tariff structures obtain. For the price-ratio lines are no longer straight lines with slope of -1, but curved lines as indicated in the discussion pertaining to Fig. 22. As a consequence, those two combinations of the two transport input variables which correspond to location at the market and location at the raw material source lie on the same price-ratio line; all other combinations lie on higher price-ratio lines.

Essentially, ubiquities which enter into the final product increase transport inputs on the finished product for any location away from the market; and the occurrence of weight-loss in the use of a localized raw material increases transport inputs on the raw material for any location away from the source. Further, the application of different transport rates to the movement of finished product and raw material can be incorporated into the problem either: (1) indirectly by the use of "ideal" weights, in which case price-ratio lines are unaffected and the relative values of transport input variables change; or (2) directly by changing the appropriate transport scales along the axes, in which case the slopes of the price-ratio lines change, and the values of the transport input variables remain unaffected. With these considerations in mind, it is easily perceived how the various correct propositions which have been advanced for the line case by Weber and others are translatable into transformation lines with respect to transport inputs and price-ratio lines.

We pass on to the use of weight triangles for the solution of the transport-orientation problem when a locational triangle is given. Dean has expounded this type of solution most precisely, and we shall have reference to his formulation.

Let us consider first the case where the weight triangle does not exist. This would obtain, for example, if Weber's material index were less than unity (and his locational weight, less than two). In this situation the ideal weight of the product exceeds the combined ideal weights of localized raw materials, the weight of the product being the *dominant* weight. When transport inputs are based on ideal weights, the price of every type of transport input is the same regardless of which raw material or finished product is being moved; and, accordingly, the problem is to minimize total transport inputs. Hence, if the material index is less than unity and if we consider a location away from the locus of consumption, it is always feasible to shift toward the locus of consumption, until that locus is reached. For, with any such shift, the total of transport inputs diminishes, since any increase in transport inputs on localized raw materials is always less than the decrease of transport inputs on the finished product. In effect such a shift corresponds to one or more movements along one or more transformation lines which involves one or more substitutions of fewer transport inputs of one type for more transport inputs of another type. This process entails a concomitant movement to lower price-ratio lines, whose slopes by definition are —1.

When transport inputs are more meaningfully based on actual weights rather than ideal weights, again it follows that if the material index is less than unity, it is not economic to locate at a site other than the locus of consumption. For, with any shift from a location not the locus of consumption toward the locus of consumption, any increase in the costs of transport inputs on localized raw materials (because of the increase in the amounts of such transport inputs) will always be smaller than the decrease in the costs of transport inputs on finished product (because of the decrease in the amount of such transport inputs). Once more such a shift involves substitutions among transport inputs which correspond to movements along transformation lines on to lower price-ratio lines whose slopes are ordinarily different from —1.

The weight triangle does not exist when Dean's *generalized* index yields a value less than unity. [In Dean's *generalized* index test the denominator is either: (1) the largest localized raw material or group of spatially localized raw materials, or (2) the product, whichever is the larger by weight.] If, for example, the weight of a localized raw material is dominant (the generalized index will then be less than unity) and if the site of production is not at the site of this localized raw material, it is always feasible to shift toward this site. With such a shift, either: (1) total transport inputs on localized raw materials and finished product will decrease, when these transport inputs are based on "ideal" weights; or (2) the decrease in the costs of transport inputs on the localized raw material (because of the decrease in the amount of such transport inputs) will be greater than any increase in the costs of transport inputs on other localized raw materials and finished product (because of an increase in the amount of such transport inputs).

Let us now turn to the general case where the weight triangle does exist. Here, the generalized index test gives values always greater than unity. Also, Weber's material index yields a value greater than unity. However, it does not follow that location cannot be at an end point (a corner of the locational triangle), and for that matter at a source of a *pure* material. The problem is one of the equilibrium of forces in which relative weights and relative distances are the basic factors.

The weight triangle is a geometric device used to obtain the point at which the several locational *forces* are in equilibrium. Its counterpart in the physical world is a mechanical model such as Varignon's which was designed to demonstrate the parallelogram of forces, and the use of which Pick describes in an appendix to Weber's book. But what are the locational *forces* in a transport-orientation problem?

If we base transport inputs on ideal weights, as Weber and Dean tend to do, the three locational forces in a locational triangle are the ideal weights of the finished product and the two raw materials. They pull against each other in a manner which minimizes total transport inputs at the point of equilibrium when that point lies within or on the locational triangle. When the point of equilibrium lies outside the locational triangle, transport inputs are minimized when location is at that corner of the locational triangle whose exterior angle is less than the corresponding angle of the weight triangle. This holds whether the corner corresponds to a pure or a weight-losing raw material.

If we base transport inputs on actual weight, as is done in the mathematical statement in Chap. 10, the three locational forces in a locational triangle are the three costs involved in moving one at a time the respective three actual weights a unit of distance. These three forces, each of which is expressed in terms of transport costs per unit of distance, interact to determine a point of equilibrium. If such a point lies within or on the locational triangle, it corresponds to a point of minimum total transport cost. If it lies outside the locational triangle, the corner of the locational triangle whose exterior angle is less than its corresponding angle in the weight triangle is the point of minimum total transport cost.

Again, one easily perceives that any shift from a location which is not a point of equilibrium within or on a locational triangle toward such a point, or toward the appropriate corner of the triangle when the point of equilibrium lies outside the triangle, entails substitutions among transport inputs which involve movements along transformation lines on to lower price-ratio lines.

In essence, the weight triangle solution shortcuts the process of determining the site of locational equilibrium. Likewise does the somewhat similar geometric construction which is based upon the use of the "pole principle," which Launhardt first sketched and Palander later amplified. However, in doing so, both the weight triangle and the pole construction fail to point up explicitly the interaction of the basic economic forces, namely, the several transport costs per unit distance. More satisfactory in this regard is the Varignon mechanical model (which can be employed for locational polygons of more than three sides), even though it is oriented to "ideal" weights rather than "economic" weights.

A third approach to the solution of the transport-orientation problem relies upon the use of isodapanes.[39] An isodapane, as used by Palander and Hoover, is a locus of points at each of which the location of the production process would incur the same over-all (combined) transport costs in the movement of both raw materials and finished product. Typically, to derive a set of isodapanes, in which each isodapane refers to a different value for total (combined) transport costs, one constructs isovectors (à la Palander) or isotims (à la Hoover) about each raw material source and finished product. An isovector is a line which, in the case of a localized raw material, connects points to which the required quantity of localized raw material may be shipped from a point source at the same transport cost. Hence, around each raw

[39] The isodapane technique is more flexible than the weight triangle method. It can encompass graduated tariff structures and transport nets composed of different media, avoid adjustment to an "ideal" weight basis, and relate to locational polygons of more than three corners. It is however a much more cumbersome technique.

material source, a set of isovectors may be drawn; to each isovector we may assign a transport cost which generally rises with distance from the raw material source. (See Figs. 48 and 49, Palander, *op. cit.*, and Fig. 15, Hoover, *op. cit.*) In the case of a finished product, an isovector is a line which connects points from which the finished product may be shipped to a specified market point at the same transport cost. Here, too, a set of isovectors may be drawn, where each represents a different level of transport cost which generally rises with distance from the market point.

Once a set of isovectors is constructed about each raw material source and market point relevant in a locational problem, isodapanes may be drawn by connecting all those points which as a location for production would incur the same sum of the several transport costs on the raw materials and finished product. The procedure of employing maps of isovectors to derive isodapanes is discussed by Palander in connection with his Fig. 52, and Hoover in connection with his Fig. 15.

Essentially, isodapanes are contour lines of a total transport cost surface. Such a surface is precisely treated in Chap. 10, and is briefly described in Pick's Appendix (Weber, *op. cit.*, pp. 244–5). Once the contour lines are mapped, the identification of the minimum transport cost point, the point of locational equilibrium in the transport-orientation problem, is a matter of course. See, for example, the situation depicted by Palander, *op. cit.*, in Figs. 53 to 68, and Hoover, *op. cit.*, in Figs. 15 and 20.

As already intimated, both the process of substitution among transport inputs, as discussed in this chapter, and isodapanes refer to the identical transport cost surface. Our substitution process refers to a path of movement along the transport cost surface in a direction *toward* the trough point of the set of isodapanes (the minimum point of the surface). An isodapane, in contrast, refers to a path of movement *around* a trough point. As such our substitution process and an isodapane represent merely two different paths of journey along the same surface.

That (1) the process of substitution among transport inputs and (2) the movement along an isodapane and from isodapane to isodapane can involve the same basic considerations is clearly demonstrated by reference to Palander's method of constructing isodapanes when three or more commodities are to be moved. Imagine a locational triangle such as Fig. 17. About each raw material source and market Palander advises as a first step the construction of a set of isovectors. As a second step, any two of the three sets of isovectors are used to derive a subset of isodapanes (partial isodapanes) which refer to the sum of only two transport costs. As a third step, the subset of isodapanes are combined with the third set of isovectors to obtain the desired set of isodapanes which refer to the sum of three transport costs.

For the moment consider (1) the subset of isodapanes derived in the second step and (2) the third set of isovectors, which, let us posit, centers around the market point. Suppose we select that isovector which corresponds to three distance units from C in Fig. 17 and thus to arc TS. Suppose also we select any one isodapane from the subset of isodapanes which intersect this isovector. As we proceed along this isovector in one direction we will be moving on to subset isodapanes of greater and greater values; and in the other direction to subset isodapanes of lower and lower values. Such movement necessarily involves a substitution between transport inputs on the raw material from M_1 and transport inputs on the raw material from M_2, since distances from M_1 and M_2 change while weights remain constant. A movement in the former direction is identical with a movement along the transformation line ST of Fig. 24 to higher and higher price-ratio (iso-outlay) lines; and in the latter direction, to lower and lower price-ratio lines. This is so because we are holding constant transport inputs on finished product to C, and, hence, the transport cost on finished product to C (since the transport rate is given). The desirability of moving along any isovector until the subset isodapane of lowest value is reached (which will be at a point of tangency) is clear. This is equivalent to substituting between transport inputs and moving along the transformation line ST of Fig. 24 until point K is reached. Of all points on the transformation line, K lies on the lowest price-ratio line and is also a point of tangency. K represents a partial locational equilibrium point.

We proceed further. Having identified the point which would be K in Fig. 17 and which is the point of tangency of the isovector of the previous paragraph with the lowest value isodapane of the subset isodapanes having a point in common with the isovector, let us select that isovector of the set of isovectors centering around raw material source M_2 which passes through what would be point K in Fig. 17. Also, construct another subset of isodapanes based upon the sum of transport costs on raw material from M_1 and finished product to C. Once again, we move along the isovector until we reach that isodapane of the new subset which has the lowest value; it will be tangent to the isovector. Once again, we are substituting between transport inputs—this time between transport inputs on the raw material from M_1 and on the finished product to C. Or, to put it otherwise, we are moving along a transformation line on to the lowest price-ratio line. We reach another point of partial locational equilibrium, partial since we hold fixed the value for the variable, transport inputs from M_2.

Next we (1) select either that isovector centering around C or that isovector centering around M_1 which passes through this new partial equilibrium point and (2) construct still another subset of relevant isodapanes. As before we move along the isovector to lower and lower subset isodapanes, etc., etc.

We can continue this procedure until we reach that point where it is no longer possible to move on to any lower subset isodapane along any of the three isovectors which can be constructed through this point. That is, it is no longer economic to substitute between any pair of transport inputs. In essence, we have a coincidence of three partial locational equilibrium points. We are at the point around which all the isodapanes center. We are at the trough of the transport cost surface.

Thus, it is clear that on a transport cost surface (1) economic movement from isodapane to isodapane and (2) economic movement which corresponds to substitution between any pair of transport inputs in our transformation sense differ in direction only. They aim at the same goal. And, in fact, when the former movement is restricted to paths along isovectors on to subset isodapanes of lower and lower value, they are identical and translatable one into the other.[40]

[40] In the above discussion we have implicitly assumed that one and only one minimum point exists. Actually, for most problems, more than one exists. However, this does not qualify our basic analysis. Following Palander and Hoover, the reader can easily reword the above statements to cover cases with several minimum points.

In this appendix an attempt has been made to translate some of the better formulations of the transport-orientation problem into substitution relations among transport inputs. It has not been the intention to treat and translate each formulation comprehensively. The discussion has not covered all the refinements of the several doctrines which are presented in Launhardt, Weber, Palander, Dean, Lösch, Hoover, and elsewhere; rather, it has sought to relate and restate only the basic threads. From here the reader can easily proceed further.

Chapter 6

The Locational Equilibrium
of the Firm:
Labor and Other Orientation

1. Introductory Remarks

In the previous chapter, we have examined the conditions for the locational equilibrium of transport-oriented processes, postulating that among sites differentials (except those arising from different transport costs on raw materials and finished product) either do not exist or are insignificant. Each productive factor and service, other than a transported raw material or finished product, was considered to be available everywhere in correct amounts and at the same price. When a raw material was present at several sources, it was taken to be adequately available at the same price for all sources. When more than one market point for a finished product existed, at each the revenue potential or the ruling price on the finished product was posited to be identical.

We now relax some of these assumptions and introduce differentials in factor costs and revenue potentials.[1] To incorporate such differentials into general locational analysis for the firm, it is necessary to think in terms of substitution between outlays, between revenues, and between outlays and revenues. It is insufficient here to speak of substitution between the commodities encompassed by our trans-

---

[1] We consider differentials in revenue potential since a firm may consider several production locations which may serve directly, or be gateway points to, different markets where different prices and demand elasticities for the firm's product(s) obtain.

formation function, for it is the variations from site to site in the prices of these inputs and outputs which, along with other forces, influence location. For example, Weber discusses the phenomenon of labor orientation where a firm does not locate at the transport optimum point representing the best combination of transport inputs but rather at a cheap labor point. When these two points are not identical, the firm thereby consumes more transport inputs and increases its transport outlays while it simultaneously holds constant (or even increases) its labor inputs but reduces its labor outlays, *ceteris paribus*. We do not have substitution between transport inputs and labor inputs but rather between transport outlays and labor outlays.

2. LABOR ORIENTATION

It is possible to develop conceptual schemes to treat substitutions between outlays, between revenues, and between outlays and revenues. Suppose within the typical Weberian framework we allow first inequalities in labor resources among sites and consequent differentials in labor costs. To every realistic point on the transformation line for a pair of transport input variables, we can assign not only a necessary transport outlay as given by the iso-outlay line which passes through it but also a labor outlay. Thus, if we take the realistic points G, F, J, E, and H on the transformation line in Fig. 23 and assume that labor outlay per ton of product is $20.00 at each of the sites represented by these points, except the cheap labor site[2] represented

[2] The term *cheap labor* is employed here in a broad sense. A site where cheap money wages are paid to labor is not necessarily a cheap labor site if the labor is inefficient; on the other hand, a site where high money wages are paid can be a cheap labor site if the efficiency of labor more than counterbalances the high money wages. The fundamental concept is the wage per labor service of a given quality or per efficiency unit.

Cheap labor areas or sites arise from a number of circumstances. Often relatively low wage payments are found to be characteristic of a surplus agricultural region. Such payments reflect the relatively small transport cost for food and drink consumed by the laborer and his family. A relatively low wage payment permits a satisfactory content of living. However, if one considers food and drink for laborers as raw materials in the production process, which conceptually is a consistent procedure, then surplus agricultural regions, which contain good assembly points for these raw materials, need not be locationally classified as cheap labor areas.

As Ohlin, Hoover, and others have noted, differences in wages which are attributable to differences in transport costs, and, therefore, total costs of the same basket of consumer goods (budget materials) at different places may be classified as "equalizing" differences. These contrast with "real" differences. Since equalizing differences arise from transport cost differentials, they represent part of the

by J where it is only \$16.00,[3] we can depict the respective transport and labor outlays incurred at these sites by corresponding points in Fig. 25. In this figure, labor outlays and transport outlays are measured along the vertical and horizontal axes, respectively. As in Fig. 23, point F is taken to be the optimum transport point.

Also in Fig. 25, we have plotted the points L, M, N, and R, which represent other cheap labor sites. These additional positions do not have corresponding realistic points on the transformation line of Fig. 23. But, in the light of all possible variations in all transport inputs (transport inputs on raw material M_1, on raw material M_2, and on finished product), such additional positions correspond to realistic points on transformation lines when the quantity of transport inputs on the finished product to C is different from that assumed in Fig. 23. Other realistic points which may or may not be cheap labor sites can also be plotted, but plotting them is not necessary to elucidate the argument.

When two or more points incur the same labor outlay, we consider only the one which involves the least transport outlay; and when, in Fig. 25, we connect these points in order according to transport outlay, we obtain the line $FJLMNR$, which may be called an "outlay-substitution" line. It presents the meaningful substitution possibilities

---

transport orientation problem and should be treated as such. Their inclusion in the transport orientation problem is, however, more complex than is often realized.

Major industrial centers based upon coal mining, iron and steel manufacture, and other primary economic activities which engage the chief breadwinners of families frequently have supplies of secondary labor available, i.e., labor which is surplus to the primary industries yet immobile because the location of the chief breadwinner determines the location of the secondary labor supplied by the family. Like any other surplus commodity, this labor can usually be purchased at bargain rates. Parasitic industry is attracted by it. But it is important to recognize that this kind of attraction is fundamentally conditioned by a site's attraction for dominant industries; it can be explained only in terms of the total situation. Basically, such parasitic industry is not a case of labor orientation. Differentials in regional development of secondary industry must be stated in terms of differentials in regional development of different primary industries.

Cheap labor sites are most often attributable to cultural factors such as are found in poverty stricken regions where long-run immobility of labor obtains. Frequently, the laborer may be willing to forego leisure and to sell his services at a low price in order to supplement his other income and thus obtain the purchasing power requisite for minimum subsistence living.

For full discussion of these and related points, refer to Dean (Selections), *op. cit.*, pp. 22–30; Ohlin, *op. cit.*, pp. 212–20; and Hoover, *op. cit.*, pp. 60–74.

[3] We repeat: Weber assumes that the wage levels of labor at the several locations are fixed and that the labor supply available at each location is unlimited. (Friedrich, *op. cit.*, p. 101.)

between transport outlays and labor outlays, just as the transformation line does for two inputs. We also construct a new set of iso-outlay (transport plus labor outlay) lines which are straight and obviously have a negative slope of unity when the same scale is used along both axes. *TU* and *CD* are two such lines representing (on transport and labor) combined outlays of $56.00 and $50.00 respectively.

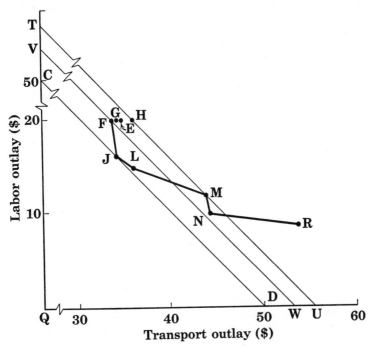

FIG. 25. An outlay-substitution line in a case of labor orientation.

Of all points on the outlay-substitution line, *J* lies on the lowest iso-outlay line. It indicates location at a cheap labor site rather than at *F*, the minimum transport cost point, and, hence, a substitution of transport outlays for labor outlays if location were initially at *F*.

If the reader cares to, he may state formal conditions for equilibrium with respect to these two outlays. These conditions might almost parallel those stated in the preceding chapter. With *Q* as origin (Fig. 25), to the left of the equilibrium point when it is not an end point, the outlay-substitution line between transport outlay and labor outlay must be steeper than the relevant iso-outlay line; and, to the right of the equilibrium point when it is not an end point, either the iso-outlay line must be steeper than the outlay-substitution line or else the outlay-substitution line must have a positive slope.[4]

Incidentally, the approach illustrated in Fig. 25 does away with the unnecessarily complex Weberian technique for determining whether or not an operation will be labor oriented and, if so, to which labor site. According to Weber, one must construct the critical isodapane[5] for each cheap labor site, consider only those sites which fall within their critical isodapanes, and select that site which in terms of "ideal" distance lies farthest from its critical isodapane. Using the above graphic technique, one needs to observe whether or not any points representing cheap labor sites lie on lower iso-outlay lines than does

[4] Along certain stretches, the slope of an outlay-substitution line may well be positive. For, in moving from one cheap labor site to another, from left to right along the outlay-substitution line of Fig. 25, not only will transport outlay rise but also labor outlay will increase if at the second cheap labor site labor is somewhat more dear. In contrast, when dealing with transformation lines for two transport inputs (or distance variables) where only a finite number of points can be considered as location sites, one would encounter positive slopes only when "unnecessary distance" is traversed, e.g., where a firm locates outside the locational polygon. This possibility has been logically excluded from our analysis except for the case where there is a particular type of irregularity in the transport rate structure.

Also, the above conditions, as in the previous chapter, may be satisfied by more than one point. It becomes necessary to select the best from among such points. For example, in Fig. 25 both J and N meet the requirements stated above. Obviously J, lying on the lowest iso-outlay line, is the more desirable site of the two.

Again it is worthy to note the extent of discontinuity involved in reality. Usually the possibilities of substitution do not permit a gradual geographic shift through sites in turn necessitating less and less labor outlay and more and more transport outlay until the optimum combination is reached. Rather, as Weber states, the problem is one of an alternative attraction (Alternativattraktion) not an approaching attraction (Annäherungsattraktion). It does no good to move from the optimum transport point to a site nearer the cheap labor location. In such a shift, labor outlays are not usually significantly affected. To derive the benefits of cheap labor, one has to migrate to the cheap labor site itself. Spatially speaking, there is no continuity in this migration. It involves in the typical case a discrete geographic jump.

[5] In contrast to Palander and Hoover, Weber uses the isodapane concept in a marginal sense rather than in the total sense as defined in the Appendix to Chap. 5. Thus according to Weber, whom we follow in this and subsequent chapters, an isodapane is a curve connecting points representing locations involving the same increases of transport cost over the cost incurred at the transport optimum point. The critical isodapane for any cheap labor site is the one which represents an additional transport outlay equivalent to the saving in labor outlay at the cheap labor site. If the site lies anywhere within the area bounded by the critical isodapane, it becomes eligible for attracting the production process under consideration (Weber, *op. cit.,* pp. 102–04).

the point representing the transport optimum site. If none does, there will be no deviation to a labor location. If more than one do, then the firm will shift to a cheap labor site and to that one which lies on the lowest iso-outlay line. In Fig. 23 such a site is J.[6]

The above presentation of the labor orientation problem, however, is inadequate. For, assuming still that all other factors are ubiquitous and available everywhere at the same cost, it is reasonable to expect another type of adjustment, specifically, a tendency for substitution at the cheap labor site of cheap labor for transport inputs, provided production coefficients and other technical relations are not fixed. This might take the form of reduction in bulk of the product, in weight, in perishability, and so forth. And, if the cheap labor site's advantage lay in the exploitability of a special class of labor, let us say unskilled labor, we might face the additional substitution problem of skilled labor vs. unskilled labor.[7] This is the type of substitution problem within a substitution problem that Predöhl had in mind. The adjustment, however, would not affect the conditions to be met by an equilibrium point. Cheap labor points would lie on lower iso-outlay lines above and to the left of their respective positions on Fig. 25. This adjustment, of course, might involve a change of the equilibrium site.

3. SOME OTHER FORMS OF ORIENTATION

In the above section we have relaxed the assumption that the costs of an efficiency unit of labor at all locations were alike. Differentials in labor costs were introduced, while, by assumption, differentials in other costs (except transport) were precluded. We now proceed to preclude differentials in labor cost, while allowing differentials in transport costs and in just one other cost item, let us say power.

It is clear that in this new situation a procedure paralleling that of the preceding section may be utilized. To every realistic point on the transformation line for a pair of transport inputs, we can assign not only a necessary transport outlay as given by the iso-outlay line which passes through it but also a power outlay. For each point, the

---

[6] Also, the above graphic approach provides a simpler framework when adjustments need to be made for transport savings from the use of replacement deposits in Weber's sense. However, logically the use of a replacement deposit signifies a shift from the supply area of one source of the raw material in question to the supply area of a second source. Such use is therefore more appropriately considered as a phase of supply area analysis to be treated below.

[7] Since for the present all other factors are considered ubiquitous and available everywhere at the same cost, there would also tend to be a substitution of cheap labor for these factors at cheap labor sites.

associated transport outlay and power outlay can be plotted on a graph along whose horizontal and vertical axes transport and power outlays are measured respectively. Also, for every realistic point on other transformation lines for any pair of transport inputs, both transport and power outlays can be derived and plotted on the same graph. When we view the entire set of points depicted on this graph and, of two or more points incurring the same power outlay, consider only the one which involves the least transport outlay, and when we connect these points in order according to transport outlay, we obtain another type of outlay-substitution line. This type presents the meaningful substitution possibilities between transport and power outlays, just as the type of outlay-substitution line in Fig. 25 presents the meaningful substitution possibilities between transport and labor outlays. We can also construct a new set of iso-outlay (transport plus power outlay) lines, which, like the iso-outlay lines in Fig. 25, are straight and have a negative slope of unity when the same scale is used along both axes.

Given the iso-outlay lines and the outlay-substitution line, it would be easy to identify in our assumed situation the optimum location. This location would correspond to that point on the outlay-substitution line lying on the lowest of the iso-outlay lines. Formal conditions of locational equilibrium could be stated. Allowance could be made for the substitution at cheap power sites of power inputs for transport inputs and other inputs, technological and economic conditions permitting. This substitution would be in addition to the substitution associated with locational shift which takes place along the outlay-substitution line.

In this way, the significance which variation in power cost has for locational equilibrium can be evaluated under our given set of assumptions. When the point on the outlay-substitution line which lies on the lowest iso-outlay line (after adjustment has been made for substitution among inputs) corresponds to a cheap power point, we have the familiar case of *power orientation*. According to Weber's terminology, the cheap power point lies within the critical isodapane; or, according to Dean's terminology, there are deviational economies, and the largest possible deviational economies, in shifting to this particular cheap power point in our assumed situation.[8]

In similar fashion, it is possible to consider formally the variation

[8] Paralleling the concept of labor coefficient and the ratio of labor savings to additional transport outlays (which are discussed in the Appendix to this chapter), one can construct a power coefficient and the ratio of power cost savings to additional transport outlays and use them as we use the labor coefficient and corresponding ratio.

in the costs of other input items resulting from diverse inequalities in mineral and human resources and from differences in cultural and political institutions. Along with variation in transport outlays, the variation of the interest rate among sites and regions might be considered in isolation. We could construct outlay-substitution lines (referring to the variation at different sites in outlays on interest and on transport) and relevant iso-outlay lines to determine which (if any) cheap interest point might deviate the location of production from the minimum transport cost point. In this problem, at least implicit consideration would have to be given to the alternatives in the use of different types of venture and other capital and to the entire set of input substitution points associated with the width and depth of capital structure.

Or we might consider in isolation variation in transport outlays and tax outlays; or in transport outlays and rent outlays; or in transport outlays and in general production outlays where differences in general production outlays obtain because of differences among sites in climatic and other environmental features, in union restrictions and diverse social burdens, in agglomeration and industrial and population density, and so forth.

Another differential that may confront the individual producer may be in the price of raw materials at different sources, whether owing to differences in fertility, richness of ore, processing costs, etc., or to imposed competitive differences. As before, assuming all other factor costs geographically uniform, one can measure transport outlay along one axis and outlay (at the source) on raw material A along the other. One can then plot the respective outlays for any possible site. However, only those sites are relevant which involve, for each possible source of the raw material under consideration, the least transport outlay for assembling all the raw materials required in production and carrying the finished product to the market. There will be a deviation from the site involving the least aggregate transport outlay of all (i.e., the best of the several relative minimum points with respect to transport cost) to an optimum position with respect to the cheaper raw material source if the saving from the lower price of raw material more than counterbalances the increased outlay on transport occasioned by the shift. The new site would lie on an iso-outlay (transport plus raw material A outlay) line lower than the first. Usually the shift would involve a discrete spatial jump, except in the case of agricultural raw materials or the like for which there are large supply areas. And similarly with sources of other raw materials, each in turn.

Again one might consider differentials in price received per unit of product at various consumption places for the case where a firm confronts a geographic pattern of market prices upon which it has little, if any, influence, and where the differential aspects of this pattern are unrelated to the given firm's transport outlays. In Fig. 26, one

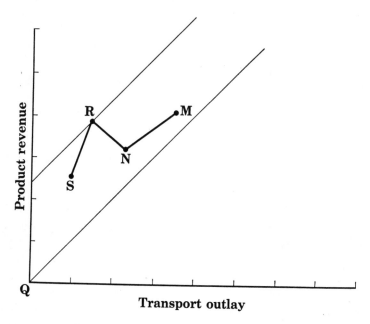

Fɪɢ. 26. A revenue-outlay substitution line.

measures total transport outlay on inputs and output along the horizontal axis and revenue from sale of product along the vertical, all other outlays and revenues being held constant. Here, one is concerned with iso-revenue-less-outlay lines, i.e., constant product revenue less transport outlay lines, with the result that of two such lines a position on the one to the left is more desirable. These straight iso-revenue-less-outlay lines, unlike those involving two kinds of outlays, have positive slopes. In Fig. 26, point S is that site which incurs the least transport outlay. However, positions R, N, and M, being "higher-price" markets or being gateway points to higher-price consumption places, all offer larger revenue from sale of the product than does point S. In the case of point R, the additional revenue more than counterbalances the additional transport outlay required for assembling raw materials at R and for shipping the product to the corresponding consumption place. R then is a preferred position

lying on a higher iso-revenue-less-outlay line than does S, N, or M.[9]
If more than one output is produced, we can construct a similar
chart for each.[10]

This sort of partial analysis, however, where all costs and revenues
but two are held constant, is inadequate and of little pragmatic value.
Weber recognized this fact when, speaking of shifts to labor locations,
he took into consideration the economies to be gained by replacement
of material deposits, that is, by utilization of new raw material sources
closer to labor locations rather than those sources which were more
favorably situated in relation to the market to be served and the
optimum transport point.   Without doubt, if a plant does find it
expedient to shift to a cheap labor site, a cheap power site, or a site
better able to serve a higher revenue consumption place, other outlays and revenues besides transport outlay do change in the usual
case.   We thus require a substitution analysis which can treat differentials in all types of costs and revenues at one time, not just differentials
in two types alone.

An extension of the analytical technique to meet this requirement
can be forced along familiar lines.   When one attacks the problem of
choosing correct quantities of physical inputs and outputs, he may first
consider the substitution point relating any two commodities, the
basket of all other commodities being given.   Then in turn he may
derive the substitution point for a second pair, a third pair, and so on.
During these latter operations, if the derived quantity of any commodity is inconsistent with the quantity previously assigned to the
same commodity within the fixed basket of goods when the substitution
relations between a first pair of goods was being considered, then one
changes the composition of the basket to make it consistent with the
new quantity.   In turn, this change is likely to lead to a new substitution point for the first two commodities and a change in the
quantities desired.   And this change in the first pair of values is likely
to alter the substitution relations between other pairs of goods, and
different quantities of these other goods might then be desirable.   This
process continues until finally a consistent set of substitution points

[9] Note also that the formal partial equilibrium conditions can be stated. They
are met in this situation. Viewed with point Q as origin, to the left of point R
the iso-revenue-less-outlay line has a slope less steep than that of the revenue-
outlay substitution line ($SRNM$); and to the right of point R the revenue-outlay
substitution line has a negative slope. R would still be an equilibrium point if
to its right the slope of the revenue-outlay substitution line were positive so
long as it were less than the slope of the iso-revenue-less-outlay line.

[10] The substitution analysis centering upon the relation between the location
of a firm and its scale of operations is considered in Chap. 8.

is obtained, wherein the equilibrium conditions are satisfied for every meaningful pair of commodities.

At the start one may be inclined to approach the problem in the same fashion when differentials in several types of costs and revenues exist between sites. One takes two outlays which are different at several sites that in other respects possess similar price and cost structures and finds the best combination of these outlays, as in Fig. 25 above. Similarly with another pair of outlays until all possible pairs are considered. However, one finds that different sets of sites pertain to different pairs of outlays. This finding means that the above procedure, though logical for certain equilibrium analyses, overlooks one important aspect of the location problem. Sites are often unlike with respect to more than two outlays. Where all sites differ in at least three outlays, the above process is inappropriate. But by lumping together two or more outlays, so that two or more sites are alike except with respect to two groups of outlays, one can still utilize this analytical technique.

It is important to recognize that this is essentially no different from the procedure where two or more commodities are used in fixed proportions. If the consumption of commodity j, belonging to a group of commodities used in fixed proportions, is increased to replace some of commodity m which is not included in the group, we cannot construct a transformation line between commodities j and m, the basket of all other commodities being fixed. For, as the quantity of j varies, so vary the quantities of those commodities used in fixed proportion to commodity j. As a consequence, the basket of all commodities other than j and m cannot be given. The only method of attack is to consider as a whole the commodities used in fixed proportions and to inquire into the substitutability of this group for commodity m, the basket of other commodities being given.

When one lumps together two or more outlays to derive an outlay-substitution line between any two groups of outlays, he is using this same technique. Here he has no such explicit constraints on the variation in quantities of commodities as those given by the transformation function. He has only a geographic pattern of resources and facilities resulting in price-cost differentials. But this does not preclude using an identical procedure. He can construct outlay-substitution, revenue-outlay substitution, and revenue-substitution lines between all possible pairs of outlays and revenues or groups of outlays and revenues. If all sites manifest price differentials with respect to only three outlays—transport, labor, and interest—one can construct an outlay-substitution line, measuring transport outlay along one axis and labor plus interest outlay along the other. The relevant price-ratio lines would be iso-outlay (transport plus labor plus interest outlay) lines.[11] If sites exhibit differences among four items—whether they be outlays or revenues—measuring along the first axis either one or the aggregate of two items and along the second axis the aggregate of respectively three or two items, one can derive a substitution line from plotting the values associated with each site to contrast with appropriately derived iso-lines. And in similar fashion one can treat the situation where differences among sites exists among five or more items.[12]

If there are differentials among all sites with respect to each cost and revenue, then, the above procedure being followed, the problem of optimum location would reduce to a simple substitution relation between two groups of outlays and revenues. At this juncture, however, cloaking the analysis in terms of substitution would be of little value. A forthright comparison of total costs at each site will achieve the desired result more readily. Likewise, the site of production being given, the substitution technique degenerates when all inputs and outputs fall into two groups, the commodities within each group being used in fixed proportions. In this situation there is only one substitution relation, namely, between the two groups of commodities. In reality, however, the various constraints to the transformation function usually leave room for many substitution relations between the different commodities. Likewise, potential sites for a production process do not manifest major price differentials in many categories of costs and revenues. The fewer constraints to the transformation function and the fewer major price differentials among all sites, the more pertinent is substitution analysis (except for the extreme case).

[11] And à la Weber, he might be inclined to compute "labor-interest coefficients." However, he would soon discover extreme difficulties in the use of such a coefficient.

[12] An alternative to this procedure is to divide sites into groups, each group containing sites which differ with respect to two items only (when sites in general differ in at least three items), or with respect to three items only (when sites in general differ in at least four items), or with respect to four items only (when sites in general differ in at least five items), and so forth. For each group of sites the optimum one can be obtained through the above substitution analysis where along each axis one, or the aggregate of two or more items, is measured. The total revenue and cost situation for each of the resulting "partial" optimum sites can be directly compared to yield the over-all optimum location. Or the over-all optimum location may be derived by a division of all the differential revenue and cost items into two groups, and by a plot for each of the "partial" optimum points of the aggregate of each group (upon a chart along whose axes the two aggregates are measured) in order to yield a substitution line to contrast with an appropriately derived iso-line.

4. A RE-EXAMINATION OF THE SUBSTITUTION FRAMEWORK FOR
SPATIAL ANALYSIS

It is appropriate at this juncture to evaluate the substitution approach developed in this and the preceding chapter. As already intimated, it may be contended that at least to some degree the substitution framework has been pushed to undesirable length. Such a view stems from a consideration of the spatial setting within which various types of costs and revenues vary.

For certain purposes it is convenient to classify location factors into three groups. These groups, though generally valid for our purposes, overlap to some degree and cannot be precisely delineated. In the first group may be included transport costs and certain other transfer costs. The distinguishing feature of these transport and transfer costs is that they vary regularly with distance from any given point of reference, usually increasing in step-by-step fashion as distance increases. Hence, given a relevant set of reference points, whether they be raw material, service, nodal, or market points, we find systematic variation of these costs over space. The structure of transport rates and the tariff structures for other transfer costs which are a function of distance being given, the systematic variation of these costs over space becomes predictable.

This is not to deny that exceptions to this systematic variation exist. Such exceptions in the transport rate structure have already been alluded to in the previous chapter, and the necessary techniques to incorporate these irregularities into the main body of rates, without jeopardizing the system of this body, have already been indicated. In similar ways, exceptions in tariff structures for other transfer costs which are a function of distance can be handled without destroying the general systematic variation of these costs over space.

A second group of location factors comprises the several costs associated with labor, power, water, taxes, insurance, interest (as payment for the services of capital), climate, topography, social and political milieu, and a number of other items. The geographic cost pattern of many of these items may be said to be relatively stable. However, in contrast to the first group, it cannot be said that the costs of any of these items generally vary systematically with distance from any given reference point. Rather, they tend to vary haphazardly, independently of direction and distance.[13] For example,

---

[13] On the surface, there appear to be exceptions to this statement. Power rates, for example, may rise regularly with distance from a generating station. Once beyond the feasible transmission range, however, the variation of power rates is

cheap labor points generally occur around any given reference point in an unpredictable fashion. There is no reason to anticipate that, given any set of spatial co-ordinates, cheap labor points will be some function of distance and direction from that defined position. Hence, in this sense, analysis of labor costs, as well as the other costs which fall in this second group, seeks in vain for any meaningful general spatial framework.

A third group of location factors comprises the diverse elements which give rise to agglomeration and deglomeration economies. Included in agglomeration economies are: (1) economies of scale; (2) localization economies; and (3) urbanization economies.[14] Deglomerative forces embrace chiefly: (1) diseconomies within a firm as its scale of operation becomes too large; (2) the rise of rents and costs of urban services as increase in the intensity of land use and population settlement leads to congestion; and (3) the rise in the cost of food supply as the increase in the size of population settlement compels resort to surplus agricultural areas farther and farther afield.[15]

It is clear from an analysis of agglomerative and deglomerative forces that their operation is independent of geographic position. Their associated economies and diseconomies are functionally dependent upon the magnitude of activities. These economies and

---

not subject to regularity, except insofar as the variation reflects differences in the transport cost of fuel. Essentially, where power transmission or transportation of fuel is possible, a regularity may ensue; where power transmission and fuel transportation are infeasible, irregularity is characteristic. It is thus transport cost which imparts to the geographic variation of power rates any regularity which it possesses, both intraregionally and interregionally. There is no inherent regularity in the geographic distribution of energy and power resources.

Likewise with labor costs. To some degree, regularity in the variation of wage rates over space may be said to have existed historically and to persist in current times. As already intimated, such regularity is for the most part related to differences in transport cost in obtaining the goods in the laborer's market basket. For a given content of living, the variation in wages resulting from these differences in transport cost have already been referred to as "equalizing" differences in money wages. They are to be distinguished from "real" differences in money wages which do not exhibit any spatial regularity. Again, it is the transport element which imparts a regularity to the spatial cost pattern of an input, which otherwise does not possess any such regularity. Compare Hoover, *Location Theory and the Shoe and Leather Industries,* Cambridge, Mass., 1937, Chap IV.

[14] See Chap. 8 for full discussion of them.

[15] To the extent that agglomerative and deglomerative forces are associated with the increase and decrease of transport cost, or of any other cost item falling in the second group, to the same extent these categories of location forces, as already suggested, overlap. However, such an overlap does not seriously interfere with our argument.

diseconomies obtain regardless of the locality at which any given magnitude and situational interaction of activities occur (though, to be sure, elements of the physical setting, such as topography and bedrock conditions can influence to some extent the intensity with which agglomerative and deglomerative forces operate). These forces are, for the most part, spatially passive. They are adaptive, and they materialize at localities where other considerations either dictate or hinder location. Their geographic pattern is a derived one, and it reflects the regularities and irregularities of spatial pattern associated with other location factors.

Hence, we are led to conclude from our general consideration of these three groups of location forces that only the transport factor and other transfer factors whose costs are functionally related to distance impart regularity to the spatial setting of activities. Substitution analysis among various transport inputs, of the type discussed in Chap. 5, is vital for understanding the spatial configuration of economic activities and its inherent order and for unearthing the pervasive impact of the friction of distance. On the other hand, substitution analysis which is more elaborate than the sort sketched in the preceding sections and which particularly treats at one time several factors that either haphazardly distort or intensify the systematic spatial arrangement imposed by the transport factor, may be judged to be less significant. Such analysis possesses less value at this stage where we are concerned with the development of equilibrium analysis for the firm as an integral part of a general theory of space-economy which is independent of any particular cultural, institutional, or geographic frame of reference.[16]

[16] For example, it may be maintained by some that, where a particular process is not transport-oriented, i.e., where transport cost differentials among sites are not the dominant ones, it is best in ascertaining the maximum profit location merely to recognize that substitutions do take place among outlays and revenues and to focus attention upon the more important substitutions. To be specific, the indirect shift of textile capacity from New England to the cheap labor point of Puerto Rico involved a substitution of transport outlays for labor outlays. The cheap labor point, however, was in no way *generally* related to a distance factor. It could have existed elsewhere. This arbitrariness, it may be contended, weakens any attempt at stating general formal equilibrium conditions regarding substitution in analyzing the spatial equilibrium of this case. This effect is even greater, it may be held, when tax outlays and other outlays are introduced into the picture.

APPENDIX TO CHAPTER 6

THE LABOR COEFFICIENT AND A RELATED RATIO

Since Weber's concept of labor coefficient has considerable significance for location analysis, it is useful to present briefly some of the connections between this concept and a related ratio directly obtainable from substitution between transport and labor outlays.

In considering the feasibility of the shift of production processes from their transport optimal points to cheap labor locations, Weber emphasizes two industrial characteristics: (1) locational weight (based upon "ideal" instead of actual weights) and (2) index of labor costs (i.e., average labor costs per ton product). Also, he considers of primary significance three environmental conditions: (1) geographic position of locational figures and labor locations, (2) transport rates, and (3) actual percentage of compression of the labor cost index. If we combine locational weight, geographic position of locational figures and labor locations, and transport rates, we obtain the set of additional transport outlays associated with any pattern of shift from the transport optimal site. [These outlays may be comprehensively depicted by a set of isodapanes. Obviously the smaller (greater) the locational weight and the lower (higher) the transport rate, the farther apart (the closer) do consecutive isodapanes lie and the greater (less) is the likelihood of deviation to a labor location. Unless the locational figure for a production process is symmetric and unit weights apply to all corners, there will not be an equal tendency to deviate in all directions. Isodapanes will not be circular; and, *ceteris paribus*, they will be pulled toward the corners with heaviest weight. For possible deviations over short distances, this distortion of circular form may be significant. As the distance of possible deviation increases, the isodapanes tend to approximate more and more a set of concentric circles, and the distorting effect of any asymmetric locational figure and pattern of weights can be increasingly neglected.]

Likewise, if we combine the index of labor costs and actual percentages of compression, we obtain the set of savings in labor outlays associated with existing labor locations. [Obviously the higher (lower) the index of labor cost and the percentage of compression, the greater (smaller) the likelihood of deviation to a labor location, *ceteris paribus*.]

To measure quantitatively the extent to which different industries may be deviated to labor locations, Weber develops the concept of labor coefficient. The labor coefficient of an industry is defined as the ratio of its labor cost per ton product to its locational weight, or labor cost per locational ton. If only deviations over significant distances are considered so that the distorting effects upon isodapanes of any particular locational figure and its set of forces can be ignored, then, according to Weber, the higher the labor coefficient the more likely that an industry will be labor oriented, given a fixed transport rate structure proportional to weight and distance and after due allowance is made for savings from replacement deposits which tend to become increasingly significant with increase of deviational distance. Weber's labor coefficient is also useful in establishing priorities for different types of industries which might be induced to locate at a cheap labor location. *Ceteris paribus*, the higher the coefficient, the higher the economic priority.

If we consider a specific labor location and if we multiply the numerator of the labor coefficient for an industry by the relevant percentage of compression and the denominator by the transport rate and distance between the labor location and the transport optimal point, we obtain a ratio of outlays—of labor savings per locational ton to additional transport expense per locational ton. So long as this ratio is greater than unity for any given industrial process and environmental situation, the labor location lies within the critical isodapane and attracts the industry in question. It pays to substitute transport outlays for labor outlays. The greater the ratio, the greater the savings achieved in shifting to a labor location.

Compared to the labor coefficient from which it is derived, the ratio per locational ton of labor savings to additional transport outlays has the virtue of being able to indicate directly whether or not a shift to a labor location is feasible. Further it can yield more directly answers to questions like these: By how much must labor costs be compressed to attract a specific industrial process to a given location, *ceteris paribus?* By how much must the transport rate be cut to allow an industrial process to be attracted to a cheap labor location, *ceteris paribus?* To which of several labor locations will an industrial process be attracted? In contrast, the labor coefficient has the major advantage of having more general applicability. It indicates relative tendency of various industrial processes to shift to labor locations and is generally independent of the percentage of compression, transport rate, or distance relations in any particular situation. (In still other contexts, another ratio might be useful, namely, one which is derived through multiplying the numerator of the labor coefficient by a relevant percentage of compression and the denominator by the transport rate. This ratio is independent of spatial situation.)

Chapter 7

Market and Supply
Area Analysis and Competitive
Locational Equilibrium

1. MARKET AREA ANALYSIS

Hitherto we have treated the firm as serving for the most part a one-point market. We now relax this simplifying postulate and consider the market as an area. Further, with the use of the concept of transport inputs it is easily shown how production analysis for a one-point consumption place may be viewed as a special case of production analysis for a market area.[1]

In Chap. 2 we have briefly sketched Lösch's conception of the

---

[1] Incidentally, for a long time, location theorists treated separately the problems of production for a one-point consumption place and production for a market area. Launhardt, who presented the first significant treatment of industrial location theory, distinguished between the partial problem of determining the site of production within or at the corners of a locational polygon, where the corners represented raw material sources and a one-point consumption place ["Die Bestimmung des zweckmassigsten Standortes einer gewerblichen Anlage," *Zeitschrift des Vereines Deutscher Ingenieure*, Bd. 26 (March 1882)], and the partial problem of supplying a consuming area from a given point of production (*Mathematische Begründung der Volkswirthschaftslehre*, Leipzig, 1885, Part III). Although he handled both problems comprehensively for his time, he made no attempt to put them together. Weber, in his analysis, treated only the first of these problems. Engländer, perhaps the first to recognize that these two problems are fundamentally one and the same (in his caustic criticism of Weber, "Kritisches und Positives . . .," *op. cit.*), nevertheless did not adequately synthesize them in this and his other works. The later writings of Palander, Hoover, and Lösch are much more satisfactory in this respect.

space-economy built upon the elements of a market area, a net of market areas, and a system of nets of market areas. We nevertheless need to start over again in order to investigate thoroughly the concept of market area and to relate it to the theoretical structure thus far developed.[2] In Chaps. 10 and 11 we shall attempt an integration of market area analysis with supply area analysis to be discussed in the next section and with other location doctrine.

Imagine that a producer secures each of his raw materials and inputs at the site of his factory (hence at zero transport cost) but serves a spatial array of consumers. If consumers come to one and only one particular site and make their purchases there, or arrange transportation from that site on the item purchased, then to the producer of this item, that site is the market. For that individual producer, whom for the present we take to be an isolated monopolist in the Chamberlinian sense,[3] our spatial equilibrium analysis need not be extended. From the standpoint of society, however, when consumers are actively responsible for the transportation of the item, another set of transport inputs may be involved. If the consumers are other producers farther along in the stage of manufacture, then this transportation appears as transport inputs on raw material from a point source in these producers' calculations; and again no extension of our analysis is required. On the other hand, if consumers are households, we are not able thus far to account for the transport inputs for which they are actively responsible.[4] However, once we make the

[2] In this section we shall cover only the more important theoretical aspects of market area analysis. For supplementary details, graphic illustrations, and more extensive discussions refer among others to W. Launhardt, *Mathematische Begründung . . .* , *op. cit.*; F. A. Fetter, "The Economic Law of Market Areas," *Quarterly Journal of Economics,* Vol. 38 (May 1924), p. 525; Tord Palander, *Beiträge zur Standortstheorie,* Uppsala: Almqvist and Wiksells, 1935, Chap. IX; Edgar M. Hoover, Jr., *Location Theory and the Shoe and Leather Industries,* Cambridge, Mass., Harvard University Press, 1937, Chaps. 2, 3, 5, and 6; C. D. and W. P. Hyson, "The Economic Law of Market Areas," *Quarterly Journal of Economics,* Vol. LXIV (May 1950), pp. 319–27; and Melvin L. Greenhut, "Integrating the Leading Theories of Plant Location" and "The Size and Shape of the Market Area of a Firm," *Southern Economic Journal,* Vol. 18 (April 1952), pp. 526–38 and Vol. 19 (July 1952), pp. 37–50, respectively.

[3] See E. Chamberlin, *The Theory of Monopolistic Competition,* Cambridge, Mass., 1938, p. 74; and "Monopolistic Competition Revisited," *Economica,* November 1951, pp. 351–54.

[4] To do so would take us into the realms of sociology and social psychology. For, to explain the spatial distribution of household consumers around focal points—for example, the population spread around any given metropolitan core—requires knowledge of the process by which tastes are molded and, in particular, understanding of the space preferences of consumers. Human ecology promises

assumption, usually considered legitimate for economic analysis, that tastes and space preferences are known, and thus demand schedules and the spatial pattern of population about any given pattern of focal points are known, we necessarily "explain" the total quantity of transport inputs for which household consumers are actively responsible.

Consider situations, where, in contrast, the producer is actively responsible for transporting his products to the places of use, where each consumer is charged a price equal to a quoted price at a focal point plus transport cost to his place, and where the producer arranges the distribution of his product from that focal point. If the consumer is an industrial producer, he has in effect made the decision to contract for the transport inputs involved in delivery from the focal point to the place of use by having chosen to locate where he is rather than at a site closer to the focal point. He incurs the expense of these transport inputs indirectly by paying a higher delivered price. From society's standpoint, we may still consider the transport cost on the product paid by the first producer as outlays by the second producer on transport inputs required to obtain one of his raw materials. Once again our analysis needs no extension. If the consumer is a household, and we take its tastes, space preference, and thus demand schedules as given, we necessarily "explain" the transport inputs involved in the delivery of the product from the focal point. The consumer's willingness to pay the delivered price signifies his willingness to incur the costs of these transport inputs. When the household is unwilling to incur these costs and when the industrial consumer finds it expedient to avoid transport inputs in obtaining the product which he uses as a raw material, the market for the producer of this product reduces to a point. Viewed in this narrow framework, production for a one-point market is thus a special case of production for a market area, continuous or discontinuous.

It is fruitful to spell out these general statements, particularly as they link up with existing market area analysis. If the producer does not encounter competition from other producers in serving consumers, to all of whom he quotes an identical factory price, his market area takes the familiar shape of a circle where consumers of like tastes and income are uniformly scattered over a plain of even topography (provided they are willing to incur the costs of transport inputs). Unevenness of consumer spread, inequalities in effective purchasing power and differences of tastes among consumers, irregu-

---

eventually to provide such an understanding. (See Bogue, *op. cit.*; McKenzie, *op. cit.*; and A. Hawley, *Human Ecology,* New York, 1950.)

larities in geographic feature, economies of scale in transport, and a host of other factors distort the "natural" circular regularity. However, the essential condition that the market boundary be a locus of consumers who are just willing to pay for the first unit of product a price which is equal to the factory price plus transport cost to the point of consumption still obtains.[5]

Introduction of a competitor producing the identical commodity alters the condition in the area in which competition is in force. Where both producers set the same factory price, effective for all consumers, and where the freight rate is invariant with direction, being a function of weight and distance only, the boundary separating the consumers served by each producer is the perpendicular bisector of the straight line joining the two producers. (For example, see the boundary line ZV of Fig. 28 which separates the markets of the two producers at A and B.) Only this perpendicular bisector yields a locus of points of equal delivered price. In the districts where competition is absent, the previous condition for the determination of the boundary line for each producer still obtains.

In the equally familiar case where one producer establishes identically for all consumers a factory price lower than the other, the locus of points of equal delivered price in the area of competition becomes an hyperbola. (For example, see the boundary line which separates the market areas tributary to production points L and M_1 in Fig. 45 in Chap. 11.) In the more unusual circumstance where both producers charge one and the same factory price but where the product of one producer bears a higher transport rate than the product of the other, the market of the former ultimately becomes enclosed by the market of the latter (provided, of course, that the area of effective consumption extends far enough in the geographic hinterland of the former); the market of the latter is limited in its outer extents only by the area of effective consumption. Finally, where inequality in factory prices as well as in transport rates obtains, the market area of the producer upon whose product the higher transport rate applies ultimately becomes contained by the market area of the

[5] Since consumers are not typically distributed so that one is at every conceivable point on a plain, the market boundary must necessarily cut through certain stretches of the plain where it does not pass through possible points of consumption. In these stretches its course is somewhat indeterminate, being restricted only by the condition that it enclose those consumers who are more than willing to pay for the first unit of product the factory price plus transport cost and that it exclude those consumers who are unwilling to do so. Because of differences of incomes and tastes and other factors, enclaves of "excluded" consumers may come to exist within a producer's general market territory.

other producer, again provided that the area of effective consumption extends far enough in the geographic hinterland of the former.[6]

At this point we pause to consider how the market area analysis thus far developed can be formulated in a substitution framework. It has already been noted that the market area of the firm which is not confronted by competitors assumes a circular form under "uniformity" conditions with respect to terrain, the geographic scatter, income and tastes of consumers, and other factors. Viewed from the firm's standpoint, for any given size of output it is always profitable, when the set of consumers it initially serves does not approximate a circular territory, to substitute transport inputs in one direction for transport inputs in another direction and to continue doing so until an approximation to a circular market area is attained. The substitution is effected simply by the curtailment of sales to the most distant consumers and the extension of sales to new, less distant consumers (transport rates being a simple function of weight and distance and invariant with direction). Viewed from society's standpoint, any given size of output can be distributed with less average cost to consumers, and hence with less effort devoted to transportation, when under the above specified situation a non-circular market territory is transformed into a circular one through the substitution of transport inputs in one direction for transport inputs in another direction. Or alternatively (and again under our simple assumptions), given a fixed amount of labor and resources devoted to both production and transportation, the path toward maximum social output and consumption of goods involves the reshaping of a non-circular market area into a circular one through the substitution of transport inputs in one direction for transport inputs in another direction.

The introduction of a competitor, as already indicated, establishes another type of boundary line, a locus of points of equal delivered price. A boundary consisting of any other set of connected points implies, in our simplified model, a social inefficiency. If such a boundary exists, it becomes economic for certain consumers to shift their buying from one producer to another. In effect society is thereby substituting trans-

---

[6] Where p_1 and p_2 are the two factory prices and r_1 and r_2 the respective freight rates on the product, the competitive boundary is defined by the equation: $p_1 + r_1 s_1 = p_2 + r_2 s_2$ where s_1 and s_2 are the respective distances from the two factory locations to any given point on the boundary line. This equation can be expressed in the form: $s_1 - h s_2 = \pm k$, where $h = r_2/r_1$; $+k = (p_2 - p_1)/r_1$ when $(p_2 - p_1)/r_1 > 0$; and $-k = (p_2 - p_1)/r_1$ when $(p_2 - p_1)/r_1 < 0$. This equation describes a family of indifference curves which the Hysons have called *hypercircles* and which comprise half the family of Descartes' ovals. See C. D. and W. P. Hyson, *op. cit.*

port inputs on the product of one producer for transport inputs on the product of the second producer and should continue to do so until a boundary comprising points of equal delivered price is attained. At the same time society is also substituting production outlays by one producer for production outlays by the second producer.

Where conditions of constant cost prevail, the marginal rate of substitution of production outlays by one producer for production outlays by the second producer is also a constant. On the other hand, the transfer of consumers from one producer's market to that of the second, as the dividing boundary line is gradually shifted, entails a changing marginal rate of substitution between transport inputs of the two producers in serving consumers on the common boundary line.[7] It is through this changing marginal rate of substitution between transport inputs of the two producers that we reach the partial equilibrium situation defined by a locus of points where the difference in transport outlays of the two producers equals the difference in their production outlays. When conditions of constant cost do not prevail, it is through the changing marginal rates of substitution both between transport inputs and between production outlays that we attain the desired locus of points.

Hoover has aptly portrayed the competitive situation for two producers with the use of graphs.[8] In Fig. 27 let a producer be located at A. Consumers are posited to be arrayed along line AB. If the producer at A were to supply the needs of consumers at A only, his marginal costs would be AK. However, other consumers not at A may wish to purchase from the producer at A. If A's market area extends as far as L, his marginal costs, owing to economies of scale, fall to AJ, assuming that the factory price he charges is equal to marginal costs.[9] Adding transport cost to the consumers along the stretch AL yields a delivered price line JG whose vertical height at any point is the delivered price to the corresponding consumer along stretch AL. JG is also a transport gradient line since it indicates how transport cost on a unit of product rises as distance from A increases.[10]

---

[7] It is implicitly assumed that each producer charges the identical factory price to all consumers and that his factory price equals his unit production cost.

[8] Hoover, *op. cit.*, Chap. II, particularly Fig. 7.

[9] If the factory price is equal to average unit cost, the factory price would be higher, sales smaller, and marginal costs higher; also, the market area would be more limited if the consumer at L were just willing to pay a delivered price equal to AH(= GL).

[10] Hoover, *op. cit.*, pp. 8–11. Where irregularities in rate structure exist, these will be reflected in the transport gradient line.

The transport gradient line of Fig. 27 is constructed to portray a rate structure

If A's market area is now enlarged to reach as far as M, sales under marginal cost pricing correspond to that output at which marginal costs fall to AE. At this output marginal costs are at a minimum, and the derived delivered price (transport gradient) line is accordingly at its lowest level (where factory price is taken to equal marginal costs).[11]

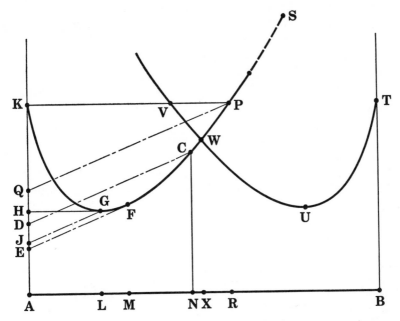

FIG. 27. Margin lines: two competitors.

For all other outputs, marginal costs (factory price) are higher and the delivered price line higher. For example, if A's market is enlarged to AN, marginal costs rise to AD, and the transport gradient line starts from point D and necessarily parallels EF at a higher level. The delivered price to the consumer at N is AD plus transport cost, or *in toto* CN.

If points G, F, and C are connected with other points, each of which by its vertical height represents for a given size market area the delivered price to the consumer on the boundary line, the curve $KGFCS$ is

---

proportional to weight and distance. If the rate structure is graduated and less than proportional to distance, the transport gradient from J would rise continuously but curve downward.

11 Obviously, under a different pricing system, sales would be of a different magnitude, and marginal costs would not be at a minimum when the edge of the producer's market is at M.

obtained; Hoover has designated this a *margin line*. It indicates how delivered price at the edge of the market varies with the geographic extent of the market. It is evident that the margin line changes in form as the basis of pricing at the factory changes.[12]

It is fruitful to point out that, in accordance with his market area theory, Lösch would maintain that the stretch of the margin line from K through G, F, and C to P corresponds to his natural market area when competition is absent and when the margin line is based upon factory prices which are equated to average unit costs.[13] Within this stretch, the economies of scale (including the advantages and disadvantages of specialization) outweigh the diseconomy of transport cost. In contrast, beyond point P, the economies of scale (which owing to rising marginal cost are less than KQ) fail to match transport costs (which exceed KQ). Consumers beyond R either produce for themselves or purchase from another producer.[14]

We may now introduce a second producer situated at B. If he confronts the same set of conditions as A—similar cost curves, types and spatial spread of consumers, transport rates—and if he, too, pursues an average cost pricing system (as is postulated for A in the preceding paragraph), his margin line for serving consumers along the stretch AB will be identical to A's. His margin line (TUV) intersects A's at

[12] Conceivably, the producer's marginal cost and average cost curves could be superimposed upon Fig. 27 if the pricing system and consumer demand curves were stipulated beforehand. Points on the horizontal axis would not only indicate distance from A but also quantity of output which would be purchased were the edge of the market at each point.

It is clear that if the pricing system is changed, the quantity purchased in each size of market area would also change; and correspondingly the shape and form of any marginal or average cost curve which might be superimposed on Fig. 27 would change. This would be so even though, in orthodox fashion, such a marginal or average cost curve is taken to be independent of price and a function of output only. Likewise, the margin line would shift since, for each size of market area, total output and hence marginal or average cost and the transport gradient starting point along the vertical axis would change (provided, of course, we retain the postulate that factory price is in some way related to costs).

If the margin line of Fig. 27 were based on a factory price equal to average cost rather than marginal cost, it would lie above the line $KGFCS$ in Fig. 27 in the initial stretch and would remain above it so long as marginal costs were below average costs. It would intersect this line were the edge of the market extended sufficiently to call forth an output at which marginal cost equals average cost. At this output the extent of the market would be identical under both a marginal cost and average cost pricing system.

[13] Though the margin line of Fig. 27 was constructed upon a marginal cost pricing system, we assume here and in the following discussion that it was constructed upon an average cost pricing system.

[14] Lösch, *op. cit.*, pp. 71–74.

W, which corresponds to point X on the straight line AB.[15] It may then be said that at X the delivered prices from the two producers are identical. Consumers to the left of X purchase from A because they bear less transport cost in the delivery of the product from A than from B. For a similar reason consumers to the right of X purchase from B.

Had B been located farther to the right so that the two margin lines would have intersected at a point to the right of P (rather than to the left), A and B would be non-competitive.[16] As already indicated, beyond P consumers in the Lösch scheme find it preferable to produce for themselves at a cost of AK rather than to purchase from A at a delivered price exceeding AK. Likewise, if any of these consumers are at the same time to the left of the new position of point V, they find it preferable to produce for themselves rather than to purchase from B. Hence, we would have had a situation (temporary in the Löschian scheme) where each producer was a monopolist within his own natural market area and where each unserved consumer lying between these two market areas produced for his own needs.[17]

We return to the situation depicted by Fig. 27 and to our substitution framework. As soon as B becomes effective as a producer, consumers along XR shift their purchasing from A to B. In doing so, they are substituting transport inputs on the product from B for transport inputs on the product from A. They are also substituting production outlays by B for production outlays by A. In this case, because of the symmetry assumptions, they are substituting lower production outlays by B for higher production outlays by A. In the more general situation, the marginal production outlays by B might be either smaller or greater than those by A. However, if they are greater, the transport inputs on product from A must exceed those on product from B to these consumers by a still greater amount if these consumers are to shift their purchasing allegiance.

In this analysis the transition from a market area which is a single straight line (as when in Lösch's scheme the y co-ordinate of every consumer's position takes the value of zero) to one which comprises any number of straight lines radiating in all directions from each of any set of focal points (where the x and y co-ordinates of consumers may take all values) is easily effected. Imagine A and B as two focal

[15] Given our assumptions, X is necessarily the mid-point of AB.

[16] Diagrammatically, V would be to the left of P (rather than to the right of P as in Fig. 27) and X would be to the left of R (rather than to the right of R in Fig. 27).

[17] In Fig. 27, AR would be A's market area; and beyond R to the edge of B's market area, consumers would be self-sufficient.

points lying on the x-axis. Radiating from each is a straight line at an angle α (less than 90°) from A and at an angle 180° $-\ \alpha$ from B. See Fig. 28. Again let Lösch's uniformity assumptions be adopted. If as a logical consequence A and B serve the same number and kinds of consumers in their respective market areas except for consumers along

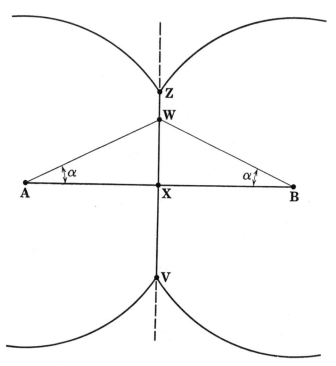

Fig. 28. The division of a spatial market: two competitors.

lines AW and BW, it also follows that B serves all the consumers along line BW and that A serves all the consumers along line AW, where $AW = BW$. For, if A were to serve a consumer on line BW (but not at W), A's delivery price to this consumer would be greater than B's.[18] Society would deem it desirable for this consumer to shift his allegiance from A to B, and thereby for him to substitute transport inputs on the product from B for transport inputs on the product from A and marginal production outlays at B for marginal production outlays at A, even though the latter might be somewhat smaller.

[18] Except perhaps in rare instances where the marginal cost curve behaves in unusual fashion.

For all values of α defined by the competitive stretch ZV (see Fig. 28) the same can be demonstrated. In short, the competitive boundary line between A and B is, as already indicated earlier in this chapter, a perpendicular bisector of the straight line connecting A and B and is a locus of points equidistant from A and B.[19] If we follow Lösch and permit complete freedom of entry and exit for many producers and impose the restraint that all consumers be served by at least one producer, we obtain boundary lines which must divide large regions into identical and regularly shaped market areas in order to be consistent with our uniformity assumptions. Only equilateral triangles, squares, and regular hexagons satisfy these requirements. And Lösch has demonstrated algebraically that the division of any large region into regular hexagonal market areas is more efficient than a division into either equilateral triangular or square market areas.[20] Put in another way, it is efficient for society to substitute among various sets of transport inputs and marginal production outlays in order to proceed to a pattern of regular hexagons from any other pattern of regularly or irregularly shaped market areas.[21]

Hence the Lösch scheme of a net of regularly shaped hexagons is a logical outgrowth of the simple Fetter-Launhardt approach when additional assumptions and restraints are introduced. As a consequence, too, it can be described in terms of simple substitution relations.

When it is additionally assumed that the production, sales, and price of any commodity are independent of the production, sales, and price of any other, and when it is recognized that differences among commodities in applicable transport rates and economies of scale will cause different sizes of regular hexagons to characterize the market areas of various commodities, a system of nets of hexagonal market areas similar to Lösch's becomes a logical derivation. (For example, see Fig. 51 in Chap. 11.) However, it does not seem fruitful for one to pursue analysis on a multicommodity basis at this level of extreme simplification. He would need to relax the assumption of the independence of the production, sales, and prices of the several commodities. In addition to economies of scale he would need to recognize other economies of agglomeration, whether they be localization, urbanization, or other forms of juxtaposition economies. He would need to eliminate among others the inconsistency between the set of uniformity assumptions, particularly with reference to population

[19] For additional details see Hoover, *Location Theory* . . . , *op. cit.*, Chaps. 2 and 3.

[20] Lösch, *op. cit.*, pp. 76–78.

[21] For a more rigorous demonstration, see Chap. 10, Sect. 4.

distribution, and the hierarchical pattern of concentrations of economic activities which results from the superimposition upon one another of nets of hexagonal market areas. This is especially so when they are ordered around a common core as Lösch is inclined to do. If one were to overcome these several obstacles, the Lösch multicommodity framework embodied in a system of nets of market areas would be a logical point of departure for the pursuit of regional analysis. Since the assumptions of the Lösch framework have most relevance to service activities (where the pull of raw materials tends to be minor) and least relevance to basic industry oriented wholly or partially to localized raw materials, the Lösch approach is most pertinent for the study of highly urbanized regions in which service activities dominate the economic structure.

2. Supply (Purchasing) Area Analysis[22]

The previous section posited that raw materials were essentially ubiquitous, available at every potential factory site at the same cost. As already intimated, this assumption cannot be tolerated for the case of wholly or partially resource-oriented industry. We must consider the theoretical significance of quantitative and qualitative inequalities in the spatial distribution of raw material deposits.

It is clear that when there are many scattered factories (manufacturers) to be served by relatively few sources of a raw material, the analysis of the preceding section applies. Each of the many factories (manufacturers) can be viewed as a consumer of the raw material, and each of the raw material sources as a production point. The problem is to define boundary lines which delineate the market area composed of industrial consumers to be served by each producing raw material source, where different extraction or production costs may obtain at the several raw material sources.[23] For example, in Fig. 46 of Chap. 11 assumed conditions lead to an hyperbolic boundary line dividing the market areas of M_1 and M_1', two sources of a first raw material, and to a straight line boundary line separating the market areas of M_2 and M_2', two sources of a second raw material.

---

[22] The term supply area or purchasing area is used here to indicate the geographic area from which a raw material is furnished to a producer. It normally consists of many sites which produce the raw material. It does *not* refer to the geographic area of consumers whose purchases of a given commodity are supplied by a specified factory. This latter area has already been designated a market area.

[23] This is the case for which Hoover initially develops his *margin line* concept. Points A and B of Fig. 27 are sites of an extractive activity. Line AB represents a locus of possible consumers, industrial or household. (Hoover, *op. cit.*, pp. 11–16.)

The case is different when each industrial consumer must procure his raw material requirements from many sources. Here, one may assert, we have market area analysis in reverse. And as with market areas, analysis of supply areas is facilitated when we proceed from the simple to the more complex situations.

Imagine an industrial consumer who does not confront competition in procuring his raw material from many potential sources of supply. If these sources are uniformly scattered in a plain, if each can yield the raw material at the same constant unit cost, and if no single source can furnish the full amount of the raw material demanded at a price which is equal to unit cost, the industrial consumer's supply area will tend to be circular.[24] Since the delivered price of the marginal unit of raw material procured rises as the radius of the supply area increases, the supply area is limited by the condition that the delivered price be consistent from a profit standpoint with the price at which the marginal unit of output can be marketed.[25]

Even in the more realistic case where increasing costs are encountered in supplying the raw material, the industrial consumer's supply area tends to be circular. The delivered price to the industrial consumer of the marginal unit from each source of raw material supply utilized will be the same. The difference in marginal costs for any two sources will equal the difference in the unit transport costs borne by these two sources. And, consequently, intensity in the utilization of any source of raw material will fall off with increasing distance from the point of industrial consumption. These latter conditions are also fulfilled when the industrial consumer can be served by only a relatively few sources.[26] Needless to say, if these conditions are

24 The supply area reduces to a point when each source can furnish the full amount of raw material demanded.

25 The industrial consumer procures the maximum possible quantity of raw material from any given source before purchasing from another, more distant source. Hence, each source lying within the circular supply area tends to be fully exploited and to generate locational rent.

26 When there are only a relatively few sources each of which operates under different cost conditions, we can graphically depict the situation with a modified Hoover-type diagram. In Fig. 29 point T is a site of industrial consumption. Points A, B, and C are raw material sources which need not be along a straight line from T but which are, respectively, AT, BT, and CT distance from T. At raw material source A, curve aa is a traditional supply curve representing the different quantities of the raw material which would be forthcoming at A at different net prices, where net price is measured along a vertical line passing through A parallel to TL and where quantity is measured along AT. At raw material source B, the corresponding supply curve is bb, where net price is measured along a vertical line passing through B parallel to TL and where quantity is measured along line BT. At raw material source C, the corresponding supply curve is cc.

Since transport costs are incurred in moving the raw material to point T, the price at T necessary to elicit the production of any quantity of raw material at A, B, or C must exceed the corresponding price at A, B, or C by an amount equal to the cost of shipping a unit from A, B, or C. In the above figure the dash-dot transport gradient lines are constructed to indicate transport costs on a unit of raw material from sources A, B, and C to T. Hence, to the industrial consumer at T, the supply curve aa appears as $a'a'$; the price at $a'a'$ associated with any given quantity of raw material exceeds the corresponding price at aa by an amount equal to transport costs which are represented by the vertical rise in the corre-

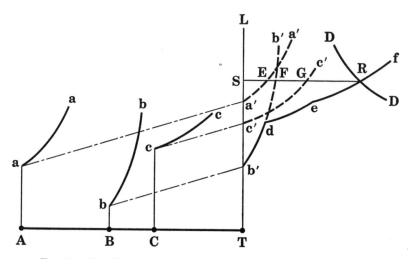

FIG. 29. The division of a market among several supply points.

sponding dash-dot transport gradient line. Likewise, to the industrial consumer at T, bb appears as $b'b'$ and cc as $c'c'$. Since for any price established at T the several quantities available from the three raw material sources are additive, we obtain at T the aggregate supply curve $b'def$. If the industrial consumer's derived demand curve for the raw material is DD, the equilibrium price and aggregate quantity are TS and SR, respectively. A, B, and C furnish respectively SE, SF, and SG quantities of the raw material ($SR = SE + SF + SG$).

With this diagram it can be easily demonstrated how shifts of demand, different transport rates, increases and decreases in transport tariffs, and changes in other elements affect the quantities produced at, and commodity flows stemming from, each raw material source.

This type of diagram can also be employed when one raw material source or producer, say at T, serves several industrial or household consumers, say at A, B, and C. At A, B, and C one constructs the respective demand curves for the raw material or commodity produced at T. Each of these demand curves can be transformed into an effective demand curve at T through depressing its vertical level by an amount equivalent to the cost of shipping the raw material or commodity from T to the corresponding point of consumption. In this case, the dash-dot transport gradient lines are downward sloping. At point T one can

not met (or if circularity of supply area is not realized in a continuous potential supply area),[27] both society and the industrial consumer will find it desirable to substitute among the various transport inputs and among the various marginal production outlays associated with the several or many sources until these conditions are fulfilled (or circularity attained).

Where the industrial consumer confronts competition from other industrial consumers in purchasing his raw materials, the boundary lines separating the supply areas of the several industrial consumers tend to be straight lines, given the Lösch type of uniformity assumptions. In contrast, when transport rates on raw material are differentiated according to the point of termination, or when prices paid at these points of termination by the several industrial producers differ, or both, boundary lines take the general form of hypercircles, which in special instances degenerate into circles, hyperbolas, and, as already discussed, straight lines.[28]

If these types of boundary lines do not obtain in the situations alluded to, once again it becomes economically feasible for society to shift raw material sources from the supply hinterland of one industrial consumer to the supply hinterland of another, and thereby to substitute among the relevant transport inputs and among the relevant marginal production outlays. It is not necessary to develop this point in detail and with the use of figures. The reasoning and graphic analysis of the preceding section, appropriately refashioned, apply here.

---

construct an aggregate demand curve by adding together horizontalwise the several *reduced* demand curves. One can also construct a supply curve and proceed in traditional fashion to determine the equilibrium price and quantity and the apportionment of the total equilibrium quantity among the several consumers. Again, one can easily demonstrate how a shift of the supply curve, different transport rates, and changes in tariff structure can affect the realized pattern of consumption and commodity flows from T.

In the situation where both consumers and producers are at different distances from a point T to which all output is transported for sale and from which deliveries to consumers are made, we can construct both the aggregate demand curve and the aggregate supply curve which obtain at T. Proceeding as above, we can determine market price at T, net price to each producer, delivered price to each consumer, the distribution of output among consumers, the allocation of sales among producers, and commodity flows to and from T.

[27] Where a continuous potential supply area encompasses subsections in which extraction costs differ, the circularity restriction must be relaxed. Also, where different transport rates apply in different directions, circularity must be expressed in terms of economic distance and not physical distance.

[28] Hyson, *op. cit.*

In a pure abstract sense one could even proceed to the analysis of systems of supply areas in a way analogous to the manner in which Lösch molds systems of market areas. But in reality, physical space restrictions essentially preclude this. It is possible to associate with any particular point a consumer who purchases a number of products and accordingly is served by a number of producers. However, for the most part it is not physically possible to associate with any particular point the production of more than one raw material or type of raw material mix. This fact raises the vital problem of competition in the use of land and logically leads to the Thünen type of agricultural location theory and to land rent analysis, which will be discussed later. Furthermore, many raw materials such as coal and bauxite are highly localized. In these cases the Weberian framework, as already discussed in Chap. 5 and as extended in later chapters, is particularly applicable rather than a Löschian system of areas.

3. Some Remarks on Spatial Pricing Systems and Competitive Locational Equilibrium

Hitherto we have avoided discussion of spatial pricing systems and competition. For the most part we have assumed that either (1) the firm establishes a price at the factory on the basis of cost or some other objectively given consideration; or (2) the firm has a negligible influence upon a ruling market price and accepts it as a datum. This latter situation obtains where a small firm and a large number of competitors are concentrated at one point, which is mostly a theoretical possibility, or where competitors' markets are concentrated at a point, as is the case with groups of farmers. In any case, our firm has not been concerned with the reactions of competitors.

Lösch has demonstrated that for the more usual case in the space-economy of reality the above assumptions are invalid. Even in the pure situation, where there are many independent producers with complete freedom of entry and exit, with complete knowledge on technology and markets, and with equal access to inputs, each firm has at least from the standpoint of classical economics a limited control over the market price it realizes. Because of the spatial spread of consumers and producers characteristic of reality, the demand curve for the individual firm's product, save for exceptional instances, is not a horizontal line of infinite elasticity at the price determined by the intersection of the demand and supply curves for the industry, as it is under the traditional pure competition. Rather, the friction of distance imparts to each producer a limited monopolistic position with regard to consumers closer to him transportation-wise than to other producers. The demand curve for the firm's product, as Lösch has neatly portrayed,[29] has a negative slope. We should therefore pursue locational analysis on the second of the four levels discussed in the early part of Chap. 5.

If reactions by competitors can be ignored, we may view the firm as weighing, for each possible location, the net revenue potentials from different possible sets of prices and outputs on the one hand and the related sets of outlays on transport and other inputs on the other. For each possible location the firm selects that price (or an array of prices in the case of price discrimination) which, in view of its estimate of the aggregate demand curve for its product (or of each individual consumer's demand curve), yields maximum net revenue. Since the firm is in a position to control prices at least to a limited extent and does tend to associate different prices with different outputs, its relevant price-ratio and iso-revenue-less-outlay lines are no longer straight as in Fig. 24 of Chap. 5 and Fig. 26 of Chap. 6. Rather they become convex and concave curves or sets of points.[30] Nonetheless, the firm's calculations can be set forth and expressed in terms of equilibrium conditions.

Having determined for each possible location the maximum net revenue, the firm selects among locations. In choosing one rather than another, the firm substitutes among potential revenues, outlays, and transport inputs. The conditions of locational equilibrium, which are satisfied by the location yielding the greatest net revenue of all, can be stated in formal terms (if the reader so desires) with the use of transformation lines, outlay-substitution lines, revenue-outlay substitution lines, price-ratio lines, iso-outlay lines, iso-revenue lines, and iso-revenue-less-outlay lines.[31]

[29] Lösch, *op. cit.*, pp. 70–74. Lösch calculates for a given factory price the amount which will be taken by each consumer along a straight line from the factory. At a lower (higher) price each consumer will take more (less), and the extent of the firm's market will be lengthened (shortened) to include more (fewer) consumers, whether or not at the expense of competitors. Hence, the aggregate demand curve for the firm's product with reference to consumers along the line is negatively sloping. Deriving the demand curve with reference to consumers along every other line which can radiate from the factory site and summing yields the total demand curve for the firm's product in the entire spatial market area. This, too, will be negatively sloping, whether or not we follow Lösch in postulating an even spatial spread of consumers of like tastes and income, a homogeneous transport network, absence of competition, etc.

[30] Each pair of consecutive points may be connected by a straight line. The resulting straight lines would have a different slope.

[31] It is implicitly assumed that the firm's operations have only a negligible effect

Once we admit the essential reality of a firm's ability to influence prices, we are logically compelled to recognize that price changes by one firm frequently provoke retaliatory measures by other firms. A firm then, in seeking to maximize its profits and to locate at the most desirable site, in many instances must take cognizance of the possible reactions of other firms, and must select its location, set its price, and determine its output after considering not only the direct consequences but also the possible indirect repercussions from the reactions of other firms. Unfortunately, our theoretical schemata for understanding the complex oligopolistic situations of reality, despite recent major advances scored by the theory of games and related studies, are rather inadequate, particularly as they pertain to locational equilibrium. We still have not developed what might be considered a pattern of rational behavior on the part of the firm in response to possible reactions of other firms, their indirect repercussions, and the many uncertainties which becloud the problem. Nonetheless, it is of value to have in mind some of the more important methodology and achievements of those who have struggled with this problem in its locational aspects. This allows a more comprehensive perspective of the space-economy of reality and a finer appreciation of the magnitude of the assignment.

We have already noted several times that Launhardt presented the earliest systematic treatment of the division of a market area among competing firms. However, in his analysis, the spatial co-ordinates of the firm were given; only variations in output and prices were considered. Fetter's attention likewise centered on firms having fixed locations; and Engländer did not explicitly analyze the combined effects of variations in both price and location in expounding his doctrine of the "local conditionality of demand and supply."[32] Hotelling was the first to allow price and location to vary simultaneously. He used a simple case primarily designed to elucidate

---

upon the local and regional income stream. Where regional income is influenced significantly by a firm's location, as in the case of the Fairless Steelworks and the Delaware River economy, then forces are generated which in turn affect price and output of the firm, as well as the prices of various other inputs such as labor, power, and transport. These indirect and cumulative effects are, at least in the traditional economic sense, beyond the pale of individual firm analysis and are judiciously relegated to the category of regional analysis. They clearly point up the close interrelation between firm and regional analysis.

[32] "Kritisches und Positives . . . ,"*op. cit.* A general, though incomplete, mathematical formulation of the problem of price policy for two or more spatially fixed competitors is given by E. Schneider, "Observations on a Theory of Space Economy," *Econometrica*, Vol. 3 (1935), pp. 79–105.

the imperfect competitive conditions of reality.[33] Palander has justly christened the following as the Launhardt-Hotelling problem.

Hotelling's simplification pictures two firms each producing a given quantity of a commodity under constant cost conditions and each competing for a market stretched along a line of length l. Corresponding to each unit length of line, one unit quantity of commodity is consumed during each unit of time. The demand from each unit of the line is infinitely inelastic. Customers' purchases are influenced only by price—factory price plus transport cost; customers are indifferent to all other circumstances surrounding the act of selling. Firms A and B are located at distances a and b from their respective ends of the line and at distances x and y respectively from a point at which the delivered prices from A and B are the same. First, Hotelling determines the set of equilibrium factory prices for A and B in terms of a, b, l, and c (the cost of transport per unit quantity, per unit distance) where costs of production are zero, assuming that neither producer attempts to drive the other out of the market by undercutting. He comes to consider the case, among others, where producer A is spatially immobilized and producer B is free to locate wherever he wishes. B proceeds on the assumption that A will not change his price in reaction to B's price or location, that is, that A trades autonomously. B therefore finds it profitable to locate as close to A as other conditions permit, on the side of A facing the more extensive market.[34] This solution of Hotelling's is also borne out by Zeuthen's graphic analysis.[35]

Both Hotelling and Zeuthen consider another type of price policy. Instead of sharing the market under the best possible terms, competitors can aim to eliminate one another by undercutting. This course of action becomes the more likely the closer the two competitors are to each other.[36] B realizes maximum profits, given A's price, when he sets his price so that his own delivered price will be

[33] H. Hotelling, "Stability in Competition," *Economic Journal,* Vol. 39 (March 1929), pp. 41–57.

[34] If B were approaching A on the short side of the market stretch, a position as close as possible to A on the short side would not represent a maximum nor a stable location. B would find it profitable to skip over A, as it were, and locate as close as possible on the other side.

[35] F. Zeuthen, "Theoretical Remarks on Price Policy: Hotelling's Case with Variations," *Quarterly Journal of Economics,* Vol. 47, pp. 231–53.

[36] Where the two firms come to be and remain fixed at locations infinitesimally close, we have a problem similar to the traditional one treated by Cournot, Amoroso, Edgeworth, and others, i.e., of two firms producing like products and located at a one-point market center.

just below A's delivered price at all points in A's hinterland when the quantity he offers corresponds to the total market demand.[37]

Where both firms are free to move, each adopting a policy of sharing the market, and where also the same given factory price is charged by each, we have a stable solution. Both firms locate at the center of the market line or, more rigorously, one at the center, the other adjacent to the first on either side.[38] For, if either firm were to serve a shorter stretch (that is, one noticeably less than one-half of the market) with factory prices given and equal and the other assumptions still valid, that firm could improve its situation by skipping over to the other side of its competitor, and thus usurping the larger market stretch. Where three or more firms serve the market line, each spatially mobile, then under the above simplified postulates Chamberlin reasons that there will not be a tendency for concentration at the market center, as Hotelling implies. Rather there will be a dispersion, the dispersion being least when sellers are grouped in pairs:

> Taking the length of the line as unity, the general conclusion for n sellers is that the space between the last sellers at either end and the ends of the line would never exceed $1/n$ (if the number of sellers is odd it can never exceed $\dfrac{1}{n+1}$), and that the space between any two sellers can never exceed $2/n$, this limit being reached only in the extreme case where sellers are grouped by twos.[39]

Anyone entering the market or any firm considering a new site, operating under the assumption that the positions of all of its competitors are fixed, will locate either adjacent to that firm which services the longest market stretch on one of its sides or, in certain likely circumstances, at a point on the longest stretch between any two consecutively placed competitors.

Palander, eschewing certain of Hotelling's, Zeuthen's, and Chamberlin's assumptions, penetrates still further this problem of spatial competition. First, he shows that Hotelling's basic solution for two firms trading autonomously is not generally valid. A stable equilibrium is reached only where the two firms are far apart and have small hinterlands. Otherwise, a constant fluctuation of price takes place within

---

[37] Apropos the applicability of conclusions relevant for a market of fixed linear extent to a market of unlimited areal character, refer to Lösch (*op. cit.*, 1st ed., 1940, pp. 12–14).

[38] See E. Chamberlin, *The Theory of Monopolistic Competition*, Cambridge, Mass., 1938, 3rd ed., Appendix C.

[39] *Ibid.*, p. 209.

limits, and price may even be cut to the level of costs (constant) if the firms lie very close to each other. The solution for two firms where one is free to locate is thus inherently unstable.[40]

Second, Palander generalizes the problem to apply when firm B, in selecting a new location, can choose (1) to eliminate its competitor from the market by undercutting; (2) to share the intermediate market with its competitor; or (3) by raising its price, to confine its sales to consumers in its own hinterland, that is, to adopt a policy of hinterland defense. Where B trades autonomously, as A does, then B adopts either (1) a policy of eliminating A from the market in which case he locates right next to A and slightly undercuts A's price; or (2) a policy of hinterland defense, in which case he may locate adjacent to A, or as far away as the mid-point on the largest market stretch—this depending upon A's price and location.[41] In these circumstances, B would never find it advantageous to share the intermediate market with A. Where B trades "superpolitisch," i.e., is aware of A's path of reaction to his (B's) choice of location and price, he will pursue a different but determinate course. He will locate relatively far away from A. Where both A and B trade superpolitisch, there results an express tendency for deglomeration.

Lerner and Singer,[42] somewhat more realistic, set an upper limit to the price which each buyer is willing to pay for one unit of the commodity (that is, limit the stretch of infinite inelasticity on the demand curve of each consumer);[43] and they have suggested analytic methods for the case where a demand with some elasticity is postulated for each consumer. As a consequence their conclusions at times differ significantly from those of the above authors. To a certain extent, too, they examine more comprehensively the range of conditions, patterns of

---

[40] Palander, *op. cit.*, Chap. IX, especially p. 248. Furthermore, Palander finds a logical inconsistency at the base of Hotelling's agglomeration tendency. Hotelling postulates that firm B trades autonomously with respect to price (assumes that A's price will not change) yet, in selecting the most desirable location, somehow comes to possess knowledge of the final equilibrium price that should result from mutual price adaptations by A and B (*ibid.*, p. 251).

[41] When A's price is relatively high and his position relatively near the center of the market, B will tend to eliminate A from the market. When A's price is relatively low and he lies relatively near one of the ends of the market line, B will tend to locate at some distance from A and set a price so high that he will just be able to retain the consumers lying in his own hinterland. (*Ibid.*, pp. 391–93.)

[42] A. P. Lerner and H. W. Singer, "Some Notes on Duopoly and Spatial Competition," *Journal of Political Economy*, Vol. 45 (1937), pp. 145–86.

[43] See also in this connection, A. Robinson, "A Problem in the Theory of Industrial Location," *Economic Journal*, Vol. 51 (June–Sept. 1941), pp. 270–75.

reaction, and possible solutions that are inherent within the problem. For example, they consider an alternative to the short-sighted policy where two mobile competitors undercut each other, being primarily concerned with short-run gains. Each producer assumes that his competitor will not respond to the sort of encroachment where the former shifts location—so long as his encroachment is limited to one-half of his competitor's customers—but that his competitor will, on the other hand, reciprocate undercutting of price with undercutting. This assumption yields the result that A and B may be located adjacent to one another or at various distances apart, depending upon transport cost, size of market, and the upper limit to price.[44]

Smithies[45] has gone farther and discarded the postulate of an inelastic demand for each consumer. He examines the case where identical linear demand functions exist at every point on the linear market and accordingly arrives at solutions different from those deduced by others. For example, the solution to the full competition case where both firms are mobile and each assumes, in any move, that the other's price and location are given, is not that one which follows Hotelling's line of reasoning. It does not conclude with the two firms adjacent—a solution which others have suggested when special conditions obtain. Instead, the two firms remain apart although less than half the linear market separates them. This is so because each producer is compelled to weigh the gains from further encroachment upon his competitor as he moves closer to the market center against the loss of consumer patronage in his own hinterland from greater freight charges.[46]

[44] In addition, Lerner and Singer have treated the question of spatial price discrimination in some detail, a question which Hotelling, Zeuthen, and Palander had already recognized to different extents. Hoover, too, has made a number of astute observations on the problem (E. M. Hoover, Jr., "Spatial Price Discrimination," *The Review of Economic Studies*, Vol. IV, No. 3, pp. 182–91). Others, such as A. Smithies ["Monopolistic Price Policy in a Spatial Market," *Econometrica*, Vol. 9 (1941), pp. 63–73], E. Schneider, in several articles, and H. Möller ["Grundlagen einer Theorie der regionalen Preisdifferenzierung," *Weltwirtschaftliches Archiv*, Bd. 58 (1943), pp. 335–90] have been concerned with the question either in a monopolistic or oligopolistic setting.

Price discrimination, which tends to be most expedient within spatial markets where distance and other geographic obstacles enable the producer to deal separately with the various sectors of his market, offers to the individual firm opportunities for additional profits. Obviously as one proceeds from a monopolistic to an oligopolistic situation, these opportunities become limited, the more so as the number of competitors increases and their locations draw nearer to that of the given firm.

[45] A. Smithies, "Optimum Location in Spatial Competition," *Journal of Political Economy*, Vol. 44 (June 1941), pp. 423–39.

[46] Smithies has also considered a more generalized set of conjectural hypotheses

Ackley[47] examines still more realistic market conditions in spatial competition. He analyzes a number of cases where there is a discontinuous distribution of customers with different demand functions, that is, cases of spatially discrete demand where the quantity sold by either seller is a discontinuous function of his own and his rival's prices and locations. He shows clearly that no precise generalized solutions emerge, even when rigid assumptions are made as to competitor's behavior. The solution of each specific discrete case needs to be worked out anew under various assumptions regarding competitor's reactions. Often the very type of market discontinuity conditions the type of assumption sellers make as to their competitor's conduct. In striving for maximum profits the sellers do not necessarily confront any less determinate or more unstable situations than where a continuous spatial market exists.[48]

Finally, we should mention a generalized approach being developed in connection with game theory, an analytical advance which has received its initial and principal stimulus from the work of von Neumann and Morgenstern.[49] Game theory pertains to situations

---

for each competitor. In addition to the full competition case cited, he examines the cases where (1) "Each competitor in making an adjustment assumes that his rival will set a price equal to his own and will adopt a location symmetrical with his own" (*ibid.*, p. 427), and (2) "each competitor assumes that his rival will have the same price reactions as above but will keep his location unchanged" (*ibid.*, p. 427). The case where each firm assumes that his competitor will not react, if he (the competitor) is cut out of the market entirely by his rival, is discarded as fantastic.

In addition, Smithies investigates somewhat the effect upon the final equilibrium relationship of changes in marginal cost of one or both firms.

47 G. Ackley, "Spatial Competition in a Discontinuous Market," *Quarterly Journal of Economics*, Vol. 56 (February 1942), pp. 212–30.

48 Möller (*op. cit.*), following H. von Stackelberg's approach, discusses at length the problem of stability of equilibrium under various regional competitive and price-setting situations.

49 J. von Neumann and O. Morgenstern, *Theory of Games and Economic Behavior*, Princeton, 1944. Also refer to the excellent and somewhat complementary expository reviews: J. Marschak, "Neumann's and Morgenstern's New Approach to Static Economics," *The Journal of Political Economy*, Vol. LIV (April 1946), pp. 97–115; L. Hurwicz, "The Theory of Economic Behavior," *The American Economic Review*, Vol. XXXV (December 1945), pp. 909–925; and C. Kaysen, "A Revolution in Economic Theory," *Review of Economic Studies*, Vol. XIV, No. 35 (1946–47), pp. 1–15. A recent survey of game theory is contained in R. Duncan Luce and Howard Raiffa, *A Survey of the Theory of Games*, Behavioral Models Project, Columbia University, 1954, hectographed. Also see John Nash, "Two-Person Cooperative Games" and J. P. Mayberry, J. F. Nash, and M. Shubik, "A Comparison of Treatments of a Duopoly Situation," *Econometrica*, Vol. 21 (January 1953), pp. 128–40 and 141–54, respectively.

of interest conflict; it has relevance to the above locational equilibrium problem where a firm, either individually or in collusion with others, competes with other firms or coalitions of firms in serving a given consumer market.

Basic to game theory in its current form are certain postulates. It is posited that the variables within a given situation are well specified and that the values which they may take and the possible outcomes of the situation can be precisely characterized. (In our spatial equilibrium problem the behavior of competitors need not be postulated as invariant, or as varying within certain limits, but can be considered an unrestricted variable.) Individuals are assumed to be completely informed about the physical characteristics of the given situation and to be "able to perform all the statistical, mathematical, etc. operations which this knowledge makes possible."[50] Further, they are able, either directly or indirectly, to assign to each possible outcome a numerical utility, for all practical purposes a money value, which in coalition activity must be transferable.

Assuming that each individual (producer) desires to maximize utility (gains), von Neumann and Morgenstern define rational behavior of an individual as the choice of that strategy which permits him the best of all possible minima, that is, the maximum of the minima. This follows since he knows that his competitors (viewed as a coalition if we wish to consider the individual competitor alone) in attempting to maximize their gains will minimize his own. On the other hand, the coalition of competitors, knowing that its rival will tend to maximize his gains, will pursue a strategy which permits its rival the least of all maxima, that is, the minimum of the maxima. When both parties pursue their respective policies simultaneously, it is conceivable that a relatively simple stable solution will be arrived at; it would be a "saddle-point" solution where the maximum of the minima coincides with the minimum of the maxima. In the usual case a saddle-point will not exist. However, the authors have abstractly demonstrated that when each party pursues a course of "mixed strategies," that is, chooses several strategies and assigns definite probabilities to each, then a solution will always exist. The competitive struggle between an individual firm and a coalition of rivals can thus be resolved. By a similar reasoning process the individual competitor may find it profitable to ally himself with others and be part of a coalition.

---

[50] Neumann and Morgenstern, *op. cit.*, p. 30. This assumption does not specify "perfect information" on the part of all competitors. The rules of the game "may explicitly prescribe that certain participants should not possess certain pieces of information" (p. 30 note).

In addition to confronting the conceptual complications of collusive action and the tremendous problem of empirical verification in a situation where the variety and complexity of solutions are overwhelming, game theorists do labor under some very unrealistic assumptions. It is difficult to accept the assigning of complex probabilities to various courses of action as characteristic of man's behavior in the competitive struggle. It is perhaps even more difficult to accept the assumption of complete knowledge in a very involved situation when experience teaches us that any human being is far more restricted in his perceptions. Moreover, empirical studies do show a great variation in individual abilities which runs counter to von Neumann's and Morgenstern's condition that all rivals are equally capable of drawing inferences from given amounts of information.[51] (Nor does the usual businessman concede the point that his competitors are his equal. Rather, it is an everyday observation that businessmen strive to outwit their competitors, being convinced of their own superiority.) Lastly, in a spatial competition setting, von Neumann and Morgenstern's approach would overemphasize the dependence of any individual's choice of strategy upon his competitors' reactions. In a social exchange economy, geographic separation of rivals acts as insulation from reactions and in many instances simplifies the problem of maximization.

Despite these difficulties and shortcomings, the contributions in the area of game theory represent an initial major achievement. As game theory develops it will undoubtedly cast considerable light upon a host of basic problems as well as the locational equilibrium problem.[52]

[51] However, J. Marschak (*op. cit.*), after presenting some simple illustrations, concludes: "it seems to us that properly stated differences in degrees of knowledge or intelligence of individual players can also be regarded as rules of the game" (p. 106).

[52] Allied to the locational equilibrium problem of this section are the contributions of S. Enke ["Equilibrium among Spatially Separated Markets: Solution by Electric Analogue," *Econometrica*, Vol. 19 (January 1951), pp. 40–47], P. Samuelson ["Spatial Price Equilibrium and Linear Programming," *American Economic Review*, Vol. XLII (June 1952), pp. 283–303], M. Beckmann ["A Continuous Model of Transportation," *Econometrica*, Vol. 20 (October 1952), pp. 643–660, and "The Partial Equilibrium of a Continuous Spatial Market," *Weltwirtschaftliches Archiv*, Bd. 71 (1953), Heft 1, pp. 73–89], K. A. Fox ["A Spatial Equilibrium Model of the Livestock-Feed Economy in the United States," *Econometrica*, Vol. 21 (October 1953), pp. 547–566], and others on spatial price equilibrium, especially as related to transportation flow patterns.

In one of its simplest forms Enke poses the problem as follows:

"There are three regions trading a homogeneous good. Each region constitutes a single and distinct market. The regions of each possible pair of regions are separated—but not isolated—by a transportation cost per physical unit which is independent of volume. There are no legal restrictions to limit the actions of the profit-seeking traders in each region. For each region the functions which relate local production and local use to local price are known, and consequently the magnitude of the difference which will be exported or imported at each local price is also known. Given these trade functions and transportation costs, we wish to ascertain:

(1) the net price in each region,
(2) the quantity of exports or imports for each region,
(3) which regions export, import, or do neither,
(4) the aggregate trade in the commodity,
(5) the volume and direction of trade between each possible pair of regions
. . . " (*op. cit.*, p. 41).

Viewed in this way the problem is essentially a transportation problem and not a basic location problem. Enke demonstrates how an electric analog can be employed to derive a solution to this problem.

As Samuelson has shown, the Enke problem contains within it the following Koopmans-Hitchcock minimum transport cost problem: "A specified total number of (empty or ballast) ships is to be sent out from each of a number of ports. They are to be allocated among a number of other receiving ports, with the total sent in to each such port being specified. If we are given the unit costs of shipment between every two ports, how can we minimize the total costs of the program?" [Samuelson, *op. cit.*, p. 284. For full discussion of this problem see T. C. Koopmans, "Optimum Utilization of the Transportation System," *Econometrica,* Vol. 17, Supplement (July 1949), pp. 136–146; and T. C. Koopmans and S. Reiter, "A Model of Transportation," Chap. XIV in *Activity Analysis of Production and Allocation,* ed. by T. C. Koopmans, John Wiley & Sons, Inc., 1951.] It should also be noted that the Enke problem contains within it a bit of the location problem. For the Enke problem determines the scale of output in each given region (the Koopmans-Hitchcock problem implicitly assumes that the scale is given).

Enke has not confined himself to only three regions. His analog solution is proposed as applicable to a problem embracing many regions. Samuelson has also probed the many-region problem, and Beckmann has gone even further and considered the case of "continuous geographical intensity distributions of production," i.e., where every infinitesimally small area in an economy which can consist of many regions both produces and consumes a commodity.

If excess supply functions could be derived for each infinitesimally small area of the world and if the Samuelson-Beckmann formulation could be considered relevant and adequate and could yield a quantitative solution, then the location problem would be solved. Corresponding to each infinitesimally small area, there would be a unique scale of output (zero or positive amount of production), such as Enke obtains for each region in his more limited model. We would have our geographic distribution of production. Theoretically, both the location and transportation patterns would have been derived simultaneously.

In practice, however, the Samuelson-Beckmann formulation ignores a number of basic locational forces, as Beckmann fully recognizes, and more important is not now able, and is not likely in the future to be able, to yield a quantitative solution for every infinitesimally small area. It is at this juncture that location theory makes its contribution. For location theory seeks principles to narrow down, and greatly narrow down, the number of points to be considered as potential locations for the production of any given commodity. Once a relatively small number of production points or regions are isolated, the Enke-Samuelson-Beck-

4. CONCLUDING REMARKS

In bringing this chapter to a close we should fully appreciate the progress which still needs to be achieved to understand rational behavior for the individual firm, even under simplified cost assumptions. When more realistic cost conditions are introduced, when geographic mobility of the firm is permitted not only along a line as in most of the discussion of the preceding section but also within a geographic area, and when the uneven areal distribution of consumer demand is recognized and different pricing policies are allowed, still greater progress is required.

From the standpoint of enabling one to reach precise results, the market and supply area analyses discussed in the first two sections of this chapter are more satisfactory than the locational equilibrium analysis following Hotelling's approach, even when the latter is supplemented by game theory. Market and supply area analyses achieve these more precise results through postulating a relatively simple problem and through abstracting from, among other factors, competitors' reactions, pricing policy as a variable, and for the most part locational mobility.

In contrast, the locational equilibrium approach stemming from Hotelling's work is much more sophisticated in its consideration of reactions and mobility. However, this approach yields results only within a very restrictive framework. It almost completely ignores the cost side of the picture and the inequalities in the spatial distribution of natural and human resources. Apart from the fact that entrepreneurial ability and organization and scale of output may vary from firm to firm and thus cause each firm to face a different cost situation, which in turn affects each one's competitive policy, it is generally true that production and distribution costs will not be the same for all sites. Access to raw material sources and power facilities, transport relations with consumers, availability of skilled and unskilled labor, labor organization, external economies from association with other industries, taxes and other social burdens, political conditions, relevant geographic features such as bed-rock conditions for power plants and soil for farming, capital supply, markets for by-products, opportunities for waste dis-

---

mann formulation may offer a more efficient approach to the determination of the resulting geographic flows of commodities (e.g., see Fox, *op. cit.*).

However, in a second volume on principles of regional science we hope to be able to demonstrate how the activity analysis approach can further regional theory and thereby our understanding of industrial location.

posal, etc., do vary from site to site and give rise to significant cost differentials. Herein lies probably the most serious weakness of the Hotelling approach.

Though the Hotelling approach does not yield as precise results as do market and supply area analyses, it can nonetheless be cloaked in a formal substitution framework for most specific situations where adequate assumptions are made about the behavior of such variables as competitors' reactions, price policies, and cost functions. For example, consider the first of Hotelling's problems discussed above. In terms of outlay-substitution lines, revenue-outlay substitution lines, and iso-revenue-less-outlay lines which relate to transport outlays and commodity revenue, in moving toward A's location, B substitutes transport outlays in one direction for transport outlays in another direction. (This corresponds to a shift along an outlay-substitution line.) B is at the same time proceeding along a revenue-outlay substitution line on to iso-revenue-less-outlay lines of higher and higher order (see Fig. 26, Chap. 6). When B finally comes as close as possible to A, on the side of A facing the more extensive market, his corresponding position on the revenue-outlay substitution line rests on an iso-revenue-less-outlay line higher in order than any other iso-revenue-less-outlay line with which the substitution line has a point in common. This point corresponds to maximum profits and stability, given Hotelling's assumptions.[53]

As already indicated game theory promises to furnish additional insights into the Hotelling locational equilibrium (interdependence) problem. When this is achieved, there still remains the task of integrating the Hotelling approach with the type of market and supply area analyses presented in the earlier sections of this chapter and with the Weberian doctrine reformulated in the preceding and later chap-

---

[53] Or consider a more complex situation in which both processing costs and transport costs on raw materials are variables. Along the horizontal axis of a relevant graph (once again see Fig. 26, Chap. 6), we would measure transport plus processing outlays. Along the vertical axis we would measure product revenue. B would then shift his location until he reached a site which would correspond to that point on his revenue-outlay substitution line which lies on the highest iso-revenue-less-outlay line. However, in this case the revenue-outlay substitution line would in turn be associated not only with a substitution line between transport outlays on product in one direction and transport outlays on product in the opposite direction but also with a second substitution line between transport outlays on product and transport outlays on raw material and a third substitution line between total transport outlays and processing outlays.

For an interesting set of graphs which illuminates this problem see Greenhut, "Integrating the Leading Theories . . ." op. cit.

ters.[54] Even allowing for progress on both these scores, we must still grapple with other variables which basically condition industrial location and regional development. Several of these are introduced into the analysis in the succeeding chapter.

[54] Greenhut, in his several articles, *op. cit.*, has explored and probed considerably into this problem.

Chapter 8

Agglomeration Analysis and Agricultural Location Theory

In his classic work on location theory, Alfred Weber emphasizes three basic location forces.[1] Two of these, transport cost differentials and labor cost differentials, interplay to determine the regional distribution of industries. We have already treated these two forces among others in the preceding chapters. The third general location factor, agglomeration (deglomeration) economies and diseconomies, acts, according to Weber, to concentrate or disperse industries within any given region. In our discussion thus far we have touched incidentally upon this third locational factor. We now probe deeper.

Following Ohlin, Hoover has neatly classified agglomeration (deglomeration) factors as follows:

(a) *Large-scale economies* within a firm, consequent upon the enlargement of the firm's scale of production at one point.
(b) *Localization economies* for all firms in a single industry at a single location, consequent upon the enlargement of the total output of that industry at that location.
(c) *Urbanization economies* for all firms in all industries at a single location, consequent upon the enlargement of the total economic size (population, income, output, or wealth) of that location, for all industries taken together.

Bearing this classification in mind, we can now examine how agglomeration theory can be reformulated in order to facilitate a more satis-

[1] C. J. Friedrich, *Alfred Weber's Theory of Location of Industries,* University of Chicago Press, Chicago, 1929.

factory integration with the previous substitution analysis and with orthodox production theory.

1. Economies of Scale

As the first step let us investigate the influence of large-scale economies upon the location of production. Let us reconsider the case to which Fig. 27 of the preceding chapter pertains. Two firms, A and B, are competing for the market along the straight line connecting their

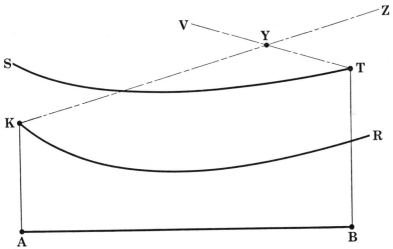

Fig. 30. A case of agglomeration from economies of scale.

factory sites. Their respective margin lines are $KGWP$ and $TUWV$. The delivered price of each to the consumer at X, when X is the marginal consumer, is the same. A comes to serve consumers lying along the stretch AX; B serves those along the stretch XB.[2]

In this case the marginal costs of both firms are rising sufficiently rapidly to make feasible a division of the market. Suppose, however, that significant economies of scale extend over a much larger range of production and that the margin lines of the two producers are as in Fig. 30. A's margin line always lies below B's; no matter which consumer is designated as marginal, A can deliver to him at a lower price than B. A usurps the entire market and can do so because production economies realized with increase of his output more than balance the mounting transport cost disadvantage as more distant consumers are served.

2 À la Hoover, it is assumed that a producer always serves first the nearer of any two consumers.

The case of Fig. 30 warrants concentration of production at A.[3] When contrasted with Fig. 27 it neatly illustrates the impulse toward agglomeration which stems from economies of scale. In another connection, namely, in determining for each commodity the appropriate size of an hexagonal market area, Lösch has also developed this point.[4]

Although the concentration of production at A (rather than a division between A and B) entails an increase of over-all transport outlays, it permits a still greater decrease in over-all production outlays. In terms of our substitution framework, transport outlays are substituted for production outlays. If we were to visualize one parent company controlling the two subsidiary firms A and B, the parent company, by concentrating production at A, would be shifting along an outlay-substitution line and proceeding on to lower iso-outlay (transport plus production outlay) lines. Viewed from society's standpoint, such concentration of production is desirable; it allows the production of any given output at lower cost and thus releases resources for other production and use.

The solution, however, does not necessarily rest with concentration

---

[3] However, in other types of situations there may not be a clear-cut indication of the location at which production should concentrate. Take, for example, the case represented by Fig. 31. A and B have identical cost curves and confront identical transport rate structures. (Consumers are uniformly distributed along

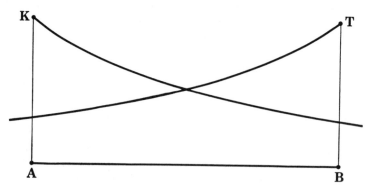

FIG. 31. A case of indeterminacy in location.

AB.) Economies of scale dictate concentration of production in one plant, but such concentration is as feasible at B as at A. In the traditional sense the solution to this problem is indeterminate; and as Hoover has pointed out (*op. cit.*, pp. 98–99), the location at which production is undertaken first is the location at which production is more likely to concentrate. (The alternative of a division of the market between the two sites involves instability.)

[4] Lösch, *op. cit.*, pp. 70–85.

of production at A. There may be other sites lying between A and B which would not labor at such high production costs as B must. Since they would occasion less transport outlays than A in serving the total array of consumers (except in extreme instances), they must be considered as potential locations. If any of these intermediate sites can produce over the relevant range of output at lower costs than A, obviously production should shift from A. If none can, then comparison must be made between savings on transport outlays engendered by any given shift from A and the corresponding increase in production outlays. If a shift were found to be desirable, the producer (parent company) would be proceeding along a revenue-outlay substitution line (as well as along several outlay-substitution lines) on to a higher iso-revenue-less-outlay line.[5]

The significant generalization which emerges from consideration of cases of this sort is that in any location decision the scale of output is one of several basic, interdependent variables. As scale varies, so may the substitution points between any pair of transport outlays, between any two sets of outlays, between outlays and revenues, and so forth.[6]

---

[5] Hoover's neat discussion (*op. cit.*, pp. 99–104) of the factors governing the location of marketing and other intermediary establishments presents another variation on this theme. He focuses upon three basic elements: (1) costs of transport (transfer) from the factory; (2) costs of operation of the intermediary establishment; and (3) costs of transport (transfer) to the consumer. His diagram illustrates how production (operation) outlays substitute for transport outlays as one shifts the intermediary establishment to successive transport junction points along the path from the factory to the consumer. At the same time it illustrates the concomitant substitution of transport outlays (inputs) on the unprocessed commodity for transport outlays (inputs) on the finished commodity.

[6] In the case depicted by Fig. 30, we considered two firms, a given linear distribution of consumers, and a fixed pattern of raw material supply. The relation between scale and location, however, can be illustrated in any number of ways. To take another example suppose we consider a single firm to whom the market and raw materials supply are variables, as well as scale. For a predetermined rate of output, an optimum site may be identified with which is associated an equilibrium relation between, let us say, transport outlays to the west and transport outlays to the east. For a larger scale of output the resources from a different source of a vital input may be required—a source, say, which lies further eastward —because the other source is taxed to capacity, or because a step-up in output at the original source involves such steeply rising costs that it becomes feasible to commence exploiting a more distant source. Or, perhaps for a larger scale of output, a larger supply area of raw materials is required, one more easily expanded in the east because of certain natural conditions. Or, perhaps the larger market area which the enterprise contemplates serving extends much farther to the east than to the west of the original site. An obvious conclusion follows. Total transport charges will increase, and if the site of production remains unchanged, most of this increase will be accounted for by greater transport outlays to the east.

This point is widely accepted and recognized, and reflects the fact that the phase of agglomeration theory which treats economies of scale is already embraced by existing production theory. It is easily incorporated into substitutional location analysis.

2. LOCALIZATION ECONOMIES

A more controversial issue in agglomeration theory revolves around the influence of localization economies. Weber raised this question early. Without clearly distinguishing among the three different types of agglomeration factors already noted, he asks under what conditions and where several units of production will agglomerate. He provides precise answers to these questions. Several individual units of production will agglomerate when (in relation to any assumed unit of agglomeration): (1) their critical isodapanes[7] intersect and (2) together

---

However, there will be a tendency for transport outlays to the west to be substituted for transport outlays to the east, that is, for the firm to shift its location eastward in order to lower total transport outlays.

It should be observed that such a shift of site can involve a considerable spatial jump. For example, until a certain size of output is reached, a dominant raw material may be supplied by a single source so that the site of production is at that source. With a larger output it may become feasible, as we have seen, to utilize a second source of the raw material and thus to locate at an intermediate site between the two sources. Or it may be that with the larger output the raw material loses its dominance and production becomes market-oriented or is most suitably located within the locational polygon of raw material sources and market points. Or it is conceivable that up to a certain output production is essentially transport-oriented, i.e., carried on at the minimum transport cost point. But with a larger output a cheap labor location, or a cheap power location, etc., becomes effective in attracting production to itself. Again all these conditions can be formally presented in terms of substitution and transformation lines which embrace all scales of output in order to point up the interrelation of scale and location.

It is also apparent that the question of the most efficient size of output to a large extent depends on the manner in which sources of raw materials and other inputs are exploitable and markets for finished goods available both in terms of their spatial distribution and their quantitative importance. And in turn the scale variable influences to a major degree the specific sources of raw materials utilized and the specific markets served.

[7] In this connection the critical isodapane for any unit of production is that locus of points for each of which transport costs in assembling the raw materials and shipping the finished product exceed the corresponding transport costs associated with the optimal transport point by a constant amount. This amount is equal to the economies of agglomeration that would be realized by association with the assumed unit of agglomeration.

See Weber for extensive discussion of the critical isodapane and of its dependence upon locational weight, transport rates, the function of economy of agglomeration, and other variables.

they attain within the common segment the requisite quantity of production.

Suppose three units of production, P_1, P_2, and P_3, each transport-oriented, are located as in Fig. 32. Around each are drawn its locational

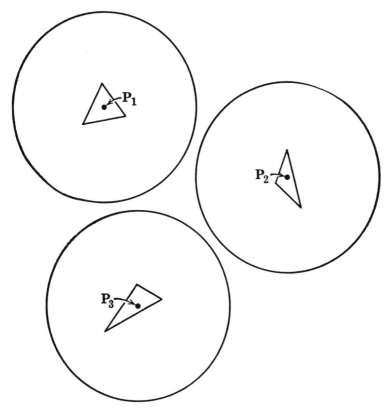

FIG. 32. Non-intersecting critical isodapanes: no agglomeration.

figure and critical isodapane. The critical isodapanes do not intersect. Agglomeration is infeasible. In contrast stands the situation depicted by Fig. 33 where these same three units are assumed initially to lie closer to one another. Here, their critical isodapanes, the heavy undashed circles, do intersect. (For the present, ignore the dashed circles). A la Weber, agglomeration will take place at a site within the common segment which is shaded.

Weber's determination of the center of agglomeration is as precise as his statement of conditions under which agglomeration will occur. The center of agglomeration "will be located at that one of the several possible points of agglomeration which has the lowest transportation costs in relation to the total agglomerated output."[8]   This point is derived by means of a locational figure and analysis of the equilibrium of forces in much the same way as is the optimal transport point

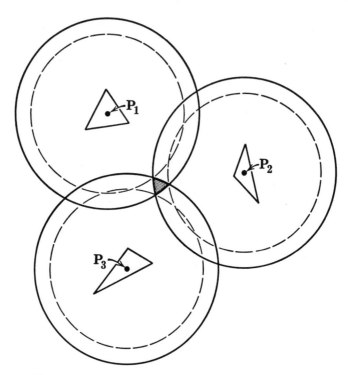

FIG. 33. Intersecting critical isodapanes: agglomeration.

for any given unit of production. However, in the derivation of this point, Weber permits the use of new sources of raw material supplies (replacement deposits) for each unit of production.

Weber gives a precise answer also to the question of the size of the unit of agglomeration to which each unit of production will be attracted. Each unit of production will select that unit of agglomeration whose center lies most distant from the relevant critical isodapane of the given unit of production.

Weber's analysis is not unsophisticated. He does consider for each unit of production a function of economy of agglomeration which varies with the size of agglomeration. He admits exceptions to his

[8] Friedrich, *op. cit.*, p. 138.

conditions under which agglomeration will be precipitated.[9] He emphasizes labor locations as centers of agglomerations, where both cheap labor and agglomeration economies are obtainable, and introduces various realities into his analysis.[10] Nonetheless it must be said that Weber's schema has limited application, especially in understanding the forces which determine the site at which agglomeration obtains in actuality.

Imagine an entrepreneur who controls three units of production and who confronts the location problem, *de novo*. Considering the locational polygon of raw material sources and markets relevant for each unit and assuming that economies of scale are not operative, he could locate each unit at its optimal transport point. Or, he could locate the three units adjacent to each other at a center of agglomeration, thereby achieving localization economies but only by incurring larger transportation costs. This is one type of situation to which Weber's schema has most application. In this type of situation, each unit of production may be visualized as substituting transport outlays for production outlays of one sort or another when it shifts to the center of agglomeration. And in this sense, that phase of agglomeration theory which concerns localization economies could be integrated into our substitutional framework just as we have integrated that phase of agglomeration theory which concerns economies of scale.[11]

[9] For example, the critical isodapane of a given unit of production may not quite reach the common segment formed by the intersection of the critical isodapanes of other units. Nevertheless, if the given unit's production is necessary for the group to attain the requisite total of production and if other units would enjoy sizable economies from agglomeration, the given unit of production can be induced to shift to the potential center of agglomeration by some form of subsidy or side payment.

[10] As with the analyses of other location factors, it is not our intention to present here these more sophisticated aspects of Weber's analysis nor to study the agglomeration factor in full. Rather, we touch upon it to the extent necessary to integrate it with our general location analysis and other existing theories. The reader is referred to other studies for more comprehensive and detailed treatments of the agglomeration and deglomeration variables. He can easily graft these more extensive treatments onto the analysis presented in this chapter.

[11] Palander contends that where the several units of production are controlled by one firm, the localization economies problem disappears. According to Palander, the firm confronts a scale problem; it must determine the amounts of production to engage in at various locations. In any case, however one views the problem, the substitutional framework applies.

The reader should also bear in mind that as soon as Weber considers centers of agglomeration where several units of production locate, his assumptions of fixed raw material prices, transport rates, wages, and other costs are less valid than when only one unit of production is associated with a given site.

However, as Engländer and Palander have rightly indicated in their sharp criticism of Weber's agglomeration theory, this type of situation is not widely characteristic of reality. Societal development is an historical process. At any given point of time there exists an inherited physical structural framework. Plants have already been erected and are producing. To relocate these plants involves opportunity costs since one would forego the use of facilities forced into obsolescence. Critics of Weber have therefore emphasized the advantages of existing production points as centers of agglomeration, whether they reflect labor or any other form of orientation. As new units of production come into existence, they will tend to gain localization economies by agglomerating around established production points. Thereby they frequently strengthen the gravitational pull of these points. From this standpoint, the evolutionary framework becomes critical as a locational factor; and any pure substitutional theory which is not linked to specific regional structure is of severely limited significance.

Moreover, even if the opportunity costs of relocation could be ignored and plants were completely mobile, the problem is not as simple as Weber depicted. In shifting to a center of agglomeration, it is to the advantage of each unit of production to deviate as little as possible from its optimal transport site. At the same time, the managers of these units of production differ in bargaining ability. Therefore, it is to be expected that the center of agglomeration will not be at the over-all minimum transport cost point of a new over-all locational polygon; rather, it will tend to lie within the common segment closer to the firms with greater bargaining ability. It could even lie at a point outside the common segment if an appropriate set of side payments were made to firms who could not otherwise be induced to agglomerate. And, if costs of relocation are reintroduced into the problem, the center of agglomeration could lie at the site of an already existing production point. Since this would eliminate one group of relocation costs, in many situations each unit of production could be made better off through an appropriate set of side payments than if all were to shift to Weber's over-all transport optimal point.

Clearly, game theory strikes at the heart of this latter type of situation. The several participants are the several units of production. Whether they be new units with whom no relocation costs are associated or existing units confronted with relocation costs, they interact engaging in various forms of collusive action. The bargaining which ensues is complicated not only because of the innumerable coalitions which are possible but also because of the different scales of agglomeration which are potentially feasible for each unit of production.[12]   As with the Hotelling and similar locational equilibrium problems examined in the previous chapter, progress in this phase of agglomeration theory and its incorporation into existing forms of analysis must await further development of game theory.

From an entirely different standpoint, however, Weber's agglomeration theory may be justly defended.   Suppose a new area is to be opened for development by a governmental planning authority.   Technological and other factors dictate, for any given commodity, the range of feasible scales for the units of production.   Should these units

[12] To spell out somewhat more the way in which game theory pertains to this phase of agglomeration theory, imagine there are three units of production (parties) placed as in Fig. 33.   Their critical isodapanes intersect with respect to two sizes of agglomeration.   (We already oversimplify the problem by considering only two sizes.)   The critical isodapanes relevant for the smaller unit of agglomeration are the dashed circles; those relevant for the larger unit are the undashed circles.   Any two parties could agglomerate to form the smaller unit of agglomeration.   The third party would consequently gain nothing.   It is therefore to his advantage to encourage the formation of the larger unit of agglomeration in which he could participate and from which he could reap gain.   Leaving aside the determination of which party is the third party, we encounter the problem of identifying types of collusive actions which might develop.   Whom will the third party approach to form a coalition?   To make an effective approach he must offer a gain to the co-operating (second) party which will be greater than what the latter obtains in the smaller unit of agglomeration.   The third party may offer a side payment.   Or he may propose to agglomerate at a site closer to the second party's initial location (optimal transport point); this proposal may, or may not, be contingent upon the participation of the remaining (first) party.   Or the second party may be strong enough to force agglomeration at his own optimal transport point, provided the first and third parties reap gain either directly or indirectly through side payments.   However, the first party cannot be presumed to be an inactive participant.   His power, like the power of any of the other two parties, rests in the fact that without his co-operation the additional gains of the larger unit of agglomeraion are not possible.   He too has bargaining power and can be presumed to exercise it.

Costs of relocation complicate the problem still more by altering the probabilities of diverse moves.   They significantly affect the range of collusive action.   Furthermore, the problem as presented is not a constant-sum game.   As Weber demonstrates, there is a center, the over-all optimal transport point, at which agglomeration can proceed with a minimum addition to the sum of the transportation costs of all parties.   Any deviation from this point reduces the "surplus" or "net gain" to be apportioned among the participants.   In certain situations it may therefore be useful to introduce a fourth participant, a dummy, in order to convert the problem into a constant-sum or zero-sum game.   This entails further complexities, as well as does any variation from the symmetrical situation presented, such as with respect to initial geographic positions, size of output of each unit of production, ability to relocate as measured by opportunity costs, and so forth.

be agglomerated to realize localization economies, or should they be spatially disconnected in order to reduce transportation costs? From this social welfare approach, irrationalities and differences among managers in bargaining ability do not enter the problem. Nor do inherited physical structures. The localization economies achievable at Weber's over-all transport optimal point (and not at any other point) must be compared with the additional transport outlays occasioned by agglomeration at this point. Moreover, this social welfare approach implicit in Weber, though not generally realistic, provides a useful guidepost; in certain contexts it can indicate directions in which existing structure should be transformed in order to approach optimum resource utilization. Hence, from these standpoints, too, the Weberian agglomeration theory is relevant,[13] and likewise the substitutional locational framework within which it fits.

3. URBANIZATION ECONOMIES

The third phase of agglomeration theory, which concerns urbanization economies, is in as unsatisfactory a state as that phase which treats localization economies. This is to be expected to some extent since the analysis of urbanization economies can be said: (1) to resemble, or (2) partially to evolve from, or (3) even to contain, according to some persons, the analysis of localization economies.[14]

In the previous section we did not specify types of localization economies (and diseconomies) which arise, such as those associated with access to a larger pool of skilled labor, with fuller use of specialized and auxiliary industrial and repair facilities, with large-lot buying and selling through common brokers and jobbers. We attacked the problem as if these economies were known and furnished us in the form of a function of economy of agglomeration (à la Weber). In the study of urbanization economies we face all these in a broader context as well as, among others: (1) economies which stem from a higher level of use of the general apparata of an urban structure (such as transportation facilities, gas and water mains, and the like) and from a finer articulation of economic activities (daily,

[13] Critics of Weber's agglomeration theory are too often inclined to forget that in his *Über den Standort der Industrien* Weber seeks a "pure" theory such as one which is relevant for social planning rather than a "realistic" theory wherein institutional forces are duly considered.

[14] The discerning reader may have already concluded that in several respects there is also only a fine line of distinction between localization economies and economies of scale. He may have observed for example that the figures used in connection with the discussion of economies of scale are also relevant, with appropriate changes in initial premises, for inquiry into localization economies.

seasonally, and interindustrially); and (2) diseconomies engendered by rises in the cost of living and money wages, in the costs of local materials produced under conditions of diminishing returns, in time-cost and other costs of transportation, and in land values and rents. Consequently, we can theoretically employ the approach linked to critical isodapanes, as developed in the preceding section, for the investigation of the impact of at least some of these urbanization economies and diseconomies. Here, the units of production need not engage in the same type of activity.

In this general sense little can be added to the existing state of analysis. It can be presumed that Weber's approach would have still less application here than in the treatment of localization economies. Cities evolve over time. They are much less subject to relocation than are individual units of production. To put it another way, the accumulated fixed investments of an urban mass in conjunction with its vested social institutions entail major geographic immobilities and rigidities and, for the most part, tend to preclude urban relocation. Cities attract or repel units of production in accordance with the urbanization (for the most part, external) economies or diseconomies relevant to each unit of production. In this sense, one concludes that agglomeration analysis, particularly that of the substitutional variety, has little to say beyond the obvious; units are attracted to or repelled from cities according to a simple comparison of advantages and disadvantages generated by these cities.

However, it is instructive to pursue a tangential extension of the above discussion. Once more we pose the following problem. A new area is to be developed. Given a full knowledge of existing technology and likely changes in this technology, of the human and natural resources of the area, and of other relevant relations and materials, how should one plan a net of cities for this area? What is the optimum spatial distribution and hierarchy of cities of different sizes? Within each urban-metropolitan region what is the best spatial distribution of different types of satellite cities and centers? Within each city what is the most desirable constellation of community and neighborhood sites of various sorts? In what ways should the intensities of land use and traffic generation be controlled to be consistent with an optimum structure of cities?

Closely allied with the above theoretical questions is a more practical one. Given a network of cities and corresponding patterns of land use, along what channels should changes in the structure of this network and these patterns be fostered in order to attain a situation closer to optimum? Since cities are conglomerations of economic activities, in what directions should the joint geographic distribution of economic activities be reshuffled when flexibility in the structure exists?

At this point, only a meager beginning can be made at answers to these basic questions, which have already been posed several times, either implicitly or explicitly. To start exploratory analysis, let there be given the economies of scale associated with every utility and service which a city provides and with every other activity or service

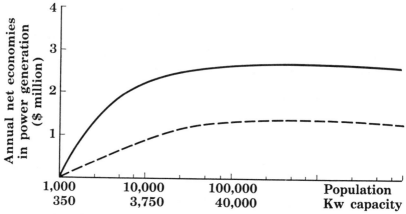

FIG. 34.   Economies of scale in power generation with urban size.

subject to urbanization economies or diseconomies. Let us focus first upon the economies and diseconomies associated with the provision of electric power. To do so we have constructed Fig. 34. Along the vertical axis we measure net economies (economies less diseconomies) in power generation. Along the horizontal axis we measure both scale of output and the corresponding size of city which can absorb any scale of output. We posit more or less representative cities for each of which an approximate level of power output can be identified. (In reality, of course, the power consumption of any city is a function of many characteristics; and consequently the kilowatt-hour requirements of any two cities of the same size can differ widely.) We also postulate that fuel of stated BTU quality is available to all sizes of cities at a fixed price or at prices which are a function of quantity of purchase but not of geographic position;[15] and that for each scale of output the most efficient power plant design is in effect. Excess capacity beyond that necessitated by peak load requirement (which is

[15] Hence, all cities are taken to be equally distant from a fuel source.

taken to exceed average load by a uniform percentage in all cities) does not exist.[16]

Given these assumptions, Fig. 34 indicates annual net economies in power generation which would be realized if any given size of population together with its associated industrial and commercial activities were concentrated in one city rather than in cities of 1000 population each.[17] The solid curve refers to a situation in which the cities of 1000 each would be too distant from one another to permit service by one or a relatively few power stations. The dashed curve refers to a situation in which the cities of 1000 each would be sufficiently close to permit some integration in power production and service.[18] Obviously, a set of curves can be constructed to depict different degrees of integration which might be feasible.

For every other service and commodity whose production or cost reflects urbanization economies and diseconomies, we can construct a similar set of net economy curves when appropriate assumptions are stipulated. One set would reflect in the early stage of each curve the general economies which arise from access to larger and more diversified pools of skilled labor, and in a later stage the diseconomies in the use of labor which stem from internal congestion and inefficiency (the journey-to-work problem), increases in money wages, and other factors as the urban mass multiplies. Another set would reflect economies and diseconomies in the operation of an urban transportation system (including streets, rail and truck terminals, parking facilities as well as bus, subway, street and electric railway, and other transit media) or of a subset of the transportation system if an identifiable subset of the transportation system can be meaningfully isolated for study. In reality the size and character of urban transportation systems vary with the spatial distribution of population, of economic, cultural, and other activities within the city, with patterns of group behavior and social organization, with topography and other geographic features, with the state of technology, and with many other factors. However, we postulate that it is possible to associate at

[16] Already the reader may seriously object to the set of postulates adopted whereby cities are standardized in terms of power consumption, price of fuel, and other factors.

[17] In Fig. 34 we depict increasing per capita consumption of power in all uses with increase in size of city in order to reflect the effect upon power consumption of the lower power rates which larger cities tend to charge because of lower unit power costs. The kilowatt capacity scale has specific reference to the solid curve.

[18] Both curves fall off slightly after a certain size of city is reached because of slowly mounting diseconomies in the co-ordination and management of larger and larger power systems.

least approximately a size and character of transportation system with each size of city, and that the difficult problem of defining a unit of transportation service can be surmounted.[19] Each curve in the resulting set of net economy curves would rise to a maximum and then fall significantly as deglomerative forces, such as congestion and co-ordination problems, grow in relative importance.

Still other sets of curves would depict economies and diseconomies in the performance of various municipal functions: in the provision of fire and police protection; in the administration and operation of an educational system; in the construction and maintenance of gas, water, and sanitation facilities; in the organization and supply of recreational facilities and services; and in other activities. Here, too, as population numbers increase, as congestion multiplies, as rents, land values, and the costs of food supply rise, diseconomies mount in relative importance.

Imagine that somehow or other it is possible a priori to identify for any large region, either already settled or about to be settled, that curve in each set of net economy curves which tends to be most relevant or representative for the situation under study. These curves (one from each set) could be plotted as in Fig. 35, where only four of them have been constructed. It is tempting to sum all these curves and to interpret the resulting total curve as an over-all index of economy or function of economy which defines the over-all urbanization economies and diseconomies associated with cities of different sizes. Unfortunately, this is not justifiable. There are many logical objections to this procedure.

To reiterate a point already mentioned, the standardization of cities is subject to serious criticism. There are no standard cities. Each is unique. Furthermore, the selection of a relevant or representative curve from any given set of net economy curves presents logical difficulties of a somewhat similar nature. It is unnecessary to spell out these fairly obvious points.

Additionally, there are a number of other objections of which at least two should be explicitly mentioned. One involves the problem of weighting. Summing the individual curves of Fig. 35 to derive the total curve depicted thereon implies that the sets of economies are of equal importance. Yet it is clearly evident that the relative importance of any set of economies depends upon many characteristics of a given situation; among others, industrial composition, income,

[19] In effect, we standardize cities in terms of: (1) the ratio of industrial activity to commercial and service activities; (2) industrial mix (heavy and light) and composition of commercial and service activities; (3) land-use patterns; (4) journey-to-work and commodity flow configurations; and many other relations.

culture and social organization, consumption patterns, and geographic setting. In a situation where cities are, or are likely to be, characterized by a heavy proportion of electro-process activities within their basic industry sectors, greater significance should be attached to the power economy curves, *ceteris paribus*. In another situation

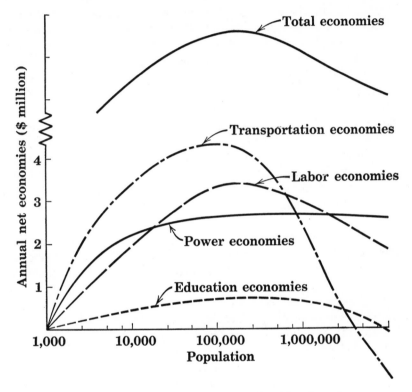

FIG. 35. Hypothetical economies of scale with urban size.

where general urban settlement is severely restricted by mountainous slopes, ocean, and other barriers, the transportation economy curves assume greater relative importance, *ceteris paribus*. Thus, some form of weighting must be introduced into the problem in a valid analytical manner.

Another objection, perhaps the most serious of all, stems from the neglect of interdependence among the sets of net economy curves (as well as interurban and urban-rural interrelations). Economies in urban transit are directly related to economies in power generation since considerable power is consumed in street and electric railways and other transit facilities. In turn, economies in power generation are directly related to economies in the operation of port and rail facilities since a significant fraction of the delivered price of fuel may consist of transportation charges. Economies and diseconomies in the educational system, in the provision of fire and police protection, and in various other municipal services are also directly influenced by the character and efficiency of the transportation system. Likewise, labor economies and diseconomies are related to a number of other sets of economies and diseconomies. In short, it is erroneous to consider the various economies and diseconomies associated with the numerous urban activities as simply additive. Rather, they are multiplicative in a complex fashion.

The above considerations are sufficient in themselves to invalidate the use, even in an approximative fashion, of a simple total curve or index of economies and diseconomies in the functioning of cities of various sizes. The construction of Fig. 35 does not answer the basic questions posed earlier in this section; nor does it cast significant light upon the third phase of agglomeration theory, which is concerned with urbanization economies and diseconomies. We are still thrown back upon the simple statement that, with respect to each firm, there are attracting and repelling forces for location in rural areas and in cities of different sizes. When the potential savings of a location shift override the additional costs involved, the firm will shift. In doing so it will be substituting one set of outlays and revenues for another set. (And, as already indicated, in the presentation of this problem the critical isodapane techniques, à la Weber, are helpful only to a limited extent.)

Nonetheless, it seems worthwhile to explore further the above approach in the analysis of urbanization economies and diseconomies. In a future volume, which will place chief emphasis upon regional analysis, it will be shown how within urban-metropolitan regions some of the complex interdependence of the sets of net economy curves can be understood and partially identified in quantitative terms. Yet, this interdependence problem, together with the problems of weighting and of introducing flexibility and non-standardization into the approach, is of tremendous scope and requires a large amount of additional research.

4. AGRICULTURAL LOCATION THEORY

As indicated at the beginning of Chap. 5, there is a traditional dualism in location theory—viz., a Thünen type of analysis for the agricultural sphere and a Weberian scheme for the industrial. Historically, the former has confined itself to an aggregative analysis; the latter primarily to individual firm analysis. Since these two schools have been concerned with two different levels of inquiry, it might appear, as it has to some in the past, that their doctrines are nonintegrable. It might seem illogical to discuss agricultural location theory in a section of a chapter where the preceding sections have centered primarily around the individual firm. However, we contend: (1) that there is a smooth transition from individual firm analysis in the Weberian sense to the analysis of the individual farm enterprise; (2) that the analysis of the individual farm enterprise must investigate the bonds which link the agricultural firm to the aggregate of agricultural activities; and (3) that casting the locational analysis of the individual farm enterprise against the background of locational forces which interplay on the aggregative level in agriculture can throw at least some light upon the way location forces which influence the individual industrial enterprise are interlocked with those governing the spatial distribution of industry on a more aggregative level.[20]

The previous discussion has emphasized the distance variable. Transport inputs and transport outlays have been given a focal position in the theoretical scaffolding. Yet the internal spatial dimensions of the firm, of industrial agglomerations, or of urban aggregates have been ignored. On the surface, at least, to ignore them was justifiable in individual firm analysis where it was implicitly assumed that the firm was associated with a factory-type operation whose requirements of land were relatively small. Differentials associated with the cost of land services were taken to be minor as they typically are for most industrial factories. In contrast this neglect is not justifiable for industrial agglomerations, for cities, and for firms whose internal spatial dimensions are relatively large. These latter firms are well typified by agricultural enterprises.

In agricultural location theory, rent differentials have always occupied a central position. Since the internal spatial extent of the typical agricultural enterprise is relatively large, differences in the price of land services associated with different spatial positions (as well as resource content) are a major location influence. However, to the agricultural enterprise, the rent differential plays the same role as the labor cost differential to an enterprise in an industry which is labor intensive, or the power cost differential to an enterprise in an industry which is power intensive. In the case of the agricultural

---

[20] The imperative need to attack the analysis of industrial agglomeration from a more aggregative standpoint has already been pointed up in the preceding sections.

enterprise, it is critical to investigate the substitution relation between rent outlays and transport outlays; in the case of textiles, it is important to examine the substitution relation between labor outlays and transport outlays; in the case of the aluminum industry, between power outlays and transport outlays. In this sense, location theory for agricultural firms is no different from that for industrial firms. Comparison of cost differentials and investigation of substitution relations among the several outlays are basic to both. The only significant difference rests, it may be contended, in the fact that the small character of the many agricultural enterprises cultivating most major crops coupled with the concentration of markets at particular points in general permits a deeper locational analysis of the agricultural sphere than of the industrial. We therefore proceed to the discussion of agricultural location theory as a logical extension of the general analytical framework evolved in the preceding pages.[21]

Consider the operator of an agricultural enterprise. Among others, his decisions regarding the location of his enterprise (in terms of distance from the market), product(s) to be cultivated, factor proportions to be used, and intensity of production are interrelated. Some of these interrelations can be neatly demonstrated with the use of a set of graphs developed by Dunn.[22]

In Fig. 36 are presented a set of price and cost curves for the individual farm operator. OE represents the price at the market for the particular product he cultivates. OD represents the net farm price, i.e., market price less the cost to transport the unit of product to the market which is indicated by ED. The solid curves, AC and MC, are respectively his average and marginal cost curves; they exclude rent payments or are relevant when the price of land is taken to be zero.

If the price of land were zero, the operator would extend output to the level, OI_1, at which level marginal costs equal net farm price (marginal revenue) and where, *ex definitione*, gross marginal costs (including cost of transport to the market) equal market price (gross

[21] In this section, we shall treat only some of the basic elements of agricultural location theory. For a full statement, see Edgar S. Dunn, *The Location of Agricultural Production*, University of Florida Press, Gainesville, 1954; August Lösch, *Die räumliche Ordnung der Wirtschaft*, G. Fischer, Jena, 1944, pp. 24–44; E. M. Hoover, Jr., *Location Theory and the Shoe and Leather Industries*, Harvard University Press, Cambridge, Mass., 1937, Chap. 2; E. T. Benedict, *et al.*, *Theodor Brinkman's Economics of the Farm Business*, University of California Press, Berkeley, 1935; F. Aeroboe, *Allgemeine landwirtschaftliche Betriebslehre*, P. Parey, Berlin, 1923, and J. H. von Thünen, *Der isolierte Staat in Beziehung auf Landwirtschaft und Nationalökonomie*, Hempel and Parey, Berlin, 1895.

[22] Dunn, *op. cit.*, Chap. III.

marginal revenue). Total surplus is represented by the area of the rectangle, *ABCD*.

To supplement Fig. 36 one can construct Fig. 37 which focuses upon other relations of this situation. Along the vertical and horizontal

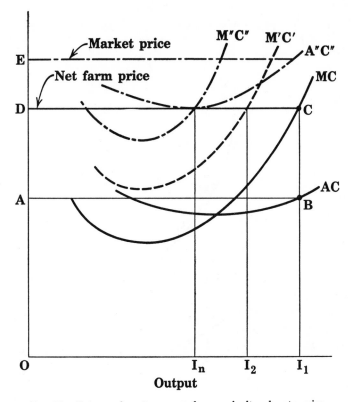

FIG. 36. Price and cost curves of an agricultural enterprise.

axes we measure respectively amounts of land inputs and amounts of a composite set of other inputs. Each of the curves $I_1 \ldots I_n$ represents an iso-product curve,[23] and, in order, they relate to decreasing levels of output. The dashed lines $OS_1, OS_2 \ldots OS_n$ are scale lines.[24]

[23] Each iso-product curve depicts the various combinations of the amounts of land inputs and of the composite set of other inputs required to produce that given level of output corresponding to the iso-product curve.

[24] Each scale line is a locus of points indicating the combinations of the amounts of land inputs and of the composite set of other inputs which involve the least total outlay for the production of each level of output, *for a given specific price-ratio of inputs.*

Since rent, the price of land services, is taken to be zero, the Hicksian price-ratio (the iso-outlay or iso-cost) lines are vertical, such as line VX. Given the level of output, OI_1, to be produced (as determined by Fig. 36), the equilibrium amounts of land and other inputs are given

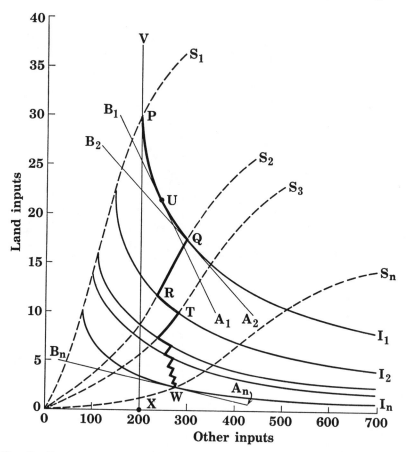

FIG. 37. Input proportions, scale, and equilibrium for an agricultural enterprise.

by the point of tangency, P, of the iso-product curve I_1 (which corresponds to an output of OI_1) with the price-ratio line VX.

Dunn has discussed the inconsistency of the above derivation. The surplus, $ABCD$ (Fig. 36), when divided by the 30 units of land utilized (as given by point P, Fig. 37) yields rent per unit of land. This rent or price for the use of the services of land may be, in certain circumstances, an opportunity cost or, in other circumstances, an actual payment by the farm operator who leases the land in full competition with other potential users. In any case, a price for the use of land services exists, and vertical price-ratio lines like VX are incorrect. As a first approximation, the rent of each of the 30 units of land under use may be taken to be $ABCD/30$. This would yield a set of price-ratio lines whose slopes are identical to that of line B_1A_1. Accordingly, U would be the new point of tangency of the I_1 iso-product curve with the relevant price-ratio line of the new set. It would be economic to reduce land inputs and increase other inputs as indicated by the shift along curve I_1 from P to U, and thereby to substitute outlays on other inputs for rent outlays.

However, if the quantities of land inputs and other inputs given by point U were to be employed to produce OI_1 of output, Dunn has shown that the resulting rent per unit of land is greater than that assumed by the price-ratio line B_1A_1. As a consequence, a new set of price-ratio lines, with less steep slope, becomes relevant. Another substitution of outlays on other inputs for rent outlays is justified. This, in turn, generates a still greater rent per unit of land and makes relevant another slope for the price-ratio lines. In Dunn's words: "a series of successive substitution adjustments is made with the tangency point moving down the iso-product line from [P to Q in Fig. 37]. Each of these successive adjustments, however, yields a rapidly decreasing increment to the rent per acre. When the point Q is reached, the rent per acre cannot be increased any further by increasing the ratio of the 'other' input factors to land."[25]

A second basic set of substitutions occurs simultaneously with these adjustments. As rent is explicitly acknowledged as a cost, the marginal and average cost curves rise. (Land inputs are a variable.) In Fig. 36, the intersection of the new dashed marginal cost curve $M'C'$, in which the rent is included as a cost, with the net farm price line suggests OI_2 as the equilibrium output, rather than OI_1. This would correspond to a shift from Q to R along scale line OS_2 in Fig. 37. However, the change of scale increases rent per unit land (when the enterprise is operating under decreasing returns to scale), decreases the steepness of the relevant set of price-ratio lines, and indicates a series of substitutions which lead to point T on the I_2 iso-product line. Once again contraction of scale is warranted. Ultimately, according to Dunn, the various scale contractions and the substitution of outlays on other inputs for outlays on land inputs lead to point W where neither scale adjustments nor outlay substitutions are prompted.[26] Corresponding

[25] Dunn, *op. cit.*, p. 30. The letters and number in brackets are mine.
[26] The reader should bear in mind that the step-by-step set of adjustments depicted in Fig. 37 is for illustrative purposes only. Both scale adjustments and

to point W are the dot-dash marginal and average cost curves ($M''C''$ and $A''C''$) of Fig. 36; the average cost curve inclusive of rent is tangent at its minimum point to the net farm price line. *Given the spatial position of the land to be used and the crop to be cultivated,* point W represents a stable equilibrium position for the agricultural enterprise.

Thus far, only part of the total problem confronting the agricultural operator has been presented. Another part concerns his location. Abstracting from changes in the resource content of the land, in position relative to fixed transport facilities, in the tax, legal, and other socio-economic and political frameworks which condition land use,[27] we can depict the impact of a shift of location upon the operation of an agricultural enterprise with the use of Fig. 36. In terms of economic distance, let the agricultural enterprise shift closer to the market. Accordingly, its net farm price line rises, the transport cost to the market being diminished.[28] A higher net farm price line would obviously permit a greater rent per unit of land if inputs and output and all other prices are constant. However, since the ratio of the price of a land input to the price of a composite of other inputs rises, the slope of the relevant price-ratio lines becomes less steep. A series of substitution adjustments leading to still greater rent per unit of land and to a higher ratio of other inputs to land inputs is warranted; and consequently the intensity with which a unit of land is cultivated increases.

Allow the agricultural enterprise to shift its location to a third site still closer to the market and in succession to a fourth and a fifth. It becomes evident that the closer the enterprise to the market the higher the rent per unit of land and the greater the intensity at which it is economically feasible to cultivate a unit of land; and, the more distant the enterprise from the market the less the rent which the operator can afford to pay for a unit of land and the less the intensity with

---

substitutions can and do take place simultaneously. Many different kinds of paths leading from the hypothetical point P to the equilibrium point W are possible.

[27] All these elements influence the firm's operations through their effect upon its cost curves. Thus, if the resource content of the land deteriorates and taxes rise as a firm shifts from one location to another, we can expect the relevant average cost curve for the second location to course at a higher level than that pertinent for the first location, *ceteris paribus.* Since the variation in the influence of these elements does not exhibit a spatial regularity, a study of their effects lies outside the scope of this volume, although for any particular situation their presence must be fully recognized. The reader interested in their effects is referred, among others, to Brinkmann, *op. cit.;* Hoover, *op. cit.,* pp. 22–33; and Dunn, *op. cit.,* Chap. 5.

[28] The extent of this diminution would be given by the typical transport gradient line over the relevant stretch.

which he cultivates it. If the rent potential per unit of land were plotted for each possible location of the agricultural enterprise along a line extending from the market, a rent function would be described such as is depicted by curve AA on Fig. 38.[29]

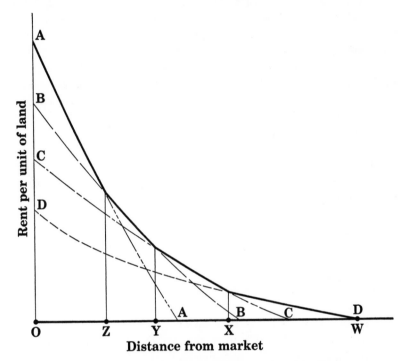

FIG. 38.   Rent functions for different agricultural land uses.

It should be emphasized that any shift of the agricultural enterprise involves the general substitution between rent outlays and all other outlays combined. Of still greater relevance are certain subsidiary

[29] Our rent function is identical with Hoover's "rent surface" and with Dunn's "industry rent function." At times this rent function has been depicted as a straight line (e.g. Lösch, *op. cit.* pp. 25–40; and Dunn, *op. cit.*, Chap. 2) when it has been either implicitly or explicitly assumed that intensity of cultivation is invariant with distance from the market. In these instances, the rent function is given as: $R = E(p - a) - Efk$ where R is rent per unit of land, k (an independent variable) is distance from the market, and E, p, a, and f (all constants or parameters) are, respectively, yield per unit of land, market price, average production cost, and transport rate (Dunn, *op. cit.*, p. 7).

Because of its emphasis upon the firm as the core unit our formulation of the problem precludes the use of a straight line rent function. A straight line rent function, although helpful for pedagogical purposes, is logically invalid.

substitutions. Viewed from the standpoint of transport orientation theory, the enterprise finds its transport optimal (minimum transport cost) point at the market. As the enterprise moves away from the market, it substitutes transport outlays for rent outlays, *ceteris paribus;* and concomitantly, because the price of land becomes more moderate, it substitutes rent outlays for other (excluding transport) outlays, *ceteris paribus.*[30] This substitution represents a deviation from the transport optimal point. This deviation is of the same order as the deviation which occurs when, following traditional Weberian dogma, a firm shifts from its transport optimal point to a cheap labor location. Among others, this latter shift involves two basic substitutions: (1) a substitution of transport outlays for labor outlays, *ceteris paribus;* and (2) a substitution of labor outlays for other (excluding transport) outlays since the price of labor is less at the cheap labor location. The only basic distinction between these two shifts, it can be maintained, is that on the one hand the shift of the agricultural enterprise can be a somewhat continuous one whilst on the other hand the shift of the industrial firm to a cheap labor location typically involves a discrete jump.

It should be borne in mind that any one farmer or agricultural operator need not approach the location decision in the comprehensive fashion depicted above. He need not be fully aware of the breadth of the problem. His vision may be narrowly circumscribed. Yet he behaves as if he were fully aware of the entire problem. This result obtains because the relative freedom of entry into and exit from agricultural production tends to force the farmer into efficient paths or to weed him out if he persistently deviates from these paths.[31] Essentially there corresponds to every site an appropriate set of characteristics relating to size of enterprise, intensity of land use, and ratios of factor inputs. This appropriate set yields, for each site, the maximum rent, all of which accrues to the landowner. The competitive process wipes away any surplus profit which might befall an operator at any site, and at the same time ensures "normal returns" or "normal profits."[32] Thus, theoretically, the farm operator is indifferent to the

[30] A move in the opposite direction, let us say from no-rent land (re: the given commodity) toward the market, involves a substitution of rent outlays for transportation outlays, *ceteris paribus,* and a substitution of other (excluding transport) outlays for rent outlays.

[31] Unless, being a landowner, he can pursue inefficient practices at the expense of economically justifiable rent.

[32] If the operator makes an abnormal profit after allowance for unusual entrepreneurial ability, etc., by implication his rent payment to the landowner is too low. Accordingly other individuals will be attracted to the use of the

position at which he is located, provided, of course, he is within the rent-yielding hinterland. Hence, observing the adjustments of the individual agricultural entrepreneur at each possible distance from the market yields, for the given crop, a theoretically valid rent function of the general order of the curve AA on Fig. 38.

As already intimated, there is another basic substitution path along which an individual farm operator can proceed. He can elect to produce a different crop. With respect to this second crop we can derive for each meaningful location the relevant net farm price line, ratios of factor inputs, scale of output, and the rent potential which through the process of competitive bidding would accrue to the landowner. As with the first crop, a rent function results, let us say curve BB of Fig. 38. Again, when production is restricted to the second crop, the agricultural operator is theoretically indifferent to location within the rent-yielding hinterland since at all locations his average unit cost curve (inclusive of rent payments) would be tangent at its minimum point to the effective net farm price line. Of course, to avoid losses and to attain a position corresponding to this tangency point, the operator is compelled to adhere to the appropriate set of substitution points, which set varies with distance from the market.

When the possibility of producing each crop is permitted, specialization in land use may ensue. Crop A should be cultivated at those sites, if any, at which the ordinate of the rent function curve AA exceeds the ordinate of the rent function curve BB. And similarly, crop B should be produced at those sites, if any, at which its cultivation yields greater rent per acre land. If the agricultural operator were to persist in the cultivation of either crop A or crop B at any location when conditions dictate otherwise, his land would be bid away from him by potential operators who channel their activity in accord with the practice which yields maximum rent per unit of land at that location. Thereby, in shifting from one crop to another, he (or the ultimate operator of the land) substitutes among various revenues and among various outlays, as generally developed in the individual firm discussion of Chap. 6.

---

given land and continuously bid up rent until the surplus profits associated with its use are eliminated. In contrast, if the operator contracts for the use of land at a price greater than its rent potential, his average unit costs (inclusive of adequate payments for entrepreneurial ability, privately-owned capital, etc.) will exceed his net farm price. He will tend to leave the industry. The land which he cultivated will tend to remain idle until the landowner reduces rent to the point where the operator's average unit cost curve can be tangent with his net farm price line. At all sites, zero surplus tends to obtain after appropriate payment is made for all inputs.

Likewise, we can derive a rent function for a third crop, a fourth crop . . . and for an nth crop. Each of these can be graphically depicted in Fig. 38.[33] Land use at any location is governed by the rent function which has the highest value at that location. For example, in Fig. 38, the stretch of land OZ should be devoted to the production of crop A, ZY to crop B, YX to crop C, and XW to crop D.[34] It is clear that the individual farmer at any one location is forced to cultivate that crop which yields greatest rent to the landowner, so long as relative freedom of entry, exit, and contract is granted. Thus, when we concentrate upon the individual farm's adjustments, we obtain the typical set of rent functions traditionally central to agricultural location theory. Further, when we rotate lines OZ, OY, OX, and OW around point O as the center, we obtain the familiar Thünen rings (concentric circles).

In the above manner, individual firm analysis moves in the direction of aggregative equilibrium analysis for the industry. The analysis of the problem on the firm level involving resources devoted to a single use is extended to encompass the problem involving competition of different uses for the same land. It is, of course, a necessary condition that the supply and demand for each crop be equated at the given market price. If not, relative market prices must change, rent functions shift, appropriate firm adjustments occur, and a new pattern of land use be established consistent with this necessary condition.[35] Thus conditions relating to the agricultural industry as a whole—conditions which the Thünen school has emphasized—are of equal importance as those governing individual firm adjustments in deriving an equilibrium land use pattern. It should be pointed out that the resulting pattern is logically more precise and different from the approximative pattern which the Thünen school derives when it abstracts from individual firm adjustments.

Where several concentrated markets, rather than one, exist for agricultural products, the problem becomes more complex graphically but remains the same conceptually. For each crop as many rent functions may be identified as there are markets, each rent function being linked to the consumption of the crop at one and only one market. Each rent function throughout its course reflects appropriate sets of individual firm adjustments. As before, any given unit of land becomes geared to that use which yields maximum rent returns within the entire range

[33] Curves CC and DD represent rent functions for two of these crops.

[34] For more extensive discussion of boundary and related conditions see Chap. 10 and Dunn, *op. cit.*, Chaps. 2 and 3 and Appendix A.

[35] For a fuller treatment which considers the income factor as well, see Dunn, *op. cit.*, pp. 16–24.

of markets and crops.[36] Furthermore, these principles governing land use apply with equal force whether we consider for each unit of land the production of single crops or any number of products in combination. In reality products in combination (farming systems) tend to characterize the operations of agricultural enterprises. However, the above analysis remains unchanged since a crop can be easily redefined as a set of products in combination.[37]

Hence we observe how the agricultural farm location problem can be viewed as an integral part of the general individual firm location problem. In the case of industrial firms, outlays on land services may frequently be less critical locationally than outlays on transport, labor, power, and other inputs. In the case of the agricultural enterprise, some of these latter outlays (excluding transport) may be the less significant ones; and typically, outlays on land are major. Despite these contrasts on the concrete level, in both cases the location problem of the individual unit involves the identical basic substitution process; the individual unit whether agricultural or non-agricultural must, explicitly or implicitly, substitute among outlays, among revenues, and among outlays and revenues.

Additionally, because of the relative freedom of entry and exit and because of the many small units which typically produce a given crop, the analysis of the adjustments of the individual farm enterprise within the full array of feasible locations, crops, and systems of crops, leads to fruitful conclusions on a more aggregative level. When combined with total conditions and restraints bearing upon supply, demand, price, income, and related variables within the agricultural industry as a whole, this analysis leads to over-all equilibrium land-use patterns within the industry and to a more precise determination of the familiar Thünen spatial configurations. However, to specify these total conditions and restraints requires the study of forces governing the interrelations of various urban-metropolitan markets, their connections with regional hinterlands, and their respective sizes. These forces operating on the more aggregative regional level will be analyzed in a future volume.

[36] This multimarket framework is dealt with at greater length in Chap 10. Also see Dunn, op. cit., pp. 57–63.

Likewise, differentials in input prices among sites at different distances from the market, an aspect of the agricultural location problem with which Brinkmann and Lösch among others have been concerned, can also be easily encompassed by the substitution framework. See Chap. 10. Additionally, other phases of the agricultural location problem can be incorporated into the above framework (see Dunn, op. cit., Chaps. 5 and 6).

[37] For further discussion, see Dunn, op. cit., pp. 46–52.

APPENDIX TO CHAPTER 8

SOME THEORETICAL NOTES ON URBAN LAND-USE

Traditionally, the analysis of urban land-use patterns has fallen outside the realm of location theory. Yet, in many respects, urban land-use theory is a logical extension of agricultural location theory. In this appendix we shall dwell upon some of the interconnections of these two forms of theories. We must leave to the reader and subsequent writers the task of comprehensively stating these interconnections and of relating the literature in these two fields.

Arbitrarily select a unit of urban land. To what use should it be put? The price each potential user is willing to bid is dependent upon many factors such as: (1) effective distance from the core; (2) accessibility of the site to

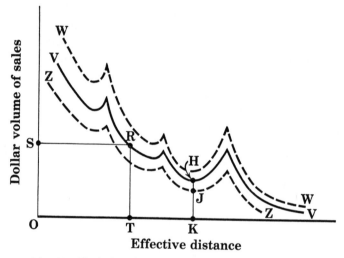

FIG. 39.   Variation of sales with distance from urban core.

potential customers; (3) number of competitors, their locations, and the intensity with which they vie for sales; and (4) proximity to land devoted to an individual use or a set of uses which are complementary in terms of both attracting potential customers and cutting costs, whether they be production, service, advertising, or other.

Couple with the selected unit of land a particular use, let us say, use A. The relations governing the decision of a businessman to bid for the unit of land and devote it to such use may be depicted by a set of graphs. In Fig. 39 we measure along the vertical and horizontal axes, respectively, dollar volume of sales[38] and effective distance from the core. (Effective distance

[38] An alternative would be to measure physical volume of sales along the vertical axis. Since retail and commercial activities tend to dominate urban economic

is not synonymous with physical distance. Rather it is physical distance adjusted in the time-cost dimensions. As a consequence, equal physical distances from the core along the several routes feeding into the core, whether directly or indirectly via other routes, correspond to different effective distances.) When the values for advertising outlays, price mark-up, quality of product or service, and other relevant variables are set, the businessman presumably estimates dollar volume of sales. This volume of sales and the effective distance separating the core and the selected unit of land may be represented, let us say, by point R, in Fig. 39.

The businessman interested in producing the commodity or service corresponding to use A also considers other sites as potential locations. Given the same set of values for advertising outlays, price mark-up, quality of product, and other relevant factors, he anticipates for each possible site a dollar volume of sales. When the effective distance and dollar volume of sales corresponding to each site are plotted on Fig. 39, we obtain curve VV. In general, it is to be expected that dollar volume of sales falls off with effective distance from the core although at times it rises to secondary peaks only to decline again.[39]

However, the potential land user can consider other sets of parametric values for quality of service, advertising outlays, price mark-up, and other relevant variables. There are, in effect, an infinite number of sets possible. For each possible set the potential land user can derive a curve similar to VV. We have added to Fig. 39 curves WW and ZZ which represent two of the infinite number possible.[40]

In addition to Fig. 39, we construct Fig. 40. Figure 40 depicts marginal cost and average cost curves in whose construction rent payments are excluded. These curves relate to that quality of product or service and that

---

activities and since the price of a retail or service activity may often be synonymous with a price mark-up based upon dollar values, we have chosen to speak in terms of dollar volume of sales and price mark-ups. The reader may do otherwise without affecting the validity of the argument.

[39] Where the urban structural pattern is set and relatively inflexible, these secondary peaks can be readily ascertained. They appear at those effective distances which separate secondary and satellite commercial and shopping centers from the core.

In contrast, where the urban structural pattern is extremely fluid and largely to be determined, it is difficult to identify the effective distances from the core at which secondary peaks occur. Since secondary peaks reflect the juxtaposition of complementary activities and since in this latter setting the spatial configurations of all economic activities including transportation patterns are interdependent, only a general equilibrium (simultaneous equations) approach, which takes into account all aspects of complementarity and competition, yields the effective distances at which secondary peaks occur.

Nonetheless, if only for purposes of exposition, we have inserted secondary peaks in Fig. 39.

[40] Rigorously speaking, the problem involves n-variables, n-dimensions, and $(n-1)$ spaces. However, the reader may care to limit the framework of reference of Fig. 39 to three variables: dollar volume of sales, effective distance, and price mark-up. In this case curves WW, VV, and ZZ refer to three different values for the variable, price mark-up, curve ZZ being associated with the highest of the three and curve WW with the lowest.

amount of advertising outlays associated with curve VV of Fig. 39. Also, they reflect variation of costs with sales volume only. Just as we assumed that agricultural cost functions (exclusive of rent) vary insignificantly with distance from the market, we postulate that the cost functions relating to land use A are invariant with distance from the core.[41] As with Fig. 36, we

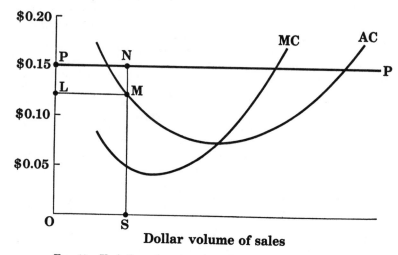

Fig. 40. Variation of cost and profit with volume of sales.

measure along the vertical axis not only costs in dollars, but also price (price mark-up).

Associated with the curve VV of Fig. 39 is a price mark-up, let us say 15 cents. This price mark-up is represented by the price line PP in Fig. 40. Therefore, for any given volume of sales, the spread between the price line and the average cost curve is profits per dollar of sales (exclusive of rent payments). Multiplying this spread by volume of sales yields total profits. Since we have posited freedom of entry, exit, and contract in the long run, this total profit in general will accrue to the landowner as rent through the process of competitive bidding.

Returning to Fig. 39, we find that the businessman estimates his volume of sales at OS if the arbitrarily selected unit of land (at effective distance OT from the core) is devoted to use A. Corresponding to this volume of

[41] As already mentioned, in reality fertility of soil, topography, labor costs, and other factors do vary in a specific regional situation with distance from a central market and thus affect agricultural cost functions. Similarly, topography, accessibility to labor force, and other factors do vary in a specific urban setting with distance from the core and do cause cost functions (excluding rent) associated with any given land use to vary with the position of the land employed. However, these features of the broad physical and social environment do not vary in a regular fashion with distance from any pertinent focal point but rather vary haphazardly. Hence, their variation cannot be incorporated into our analysis which aims at generality and which abstracts from specific environmental situations.

sales in Fig. 40 is the spread (profit per dollar of sales) MN and, therefore, a rent (total profits) which is represented by the area of the rectangle $PNML$. Accordingly, we can plot in Fig. 41 point F which indicates that a total rent OJ (= $PNML$) is yielded by the arbitrarily selected unit of land (at OT distance from the core) if devoted to use A. In Fig. 41, we measure effective distance along the horizontal axis and rent along the vertical.

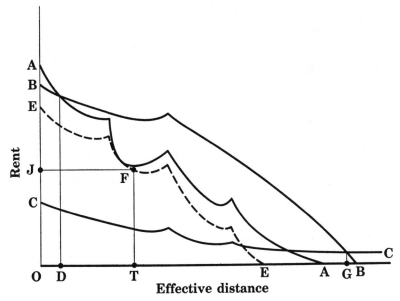

Fig. 41. Rent functions for different urban land uses.

For every other unit of land, the businessman, who has already estimated volume of sales corresponding to any effective distance from the core (as given by curve VV, Fig. 39), can determine profits per dollar sales and total profits (rent) in accordance with Fig. 40. We can therefore plot in Fig. 41 the rent corresponding to each effective distance separating any relevant unit of land from the core. We obtain the dashed curve EE. It depicts rent generally declining with increase in effective distance though rising to secondary peaks at satellite centers where sales volume also attains secondary peaks.

Curve EE might be construed as the rent function relating to use A, much as curve AA in Fig. 38 was construed. Except in a very limited sense, this interpretation would be incorrect. In considering the employment of different units of land in use A, the businessman would not confine his potential operations to the values for price mark-up, quality of product or service, advertising outlays, and other variables which underlie curve VV of Fig. 39. He would find that total profits could be enhanced if one or more of these values were varied at each potential location. Simultaneously, of course, his cost functions would be altered.

For example, the businessman might realize greater profits at effective distance OK (Fig. 39) if he operated under conditions specified by curve ZZ rather than by curve VV. His profit could be greater even though his volume of sales would not be HK, but only JK, since the cost curves associated with curve ZZ would be significantly lower than those in Fig. 40.[42]

Hence, at this and most locations the rent which could potentially accrue to the landowner would exceed that indicated by curve EE (Fig. 41); at no location would rent be less. We therefore let curve AA be the locus of points, each of which depicts at the given effective distance the maximum rent obtainable from the variation of all factors under control of the businessman. It is the relevant rent function for use A.[43]

In similar fashion we can derive for each possible use—retail, commercial, wholesale, industrial, residential, cultural, etc.—a rent function which would depict the maximum rent potential at each possible site. For purposes of illustration, we have added two of these functions, BB and CC, to Fig. 41. As with Fig. 38, at each effective distance, that use whose rent function has the highest ordinate wins out in the competition. For example, if there were only three possible uses of urban land and if at each effective distance the rent potential in any use were completely independent of the uses to which other land was put, the units of land along stretch OD would be channelled into use A, along stretch DG into use B, and beyond G into use C. In reality, at any effective distance the rent potential of land in a given use may be significantly affected by the uses, whether competitive or complementary, to which adjacent and other units of land in the urban area are put. Competition coupled with limited volume of sales is likely to depress markedly the rent potential of any given unit of land when decisions are or have been made to devote other units to the same use.[44] Furthermore, innumerable rent functions obtain, each of which corresponds to a unique use to which urban land can be put. Thus, aside from general residential and industrial land, only a relatively few sites of the many possible ones are allocated by the market mechanism to any particular use. Such sites may comprise clusters

[42] For related discussion on the problem of choosing for any given location the correct set of values for price mark-up, advertising outlays, and quality of product, the reader is referred to, among others: Kenneth E. Boulding, *Economic Analysis*, Harper & Brothers, New York, rev. ed. 1948, Chaps. 31 and 32, especially pp. 717–727; Edward Chamberlin, *The Theory of Monopolistic Competition*, Harvard University Press, Cambridge, Mass., 1938, Chaps. V and VI; L. Abbott, "Vertical Equilibrium Under Pure Quality Competition," *American Economic Review*, Vol. XVIII (December 1953), pp. 826–845; and R. Dorfman and P. O. Steiner, "Optimal Advertising and Optimal Quality," *American Economic Review*, Vol. XLIV (December 1954), pp. 826–836.

[43] If there were plotted in Fig. 41 an infinite number of curves, each corresponding to the relevant conditions depicted by one of the infinite number of curves which we can draw in Fig. 39, we would find that at each effective distance curve AA passes through the maximum of the infinite number of values of the ordinate given by these curves at that effective distance.

[44] This is not to deny that the rent potential of certain units of land in a given use may be greatly enhanced when the use (whether like or unlike) of adjacent land results in increasing the attractive power (dollar volume of sales) of the several juxtaposed units as a whole.

of adjacent units, units spatially distributed throughout the urban area in more or less regular fashion, or both.[45]

In the above fashion, it is thus possible to proceed with the derivation of optimal land-use patterns for different urban settings. Only a skeletal framework has been traced in this appendix. Yet it suffices to disclose the rather obvious interconnections of agricultural location theory and urban land-use theory. In each, rent functions (surfaces) guide the allocating hand of the market. For both, relations to transportation facilities and systems are critical in the definition of effective economic distance; and changes in the transportation grid provoke in each a dynamic pattern of adjustments whose outline is difficult to unravel *ex post*, let alone anticipate. In agricultural location theory, transport outlays are explicitly considered; they depress net farm price. In urban land-use theory, transport outlays enter into the picture just as forcefully, though only implicitly. Transport outlays in terms of both time and cost are borne by the consumer but strategically condition revenue potentials of the business firm through affecting the accessibility of his location to customers and, hence, his volume of sales.

Both agricultural location and land-use theory must be concerned with complementarity and competitive relations. On the farm, complementarity revolves around the full utilization of the farmer's time, equipment, land, and other indivisible units, and it customarily results in the cultivation of a system of crops rather than a single crop. In the urban setting, complementarity in terms of configuration of uses spatially juxtaposed critically affects both costs and accessibility.[46] Finally, technology, the legal framework, and other institutional and cultural factors in their full dynamic setting establish constantly changing limits to which a given unit of land, whether rural or urban, may be put. In many cases, these limits are rational so far as the commonweal is concerned; in other instances, irrational. Where rational, they too add to the similarities of and interconnections between agricultural location theory and urban land-use theory.

In bringing this appendix to a close, we wish to state that the urban land-use problem can be presented in terms of substitution analysis and as an integral part of general location theory, much as agricultural location theory has been. In essence the businessman substitutes among various outlays and

---

[45] The reader is referred to Hoover, *op. cit.*, Figs. 11 and 12, for suggestive graphic illustrations.

To avoid complicated diagrams we have presented the analysis in terms of effective distance along only one line radiating from core point O. A more comprehensive presentation would have considered units of land along all possible lines radiating in different directions both directly and indirectly from point O. Such a presentation (in which, to reiterate, equal physical distances would correspond to different effective distances) would have yielded rent surfaces for each of the innumerable uses. However, the analysis would not have been altered and would have led to similar general results.

[46] The complementarity problem is as difficult to attack as the agglomeration problem. In many respects, these two problems are two sides of the same coin. Both require an analytical approach which looks at each individual activity not in vacuum but as an element of a complex of activities. Such a complex approach will be explored in a future volume.

revenues when he selects both the commodity (product or service) to be produced and his location. He may substitute rent outlays for advertising outlays or for outlays to alter the quality of his commodity when he considers shifting his location to any site closer to the core; or, if he maintains quality and advertising outlays, he incurs additional rent outlays to acquire additional revenue potentials. In weighing the several commodities which he might produce, once again he substitutes among the outlays and revenues associated with the several commodities, much as the farmer does in selecting the particular set of crops to be cultivated. And so forth. Thus, although the typical businessman may not attack his problem in such a comprehensive fashion, tracing out in a substitution framework what his logical reactions would be allows us to arrive at optimal patterns of land use.

It must constantly be borne in mind, however, that the businessman operates within a setting of restraints. Certain of these restraints are imposed by the features of his physical environment, such as topography and existing structures. Certain are associated with social and economic conditions which relate to such factors as total demand, total income, tastes, and cultural patterns, whose treatment falls within the scope of a volume on regional analysis. These restraints are of as great importance in shaping land-use patterns as are the businessman's own decisions. Since these restraints differ from urban area to urban area, they in turn induce logical patterns of land use which differ from area to area. They furnish a partial justification for the kaleidoscopic variety of reality.

Chapter 9

Some Basic Interrelations
of Location and Trade Theory[1]

1. PRELIMINARY REMARKS

Heretofore, we have treated trade rather incidentally. We have focused upon the location of the individual industrial or agricultural enterprise (or group of enterprises) with respect to markets, whether one-point or areal. We have implicitly posited that once locations are determined, the associated flows of commodities, both as inputs and products, are likewise determined. This postulate is consistent with the statement in Chap. 2 that "(1) location cannot be explained without at the same time accounting for trade and (2) trade cannot be explained without the simultaneous determination of locations."

Although trade and location are as the two sides of the same coin, it does not follow that the general location theory developed thus far is adequate to explain all forms of trade. First, the general theory of location developed in this volume does not consider, except in minor fashion, the aggregate demand and income side of the picture, particularly as they relate to regions and to interregional trade. These aspects of both the location and trade problem are to be considered in another volume.[2]

[1] The contents of this chapter are largely drawn from a manuscript written jointly with Merton J. Peck.

[2] The reader will find some of these aggregative demand and income aspects treated in W. Isard, "Location Theory and Trade Theory: Short-Run Analysis," *Quarterly Journal of Economics*, Vol. LXVIII (May 1954), pp. 305–320.

Second, trade may be international as well as intranational. An international setting introduces into our conceptual framework certain additional basic factors. Nonetheless some of these factors can be incorporated into our analysis, as we shall now attempt to demonstrate in this chapter.

In Chap. 2 we have already noted that Weber criticized classical trade theory for ignoring the significant amount of industry which is transport-oriented, and whose geographic distribution, internationally speaking, is governed primarily by considerations of transport cost of raw materials, fuel, and finished product. This criticism was undoubtedly a major source of inspiration for Ohlin's attempt "to demonstrate that the theory of international trade is only a part of a general localization theory."[3] This attempt has already been discussed in Chap. 2. Other location theorists—Furlan, Engländer, Weigmann, Predöhl, and particularly Lösch[4]— have reiterated Weber's contention. But despite Ohlin's excellent formulation of the problem, Williams' classic criticism of the mobility and immobility premises of trade theory,[5] and Lösch's major contribution in visualizing and portraying the spatial structure of an economic system, the presentation of the basic interrelations which should logically obtain between location and trade theories, and which should lead to improvements in both, is still wanting. As one of the objectives of this chapter we hope to cast additional light on these basic interrelations.

2. A FUSION OF OPPORTUNITY COST DOCTRINE AND TRANSPORT-ORIENTATION

The empirical materials presented in Chap. 3 testify to the significance of the friction of distance both in interregional and in inter-

---

[3] Bertil Ohlin, *Interregional and International Trade,* Harvard University Press, Cambridge, Mass., 1933, p. vii.

[4] V. Furlan, "Die Standortsprobleme in der Volks- und Weltwirtschaftslehre," *Weltwirtschaftliches Archiv,* Vol. II (1913), pp. 1–34; O. Engländer, "Kritisches und Positives zu einer allgemeinen reinen Lehre vom Standort," *Zeitschrift für Volkswirtschaft und Sozialpolitik,* Vol. V (Neue Folge), Nos. 7–9 (1926); H. Weigmann, "Ideen zu einer Theorie der Raumwirtschaft," *Weltwirtschaftliches Archiv,* Vol. XXXIV (1931), pp. 1–40; and "Standortstheorie und Raumwirtschaft" in *Johann Heinrich von Thünen zum 150 Geburtstag,* ed. W. Seedorf and H. Jurgen, Rostock, 1933, pp. 137–57; A. Predöhl, "Aussenwirtschaft," *Grundriss der Sozialwissenschaft,* Bd. 17 (Göttingen, 1949); A. Lösch, *Die räumliche Ordnung der Wirtschaft,* Jena, 1944, Part III.

[5] J. H. Williams, "The Theory of International Trade Reconsidered," *Economic Journal,* Vol. XXXIX (June 1929), pp. 195–209.

national trade. The "falling off with distance" effect is pronounced.[6] Yet how incorporate this effect in both location and trade theory?

In the previous chapters, especially in Chap. 5, the distance variable has already been partly incorporated into location theory via the concept of transport input. Fuller treatment of this variable by location analysis lies in that direction which would involve the development of gravity models and models of other types.[7] (These models are to be discussed in a subsequent volume.) In contrast, in international trade theory the distance variable has hardly been explicitly recognized. This situation reflects the fact that the various international trade doctrines have been pushed along certain channels to extreme refinement but left in a primitive stage of development in other channels. Those aspects of trade theory which have remained undeveloped are the very ones which would involve the explicit treatment of the distance variable and which would thereby contribute to the fusion of trade theory and location theory. Hence an attack must be made on these aspects.

A major obstacle to such an attack is the disagreement among trade theorists as to what is "good and relevant" trade theory. Into such a controversy we do not wish to enter, particularly since we feel that, for the most part, whatever the trade theory considered, improvement can be effected when attention is paid to the spatial aspects of the economy and when the techniques and concepts of location theory are embraced. For our purposes, however, it seems sufficient to proceed with a very crude classification of trade doctrines, namely, those which are concerned with or emphasize long-run effects and adjustments, and those which attribute greater, though not exclusive, significance to short-run repercussions and forces. Since the extension of the latter set of trade doctrines to incorporate more explicitly the distance variable revolves around the appropriate development of gravity models, modified interregional input-output schemes and activity analysis, which are to be discussed in a subsequent volume, we shall confine ourselves in this chapter to the extension of the first type of trade doctrine.[8] This type is best exemplified by Graham's work.[9]

[6] Also, see W. Beckerman, "Distance and the Pattern of Intra-European Trade," *Review of Economics and Statistics*, forthcoming.

[7] See W. Isard and G. Freutel, "Regional and National Product Projections and Their Interrelations," *Long-Range Economic Projection,* Studies in Income and Wealth, Vol. XVI, Princeton University Press, Princeton, N.J., 1954, pp. 434–439.

[8] For some preliminary extension of the latter set of trade doctrines the reader is referred to W. Isard, *op. cit.*

[9] Frank D. Graham, *The Theory of International Values,* Princeton University Press, Princeton, N.J., 1940.

Graham's approach has strong appeal to location theorists since he adopts a multicountry, multicommodity approach (one which until recently has not been common among trade theorists) and since he emphasizes supply and cost conditions.[10] However, Graham ignores the very heart of location analysis, namely, that sector of any national or international economy for which transport costs are the primary location factor and which is characterized as transport-oriented. As pointed out above, if there is any significance to location analysis, it lies in the fact that transport costs vary systematically with distance and thus provide an underlying stratum for systematic analysis.

Though transport-orientation analysis should be included in trade doctrine in order to facilitate the understanding of flows of commodities, it must be admitted that existing location theory does not readily adapt itself to being so included since it treats costs only in terms of a given currency. We wish now to demonstrate that, by extending the analytic framework of transport-orientation to consider not costs in any particular currency (as dollars or sterling) but *rather opportunity costs*, it is possible to incorporate transport-orientation into existing trade theory. We illustrate by an extended, though simple, example.

Assume three countries, *A*, *B*, and *C*, each possessing, as with Graham, 12 productive units. After trade, two finished goods, steel and textiles, are consumed by each. To produce 1 weight unit of steel requires 2 weight units of ore and 4 weight units of coal and, in addition, shipping for the finished steel and for one or both raw materials. If production is at *A*, coal which is assumed to exist in *B* alone will need to be shipped as well as finished steel. If production is at *B*, ore which is assumed to exist in *A* alone will need to be shipped as well as steel. If production is at *C* which possesses neither coal nor ore, both raw materials and steel will need to be shipped. To simplify computations, shipping requirements on textiles are assumed to be negligible.[11]

[10] By and large, the traditional location theory of the Launhardt, Weber, Palander, and Hoover type has posed the problem of finding the point of minimum cost for assembling raw materials, processing them, and distributing the finished product to the market point or area. For the most part, demand has been taken as given, or its variation as of minor consequence for determining the optimum plant location. Even agricultural location theory of the Thünen type takes prices and hence demand at the city market as set. The problem is essentially to consider the variation in transport and production costs associated with the various possible patterns of zones in the cultivation of several crops and to select that pattern which maximizes rent for each unit of land.

[11] The reader may wish to consider not only shipping requirements on textiles, but also the raw material and other factor requirements in both textile and steel production, as one must in reality. To do so complicates manyfold the computations and does not affect the essential nature of the conclusions to be derived.

In each country let a productive unit, when devoted to the production of a given commodity alone, produce under conditions of pure competition and constant cost, the quantities (in standard weight units) of each commodity as listed in Table I. Shipping is necessarily expressed in terms not of weight units but of transport inputs where a transport input (say a ton-mile) is defined as the movement of a weight unit (a ton) over a unit of distance (a mile). Also, although a productive unit in each country can produce 8 units of steel when the ore and coal are at hand, the ore, coal, and transportation of the ore, coal, and finished product must be purchased. Hence, a productive unit in countries A, B, and C produces respectively $8 - X_A$, $8 - X_B$, and $8 - X_C$ units of steel where X_A, X_B, and X_C correspond to the amounts of steel (or their equivalents in terms of textiles or shipping)

TABLE I. AMOUNT OF EACH COMMODITY A PRODUCTIVE
UNIT IN EACH COUNTRY CAN PRODUCE WHEN DEVOTED
TO THE PRODUCTION OF ONE COMMODITY ALONE

Commodity	Country		
	A	B	C
Ore	30	0	0
Coal	0	20	0
Textiles	5	4	2
Shipping (in transport inputs)	2500	600	600
Steel	$8 - X_A$	$8 - X_B$	$8 - X_C$

exchanged for the coal, ore, and associated shipping required if a particular country were to produce and deliver the steel. The figures of Table I, once the values of the variables X_A, X_B, and X_C are determined for any given situation, express for each country the opportunity costs in the use of a productive unit for the production of any commodity.

In determining the values of X_A, X_B, and X_C we must construct a table on shipping requirements of steel in terms of transport inputs. For this to be done, however, the distances separating countries must be specified. For the moment, posit that each country is 100 distance units from each of the other two, so that their geographic position is

---

The two activities, textile and steel production, are purposefully chosen. The former typifies an industry usually treated by trade theorists and is one in the location of which labor and other immobile local (national) resources are dominant factors while transport cost is, at most, minor. The latter represents a transport-oriented industry, in the location of which labor and other immobile resources have been considered incidental (W. Isard, "Some Locational Factors in the Iron and Steel Industry since the Early Nineteenth Century," *Journal of Political Economy*, Vol. LVI (June 1948), pp. 203–217).

as the corners of an equilateral triangle. See the figure at the upper right hand corner of Table II. Immediately Table II can be filled in. Since in serving any market B has less shipping expense (incurs fewer transport inputs) than either A or C, and A less than C, and since the

TABLE II.   TRANSPORT INPUT REQUIREMENTS PER WEIGHT UNIT OF STEEL, GIVEN RELATIVE POSITION:

Country to Which Delivered		On Coal	On Ore	On Steel	Total
A	If production at A	400	0	0	400
	If production at B	0	200	100	300
	If production at C	400	200	100	700
B	If production at A	400	0	100	500
	If production at B	0	200	0	200
	If production at C	400	200	100	700
C	If production at A	400	0	100	500
	If production at B	0	200	100	300
	If production at C	400	200	0	600

mine prices of ore and coal wherever steel may be produced will be identical for the three countries,[12] it follows that:

$$8 - X_B > 8 - X_A > 8 - X_C.$$

To derive the values of X_A, X_B, and X_C as well as the patterns of production and trade, demand conditions must also be specified since otherwise exchange ratios cannot be obtained. To simplify the problem assume, within the range of variation of real income considered below, that each country desires to consume twice as much textiles as steel.[13] It then follows that:

[12] The mine prices of ore and coal in terms of finished steel will, of course, depend upon which country or countries produce steel.

[13] It is traditional to posit that variation of real income, within definite limits, does not affect the simplified expenditure (demand) pattern usually assumed. See, for example, Graham, *op. cit.*, Chap. V, or L. Metzler, "Graham's Theory of International Values," *American Economic Review*, Vol. XL (June 1950), pp. 304–13.

(1) A produces all the ore required; also she furnishes all the shipping (since, given demand conditions, her 12 productive units are not completely utilized in both ore production and in shipping and since she has greater advantage compared to B and C in shipping than in any other activity except ore production) ; and in addition she engages in some textile production (since she has greater comparative advantage in textiles than in steel or coal).

(2) B produces all the coal required and some textiles (since even if B were to produce all the steel required in addition to the coal, she would have left over some productive units, given the demand conditions, and since relative to A she has less disadvantage in the production of textiles than in shipping or ore production).

(3) C produces some textiles (since even if C were to produce all the steel required, she would have unutilized some productive units, and, since relative to A or B, she has less disadvantage in the production of textiles than in shipping or ore production or coal production).

Since each country produces textiles, exchange values are, as with Graham, 1 unit of textiles for 6 of ore, for 500 of shipping,[14] for 5 of coal and for $(8 - X_B)/4$ or $(8 - X_C)/2$ of steel. However, it is not clear whether B or C will produce steel, even though B has absolute advantage over C in steel production and is the point of minimum transport cost for serving each steel market. The answer hinges upon whether B's productivity in steel $(8 - X_B)$ is more than twice C's $(8 - X_C)$. Simple calculation shows that this is the case.[15] As a

[14] Traditional location theory assumes a given transport rate structure which applies to the movement of a commodity whether or not the commodity represents return cargo on a ship which otherwise might make the trip empty. This procedure assumes certain monopolistic elements and inefficiencies in rate-making which to some extent at least exist in reality.

Logically, the entire pattern of commodity movements and requirements for transport services in all directions should be considered in setting rates, as, for example, Koopmans has done (T. C. Koopmans and S. Reiter, "A Model of Transportation," in *Activity Analysis of Production and Allocation*, ed. by T. C. Koopmans, New York, 1951, Chap. XIV). To do this here, however, would require an extension of location theory in a direction which is beyond the scope of this chapter. The rate of 500 transport inputs for 1 unit of textiles is taken as fixed.

[15] From Table II it is seen that in producing and delivering steel to any market C's absolute disadvantage relative to B is *least* with respect to the market in C, the absolute disadvantage in this case being measured by 300 transport inputs. Consider then the question of productivity in producing and delivering steel to C. To produce and deliver 8 units of steel to C, B requires: (1) 16 units of ore for which, according to the above exchange ratios, she must pay A 2.7 units of textiles (or its equivalent); (2) 32 units of coal for which she must pay her coal producers 6.4 units of textiles; and (3) 2400 transport inputs for which she must

consequence, B produces steel and C textiles since C has comparative advantage in textiles alone.

It is not necessary to show here how one derives the equilibrium situation consonant with the several postulates on demand,[16] opportunity costs, and relative position of countries.[17] Suffice it to indicate that country C consumes 5.7 units of steel and twice as much textiles; B, 11.9 units of steel, and twice as much textiles; and A, 14.2 units of steel and twice as much textiles. C exports to B 12.7 units of textiles in exchange for 5.7 units of steel. B exports to A 14.2 units of steel in exchange for 63.5 units of ore, 4.4 of textiles, and 8331 transport inputs. (These data together with data on outputs and raw materials and shipping consumption are recorded in Table IV.)   In addition, the exchange ratio of textiles for steel at the point of consumption is 2.2 to unity in A and C, and 2.0 to unity in B.[18]

---

pay A 4.8 units of textiles. Thus, to obtain the ore, coal, and shipping, she must pay out 13.9 units of textiles (or its equivalent) which requires the employment of 3.5 of her productive units since, according to Table I, each of her productive units can produce 4 units of textiles. In addition another productive unit is engaged in the actual manufacture of 8 units of steel. All told, B must devote 4.5 of her productive units to the task of producing and delivering 8 units of steel to C. Her productivity in steel relative to the market in C is 1.8.

To produce and deliver 8 units of steel to C, C requires: (1) 16 units of ore for which she must pay A 2.7 units of textiles; (2) 32 units of coal for which she must pay B 6.4 units of textiles; and (3) 4800 transport inputs for which she must pay A 9.6 units of textiles. Thus she must pay out 18.7 units of textiles (or its equivalent) which, according to Table I, requires the employment of 9.3 of her productive units. In addition, one more productive unit is engaged in the actual manufacture of steel. All told, C must apply 10.3 of her productive units to the job of producing 8 units of steel for her own consumption. C's productivity in steel relative to the market in C is 0.8. Since C's productivity in this case is less than one-half of B's (1.8), B has comparative advantage in producing steel.

If B has comparative advantage over C in producing and delivering steel to the market in C, for which market B has least absolute advantage over C, it follows that B has comparative advantage over C in producing and delivering steel to the markets in A and B, for which markets B's absolute advantage is greater. Hence, B produces all the steel, and C produces only textiles. (The above numerical results and those to follow are rounded to the first decimal point.)

[16] The reader should bear in mind that the simplifying assumption concerning demand is not basic to the argument. Any other assumption is equally suitable, provided it does not unduly complicate computations.

[17] The reader can refer to Graham, op. cit., pp. 76–82, for a demonstration of how a final, stable exchange situation may be derived.

It should also be noted that the problem can be set up in a linear programming form. This has been done by John S. Chipman, who has verified in this manner some of the results obtained.

[18] The ratio is smaller in B since transport input requirements are smaller in delivering to the market in B. See Table II.

The above example illustrates how the basic core of location theory, namely, transport-orientation, can be fused with the opportunity cost doctrine of trade theory to yield a superior understanding of the simultaneous determination of the location of economic activities and of trade. Steel production is concentrated at B. This result is obtained and represents a case of transport-orientation, whether we employ the traditional (intranational) location approach which minimizes the cost of transport inputs or the superior approach which considers opportunity cost as well. From the standpoint of trade theory we have introduced explicitly the distance factor (in the concept of transport inputs) and shown how the opportunity cost formulation can be easily extended to embrace industries which are typically transport-oriented intranationally. The extended opportunity cost formulation and the improved formulation of transport-orientation are, of course, one and the same.

3. The Effects of a Change in the Distance Variable Upon Trade, Industrial Location, and Geographic Specialization

We now consider the implications of a change in distance relations. Are trade and geographic specialization among nations and regions significantly dependent upon their relative position, upon the absolute distances separating any pair?[19] To answer this basic question, alter the relative positions of the three countries so that they are as a straight line, 200 distance units separating A and B, with C at the midpoint, 100 distance units from both A and B. See the line diagram at the upper right hand corner of Table III. Transport input requirements are simultaneously changed and are recorded in Table III. Note that once again B has an absolute advantage over all countries in producing steel for all markets because (1) the prices of coal, ore, and transport inputs and the unit requirements of coal and ore are the same for all countries as potential producers, and (2) the transport input re-

[19] Again the reader is reminded that provided distances are not so great as to make transport cost prohibitive for certain commodities and thus stifle trade in these commodities, trade theory (aside from Ohlin's contribution) has usually presumed that variation in distances and hence transport costs will cause variation in the divergences of exchange values in the several countries but will not affect the commodities produced and traded by each country. See, for example, R. F. Harrod, *International Economics*, London, 1947, p. 20; Haberler, *op. cit.*, pp. 140–42; Viner, *op. cit.*, pp. 314–18 and 467–70; and even Graham, *op. cit.*, pp. 139–46, who perhaps treats transport cost more realistically than any of the above. It should be noted that at one point Viner writes: "In fact, differences in freight costs may create a comparative advantage which in the absence of freight costs would not exist at all" (p. 470 note). However, this pregnant statement is left undeveloped.

quirements in serving each market are least for B. Thus, B, according to orthodox location doctrine, is the optimal transport point. It should be the point of steel production for all markets (as it was in the triangular situation) *provided the net deviating force of cheap sites of*

TABLE III. TRANSPORT INPUT REQUIREMENTS PER WEIGHT UNIT OF STEEL, GIVEN RELATIVE POSITION:

Country to Which Delivered		On Coal	On Ore	On Steel	Total
A	If production at A	800	0	0	800
	If production at B	0	400	200	600
	If production at C	400	200	100	700
B	If production at A	800	0	200	1,000
	If production at B	0	400	0	400
	If production at C	400	200	100	700
C	If production at A	800	0	100	900
	If production at B	0	400	100	500
	If production at C	400	200	0	600

(Relative Position: A •——100——• C ——100——• B)

labor and other inputs does not offset the transport minimizing force.

The resulting stable exchange situation, *which does testify to the partial dominance of the deviating force of cheap labor at C,* is presented in Table IV, along with the old exchange situation of the triangular setup.[20] The new situation strongly contrasts with the old. C now produces steel for both itself and A. There are new geographic flows of ore, transport inputs, and textiles from A to C, of coal from B to C, of steel from C to A, and of textiles from B to A. The old flows of steel from B to A, of textiles from A to B, and of steel from B to C have been eliminated. The only flow which has not been subject to major change is that of textiles from C to B. In sum, changing the distance variable as we did almost completely revamps the geographic flow of commodities and the structure of trade. In contrast, the

[20] As in the old situation, we quickly perceive in the new that: (1) A should produce all the ore, all the shipping, and some textiles; (2) B should produce all the coal and some textiles; and (3) C should produce some textiles. Again, the critical question is: should B, C, or both produce steel? If he cares to, the reader can make the necessary computations to derive an answer to this question in the same manner as was done in an earlier footnote for the triangle situation (the following footnotes also indicate another computational approach). The results are: (1) B produces steel for its own market; (2) C produces steel for both its own and A's market.

resulting changes in real income (consumption of the finished goods, textiles, and steel) are relatively minor.[21]

Thus we see how, once trade theory is extended to embrace the realistic situations of commodities sensitive to differentials in transport cost, the distance variable can have a major influence on trade as it does in fact. With such an extension the criticisms of Weber are met, and the vague intuitive formulation of Ohlin can be concretely expressed. Although one example (to which we limit ourselves in this chapter) is inadequate to point up in full the implications of such an extension, it develops the required procedure and the significance of the distance factor.

At the same time this extension represents an extension of location theory. As already noted in the line position case, B by orthodox location doctrine is the optimal transport point for steel production. However, it develops that B produces steel for its own consumption only and not for A and C. This result obtains because B has comparative advantage over C in producing steel for B's internal market (costs being expressed in terms of textiles) but comparative disadvantage (though still absolute advantage) in producing steel for A and C.[22] The required restatement of location doctrine is immediately apparent: costs must be expressed as opportunity costs. Thus, a transport-oriented industry must be defined as one in which the differential advantage of the optimal transport point completely offsets the net differential advantage of any other site *where costs are expressed in terms of a commodity produced in common by two or more nations.* And a labor-oriented industry must be defined as one in which the differential advantage of a cheap labor point completely offsets the net differential advantage of any other site, *again where costs are expressed in terms of a commodity produced in common.* In the triangle case, B was the optimal transport point, and in terms of each market its transport cost advantage more than offset the labor cost advantage of C. In the line case B is still the optimal transport point, but, in serving the markets at A and C (but not at B), its transport

21 The exchange values also are subject to some change. One unit of textiles still exchanges for 6 of ore, for 500 of shipping, and for 5 of coal. However, in A, 1 unit of textile exchanges for 0.359 units of steel as against 0.448 of steel in the triangular situation; in B, for 0.411 as against 0.492; and in C, for 0.387 as against 0.448.

22 In terms of the market at B, 1 productive unit in B (whose opportunity cost is 4 units of textiles) can produce 1.64 units of steel; and 1 in C (whose opportunity cost is 2 units of textiles), 0.72 units of steel. In terms of the markets at A and C, 1 productive unit in B can produce respectively 1.41 and 1.52 units of steel; and in C, 0.72 and 0.77 units of steel.

TABLE IV. PRODUCTION, CONSUMPTION AND TRADE FLOWS CONTRASTED FOR THE TWO DIFFERENT RELATIVE SPATIAL POSITIONS OF COUNTRIES

Country	Commodity	Production (Units) Triangle Position	Production (Units) Line Position	Net Imports from A Triangle Position	Net Imports from A Line Position	Net Imports from B Triangle Position	Net Imports from B Line Position	Net Imports from C Triangle Position	Net Imports from C Line Position	Consumption (Units) Triangle Position	Consumption (Units) Line Position
A	Textiles	32.7	17.9							28.3	25.1
	Steel					14.2	12.3		12.5	14.2	12.5
	Ore	63.5	57.2								
	Coal										
	Shipping	8331	16,248								
B	Textiles	6.8	19.7	4.4				12.7	14.2	23.8	21.7
	Steel	31.7	10.8							11.9	10.8
	Ore			63.5	21.7					63.5	21.7
	Coal	127.0	114.4							127.0	43.3
	Shipping			8331	4332					8331	4332
C	Textiles	24.0	19.5							11.3	10.5
	Steel		17.8		5.1	5.7				5.7	5.2
	Ore				35.5						35.5
	Coal						71.1				71.1
	Shipping				11,916						11,916

cost advantage is more than offset by C's labor cost advantage.[23] Hence the steel industry in the straight line case is partially transport-oriented and partially labor-oriented. Incidentally, expressing costs as opportunity costs brings out the significant conclusion that industries which have traditionally been considered transport-oriented within a national framework may, because the international set of cost differentials diverge considerably from the national, be oriented otherwise within an international framework.

4. Some Conclusions

For long-run analysis it is shown how, with the use of the concept of transport inputs, transport-orientation and the opportunity cost doctrine can be fused to yield a superior set of tools. It becomes possible to trace the impact of change in the distance variable upon the industrial structure (geographic specialization) of each country, the composition of trade, exchange values, and the magnitude and characteristics of other significant elements associated with the simultaneous determination of location of economic activities and commodity flows. At the same time this fusion represents, on the one hand, an extension of location theory since the traditional cost approach of location theory is reformulated in terms of opportunity costs, and, on the other hand, an extension of long-run trade theory since commodities sensitive to differentials in transport costs are introduced into the traditional comparative cost framework. By this achievement the way is paved for each type of theory to take over many of the sound doctrines of the other. Practically all location doctrine, such as labor orientation, power orientation, agglomeration, etc., can now be adapted and employed in trade theory; and, similarly, all developments in long-run trade theory can be adapted and employed in location

---

[23] In the triangle case, to produce and deliver 8 units of steel to C requires: (1) shipping which costs 4.8 units of textiles if production is at B and 9.6 units of textiles if at C; (2) 1 productive unit which costs 4 units of textiles at B and 2 at C; and (3) ore and coal whose prices are identical for both B and C. Thus, B has a differential advantage of 4.8 units of textiles with regard to transport and a differential disadvantage of 2 units of textiles with regard to labor and other resources contained in a productive unit. The transport differential is the greater; hence, the industry is transport-oriented at B.

In the straight line case, shipping costs 8 units of textiles if production is at B and 9.6 units if at C; 1 productive unit is still required whose cost is 4 at B and 2 at C. The differential in the cost of the productive unit is now greater. As a result, in serving the market at C the industry becomes oriented (presumably labor-oriented) to the cheap site of the productive unit, namely C.

theory. Actually to perform this adaptation, however, would require more extended treatment than is possible in this volume.[24]

[24] The reader is again reminded that other relations of location theory and trade theory, particularly the short-run aspects of trade theory, will be discussed in a second volume. Certain of these have been pointed up in W. Isard, "Location Theory and Trade Theory . . .," *op. cit.*

Also the reader is referred to Gottfried von Haberler's "A Survey of International Trade Theory," *Special Papers in International Economics*, No. 1, September 1955, Princeton University Press, Princeton, New Jersey, for a brief, but penetrating, statement on the directions in which one should approach the goal of fusing trade and location theory.

Chapter 10

Aspects of General Location Theory: A Mathematical Formulation

The previous chapters, particularly Chaps. 5 to 8, have treated several types and elements of location theory in a manner which emphasized their interrelations and interconnections. The substitution framework was advanced as a means of pointing up these interrelations and interconnections better. In this chapter we shall, in one sense, repeat the argument, though more explicitly and cogently through the use of mathematical symbols. Yet, more important, we shall try to probe deeper and indicate more effectively how the substitution framework coupled with the concept of transport inputs permits at least a partial fusion of the several location dogmas not only with each other but also with much of production theory. We hope (1) to demonstrate more satisfactorily the pervasiveness of a general principle of an optimum space-economy,[1] and (2) to signify how, when supported by appropriate

---

[1] The space-economy will be assumed to operate under a set of conditions customarily postulated by economists. To the same extent that the postulates are unacceptable to the reader, the ensuing analysis will be devoid of significance. For a dissent from the profit maximization (or cost minimization) principle typical of human ecologists and economists of similar inclinations, see Kenneth E. Boulding, *A Reconstruction of Economics*, John Wiley & Sons, Inc., New York, 1950, Chaps. 1 and 2.

Also, it is recognized that the term *optimum* can be interpreted in several different ways. The analysis that follows will be concerned with an optimum space-economy, primarily from a location standpoint with emphasis on transportation costs. Further, we approach the problem only in terms of an economy with given transport facilities and rate structure. Equally important, however, is an approach which attempts to

side conditions and other hypothesized relations, this principle implies various existing location theories, and therefore must be considered a core element of a general theory of location.

1. Weberian Theory Restated and Generalized

Imagine a general spatial transformation function as

$$(1) \quad \phi(y_1, y_2, \cdots, y_k; m_A s_A, m_B s_B, \cdots, m_L s_L; x_{k+1}, x_{k+2}, \cdots, x_n) = 0$$

where the variables $y_1, y_2, \cdots, y_k$ represent quantities of various inputs other than transport inputs; $m_A s_A, m_B s_B, \cdots, m_L s_L$ represent quantities of various transport inputs, and $x_{k+1}, x_{k+2}, \cdots, x_n$ represent quantities of various outputs. In this formulation, $m_A, m_B, \cdots, m_L$ represent the weights of various raw materials and finished products subject to shipment, and $s_A, s_B, \cdots, s_L$ represent the distances the respective raw materials and products are moved. By definition, $m_I s_I$ represents transport inputs (say, ton-miles of transportation) involved in the shipment of the raw material I from its source(s) to the site of production, or the product I from this site to the consumption point(s).

Transport inputs are explicitly set apart in this function, for a study of their variation is basic to an understanding of the operation of the space-economy. To facilitate this study, we shall start the analysis at a very simple level and assume the Weberian problem of transport orientation.[2]   Given the locational triangle IJC in Fig. 42 where points I and J each represent a unique source of a raw material and C the market point, find in this enclosed area the location for the point of production that minimizes total transportation costs per unit of output. This problem is subject to the postulate that prices and the required amounts per unit of output of all inputs (including raw materials) except transport inputs are invariant with the site of production. The

---

determine the transport network and rate structure simultaneously with the location of economic activities.   Excellent analyses of an optimum transportation system, given the geographic distribution of economic activities, are to be found in T.C. Koopmans, "Optimum Utilization of the Transportation System," *Econometrica*, Vol. 17 (July 1949), Supplement, pp. 136–46; and T. C. Koopmans and S. Reiter, "A Model of Transportation" and G. B. Dantzig, "Application of the Simplex Method to a Transportation Problem," in *Activity Analysis of Production and Allocation* (ed. by T. C. Koopmans), John Wiley & Sons, Inc., New York, 1951, Chaps. XIV and XXIII, respectively.   Also, see M. Beckmann, "A Continuous Model of Transportation," *Econometrica*, Vol. 20 (October 1952), pp. 643–60.

It seems very likely that the analysis developed in this chapter will also prove valid for an optimum space-economy where the character of the transport rate structure is also viewed as variable and to be determined.

[2] *Alfred Weber's Theory of Location of Industries*, ed. by C. J. Friedrich, University of Chicago Press, Chicago, 1929, Chap. III.

only variables are the three transport inputs $m_I s_I$, $m_J s_J$, and $m_C s_C$; since m_I and m_J are fixed and m_C is taken as unity, transport inputs vary simply because distances vary.

Since total revenue and costs on all inputs (except transport inputs) are thus fixed, the firm's customary problem of maximizing profits

$$V = -p_1 y_1 - p_2 y_2 - \cdots - p_k y_k - r_A m_A s_A - r_B m_B s_B - \cdots$$

(2)

$$-r_L m_L s_L + p_{k+1} x_{k+1} + p_{k+2} x_{k+2} + \cdots + p_n x_n,$$

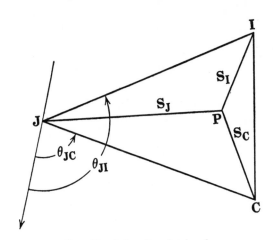

FIG. 42. A locational triangle.

where $p_1, p_2, \cdots, p_n$ are prices, and $r_A, r_B, \cdots, r_L$ are transport rates, is reduced to the problem of minimizing transport costs,

(3) $$K = r_I m_I s_I + r_J m_J s_J + r_C m_C s_C.$$

Either in maximizing profits or minimizing transport costs, the firm is restrained by the spatial transformation function of Eq. 1 which in the latter case becomes simply

(4) $$f(s_I, s_J, s_C) = 0,$$

and implies that the firm must choose quantities of transport inputs consistent with measuring the three distances s_I, s_J, and s_C from a common point P within the locational triangle (see Fig. 42).

A necessary and sufficient condition that within the locational triangle P be a stationary point of K is that

(5) $$dK = d(r_I m_I s_I) + d(r_J m_J s_J) + d(r_C m_C s_C) = 0$$

or that

$$\frac{r_I}{r_J} = - \left. \frac{d(m_J s_J)}{d(m_I s_I)} \right| (m_C s_C) = \text{const.}$$

(6)

$$\frac{r_I}{r_C} = - \left. \frac{d(m_C s_C)}{d(m_I s_I)} \right| (m_J s_J) = \text{const.}$$

$$\frac{r_J}{r_C} = - \left. \frac{d(m_C s_C)}{d(m_J s_J)} \right| (m_I s_I) = \text{const.}$$

Equations (6) obtain since

(7) $$d(r_i m_i s_i) = r_i d(m_i s_i) \qquad (i = I, J, C),$$

for, by definition, r_i is fixed. The right-hand terms in Eqs. 6 represent the marginal rate of substitution between the respective transport inputs. Of Eqs. 6, any two conditions are necessary and sufficient, since with Eq. 4 any two imply the third.[3] We thus have three equations to determine the three unknowns.

For the stationary value to be a minimum, i.e., a point of minimum transport cost, it is sufficient that the second derivative be positive along any arbitrary straight line through P.[4] Since along any such line

(8) $$\frac{d^2 s_i}{du^2} \geqslant 0 \qquad (i = I, J, C),$$

where u is the arc length on an arbitrary line along which the derivative is evaluated and where the equality cannot hold for all values of i in this Weberian problem of fixed m_i and r_i,

(9) $$\frac{d^2 K}{du^2} = \sum m_i r_i \frac{d^2 s_i}{du^2} > 0 \qquad (i = I, J, C).$$

The transport cost surface is everywhere convex downward and of necessity there is only one minimum point.

In terms of the space-economy, Eqs. 6 state the important condition that *at the point of minimum transport cost, the marginal rate of substitution between any two transport inputs, the other held constant, must equal the reciprocal of the ratio of their prices, namely, the corresponding transport rates.*

[3] For, since all directional derivatives of the transport cost function are continuous, the vanishing of the derivative of the function in two directions at point P (in our case, let us say along the two arcs where s_C and s_J in turn are constant) implies that the derivative vanishes in all directions (for example, along the arc where s_I is constant).

[4] If such is the case, it follows that in a neighborhood of P, total cost increases with any arbitrary movement away from P. Therefore P must be a minimum point.

The above condition, it must be emphasized, holds when the minimum transport cost point is not at one of the vertices of the triangle, i.e., when

(10)
$$(r_i m_i)^2 < (r_j m_j \cos \theta_{ij} + r_k m_k \cos \theta_{ik})^2$$
$$+ (r_j m_j \sin \theta_{ij} + r_k m_k \sin \theta_{ik})^2$$
$$(i \neq j \neq k; i, j, k = I, J, C),$$

where θ_{ij} and θ_{ik} are angles cut off by an arbitrary straight line through i and directions i to j and i to k, respectively.[5]

In words, if we conceive the problem as one of the equilibrium of forces,[6] the magnitude of the resultant of the forces (locational pulls) acting from any two corners on the third corner is greater than the magnitude of the force (locational pull) acting from the third.[7]

The fact that any one of the inequalities of Eqs. 10 does not hold is necessary and sufficient that the point corresponding to i be the minimum transport cost point. In a movement away from i the marginal rate of substitution between transport inputs associated with i and transport inputs associated with any other corner j is then given by:

(11)
$$\frac{r_i}{r_j} \geq - \frac{d(m_j s_j)}{d(m_i s_i)} \bigg|_{m_k s_k} = \text{const.}$$

Economically speaking, this means that any small movement away from the transport optimum point along a path for which transport inputs to

---

[5] In Fig. 42 we illustrate for $i = J, j = C$, and $k = I$.

[6] See *Alfred Weber's Theory of Location of Industry*, op. cit., pp. 227–32.

[7] When any one of the inequalities of Eqs. 10 does not hold, and this can be true of only one of the three which compose the set, three types of cases may be distinguished (1) when $m_i r_i > m_j r_j + m_k r_k$. This corresponds to the Weberian category where one raw material or the product is dominant; (2) when one of the inequalities of Eqs. 10 becomes an equality. Here, in the direction of the resultant force, the slope of the transport cost surface vanishes as point i is reached from within the triangle. However, in all other directions, the directional derivative $\neq 0$ as i is approached; (3) when one of the inequalities of Eqs. 10 is reversed but type (1) does not obtain. Here, as in type (1), all directional derivatives $\neq 0$ as i is approached.

As Dean has neatly pointed out, in cases of type (1) Weber's emphasis on weight loss, purity, and addition of ubiquities is correctly placed; however, in cases of types (2) and (3) "the only pertinent concerns are relative gross weight and relative distance." (W. H. Dean, Jr., *The Theory of the Geographic Location of Economic Activities*, Selections from the doctoral dissertation, Edward Brothers, Inc., Ann Arbor, Mich., 1938, p. 19.) This is clear from inequalities of Eqs. 10. Weber and others who have employed his concepts have ". . . seriously overestimated the determinate influence upon location of weight-losing materials, when they are not dominant, and underestimated the attractiveness of pure materials, which are never dominant" (*ibid.*).

or from k is constant involves savings of transport cost on one set of transport inputs which are smaller than (or in an extreme case, equal to)[8] the additional outlays on the other set of transport inputs.

We now extend the problem and consider the shipment of many raw materials to a production point and of product(s) to many consuming points (l variable distances).

The transport cost equation with l terms

$$(12) \qquad K = r_A m_A s_A + r_B m_B s_B + \cdots + r_L m_L s_L$$

is subject to ($l - 2$) restraints

$$(13) \qquad \phi_i(s_A, s_B, \cdots, s_L) = 0 \qquad (i = 1, \cdots, l - 2),$$

since the determination of the values for any two of the distance variables necessarily determines the values of all the others. There are only two independent variables.

As in the case of three distance variables, a necessary and sufficient condition that a point P, not coinciding with any raw material or consumption site, be a stationary point is that

$$(14) \qquad \frac{r_i}{r_j} = - \left. \frac{d(m_j s_j)}{d(m_i s_i)} \right| \sum_{k=A}^{L} r_k m_k s_k = \text{const.}$$

$$(j \neq k \neq i)(i, j = A, \cdots . L).$$

Of these equations, any two imply the rest.[9] These two together with the $l - 2$ restraints determine the l unknowns.

For the stationary point to be a minimum it is sufficient that the second derivative be positive along any arbitrary straight line through P, which is the case as shown above.

However, the above conditions exist only when P does not coincide with any raw material or consumption site. The sufficient and necessary conditions that P does coincide with any such site are exactly analogous to those stated above for three distance variables except that there are ($l - 1$) terms in each of the parentheses of inequalities of Eqs. 10. In a movement away from corner i the marginal rate of

---

[8] This extreme case occurs when one of the inequalities of Eqs. 10 becomes an equality and when the movement is at the same time along the path of the resultant acting on corner i.

[9] Except in the extreme case where the curve (defined by $\sum_{k=A}^{L} r_k m_k s_k = \text{const.}$; $j \neq k \neq i$) along which the first of the derivatives is taken is tangent at P to the other curve along which the second of the derivatives is taken. In such a case the two equations are not independent, and a second independent equation must be introduced.

substitution between any two transport inputs is then given by:

(15)
$$\frac{r_i}{r_j} \geqslant - \left.\frac{d(m_j s_j)}{d(m_i s_i)}\right|_{\sum\limits_{k=A}^{L} r_k m_k s_k} = \text{const.}$$

$$(j \neq k \neq i)(i, j = A, \cdots, L).$$

In words, Eqs. 14 state that at the point of minimum transport cost, the marginal rate of substitution between any two transport inputs, total cost on all other transport inputs being held constant, must equal the reciprocal of the ratio of their prices, namely, the corresponding transport rates. This statement applies, however, only to a minimum transport cost point which does not coincide with a raw material or consumption site. Such correspondence will exist when the locational pull at any site exceeds (or in an extreme case, just equals) the combined locational pulls of other sites. Then, according to Eqs. 15, any small movement away from such a site along any path for which total costs on all transport inputs but two are constant may involve a saving on expenditures for one of these transport inputs, but a saving which is less than (or, in an extreme case, just equal to) the additional expenditures on the second of these transport inputs.[10]

Equations 14 have some interesting implications. If the l transport inputs are arbitrarily divided into any two groups,[11] say, for example, transport inputs on raw materials and transport inputs on products, and if for each group a set of constant total cost curves (generalized isotims) is constructed, the point of minimum transport cost P is a point of tangency between two of these constant total cost curves, one from each set. For, employing vector notation, at P

(16) $$\text{grad } K = \text{grad} \sum_{i=A}^{F} m_i r_i s_i + \text{grad} \sum_{j=G}^{L} m_j r_j s_j = 0$$

and by hypothesis each constant total cost curve in groups one and two is of the form

(17) $$\sum_{i=A}^{F} m_i r_i s_i = C_1$$

(18) $$\sum_{j=G}^{L} m_j r_j s_j = C_2$$

---

[10] See Chap. 5 for some parallel geometric presentation.

[11] It is relevant to consider this phase of the problem since in reality there are marked differentiations in transport rate structures. For example, on the whole raw materials bear a significantly lower rate than finished products; movement in one direction may entail rates markedly different from those for movement in a second direction; shipments over one major type of transport facility usually incur charges different from those for shipments over a second major type. We shall merely sketch how analysis of substitution between groups of transport inputs may proceed.

respectively, where C_1 and C_2 are constants. Since at each point of any curve defined by Eq. 17, grad $\sum\limits_{i=A}^{F} m_i r_i s_i$ has a direction normal to the curve, and likewise for grad $\sum\limits_{j=G}^{L} m_j r_j s_j$ at each point of each curve defined by Eq. 18, these two gradients can be in opposite directions at a point (as required by Eq. 16) only when the respective curves passing through that point are tangent to each other. In terms of the familiar Edgeworth-type box diagram,[12] where the two families of curves may be for illustrative purposes alone taken to represent Eqs. 17 and 18, it is always possible to reduce total costs on each of the two groups of transport inputs by shifting location from a point not a point of tangency to some point which is a point of tangency. However, in contrast to the Edgeworth solution Eq. 16 states more. Of all the possible points of tangency there is one which is the best, namely, the one at which the two gradients are not only opposite in direction, but also equal in magnitude.

For policy purposes, a more generally useful approach in treating groups of transport inputs is to replace actual weights by ideal weights à la Weber. A finished product with a representative transport rate may be taken as the standard for all finished products. The weight of any given finished product can be adjusted upward or downward according as its rate is greater or smaller than that for the standard finished product. One thousand tons of product X moving at a rate three-quarters that of the standard product would have an ideal weight of 750 tons. Likewise, ideal weights of raw materials can be derived with respect to a standard raw material.

It then follows from Eq. 12 that since the rates are the same for all transport inputs of a group, at P

$$(19) \qquad \frac{r_i}{r_j} = -\frac{d \sum\limits_{j=G}^{L} m_j{}^* s_j}{d \sum\limits_{i=A}^{F} m_i{}^* s_i}$$

where $m_i{}^*$ and $m_j{}^*$ are ideal weights.

Under this circumstance, at the optimum location, the marginal rate of substitution between the two groups of transport inputs must be equal to the reciprocal of the ratio of the corresponding transport rates.

Hitherto, transport rates proportional to distance and a space-

---

[12] For example, see W. F. Stolper and P. A. Samuelson "Protection and Real Wages," *Review of Economic Studies*, Vol. IX (November 1941), p. 67.

economy which is continuous transportationwise have been postulated. Needless to say, the real world differs considerably from such a fiction and accordingly it is important to explore needed modifications of the above analysis. We wish to make a few preliminary comments here.

Typically, with modern transport media, there is an initial terminal and loading charge incurred by any shipment, invariant with distance of the shipment, and in addition a line charge where the rate per ton-mile tends to be a decreasing function of distance. Consider first the effect of the line charge alone.

Letting, $r_i = r_i\,(s_i)$, from Eq. 12 we have:

$$(20) \qquad dK = \sum_{i=A}^{L} m_i(r_i + s_i r_i')ds_i$$

where $r_i' = \dfrac{dr_i}{ds_i}$.

The necessary and sufficient condition that P not coinciding with any raw material or market site be a stationary point of K is that the following relations hold at P:[13]

$$(21) \qquad \frac{r_i + s_i r_i'}{r_j + s_j r_j'} = - \frac{d(m_j s_j)}{d(m_i s_i)} \Bigg|_{} \sum_{k=A}^{L} r_k m_k s_k = \text{const.}$$

$$j \neq k \neq i$$
$$i, j = A, \cdots, L.$$

Here, in contrast with the situation where transport rates are proportional to distance there need not be one and only one stationary point and a stationary point which is necessarily a minimum. For along any arbitrary straight line through P,

$$(22) \qquad d^2K = \sum_{i=A}^{L} m_i[(r_i + s_i r_i')(d^2 s_i) + (2r_i' + s_i r_i'')(ds_i)^2].$$

The first term in the brackets is necessarily non-negative, whereas the second term can be both positive and negative, though usually negative.[14] Thus d^2K can be both positive and negative. For point P to be a transport optimum point, the usual second-order quadratic form

---

[13] Provided the two relations are independent. See footnote 9 of this Chapter.

[14] The first term is non-negative since $d^2 s_i$ is non-negative, and since $m_i\,(r_i + s_i r_i')$ is the partial derivative of total transport cost (K) with respect to s_i and thus necessarily positive.

The expression $(2r_i' + s_i r_i'')$ measures the rate of change of slope of $m_i\,r_i\,s_i$ as s_i and r_i alone vary. In modern rate structures r_i' tends to be negative. Also, r_i'' is typically positive but not sufficiently so that $s_i r_i'' > - 2 r_i'$; i. e., $m_i\,r_i\,s_i$ is typically concave downward as a function of s_i.

conditions for a minimum must be satisfied; if more than one stationary point satisfy these conditions, then, obviously, by direct calculation, of these points P must incur least total transport cost.[15]

In economic terms, the first-order conditions of Eqs. 21 state that the marginal rate of substitution between any two transport inputs must equal the reciprocal of the ratios of their *modified transport rates*, each modified transport rate being equal to the actual transport rate for distance s_i adjusted for the saving or added expense per ton-mile resulting from the change in the rate that would ensue from a small change in the distance variable s_i.

When, in addition to a line charge, there is an initial terminal and loading charge, a minimum must exist at each raw material and market site. An infinitesimal movement in any direction from such a site involves a significant initial charge which, in reality, far exceeds the transport cost savings that may be realized by diminishing other transport inputs. Also, for the same reason, a minimum will exist at each point corresponding to a break in the transportation network, where an additional transshipment, loading, or other charge is levied. However, the conditions that P not coinciding with any raw material or market site or break be a minimum point remain unaltered.[16]

Thus, terminal and loading charges, transshipment expenses at breaks, special transit privileges at particular junction points, and other transport rate abnormalities introduce discontinuities into the transport cost surface. Pictorially the entire transport cost surface is raised by the sum of all the initial terminal and loading charges, transshipment expenses, and the like except at each raw material, market, junction, or special privilege site where the surface is punctured. Each punched out point is raised not by the sum of these charges and expenses but by the sum less the charge or expense encountered in movement from the corresponding site. As a consequence, the space-economy tends to comprise a hierarchical set of focal points of different degrees of dominance.

---

[15] The full statement of second-order conditions may be found, for example, in P. A. Samuelson, *op. cit., Mathematical Appendix A.*

It should be noted, however, that in a specific location problem one can avoid the cumbersome quadratic form conditions with complicated side relations by calculating d^2K directly with d^2s_i and ds_i expressed as trigonometric functions of angles formed at P by the lines from P to P_i and the line along which d^2K is evaluated.

A necessary and sufficient condition that P coinciding with a raw material or market site P_i be a minimum point is that the inequalities of Eqs. 10 extended to embrace ℓ variables is not valid where r_j is replaced by $(r_j + s_j r_j')$, $j = A, \cdots, L$.

[16] However, it is unlikely with modern rate structures that P will be an absolute minimum point. For full elaboration of this point see Chap. 5.

2. Inclusion of Market and Supply Areas as Variables

In the previous section the market points to be served are stipulated beforehand. To the extent that there are many, and particularly if there is an infinite number in an area of approximately continuous density, the above location analysis may be said in a sense to embrace market area theory. But in a major respect such a statement would be invalid. Market area analysis has as its essential core the problem of demarcating boundaries and consumers to be served. The problems of determining transport relations and sites of production are also vital, but only in a framework where the area itself is a variable.[17] The analysis hitherto developed posits a fixed market area and is thereby inapplicable.

However, it is not difficult to extend the analysis to encompass the market area (and later, the supply area) as a variable. The initial step is to state the condition of indifference that defines the market boundary, which we take to be:

$$(23) \qquad r^*s^* + \sum_{i=A}^{F} b_i r_i s_i = T,$$

where r^* represents transport rate (with regard to the unit of product) to the boundary line, being invariant with direction;[18] s^* represents radius of circle defining boundary line; $A, \cdots, F$ denote the various raw materials required; b_i represents a constant coefficient indicating the number of units of raw material i used per unit of product; r_i represents transport rate on a unit of raw material i; and T represents the difference between the maximum price p_0 the consumer is willing to pay and the unit costs of production π (excluding transport costs) which are held constant throughout this section of the analysis. Equation 23 states that at the market boundary the sum of the transport costs on the unit product and on the raw materials required to yield the unit product is

[17] See, for example, W. Launhardt, *Mathematische Begründung der Volkswirtschafts-lehre*, Leipzig, 1885, Part III; F. A. Fetter, "The Economic Law of Market Areas," *Quarterly Journal of Economics*, Vol. XXXVIII (May 1924), p. 525; O. Engländer, *Theorie des Güterverkehrs und der Frachtsätze*, Jena, 1924; T. Palander, *Beiträge zur Standortstheorie*, Uppsala, 1935, Chaps. IX and XII; E. Schneider, "Bemerkungen zu einer Theorie der Raumwirtschaft," *Econometrica*, Vol. III (January 1935), pp. 79–89; E. Hoover, *Location Theory and the Shoe and Leather Industries*, Cambridge, Mass., 1937, Chaps. III and V; A. Lösch, *Die räumliche Ordnung der Wirtschaft*, Jena, 1944, Part II; and C. D. Hyson and W. P. Hyson, "The Economic Law of Market Areas," *Quarterly Journal of Economics*, Vol. LXIV (May 1950), pp. 319–327.

[18] When r^* is not invariant with direction, the resulting market area is non-circular. The ensuing analysis, however, is not altered save that visual conception becomes more difficult.

just equal to the difference between unit costs of production and the maximum price the consumer is willing to pay.

For the moment it is useful to consider the simplified case where each consumer purchases one and only one unit of product, for which he is willing to pay a maximum price p_0, ($p_0 = T + \pi$), but for which he actually pays a delivered cost price (i.e., π plus transport costs on raw materials and the unit of product he purchases). The resulting total (consumer or social) surplus is:[19]

$$(24) \qquad Tm - K = Tm - \sum_{i=A}^{F} m_i r_i s_i - \int rs \, d\psi(s)$$

where m represents number of units produced (consumed), r represents transport rate (with regard to the unit of product), s represents distance from P to the consumer, $\psi(s)$ represents the quantity consumed inside circle with radius s and center at P, and the Stieltjes integral is evaluated over an area with P as center and s^* as radius.

Since, by definition,

$$(25) \qquad m = \int d\psi(s)$$

we rewrite Eq. 24:

$$(26) \qquad Tm - K = Tm - \sum_{i=A}^{F} m_i r_i s_i - m\overline{rs}$$

where $\overline{rs}$ represents the average unit cost of transporting the product from P to all consumers.

To maximize surplus,[20] we set:

$$(27) \qquad d(Tm - K) = d(Tm) - \sum_{i=A}^{F} r_i d(m_i s_i) - d(m\overline{rs}) = 0$$

which with Eq. 23 is subject to $(f - 2)$ restraints expressing as before the fact that only two of the s_i can be independent. Equation 27 implies:

$$(28)$$

$$\frac{r_i}{r_j} = -\left.\frac{d(m_j s_j)}{d(m_i s_i)}\right| \; Tm - \sum_{k=A}^{F} r_k m_k s_k - m\overline{rs} = \text{const.}$$

$$(j \neq k \neq i)(i, j = A, \cdots, F),$$

$$\frac{r}{r_j} = -\left.\frac{d(m_j s_j)}{d(m\overline{s})}\right| \; Tm - \sum_{k=A}^{F} r_k m_k s_k = \text{const.}$$

$$(j \neq k)(j = A, \cdots, F).$$

[19] See below in text and footnote 25 for some discussion of the concept of surplus.

[20] The problem is not to minimize total transport cost subject to Eq. 23 and the $(f - 2)$ restraints. For in such a problem P would *tend* to be a center in a market area containing as sparse a population as the restraints permit. Clearly, this is not optimum from a social standpoint.

Of Eqs. 28 any two independent ones imply all the rest.[21]   These two in addition to Eq. 23 and the $(f - 2)$ restraints on the variation of the s_i determine the f unknown distances and s^*.   Equations 28, however, are only necessary and not sufficient conditions for a maximum point except where the density of consumption is constant throughout the region,[22] and perhaps certain other special cases.   It is easily seen, for example, that variation in consumer density over a region may lead to relative maxima at points tending to be central with respect to districts of heavy density and to relative minima in sparsely populated districts in between.   As before, second-order conditions can be stated to distinguish between stationary points, and the best of the maxima can only be determined by direct computation.

Equations 28 state that at the point of maximum surplus the marginal rate of substitution between any two transport inputs (transport inputs on the product being equal to the sum of transport inputs involved in delivering each individual unit from P) is equal to the reciprocal of the ratio of their transport rates, the difference between Tm and total costs on all other transport inputs held constant.[23]   Also, it logically follows that the point of maximum surplus is the point of minimum total transport cost for serving the market area defined with P as center.[24]

[21] Equations 27 and 28 and others to follow which are based upon Eq. 24 and others which employ the Stieltjes integral are valid only when the Stieltjes integral $\int rs \, d\psi(s)$ is differentiable in the relevant region.   The Stieltjes integral rather than the Riemann is employed since the Riemann is a special case of the Stieltjes and since the Riemann cannot be used as the Stieltjes can for cases where discrete consumption points exist at finite distances from the boundary line within a market (or supply) area.

[22] When such is the case, the point of minimum transport cost on raw materials is the point of maximum surplus P.   Any movement away from P increases average cost (K/m) and decreases m, and thereby decreases surplus $(Tm - K)$.   Thus P is a maximum.

[23] Any movement away from P resulting from the substitution of a transport input on one raw material for a transport input on a second raw material may involve a shrinking or expansion of the circular market area and change in m as well as change in the other distance variables.   The market area itself can of course encompass raw material sites.

[24] Suppose the m consumers, contained in the circle with P as center and s^* as radius, could be served with lower total transport costs from P', necessarily not forming a circular area around P'. P' would then yield greater surplus.   But since a circular area with center at a production site will, by our equations, always yield greater surplus than a noncircular area around the same point, a circular area around P' must then yield still greater surplus than that around P.   But this contradicts the fact that P is the point of maximum surplus.   Thus P must be the point of minimum transport cost for the m consumers.

It also follows that at P average transport cost (K/m) for the given market is

The simplification that each consumer purchase one and only one unit can now be relaxed. Without specifying the nature of each consumer's demand function, we can conceive of: (1) a firm, located at one site only, levying a fixed profit α per unit; or (2) each consumer, except when he is on the boundary, obtaining per unit product purchased a surplus β measured, let us say, by the difference between some given price and the lower delivered price (π plus costs of transportation); or (3) society attributing a value γ (in addition to the delivered price the consumer pays) to the consumption of each unit.[25] In each of these cases and a multitude of others that the reader may wish to construct, the form of the necessary conditions for equilibrium is not altered though their content is.

In the first case we maximize

$$(29) \qquad \alpha m = \int (\alpha + p - \pi)\, d\psi(s) - K = (\alpha + \bar{p} - \pi)m - K$$

where p represents the delivered price (excluding the profit charge) to consumers at s, the distance from P, and $\bar{p}$ represents an average delivered price (excluding profit charge) over all units sold. In effect, Eq. 29 resembles Eq. 26 except that $(\alpha + \bar{p} - \pi)$ has been substituted for T. The form of the necessary conditions for a maximum in this problem resemble those expressed in Eqs. 27 and 28 for the previous problem, save that $(\alpha + \bar{p} - \pi)$ is always substituted for T.[26] However, the path along which substitution of transport inputs on raw material i for transport inputs on raw material j can take place is totally different. In such a substitution, the market area tends to shift, expand, or contract; each consumer tends to alter the number of units he pur-

---

at a minimum which, since

$$d\left(\frac{K}{m}\right) = d \sum_{i=A}^{F} b_i r_i s_i + d(\overline{rs}) = 0$$

yields the relations,

$$\frac{r_i}{r_j} = - \frac{d(b_j s_j)}{d(b_i s_i)} \Bigg|_{} \sum_{k=A}^{F} b_k r_k s_k + \overline{rs} = \text{const.} \qquad (j \neq k \neq i)(i, j = A, \cdots, F).$$

These relations which are implied by, but do not imply, Eqs. 28 may facilitate testing the stationary character of points.

[25] We fully appreciate the unreality of these conceptions. However, since economics has not yet reached the stage where the welfare of a group of consumers can be quantitatively evaluated, and since the validity of the relations emphasized in this paper is independent of the nature of any welfare function, these simple conceptions suffice for the immediate purpose.

[26] Also, α must be subtracted from T in Eq. 23.

chases; and thus $\bar{p}$ and m tend to change. To determine a path of substitution becomes more difficult.

In the case of (2) or (3) above, we merely substitute β or γ for α in all the equations. The form of the necessary equilibrium conditions remains the same, although again the content differs.[27]

Heretofore, we have posited that each raw material originates at a single point. The analysis can now be extended to embrace raw material supply areas, each composed of any number of originating sites. To do so with respect to any raw material i requires the substitution of $\int r_i s_i \, d\psi_i(s_i)$ or $m_i \overline{r_i s_i}$ for the term $m_i r_i s_i$ in the above equations where $\psi_i(s_i)$ is the quantity of raw material i supplied within a circle of radius s_i and P as center. With the introduction of a supply (or purchasing) area for any raw material the problem is changed in a way exactly analogous to the way it was changed with the introduction of a market area. The reader will find, if he cares to reformulate the problem mathematically, that the fundamental form of the substitution relations remains unchanged, though these relations bear upon different paths and have different content.[28]

3. The Analysis Extended to the Case of Many Producers

Having generalized the analysis to embrace a market area, variation in consumption patterns over space, and a supply area for each raw material where such areas overlap so that a point may be both a market site and a site at which several raw materials originate, we now proceed to allow more than one production site. In doing this we could maintain the postulate of constant unit production cost (excluding transportation). We would then obtain a statement implying geographic patterns such as those depicted in Palander and Hoover[29] where, for example, we may have at one and the same time production: (1) at raw material sites, each serving a district of consumers, (2) at each point along a closed elliptical-shaped curve, each point serving the consumers in the

---

[27] Where no raw materials are required in production, Eqs. 23 and 27 become $r^* s^* = T$ and $d(Tm - K) = d(Tm) - d(m\overline{rs}) = 0$. The radius s^* is thus invariant with production site. However, if we wish to express equilibrium conditions in terms of transport inputs and not in terms of the vanishing of the partial derivatives in the x and y directions, we can divide transport inputs on the product into three or more subdivisions of transport inputs, each corresponding to a set of consumers asymmetrically located. The analysis would proceed as above where there are several transport inputs to consider.

[28] Of course, substitution can now involve change in one raw material supply area vis-à-vis change in another raw material supply area, or in the market area, and so forth.

[29] T. Palander, op. cit., Chap. VI; and E. M. Hoover, op. cit., pp. 53–55. Also see Fig. 44 below and the accompanying discussion in Chap. 11.

hinterland along its pole line only, and (3) at each consumption site contained in the elliptical-shaped curve, each such site meeting its own needs only.

However, we shall not dwell upon this unrealistic situation which can be considered a special case of the more general type which allows variation in the unit cost of production (as Lösch does). A region may be conceived as divided into several market areas, each served from a production site and bounded on all sides. As before, any boundary line, not a boundary line between two producers, is defined by a condition corresponding to Eq. 23, namely,

$$(30) \qquad \sigma_\mu + r_\mu{}^* s_\mu{}^* + \sum_{i=A}^{F} b_i r_i s_{i\mu} = p_0, \qquad (\mu = 1, \cdots, \eta),$$

where σ_μ represents the marginal production costs (excluding transportation) at site P_μ, and $s_{i\mu}$ represents the distance between P_μ and the site of raw material i.[30]

Our problem is to maximize, let us say, *social* surplus:

$$\gamma m = m(\gamma + \bar{p} - \bar{\pi}) - K$$

$$(31)$$

$$= m(\gamma + \bar{p} - \bar{\pi}) - \sum_{i=A}^{F} \sum_{\mu=1}^{\eta} m_{i\mu} r_i s_{i\mu} - \sum_{\mu=1}^{\eta} m_\mu \overline{rs}_\mu,$$

where $\bar{p}$ represents the average delivered price on all units produced (consumed); $\bar{\pi}$ represents the average unit production costs on all units; $m_{i\mu}$ represents the total weight of raw material i used by producer μ; m_μ represents the total units (weight) of product consumed in market area served by producer μ; and $\overline{rs}_\mu = \dfrac{1}{m_\mu} \int rs_\mu \, d\psi_\mu(s_\mu)$ represents the average transport cost per unit of product in shipping the product from P_μ to customers in the corresponding market area.

[30] We have defined the boundary in terms of marginal production cost plus unit transport cost rather than average unit production cost plus unit transport cost. This ensures an optimum spatial arrangement for society as a whole, but involves a net loss for each producer when he is producing on the falling section of his average cost curve and when delivered price is based on marginal cost at P_μ. The reader may substitute π_μ (average unit production cost) for σ_μ in Eqs. 30 and in subsequent equations which define boundary conditions among producers. This, however, would not be consistent with an optimum space-economy, though of course it would be consistent with an optimum space-economy subject to the restraint that delivered prices be based on average unit production cost.

This problem, which lies outside the scope of this book, has been treated at length in the literature on welfare economics. Refer, for example, to A. Bergson, "Socialist Economics," in *A Survey of Contemporary Economics*, ed. by H. S. Ellis, Blakiston, Philadelphia, 1948, pp. 424–28, and the literature cited therein.

First, it should be noted that since there is an infinity of market sites (consumers) in our wholly or partially continuous areas, one may treat an infinity of variables, the distance from any consumer to a corresponding producer being a variable. However, it is immediately possible to reduce the infinity of variables to a finite number through considering each market area as a whole and introducing boundary conditions between the market areas of any two producers. Imagine that any two producers shift their common boundary within any small element of area without affecting the market areas and outputs of other producers. Let the first obtain dm_ρ new sales from this element while the second lose $dm_\rho \; (= -dm_\nu)$ sales. If γm is a maximum, such a shift should not reduce total costs when through some pricing arrangement the intensity pattern of consumption of all other elements in the two market areas is held unchanged, as it can be. For, if this were not so, the resulting decrease in total costs would make possible an increase in m and thus in γm. Therefore, with such a shift, for $d(\gamma m) = 0$, we must have:

$$d(\pi_\rho m_\rho) + d(r_\rho m_\rho \bar{s}_\rho) + d\left(m_\rho \sum_{i=A}^{F} b_i r_i s_{i\rho} \right)$$

(32)

$$= -d(\pi_\nu m_\nu) - d(r_\nu m_\nu \bar{s}_\nu) - d\left(m_\nu \sum_{i=A}^{F} b_i r_i s_{i\nu} \right)$$

where π_ρ and π_ν represent the average unit production costs (excluding transportation) of producers at sites P_ρ and P_ν, respectively. Since

$$d(\pi_\rho m_\rho) = \sigma_\rho \, dm_\rho,$$

(33)

$$(d\pi_\nu m_\nu) = \sigma_\nu \, dm_\nu = -\sigma_\nu \, dm_\rho,$$

and since

$$d(m_\rho \bar{s}_\rho) = s_\rho{}^0 \, dm_\rho,$$

(34)

$$d(m_\nu \bar{s}_\nu) = s_\nu{}^0 \, dm_\nu = -s_\nu{}^0 \, dm_\rho,$$

where $s_\rho{}^0$ and $s_\nu{}^0$ represent the distances from P_ρ and P_ν, respectively, to any point on their common boundary line, Eq. 32 becomes, after cancelling dm_ρ,

$$\sigma_\rho + r_\rho s_\rho{}^0 + \sum_{i=A}^{F} b_i r_i s_{i\rho} = \sigma_\nu + r_\nu s_\nu{}^0 + \sum_{i=A}^{F} b_i r_i s_{i\nu}$$

(35)

$$(\rho \neq \nu)(\rho, \nu = 1, \cdots, \eta).$$

Equations 35 furnish the boundary (indifference) conditions dividing a market domain between any two producers, each boundary representing a locus of points of equal delivered prices.

The problem is now reduced to one involving a finite number of variables, namely, to that of maximizing γm (where the η market areas are defined by Eqs. 30 and 35), subject to $\eta(f-2)$ restraints on the variation of the distances, which express for each producer the fact that in choosing his production site only two of his f distance variables can be independent. Thus γm can be considered as a function of independent coordinates in 2η dimensional space.

In this new framework, setting $d(\gamma m) = 0$, we obtain:

$$(36) \qquad \frac{r_i}{r_j} = -\frac{d(m_{j\rho}s_{j\rho})}{d(m_{i\nu}s_{i\nu})}$$

evaluated along the path

$$m(\gamma + \bar{p} - \bar{\pi}) - \sum_{k=A}^{F} \sum_{\mu=1}^{\eta} m_{k\mu}r_k s_{k\mu} - \sum_{\mu=1}^{\eta} m_\mu \overline{rs}_\mu = \text{const.}$$

$$(j\rho \neq k\mu \neq i\nu).$$

Of Eqs. 36,[31] each of which holds in $2\eta - 1$ independent directions, and yields $2\eta - 1$ independent equations, any two together holding in 2η and only 2η independent directions are required to provide necessary and sufficient conditions for a stationary point. These provide the equations for determining the 2η independent unknowns. Again, complex second-order conditions are required to distinguish among maxima and other stationary points, and only direct computation will yield the best of the maxima points.

Economically speaking, Eqs. 36 state that in a small variation of any production site from its corresponding position in a geographic pattern of production sites which yields maximum surplus, the marginal rate of substitution of one transport input for another must be equal to the reciprocal of the ratio of their transport rates, *social* surplus plus total revenue less total production costs and less total cost on all other transport inputs being held constant. It should be emphasized that variation of any production site tends to entail variation in all production sites, as well as market areas, and so forth.

In order to avoid further complications in detailing the above relations, it has been postulated that each raw material originated from one fixed site only. However, just as we have treated many producers serving a spatially extended market, we can treat many producers procuring their supplies of each raw material from a spatially extended supply area. New unknown boundary equations are introduced, but so are new

---

[31] Analogous to the second of the Eqs. 28 the ratios in Eqs. 36 should be viewed as involving transport inputs on product [e.g. $d(m_\mu \bar{s}_\mu)$ vis-à-vis $d(m_{i\nu}s_{i\nu})$ or vis-à-vis $d(m_\nu s_\nu)$] as well as transport inputs on raw materials.

conditions to determine them.   The reader can easily develop analysis in this direction.

One further salient point must be noted.   The derived boundary (isotant) Eqs. 35 contain market area theory, developed by Launhardt, Fetter, Palander, Hyson, and others.[32]   In the usual case, only two producers, each at a particular site, are considered, and transport costs on raw materials are neglected or assumed to be zero or already accounted for in the price which each producer charges.   Where marginal cost is the basis for determining the price at the factory[33] then Eqs. 35 are relevant and they will yield (1) straight line boundaries, when $\sigma_\rho = \sigma_\nu$ and $r_\rho = r_\nu$, (2) hyperbolic boundaries when $\sigma_\rho \neq \sigma_\nu$ and $r_\rho = r_\nu$, (3) circular boundaries when $\sigma_\rho = \sigma_\nu$ and $r_\rho \neq r_\nu$, and (4) Descartes ovals or hypercircles as boundaries when $\sigma_\rho \neq \sigma_\nu$ and $r_\rho \neq r_\nu$.[34]

4. Lösch Market Area Analysis Encompassed

In this section we wish to demonstrate that the principle and general analysis thus far developed logically embraces the Lösch system of market areas.

In Chap. 2 we have sketched Lösch's elaborately developed theory of market areas based upon empirical evidence and deductive reasoning. Assuming raw materials equally and adequately present at any site, population uniformly distributed and having like tastes and of like stamp, full technical knowledge and other resources available to everyone, transportation possible in all directions at a fixed rate, and complete freedom of entry and exit for producers, Lösch has demonstrated how a regular hexagonal net of market areas will evolve.[35]   It can be shown that such a net of market areas, given Lösch's restraining postulates, is implied by the general relations in Eqs. 35 and 36.

First, the assumption of raw materials equally and adequately present at every site reduces transport inputs on raw materials to zero and

---

[32] See footnote 17.

[33] Where another method of pricing is employed, the process of maximizing social surplus γm will be constrained by such a method and will yield boundary equations similar to Eqs. 35 except that the factory price charged the peripheral consumer by each producer will substitute for marginal cost.   The boundaries yielded by these new equations will still be of the same type as those derived by traditional market area analysis.

[34] Where the transport rate is a function of distance, then the hyperbolic, circular, and hypercircular boundaries become distorted and need to be described by more complex functions.

[35] Lösch, *op. cit.*, Part III.   Also contrast with the empirical materials in: W. Christaller, *Die zentralen Orte in Süddeutschland*, Jena, 1935; and E. Ullman, "A Theory of Location of Cities," *American Journal of Sociology*, Vol. XLVI (May 1941), pp. 853–64.

eliminates transport inputs on any raw material as a variable. Equations 36 can now be simply stated:

$$(37) \qquad 1 = \frac{r_\nu}{r_\rho} = -\left.\frac{d(m_\rho \bar{s}_\rho)}{d(m_\nu \bar{s}_\nu)}\right| m(\gamma + \bar{p} - \bar{\pi}) - \sum_{\mu=1}^{\eta} m_\mu \overline{rs}_\mu = \text{const.}$$

$$\rho \neq \mu \neq \nu$$
$$\rho, \nu = 1, \cdots, n$$

where $r_\nu = r_\rho = r$, a constant rate per unit product; or the marginal rate of substitution between any two transport inputs on product from any two production points is unity along a path where social surplus plus total revenue less total production costs less total costs on all other transport inputs is held constant. Boundary Eqs. 35 become

$$(38) \qquad \sigma_\rho + rs_\rho{}^0 = \sigma_\nu + rs_\nu{}^0$$

$$\rho, \nu = 1, \cdots, n$$

Lösch's assumption of free entry and exit of producers ensures that there will be no profits, namely, that price will equal average unit production cost for any producer. Furthermore, in Lösch's schema the delivered price is equal to average unit production cost (factory price) plus transport cost (the consumer is responsible for the transportation of the product he purchases). Hence, the boundary (indifference) line between the market areas of any two producers, which is a locus of points of equal delivered price, is given by:

$$(39) \qquad \pi_\rho + rs_\rho{}^0 = \pi_\nu + rs_\nu{}^0$$

Consider for the moment all situations, whether optimum or not, where Eqs. 38 are satisfied. If the Löschian schema necessitating the conditions of Eq. 39 is to be simultaneously satisfied, then, by subtraction:

$$(40) \qquad \pi_\rho - \sigma_\rho = \pi_\nu - \sigma_\nu$$

$$\rho, \nu = 1, \cdots, n$$

This states that the difference between average and marginal costs is the same for all producers. Such can be the case, when each producer confronts the same regular demand and U-shaped average cost functions, if, and only if, as Lösch posits, the outputs of all producers are of the same size; and thus where each produces at a point where the demand curve is tangent to the average cost curve. Furthermore, with a uniform distribution of consumers and producers of the same size, Eqs. 38 as derived from the general problem ensure a straight line boundary between any two producers which is a perpendicular bisector of the straight line joining the two.   Of the various regular[36] geometric shapes which possess such boundary lines, only the equilateral triangle, square, and regular hexagon can exhaust any given domain, *as required by Lösch*. Equations 38 do not constitute sufficient conditions for an optimum areal distribution.   A distribution, under Lösch's restraint that all producers be of the same size, must also satisfy the relations in Eqs. 37 to ensure necessary (though still not sufficient) conditions for a maximum.   We do find that the distribution of a domain into squares verti-

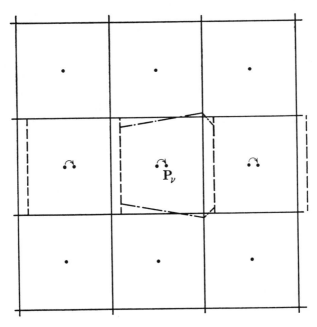

Fɪɢ. 43. Change in market boundary pattern with shift of production points in a square matrix.

cally and horizontally aligned as in Fig. 43 (unbroken lines) does, because of pattern symmetry, satisfy Eqs. 37 as well as boundary Eqs. 38 and 39 and Lösch's other postulates.   However, we can easily demonstrate that this distribution is not a maximum one.

Let all producers and their associated consumers in the second row of Fig. 43 shift their positions equally to the right by a small arbitrary amount so that the dashed lines become the boundary lines separating the market areas of producers in the second row.   Since any consumer is no more distant from his respective producer in the

---

[36] Competition compresses irregular shapes into regular areas.

new situation than in the old, m and m_μ are unaffected and likewise σ_μ, π_μ, and the profit of each producer. It also follows that since consumers of like tastes and stamp are uniformly distributed throughout the area, the same variables are unaffected if no consumers are shifted when all producers in the second row and their mutual boundary lines are shifted as above.[37] But this new situation does not fulfill Eqs. 38 and 39. These equations require that the boundary separating any two producers be a perpendicular bisector of the line connecting the two, and require that, given the new (shifted) pattern of production sites, the market area of any producer in the second row take on an irregular hexagonal shape as indicated for the producer at P_ν in Fig. 43. Therefore the new pattern of production sites with irregular hexagonal market areas for the second row producers involves a greater m and a greater social welfare than the same pattern of production sites with rigid square market areas and thus than the old pattern of production sites with square market areas vertically and horizontally aligned. Hence this latter square pattern is not a maximum one. Likewise with the pattern where a domain is divided into equilateral triangles.

A distribution into regular hexagons, too, satisfies Eqs. 37 because of pattern symmetry. However, unlike the square and equilateral triangle distributions, it does represent a maximum, given producers of like size. Any substitution of transport inputs on the product of one producer for that on the product of another which entails small shifts of a number of production sites leads to six-sided polygons which are not regular hexagons[38] (as can be easily verified by the reader). Since a regular hexagon is more efficient (requires less transport inputs) in serving any area of given size than any other six-sided polygon, the regular hexagonal pattern corresponds to a minimum transport cost, or maximum surplus arrangement. Thus, given Lösch's restricting postulates, the regular hexagonal, and only the regular hexagonal, pattern is implied by the derived general location principle and analysis.[39]

[37] Producers in the second row will, it is true, serve different consumers; and some consumers will become worse off, while others better off. However, overall consumption and social welfare will not have been changed by the shift.

[38] This contrasts with the situation where in certain directions small shifts in production sites transform a square or equilateral triangle pattern into a pattern of more-sided polygons which is more efficient than the initial pattern.

[39] However, the Lösch hexagonal pattern is not *in general* consistent with an optimum space-economy if Lösch's restraining postulates are relaxed.

Imagine average unit production cost falls in such a way with increase in output (engendered by extending the radius of a circular market area) that the sum of average unit production cost and average transport cost of product to consumers contained in any size market area yields a cost function which decreases only slightly as the size of the circular market area increases. Also, for simplicity, imagine each consumer buys one and only one unit. The market domain then can

5. Agriculture Location Theory Embraced and Generalized

Another major branch of location theory, stemming from the work of von Thünen, developed by Aereboe and Brinkmann and most recently by Dunn,[40] has as its object the explanation of the geographic pattern of agricultural activities. Immediately, it is seen that, since the von Thünen problem concerns itself with the formation of zones each devoted to the cultivation of a particular crop or combination of crops, the general location statement hitherto developed must be extended to treat more than one commodity if it is to encompass agricultural location theory.

As in the previous analysis, we shall abstract from price changes, prices being determined and fixed beforehand. However, this position is much less tenable in the case of agricultural location theory. Since several commodities vie for the purchasing potential of the city market and since significant changes in the outputs of the various agricultural commodities may be involved in spatial (zonal) shifts, it is only by price changes, direct and indirect, and their resultant effects upon the several outputs that appropriate and complete adjustments can be made to locational shifts. To account for repercussions through price changes, as a truly general equilibrium system would, is, however, beyond the scope of this chapter.[41] Since agricultural location theorists have traditionally omitted price changes from their formulations of concrete

be overlain with non-overlapping circles of different sizes, tangent to one another, and which at the same time satisfy boundary conditions in Eqs. 38. Any unfilled gap between any three circles, each tangent to the other two, can be partially filled with a circle of still smaller size, even to the extreme where the circles themselves become infinitesimal in area. For practical purposes, however, we can allow slight distortions of the circles well before such an extreme is reached. Since a circle can more efficiently serve a given size area (consumers) than a regular hexagon (see Lösch, op.cit., pp. 76–78) and since, in this example, the distortions of circular form are minor and the variation in total average cost (including transport) associated with the various sizes of circles is but slight, each size circle is more efficient than any regular hexagon which may be derived as optimum size. Hence, a pattern of circles, slightly distorted to exhaust the area, serves the area more efficiently than any pattern of regular hexagons.

[40] J. H. von Thünen, *Der isolierte Staat in Beziehung auf Landwirtschaft und Nationalökonomie*, Hempel and Parey, Berlin, 1895; F. Aereboe, *Allgemeine landwirtschaftsliche Betriebslehre*, P. Parey, Berlin, 1923; E. T. Benedict, H. Stippler and M. R. Benedict, *Theodor Brinkmann's Economics of the Farm Business*, University of California Press, Berkeley, 1935; and Edgar S. Dunn, Jr., *The Location of Agricultural Production*, University of Florida Press, Gainesville, 1954.

[41] The reader may refer to the non-operational general equilibrium statements, involving the simultaneous determination of price and spatial structure, in Lösch, *op. cit.*, 1st ed., 1940, pp. 57–63, and Dunn, *op. cit.*, Chap. 2.

equilibrium conditions, there is no inconsistency in demonstrating how their analysis is implied by our general analysis.

We shall proceed from the simple to the more complex. Imagine a single city, surrounded by land of uniform quality, consuming commodities $k + 1, \cdots, n$ whose prices $(p_{k+1}, \cdots, p_n)$ are set. Our problem is to determine the location and the quantities $(m_{k+1}, \cdots, m_n)$ of the agricultural commodities which will be produced, given the freight rate $(r_{k+1}, \cdots, r_n)$ and cost function for each commodity, $\pi_{k+1}, \cdots, \pi_n$, and $\sigma_{k+1}, \cdots, \sigma_n$ representing their average unit and marginal costs, respectively.

Discarding the assumptions of constant yield of a given crop per acre, regardless of distance from the city, and of constant average unit cost—assumptions which have characterized the algebraic statements of Brinkmann, Lösch, and Dunn[42]—we have for the given commodity a unique marginal rent function, which traces out the amount of rent which would be yielded by each unit circumferential band of land as we proceed radially outward. Each marginal rent function declines continuously since local price (net of transport cost) falls off with distance from the city market and since, too, as a result intensity per unit of land falls off given uniform fertility of land and hence a production function invariant with distance.[43] However, since only one commodity (or one combination of commodities that is fixed proportionally and thus can be viewed as a single commodity) can be cultivated on any given piece of land, it is necessary to think in terms of stretches of land devoted to the cultivation of one and only one commodity.

Consider total rent for society

$$(41) \qquad R = \sum_{\tau = k+1}^{n} \left[\int_{\tau} \Gamma_\tau (p_\tau - \pi_\tau) \, dW - \int_{\tau} \Gamma_\tau r_\tau s \, dW \right]$$

under the simplification that no transportation costs are incurred on raw materials, labor, and other inputs[44] and where the Riemann integral

[42] As previously noted, Dunn has pushed the analysis on to the individual firm level and has shown the inconsistency of these assumptions for firm analysis. Thereby, he has been able to sketch graphically the approximate character of the necessary modifications of analysis on the industry level. A revision of his mathematical statement, however, was not made.

[43] Under the usual assumption that the farmer is not incurring loss and, thus, is operating at a point on the rising section of his marginal cost curve.

[44] The simplification is made merely to facilitate presentation. As will be shown later, another term representing transport costs on raw materials and on labor can be brought into the brackets of Eq. 41; the analytical technique remains unaffected.

It should be noted that von Thünen and Brinkmann would insist upon two additional terms, a *negative* one for transport costs on industrially produced goods

$\int_\tau$ is taken over the area devoted to the production of the τth commodity, Γ_τ representing the intensity of production of τ associated with the element of area dW.[45] Setting $dR = 0$, we obtain

(42)
$$\frac{r_i}{r_j} = - \frac{d \int_j \Gamma_j s \, dW}{d \int_i \Gamma_i s \, dW}$$

evaluated along the path

$$\sum_{\tau=k+1}^{n} \int_\tau \Gamma_\tau (p_\tau - \pi_\tau) \, dW - \sum_{\substack{\tau=k+1 \\ j \neq \tau \neq i}}^{n} \int_\tau \Gamma_\tau r_\tau s \, dW = \text{const.}$$

$$(i, j = k + 1, \cdots, n).$$

Immediately, it is seen that these relations imply a concentric circular zone (in the extreme case approaching a line) pattern of cultivation. First, zones, whatever their shape, must be contiguous to each other and to the city market. Otherwise, there would be empty spaces which would then permit a shifting of some zone closer to the city market thereby reducing transport costs on one commodity without affecting transport costs on any other commodity. But this is inconsistent with Eqs. 42. Second, since the transport rate is independent of direction, the contiguous zones must also be concentric and circular because Eqs. 42 also imply pattern symmetry.[46]

Of Eqs. 42, only $n - k$ are independent, and they determine the $n - k$ variable boundaries separating the zones in which the $n - k$ commodities

used as inputs and shipped from the city market, and a *positive* one for transport costs of the agriculturally produced inputs from any element of area to the city market. The latter positive term represents the differential price advantage any element of area has over the city market in procuring agricultural raw materials (including food for labor), since the difference between the price at the city market and the local price at the element of area for any such raw material is the cost of shipping that raw material from the element of area to the market.

[45] We employ the Riemann integral throughout this section since intensity of production on any element of area (farm) is a critical issue in agricultural location theory. The use of the Stieltjes integral would conceal the intensity variable. Also, since agricultural production tends to assume a continuous character, the Stieltjes integral would in any case tend to reduce to a Riemann integral. However, in the latter part of this section where a continuous market area is considered, the use of the Stieltjes integral would have definite advantage in an extension of the analysis to include cities as discrete consumption points within the market area, provided the integral is differentiable in the relevant region.

[46] Thus the analysis in its more vital aspects can be reduced to the problem of examining relations along any straight line through the point representing the city market.

are produced. These equations are only necessary conditions for maximum rent. Elaborate second-order conditions are required to distinguish a maximum from other stationary points. With marginal rent functions for all commodities plotted on a single graph (marginal rent measured along the ordinate), the absolute maximum obtains when the commodity produced on any given unit of land corresponds to the marginal rent function having the highest ordinate for that unit of land.[47]

Economically speaking, Eqs. 42 state that for maximum rent the marginal rate of substitution between any two transport inputs, each on a particular crop, must equal the reciprocal of the ratio of their transport rates, the sum of rent on all other commodities plus the total difference between sales value and production costs for the two crops being held constant. It must be borne in mind that the path along which the sum is held constant may involve shifts of the zonal boundaries of other crops as well as of the two explicitly considered and may call for changes in the intensity of cultivation and in unit production costs of other crops as well as of these two. Thus the path may be quite complex.

Despite this complexity, Eqs. 42 imply relatively simple boundary determining equations. Imagine that only two boundaries shift, namely, those s_ρ and s_μ distances from the city, representing respectively the outer boundaries of the zones producing crops ρ and μ. Further, let at least one other zone intervene, ρ being nearer the city. From Eqs. 42 where $i = \rho$ and $j = \mu$ we would have with a small change of s_ρ and corresponding change of s_μ:

$$(43) \qquad r_\rho \Gamma_\rho s_\rho{}^2 \, ds_\rho = -r_\mu \Gamma_\mu s_\mu{}^2 \, ds_\mu$$

where $2\pi s \, ds$ substitutes for dW and 2π is cancelled. Also from the restraint of Eqs. 42 defining the path, we have, after cancelling 2π,[48]

$$
\begin{aligned}
(44) \quad & \Gamma_\rho (p_\rho - \pi_\rho) s_\rho \, ds_\rho - \Gamma_{\rho+1}(p_{\rho+1} - \pi_{\rho+1}) s_\rho \, ds_\rho + \Gamma_\mu (p_\mu - \pi_\mu) s_\mu \, ds_\mu \\
& - \Gamma_{\mu+1}(p_{\mu+1} - \pi_{\mu+1}) s_\mu \, ds_\mu + r_{\rho+1}\Gamma_{\rho+1}s_\rho{}^2 \, ds_\rho + r_{\mu+1}\Gamma_{\mu+1}s_\mu{}^2 \, ds_\mu = 0
\end{aligned}
$$

where $\Gamma_{\rho+1}$ and $\pi_{\rho+1}$ are evaluated at s_ρ, and $\Gamma_{\mu+1}$ and $\pi_{\mu+1}$ at s_μ. Similarly two equations of like form are obtained when in Eqs. 42 we let

---

[47] Given any position other than the absolute maximum already described, there is always at least one way in which a substitution of transport inputs on one commodity for transport inputs on another can increase rent. This may involve a shift of some element of area from the cultivation of one crop to the other, the formation of new, or deletion of old, zones, and a corresponding increase or decrease in the number of boundary variables.

[48] In Eq. 44 are contained all the elements which change in the restraint governing the path, namely, the sales revenue and production costs associated with crops ρ, $\rho + 1$, μ, and $\mu + 1$ and transport costs associated with crops $\rho + 1$ and $\mu + 1$. Since the path defines a constant sum, the total of these changes must be zero.

$i = \rho$ and $j = \mu + 1$, and where as before distances s_ρ and s_μ only are varied. These latter two equations, with Eqs. 43 and 44, yield algebraically:[49]

$$(45) \quad r_\mu s_\mu \Gamma_\mu - r_{\mu+1} s_\mu \Gamma_{\mu+1} = \Gamma_\mu(p_\mu - \pi_\mu) - \Gamma_{\mu+1}(p_{\mu+1} - \pi_{\mu+1}).$$

Equations of the type of Eqs. 45 represent another way of expressing necessary conditions for maximum rent.[50] Each such equation states that with a small shift of the boundary line between any two zones, the change in over-all transport costs for the two crops is equal to the change in the sum of the difference between sales value and production costs for each of the two crops. Or, if in each of Eqs. 45 the first term on the left side is carried over to the right and the last term on the right to the left, the necessary conditions for maximum rent are that with any infinitesimal shift of the boundary between two zones, marginal rent on the one crop must equal marginal rent on the other. In graphic terms, the marginal rent functions of the two crops must intersect or be tangent at the boundary line.[51]

These boundary conditions, implied by Eqs. 42, are identical with those obtained by Lösch and Dunn,[52] except that Γ_i and π_i are constants in Lösch's and Dunn's schema whereas they are variables in our formulation. Treating intensity and unit production costs as variables not only is realistic but has the distinct advantage, as Dunn noted, of facilitating the unification of theory for the industry and for the individual farm unit.[53] Postulating Γ_i and π_i as constants throughout a zone precludes any such thing as a firm adjustment to a lower or higher local (net) price for product and rent payment for land and, thus, in essence is inconsistent with customary firm analysis. However, with Γ_i and π_i as variables, we derive that, since a farmer will produce on the rising section of his marginal cost curve up to the point where his marginal costs (σ_i) just equals the local (net) price ($p_i - r_i s_i$), $d\sigma_i/ds_i = -r_i$; and therefore, $d\Gamma_i/ds_i = -r_i \, d\Gamma_i/d\sigma_i$. As $d\Gamma_i/d\sigma_i$ is positive on the rising section of the marginal cost curve, $d\Gamma_i/ds_i$ is negative. Thus intensity of cultivation falls off in any zone from land unit to land unit, or farm unit to farm unit with increase of distance from the market.[54]

[49] By eliminating the three unknowns ds_ρ, ds_μ, and s_ρ.

[50] These equations are also obtainable when more than two boundaries are shifted.

[51] This condition also characterizes stationary points other than the absolute maximum, including relative maxima when each crop is restricted to production within one zone only.

[52] Lösch, op. cit., pp. 28–32; Dunn, op. cit., Chap. 2.

[53] Though, of course, when there is no definite bunching of firms with respect to similarity of product or output mix, there may not be any justification or meaning in the distinction between firm and industry.

[54] However, because of differences in production cost functions, transport rates,

And thus we have an adjustment to the fall in local price appropriate to both firm and industry analysis.

When within any zone it is desirable to consider each firm by itself, because outputs or output combinations for various firms are too heterogeneous or for other reasons, each firm can be considered an industry. More boundary variables are introduced but so are more equations to determine the boundaries. Boundary Eq. 45 comes to hold between firms whether or not they produce a homogeneous output as well as between groups of firms (industries), each corresponding to a zone. Thus firm and industry analysis are mutually consistent in this spatial framework, and in the extreme case, may be considered as one and the same thing.

Hitherto, we have excluded consideration of transport costs on raw materials. Such can easily be introduced explicitly into the analysis by inserting into the brackets of Eq. 41 the term

$$-\int_\tau \sum_{i=1}^k \Gamma_\tau b_{i\tau} r_i s_i \, dW,$$

where s_i is the distance of the source of raw material i from the element dW. With this term inserted, marginal rates of substitution between transport inputs on raw materials, and between transport inputs on a raw material and transport inputs on a product, are obtainable from the required revision of Eqs. 42. It should be noted that in general the zonal boundaries will no longer be concentric circles because pattern symmetry will have been lost.[55]

If, however, raw material i is supplied not from a single point source but from an area, s_i becomes a variable for any given element, dW, representing the distance from dW of the element of the raw material supply area, dU, which furnishes the i required by dW. As a result additional equations of the order of Eqs. 42 result which relate, for example, transport inputs on raw material i used by crop τ,[56]

$$\int_{U_\tau} \Gamma_i s_{i\tau} \, dU,$$

---

and market prices, intensity per land unit, however measured, need not fall off from zone to zone or from a farm unit in one zone to a contiguous farm unit in the next zone.

[55] Hence, it becomes necessary to think in terms of a boundary defined by an equation rather than by a radial distance alone. Analysis along a straight line is in general no longer valid.

[56] This is, of course, equivalent to $\int_\tau \Gamma_\tau b_{i\tau} s_i \, dW$.

and transport inputs on raw material i used by crop $\tau + 1$,

$$\int_{U_{\tau+1}} \Gamma_i s_{i_{\tau+1}}\, dU.$$

These determine the boundary lines cutting off the portion of the supply area of raw material i which serves each crop.[57]

A still more general framework, encompassing more than one city market, can be handled. Consider first a relatively small number of city markets close enough to compete for the potential crops of at least some land. Here an industry (agricultural activity) and its corresponding zone of cultivation must be defined not only in terms of the crop produced but also the city market served. The number of industries is thus multiplied but so also is the number of Eqs. 42 to determine boundary lines.[58]

Where the number of city markets becomes large and attains the approximate continuity of a market area, we reach the most general type of framework, that is, many markets each consuming many products, many producers of any given product, many raw materials used by each producer, and many sources (a supply area) of each raw material. An alternative approach to this most general framework follows from the analysis of Sect. 3. There we considered many producers of a single commodity demanded by a population spread over an area and requiring many raw materials, each furnished from a supply area. By introducing many commodities in this framework we reach the same problem as when we inject the market area into the Thünen type of framework. It seems, however, more desirable to generalize from the Thünen type of framework. In this framework prices are explicitly assumed as given and we avoid the problem, which thus far has not been satisfactorily handled, of relating social surpluses, or consumer utilities, or satisfactions derivable from several commodities.[59]

[57] Also, $dR = 0$ implies equations guaranteeing the appropriate pairing off of elements of area in any portion with the elements in the crop zone which the portion serves.

[58] In the case of only two cities, in which the ruling market prices are different, there will tend to be two hinterlands, one corresponding to each city. In each hinterland, zonal pattern symmetry will exist with respect to the cultivation of any given crop when no raw materials are employed. However, on the two sides of any small stretch of the border separating the two hinterlands, in general different types of crops will be cultivated at different intensities per unit of land, though marginal rent is the same.

[59] In essence, the Thünen framework assumes away this subjective evaluation problem. It treats only objective, measurable elements and, on the basis of these latter alone, yields a spatial pattern of economic activity and land use.

This problem would confront us if we were to proceed from the analysis of Sect. 3.

Generalizing the Thünen analysis we have for total rent:

$$
R = \sum_{\tau=k+1}^{n} \left[\int_H \Gamma_{H\tau}(p_\tau - \pi_\tau)\, dH \right.
$$
$$
\left. (46) \qquad - \int_H \Gamma_{H\tau} r_\tau s_\tau\, dH - \int_\tau \sum_{i=1}^{k} \Gamma_\tau b_{i\tau} r_i s_i\, dW \right],
$$

where $\Gamma_{H\tau}$ represents the intensity of the effective demand for product τ in the element dH of the consumption market area at the price p_τ, p_τ being fixed for each element but varying from element to element; π_τ represents the average production cost of τ at the element dW, where an element dW may serve more or less than one element dH; and s_τ represents the distance from the element dH of the element dW producing the τ which is demanded at element dH.

Setting $dR = 0$ yields again equations of the order of Eqs. 42, though more complex. These, nonetheless, can be easily set down by the reader. A whole new set of substitution relations, however, is embraced. For example, there may be substitution between transport inputs on the product τ going to city A, $\int_{\tau A} \Gamma_\tau s_{\tau A}\, dW$,[60] and transport inputs on the product τ going to city B, $\int_{\tau B} \Gamma_\tau s_{\tau B}\, dW$, or on the product $\tau + 1$ going to city B, etc. More generally, the consumption market area may be divided into any two or more meaningful parts and transport inputs on product τ going to any α part can be considered vis-à-vis transport inputs on any other product going to any area or meaningful part of an area, or on any raw material going to any production area or meaningful part of a production area of any good,[61] and so forth. In this way, within the hypothesized framework of the space-economy, one can make the most comprehensive statements concerning equilibrium conditions and

[60] Equivalent to $\int_H \Gamma_{H\tau} s_\tau\, dH$ where the integral $\int_H$ is evaluated over the area of city A.

[61] As a consequence, if attention is paid to a given crop alone without regard to destination or market, multiple zones of cultivation will appear, each in general asymmetrical with respect to any selected focal point.

Where a given good is produced at a finite number of plants, as in the analysis of Sect. 3, the cultivation zone or production area of that good has in effect been reduced to a finite number of points, the intensity of cultivation or production at other points being zero. Any one point may still be a potential site of production of all other goods, a potential source of all raw materials, and a potential market for all goods.

substitution relations among transport inputs.   This the reader can easily do by setting down equations of the order of Eqs. 42 that, however, correspond to total rent as defined in Eq. 46.

6. CONCLUDING REMARKS

We have treated what may be called a continuous space-economy, continuous transportationwise and continuous to some extent at least with respect to market and supply areas.   This stands in strong contrast to the highly discontinuous realistic one.   We have noted how modern rate structures in effect yield a transport cost surface punctured at terminal sites, the transport cost for each such point being significantly below that for points contiguous in space.   The fact that in reality transport routes radiate from one point not in all directions but in only a few, particularly in modern industrial societies with a relatively small number of fixed trunk routes, means that the transport cost surface is punctured linearly, too.   Each locus of points corresponding to an existing transport route lies significantly below any locus of points through which no transport route courses.   The presence of junction and transshipment points, of loading and unloading facilities, of various auxiliary transport services, and of the whole complex of agglomeration economies, as well as of varying topography, back-haul and other abnormal rates, special transit privileges, and other factors, imposes still larger discontinuities and distortions upon the transport cost surface derived from simplifying assumptions.   Hence we discover in the space-economy of reality hierarchies and different degrees of dominance in sets of focal points and channels of movement.[62]   To a large extent substitution among transport inputs is not in the small but rather in the large, entailing geographic shifts over substantial distance from one focal point to another.   To this extent the preceding analysis is not directly relevant.

However, the extent of discontinuity must not be exaggerated.   The demarcation of many agricultural and raw material supply areas and many industrial market areas can be handled in terms of substitution in the small.   Likewise with many industrial location problems.   It should be kept in mind that the extent to which spatial continuity and discontinuity exist is yet to be determined or even approximately estimated by empirical study.

[62] For an excellent pictorial presentation, refer to "Interregional Highways," *House Document* 379, 78th Congress, 2nd session, Washington 1944, Fig. 22.   For discussion, see A. Hawley, *Human Ecology; A Theory of Community Structure,* New York, 1950; D. J. Bogue, *The Structure of the Metropolitan Community,* Ann Arbor, 1949; and W. Isard and G. Freutel, "Regional and National Product Projections and their Interrelations" in *Long-Range Economic Projection,* National Bureau of Economic Research, Studies in Income and Wealth, Vol. 16, Princeton University Press, Princeton, 1954, pp. 427–471.

To analyze the space-economy in terms of geographic shifts in the large, from focal point to focal point, is highly desirable and will be partially attempted in a future volume. In this chapter we have tried to demonstrate the usefulness of the concept of transport inputs in deriving conditions for the efficient operation of a space-economy. A basic principle—in a sense an intuitively obvious one—has emerged, namely, that the marginal rate of substitution between any two transport inputs or groups of transport inputs, however the transport inputs or groups of transport inputs may be defined, must equal the reciprocal of the ratio of their transport rates, social surplus (however defined) less transport costs on all other transport inputs being held constant. This principle implies a large part of existing location theory. Weberian transport orientation is embodied in such a principle, and with this principle we are better able to take transport orientation out of the narrow geometric framework in which it has hitherto been confined and determine the optimal transport point for the more generalized case when many raw material and market points are involved. The principle, too, encompasses all market (and purchasing) area theory, implying the customary boundary conditions which separate the market areas of producers (and hinterlands of focal points). Likewise, Lösch's spatial designs are embraced as well as the von Thünen type of agricultural location theory. Both the Lösch and the von Thünen types of theory can be generalized to harbor a much broader range and a more realistic set of situations.

More important, this general principle fuses the separate partial location theories. It thus serves as a basic core of a general location theory from which, for the most part, existing location theories are derived as special cases of the most general situation, embracing many market points, each consuming many commodities, each of which is produced by many producers, each of whom uses many raw materials and inputs, each of which is furnished by a supply area.[63]

Perhaps most important is that this principle allows existing location theory to be stated in a form comparable to that of production theory. By incorporating transport inputs into the transformation function, and thereby yielding a spatial transformation function, we can extend existing production theory so that to a large extent it embodies the location factor explicitly. At the same time location theory can now consider change in a number of parameters. For example, the relation between

---

[63] For example, one can derive Weber's theory of transport orientation by making assumptions such as the existence of a single market point, consuming one unit of one commodity, produced by a single producer, using two raw materials, each obtainable at a single source.

economies of scale and the number and geographic distribution of plants can be examined through substitution between transport inputs and all other inputs as a whole; or the relation between the spatial extent and capital intensity (time extent) of production, through substitution between transport inputs and capital inputs.   Thus a more comprehensive framework emerges for both types of theory.

Chapter 11

Partial Graphic Synthesis
and Summary

We must now take stock. *What has been accomplished?* In attacking this question we shall, where the use of illustrations makes it possible, attempt a finer integration of the materials than has thus far been achieved. However, in order to keep repetition at a minimum we shall be brief. We shall assume that the reader has thoroughly digested previous materials.

In Chap. 2 we have envisaged the general theory of location and space-economy as embracing, within a temporal (dynamic) framework, the total spatial array of economic activities and their interrelations, both aggregatively and atomistically, with attention paid to the geographic distribution of inputs and outputs and to the variations over space in prices and costs. This theory eschews the narrow framework of Marshallian doctrine. In many ways it includes modern general equilibrium theory as but a special case; in other respects it becomes synonymous with a broadly defined trade theory and a broadly defined theory of monopolistic competition.

The empirical materials of Chap. 3 strongly testify to the fact that there are significant regularities associated with the distance variable and that in many important respects there is a basic structure to a space-economy. To understand this structure and to analyze the current and anticipate the future functioning of a space-economy, we adopt a substitution approach as initially suggested by Predöhl. The substitution approach, covering substitution in the large as well as substitution in the small, is familiar to economists and needs no further comment.

Coupled with the substitution approach is the concept of transport inputs. A transport input is defined as the movement of a unit weight over a unit distance. In the growth of a simple nucleus of population, transport inputs early become basic elements. They permit the increased productivity which accrues from (1) postponing and mitigating diseconomies from excessive agglomeration and the forces of diminishing returns and (2) exploiting the unequal distribution of natural resources. These same basic forces operate in our modern world-economy with its complex hierarchy of cities and spatial distributions of population.

As with capital inputs, transport inputs can be thought of as derived and as indicating roundaboutness in the production process. Corresponding to transport inputs there are such concepts as spatial extent of production, space discount, and space preference. The transport rate is the price of a transport input. The determination of this price may be accounted for by a conventional demand and supply analysis for transport inputs. A fall in the price of a transport input induces a spatial lengthening of production and may be associated (as is historically the case) with both a scale and substitution effect.

In Chap. 5 we couple the substitution approach and the concept of transport inputs in order to restate and reformulate transport-orientation doctrine. The problem of finding the transport optimal point reduces to a problem of finding the correct substitution points between pairs of transport inputs. This is so whether one treats simplified transport rate structures or the complicated ones of reality, whether one assumes uniform transport facilities radiating in all directions from all points or the discontinuous and heterogeneous network of reality, whether one analyzes a process using one localized raw material or many, and whether one considers one market point or many. It is demonstrated how the various geometric, graphic, and physical solutions propounded are translatable into substitution points among transport inputs. The most rigorous presentation of the solution to the transport-orientation problem in terms of substitutions among transport inputs is found in Sect. 1 of Chap. 10. The formulation of the transport-orientation problem as well as other problems of location in terms of substitution among transport inputs, where transport inputs are viewed as any other set of inputs embraced by a transformation function, has the decided advantage of permitting at least a partial fusion of production theory and location theory.

Much of the argument of Chap. 5 centers around the locational triangle, as has historically been the case with transport-orientation analysis. However, the argument does embrace more than one market point and a single source of each of two raw materials. n market points and raw materials are considered, and in Sect. 1 of Chap. 10 this extension of the argument is most rigorously presented. Yet another useful way of presenting the problem of transport-orientation when no weight is dominant and when there exist many market points, or in essence an area of consumers, has been developed by Launhardt and Palander. Their graphic presentation can be extended to portray in a forceful manner the interrelations and influences of the various location factors.

In constructing his basic diagram which we largely depict in Fig. 44, Palander, following Launhardt, in effect postulates (1) the absence of

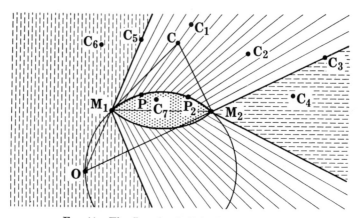

Fig. 44. The Launhardt-Palander construction.

the various agglomeration economies and of geographic variations in the prices of various inputs and outputs except those resulting from transport cost on the product and on the two raw materials considered, and (2) uniform transport facilities radiating in all directions from all points.[1] Given M_1 as the only source of the first raw material and M_2 as the only source of the second raw material, at what points should production occur to serve consumers? Starting with consumer at C, we construct the locational triangle CM_1M_2 and the corresponding weight triangle OM_1M_2 erected upon the side M_1M_2 of the locational triangle. O is one of Launhardt's poles. We circumscribe a circle around the weight triangle and connect the pole O with the point of consumption C by a straight line. P, the point of intersection of the pole line OC and the circumscribed circle, is the desired location, the transport optimal point, for serving the consumer at C.

[1] Palander, *op. cit.*, pp. 143–146.

Take another consumer at C_1. We could construct a second locational triangle $C_1M_1M_2$. Its weight triangle, too, would be OM_1M_2. We find that the relevant pole line OC_1 coincides with pole line OC. Since the point of intersection with the unchanged circumscribed circle remains the same, P is the logical production point to serve not only C but also C_1. Likewise, it can be demonstrated that P is the optimal transport point for all consumers along the pole line OC_1 from P to C_1 and beyond.

Take still another consumer at C_2. We could construct the locational triangle $C_2M_1M_2$. Its weight triangle erected upon side M_1M_2 would as before be OM_1M_2, since the relevant weights have not changed. The corresponding circumscribed circle therefore remains the same. Thus, to derive the production point for serving C_2, we need not construct locational triangle $C_2M_1M_2$. We simply connect the pole O and C_2 with a straight line and locate P_2, the point of intersection of the pole line OC_2 with the circumscribed circle.

Take a fourth consumer at C_3. Connecting C_3 with the pole O yields pole line OC_3 with M_2, the source of the second raw material, as the point of intersection and thus the logical production point for C_3. For C_4, M_2 is the transport optimal point, too. This is so even though the pole line OC_4 does not intersect the circumscribed circle at M_2 but rather at a point outside the locational triangle $C_4M_1M_2$. At M_2 the external angle of the locational triangle is less than the corresponding angle of the weight triangle. This fact indicates production at M_2.

As with C_3 and C_4, we derive that consumption points C_5 and C_6 should be served by a producer at a raw material source, this time M_1, the source of the first raw material. When we consider the consumer at C_7, once more we have the situation where the pole line OC_7 does not intersect the circumscribed circle at a point within the locational triangle $C_7M_1M_2$. Angle conditions yield C_7 as the logical point of production for the consumer at C_7.

Since it can be demonstrated that the breakdown of situations for the consumer field lying below a straight line coursing through M_1 and M_2 is an exact reflection of the breakdown of situations above the line, we can generalize. For all consumers in the horizontally dashed area, including the boundary lines, production should be at M_2. For all consumers in the vertically dashed area, production should be at M_1. For all consumers along any given pole line, production should be at the intersection of that pole line and the relevant circumscribed circle. For each point of consumption in the dotted area, production should be located at that very point. Thus we obtain an infinite number of logical production points contained within and lying on the two relevant circular arcs of Fig. 44. In this way the graphic presentation of transport-orientation when a weight triangle generally exists is extended to embrace an area of consumers, whether or not consumers are actually spread continuously throughout the area.[2]

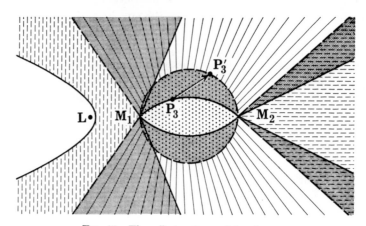

FIG. 45. The effects of a weight change.

Despite its unreality, this derivation of Launhardt and Palander can yield fruitful insights, as Palander has demonstrated. For example, consider the effect of technological change. Such change may result in the use of a new raw material source, or the use of a new process of production utilizing the same or different raw materials, or some other change in the transformation function. Suppose we take a situation where the efficiency in the use of a material, say coal, is increased, *ceteris paribus*. Coal is located at M_1 in Fig. 45 drawn largely from Palander.[3] Before the technological change, the spatial production and market patterns are given by the heavy lines. (For the moment ignore the unmarked area around L.) The new spatial patterns consequent to the reduction in the weight of coal per unit product are given by the dashed lines. The shaded areas indicate changes. The area tributary to M_1 (the source of coal) contracts, that to M_2 increases. The area in which production is market-oriented also expands. Simultaneously, all the production points de-

---

[2] When a weight triangle does not exist, i.e., when the weight of a raw material or the product is dominant, production for all consumers whether they are concentrated at a point or scattered takes place at a raw material source (when a raw material is dominant) or always at the market (when the product is dominant).

[3] Palander, *op. cit.*, p. 153.

pendent on markets along a pole line shift position, e.g., P_3 loses its market along a pole line and $P_3{}'$ comes to serve consumers along such a line.

It could have been the case that before the technological change coal was dominant. The entire area under consideration would have been tributary to M_1 (vertically dashed). With technological change coal loses its dominance, and this Palander-type diagram suggests a theoretical location pattern that might emerge. Or, given the situation as initially depicted, the technological change might have completely eliminated the use of the raw material at M_1. The resulting new pattern would not have a vertically dashed area.

In this way and others the Launhardt-Palander construction can give insights into locational shifts. It particularly points up some of the *dynamic* locational implications of *changing weight relations* whether the changes are due to technological advance or to other forces. It also can be employed theoretically to anticipate some of the locational effects of the exploitation of a new raw material source[4] or market potential.

In Chap. 6 we treat the case of labor and other similar types of orientation. The shift of a production process from the transport optimal point to a cheap labor point lying within the critical isodapane of the relevant locational figure is depicted as the substitution of transport outlays for labor outlays. In addition to permitting both a more direct attack upon the problem when several cheap labor points exist and a more comprehensive presentation of the interrelations of labor outlays and other types of production outlays as well as of the different kinds of labor outlays, the substitution approach allows a closer tie with production theory in general.

Somewhat similar statements relate to orientation to a cheap power site, to a low tax site, to a low rent site, or to any site at which a significant saving in a given type of production outlay (or increase in revenue) is obtainable. Substitution between transport outlay (which tends to vary systematically with distance from a given reference point) and any other outlay or revenue (which tends to vary haphazardly with distance from a reference point), whether or not depicted in terms of outlay-substitution, iso-outlay, and other lines of like character, is a fruitful alternative to the critical isodapane technique. It can be extended, though with decreasing returns, to embrace meaningful groups of outlays (and revenues).

Incorporation of labor or a similar type of orientation into the Launhardt-Palander construction is easily achieved. In Fig. 45 let

[4] In this connection, see Palander, *op. cit.*, pp. 157–162.

L be a cheap labor location. For each of the innumerable points in the market region, we construct a locational triangle as before. Around each locational triangle, we construct the critical isodapane with reference to point L. We group together those locational triangles within whose critical isodapanes point L falls. The market points corresponding to these locational triangles together comprise the consumer market served by the cheap labor location. They are indicated in Fig. 45 by the unmarked area centering around L. The boundary line between the market area tributary to L and that to M_1 is a locus of market points corresponding to the locational triangles whose critical isodapanes course through point L.

Clearly, if the labor cost advantage of L increases, the consumer market tributary to L expands. At one extreme the total area becomes tributary to L. At the other extreme, as the labor cost advantage of L diminishes, the consumer market served by L is entirely regained by M_1.

In like manner, we can insert other cheap labor sites, cheap power sites, cheap tax sites, etc. into Fig. 45 and determine the consumer points, if any, which might be served by these sites. In this way, the transport-orientation problem already extended to embrace many market points, is converted into a more generalized location problem which considers the pull of sites possessing advantages with reference to factors other than transport and relative spatial position.

Viewed from a different angle, the location of production at L plays up another phase of location theory, namely, market area analysis. The market area variable does not crop up when we consider the typical Weberian problem where the market is concentrated at a point. Point L either is or is not the best site at which to produce to serve that point. When many market points exist, the identification of those points to be served by production at L becomes a problem of defining a boundary line cutting across a market region. In Fig. 45 we need not adopt the cumbersome procedure of constructing for each market point a locational triangle and its critical isodapane to determine points to be served by L. Rather we can view L and M_1 as two points, each producing at constant though different unit costs and competing for the market in M_1's hinterland. This is a customary market area problem.

In Chap. 7, we treat market and supply area analysis. Once again it is demonstrated that all such analysis can be embraced by a general substitution framework involving substitution among transport inputs and among outlays and revenues. This can be shown whether we consider a single isolated monopolist, a set of competing firms producing at constant or variable unit costs, a single consumption market, or several competing markets offering the same or different prices for a commodity. The substitution relations among various types of transport inputs in the analysis of market and supply areas are particularly pointed up in Sect. 2 of Chap. 10.

As already indicated, the introduction of a cheap labor point into the Launhardt-Palander construction can simultaneously introduce a market area problem. It is instructive, however, to inject the market area problem into this construction in another way.

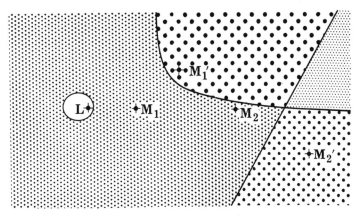

FIG. 46. Division of a market region between two sources of each of two raw materials.

Suppose we have a situation where, owing to the addition of ubiquities, the weight of product becomes dominant. Production becomes market-oriented, except for a small area tributary to L. The dotted area bounded by the two circular arcs in Fig. 45 expands to include almost the entire region. See Fig. 46. Into this situation we now allow a second deposit of each raw material, which we designate M_1' and M_2' respectively. Since we still postulate that the transport rate structure is proportional to weight and distance and since we take the price (unit cost) of the first raw material to be less at M_1 than at M_1' we obtain a hyperbola as a boundary line (the locus of equal delivered prices). It delineates the market area of industrial consumers tributary to source M_1 and that tributary to M_1'. Additionally, since we take the price of the second raw material to be the same at both M_2 and M_2', we obtain a straight line boundary which marks off the market areas of industrial consumers served by each of these two sources. Except for the small district of household consumers oriented to production at L, we demarcate altogether four districts of industrial consumers, each employing the same combination of raw materials, but each procuring them from a different combination of sources. Since production is market-oriented, there is spatially coincident with each district of industrial consumers a district of household consumers. It is hardly necessary to repeat that, if an industrial consumer procures

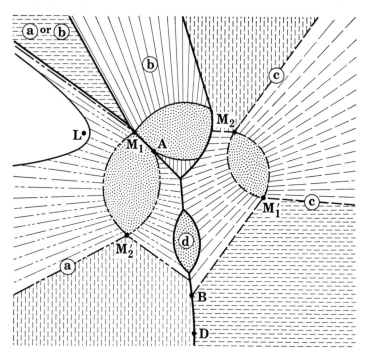

FIG. 47. Spatial production patterns: two sources of each of two raw materials, one labor location.

any raw material from a source other than indicated, he will find it profitable to switch his allegiance. In doing so, he will effect the socially desirable substitutions between transport inputs on raw material from one source and the other and between production outlays at one source and the other.

Figure 46 presents a rather simple and conventional case of market delineation. It is fruitful to investigate a more complicated situation. Suppose we eliminate the ubiquities required in production and postulate that equal weights of the two raw materials and finished product are pertinent. Further, let us follow Palander and add to Fig. 45, as he has done, an additional source of the first raw material at M_1'; and of the second at M_2'. Accordingly, we derive Fig. 47 which is largely taken from Palander. Once again, aside from the district of household consumers served from the cheap labor point L, we obtain four groupings of industrial consumers, whose respective districts of household consumers are indicated by double-weight solid lines.[5] This time, however, production in each of these four districts need not be market-oriented.

In district a, households are served by producers who utilize raw materials from sources M_1 and M_2'.[6] Production takes place at the raw material sources, at market points, and at points where relevant pole lines intersect with an arc of a circle circumscribed about the relevant weight triangle. At the lower right, district a is partly bounded by district c. In district c producers at raw material sources, market points, and intersection points procure their raw materials from M_1' and M_2. District a is also partly bounded by district d. In district d all producers are market-oriented; they obtain raw materials from M_1' and M_2'. Because this pair of raw material sources is separated by a greater distance than any other relevant pair, its competitive ability is not so great.[7] The district of household consumers which this pair of sources can indirectly serve with economy is the most restricted of the four. It contrasts with the pair of sources, M_1' and M_2, which being the closest of any relevant pair serves indirectly the largest district of household consumers.

Finally at the upper right, district a is bounded by district b. Since M_2 and M_2' are equally distant from M_1 and since they supply the second raw material at the same price, it is indifferent whether production at M_1 is based upon either of these sources of the second raw material. Therefore, the subdistrict served by M_1 can be part of either a or b.

Figure 47 neatly illustrates how a market region of household consumers can be *indirectly*, via industrial producers, assigned to the market areas of competing raw material sources. For example, in district c none of the ultimate consumers procures his raw materials directly from M_1' and M_2. Rather, household consumers are served by industrial producers who directly consume the raw materials from M_1' and M_2 and who at times may be located at the point of ultimate

---

[5] These lines are loci of equal delivered prices to household consumers.

[6] Sources M_1 and M_2' also furnish the raw materials for the production of the goods consumed by households in the unmarked area tributary to L.

[7] Palander's diagram and discussion suggest that he postulates for the first raw material the same price at each of its two sources, and likewise for the second raw material.

consumption. Thus, boundary lines which pertain here to the division of a market region of ultimate consumers are more complex than those discussed in the first two sections of Chap. 7 and illustrated in Fig. 46. This is so because a complex transport-orientation problem as well as a market área problem is involved. Boundary lines come to be defined by substitution points which have reference to transport inputs on the finished product, transport inputs on the first raw material, transport inputs on the second raw material, and, if a cheap labor location exists, labor outlays and transport outlays.

It is to be noted that when we consider the market of industrial producers who are supplied with raw materials we find it to be discontinuous because of the transport-orientation problem which is involved. Industrial production occurs only on the four pairs of circular arcs, or within the areas contained by them, and at L. The sole section at which there is effective competition between alternative sources of a raw material, of the sort illustrated by Fig. 46, is along the straight line from M_1 to A. Along this stretch, industrial producers are indifferent as to the source of their second raw material.[8]

As is widely recognized, the sharpness of the boundary lines presented in Fig. 47 as well as in preceding figures is much exaggerated. Producers who compete for the household market do not behave according to the criteria which have been implicitly assumed. They generally do not establish at the factory a single price based on unit cost and applicable to all customers. They typically are able to influence price, to discriminate among consumers, to induce consumers by advertising, price cuts, or other means to shift their allegiance from a competitor. Producers relocate at times, take cognizance of each other's reactions, form coalitions, set prices and quotas. All these types of monopolistic and oligopolistic behavior tend to invalidate the simple, clear-cut boundary lines customarily depicted. At best boundary lines are blurred and tend to degenerate into overlapping zones.

Even if we were to allow zonal types of boundaries, cross-hauling, and market interpenetration in the above diagrams, we must recognize that the geographic patterns of production which they would depict have limited validity. When we treated, in Sect. 3 of Chap. 7, the simple case of locational equilibrium along a line where pricing policy and firm

---

[8] When the raw material sources are pulled farther apart, even this competitive stretch disappears. See Palander, *op. cit.*, Figs. 27 and 28.

It should also be noted that along stretch BD of Fig. 47, the two producers located at M_1' and M_2' compete for household consumers in a way consistent with the simpler framework discussed in Chap. 7.

location were variables, as they are in reality, we noted that many types of location patterns were possible, depending upon one's set of initial assumptions. Even the application of the powerful tools of game theory does not, at the present time, cast additional light on the elusive problem of rational behavior for a group of firms in terms of their pricing and location policies. Thus we must contantly bear in mind that Fig. 47 and similar diagrams pertain to a situation which abstracts from interest conflicts, undercutting and retaliation, advertising strategies, collusive action, market encroachment, and similar phenomena characteristic of firm behavior.

In addition to exaggerating the sharpness of boundary lines and the determinateness of locational equilibrium, we greatly overstate in Fig. 47 the number of producers. We derive this unrealistic result because Fig. 47 is a theoretical construction which abstracts from a number of forces, especially economies of scale both in production and transportation.

In Chap. 8 we treat economies of scale as a subset of agglomeration factors, localization economies and urbanization economies being the other two subsets. We recognize that these three subsets are not always clearly distinguishable from one another. Section 1 of Chap. 8 demonstrates how the economies of scale factor can be frequently embodied in a substitution of transport outlays for production outlays in general. The achievement of these economies of scale can be visualized in many instances as a movement along an outlay-substitution line on to a lower iso-outlay line.

The impact of economies of scale can be easily portrayed. In Fig. 47 the smallest scale of output is associated with those producers who are market-oriented. Granted significant economies of scale, we have postulated that output in each of the three largest market-oriented production areas will be concentrated at a single (central) point. These points are designated as I_1, I_2, and I_3 in Fig. 48.[9] We also assume that the smallest market-oriented production area, the d district, does not have a demand sufficient to justify a production point within its bounds when economies of scale exist.

In Fig. 47, the production points serving consumers along one and only one pole line also operate at a small scale. In a setting in which there are significant scale economies, we postulate that along any one arc production will be concentrated at a single point. Thus

---

[9] These points as well as others which are identified are only roughly located. We do not attempt in this and the following figures to determine a set of production points and market areas consistent with a given scale economy function. These figures are for illustrative purposes only.

we account for points P_1, P_2, P_3, P_4, and P_5 of Fig. 48.[10]   Finally, we posit that the scale of output at each of the raw material points and the cheap labor point in Fig. 47 is large enough to warrant the retention of each as a production point in Fig. 48.

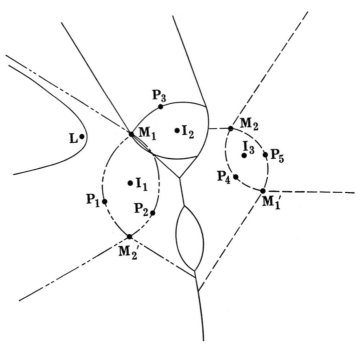

FIG. 48. Spatial production patterns: scale economies introduced.

Thus Fig. 48 depicts a situation reflecting the impact of the scale variable.   It portrays a much more realistic production pattern than that of Fig. 47.   Because only a relatively few production points are justified, each production point comes to serve a market area. The cases of production for a single market point or a single pole line are eliminated.   Market boundary lines, of the type illustrated in Fig. 46, become significant once again, as they are in blurred form in reality.   However, since there are many competing production sites surrounding any given producing location, the boundary line determining the market area served by this location is a connected series of different types of boundary stretches, where each stretch pertains

[10] We do not allow for any production points on the circular arcs enclosing district d and on the lower circular arc of district b.   There is no pole line market for the former and too small a market to justify the latter.

to the competition between the given location and one other producing site.[11]

As the next step in our graphic presentation, imagine that the sources of the two raw materials are multiplied many times so that for all practical purposes the two raw materials become ubiquities, each available everywhere at the same price. Further, take consumers of like taste and stamp to be uniformly distributed, and adopt Lösch's various other assumptions and conditions pertaining to his market area analysis, which we have noted several times. One can easily visualize how the pattern of production sites takes on a uniform character such as to yield the logically derived pattern of hexagonal market areas.[12] Thus, from this angle, the Lösch derivation can be considered as a special case of the Launhardt-Palander construction into which the factor of economies of scale has been injected. In his derivation Lösch has pointed up the conflicting pulls of the scale variable and the transport outlay variable; in essence, the basic substitution relation between transport outlays and production outlays. As with the Launhardt-Palander construction, the Lösch derivation is implied by the principles governing substitution among transport inputs once Lösch's set of assumptions is admitted. This is demonstrated in Sect. 4 of Chap. 10.

We proceed with the summary discussion of Chap. 8. Section 2 of this chapter treats localization economies, a second subset of agglomeration economies. In contrast to scale economies which are internal to a firm, localization economies are external to a firm. They are contingent upon the spatial juxtaposition of several firms of like character. They are reflected, for example, in lower cost service inputs when such juxtaposition permits the more efficient use of an auxiliary repair facility.

The realization of localization economies involves a physical move and additional transport outlays by at least one firm. At least one firm must and will find it profitable to substitute transport outlays for production outlays in general. Exactly which firm or firms will relocate and exactly which points will prove to be the points of agglomeration are questions which revolve around a complex interplay of historical and institutional forces relating to decision making and

---

[11] The interested reader may construct these boundary lines for himself. He is reminded that the market areas of the raw material sources and the cheap labor site are greater than the corresponding ones of Fig. 47. Production sites which effectively compete with the raw material sources and L are farther removed from them in Fig. 48 than in Fig. 47.

[12] See Fig. 51 below for an illustration of several nets of hexagonal market areas.

rational behavior by the firm. We have as yet been unable to unravel the concrete manifestations of this interplay. The clearest picture of the degree and pattern of localization and of specific substitutions emerges when we abstract from these forces and approach from a social welfare standpoint the problem of industrial planning for a completely undeveloped region.

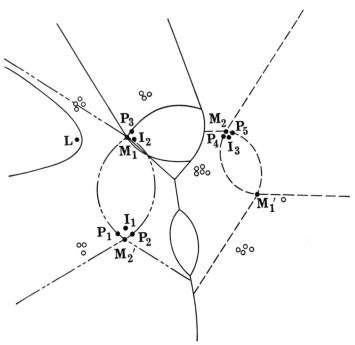

Fig. 49. Spatial production patterns: localization and scale economies introduced.

For illustrative purposes, we posit as only one of many possible situations that depicted by Fig. 49. (For the moment ignore the small circles which are not filled in.) In this situation, firms I_1, P_2, and P_1 have relocated around M_2' to realize localization economies; P_3 and I_2 around M_1; P_4, P_5, and I_3 around M_2; and none around M_1' and L.

Into the locational pattern of Fig. 49, we can introduce the forces associated with urbanization economies, the third subset of agglomeration economies. To do so compels us to expand into a multicommodity framework since, as already noted, urbanization economies refer to those savings in production outlays which are realizable when firms producing a variety of commodities agglomerate around a point. As we have discussed in Sect. 3 of Chap. 8, urbanization economies, like localization economies, reflect a complex interplay of historical and institutional forces. The factors governing the *specific* localities at which different degrees of urbanization economies become obtainable are beyond the pale of our current analytic frameworks. We can only make the simple statement that for many firms the advantages of

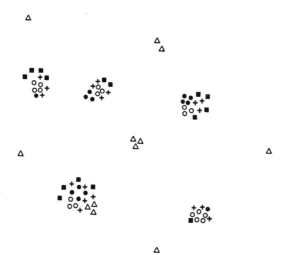

FIG. 50. Spatial production patterns: urbanization, localization, and scale economies introduced.

locating at an urban center outweigh the advantages of a non-urban location. The decision to settle in an urban area thereby involves substitutions among various outlays and revenues.

We portray the impact of urbanization economies with the use of Fig. 50. In Fig. 49 we have already noted the fairly concentrated geographic pattern of production to which localization economies lead when only a single commodity is considered. Suppose in Fig. 49 we also depict, for the given region or nation, the geographic pattern of firms producing a second commodity. These firms are represented by the small circles which are not filled in. Their pattern also reflects localization economies. A geographic pattern of firms producing a third commodity could be marked in Fig. 49. Likewise, for a fourth, fifth . . . and *n*th commodity. To avoid confusion these have not been presented in Fig. 49.

In Fig. 50 urbanization economies act to bring together the firms represented by the small black and white circles which would otherwise be separated as in Fig. 49. In some instances the firms producing the second commodity shift to a center of production of the first commodity; in other instances the firms producing the first commodity shift to a center of the second. To these sets of locations on Fig. 50 we have added sets of locations of firms producing a third, fourth, and fifth commodity, represented respectively by small black squares, crosses, and white triangles. In the absence of urbanization

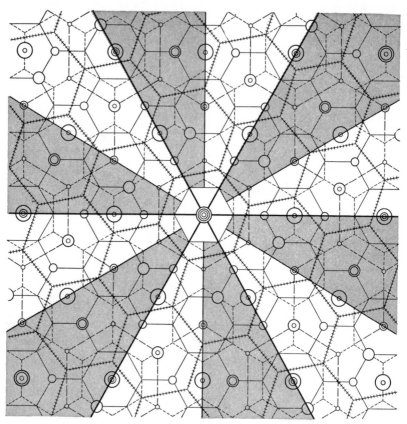

FIG. 51. A simple Lösch system of nets of market areas. (Source: Adapted from A. Lösch, *The Economics of Location,* Yale University Press, New Haven, Conn., 1954, Fig. 28.).

economies, many of the firms producing the third and fourth commodities would be situated differently. Not so, however, with the firms producing the fifth commodity, whose locations are indicated by white triangles. They are not led to relocate because of the pull of urbanization economies. Moreover, they are not very sensitive to localization economies. They retain a fairly dispersed pattern.

A second, less satisfactory way of graphically depicting the impact of urbanization economies is to follow Lösch. In Fig. 51, we reproduce one of Lösch's inconsistent diagrams. This diagram involves the superimposition of several nets of hexagonal market areas.[13] Associated with each net is a set of commodities resembling each other only in that they have market areas of the same size and are produced at each of the same set of production points. The several nets of market areas are arranged with at least one production center in common and so that, according to Lösch: (1) the greatest number of locations coincide; (2) local effective demand is at a maximum; (3) the sum of the shortest distances between industrial locations is at a minimum; and, as a consequence, (4) shipments and total length of transport lines are at a minimum. To this diagram we have added Lösch's twelve major radial transport routes; and we have indicated his six sectors rich in number of production sites (shaded) and his six sectors poor in number of production sites (unshaded).

Perhaps the most serious deficiency of this Löschian construction is that it yields different sizes of concentrations of industrial activity and thus jobs at various production centers, and yet it postulates uniform distribution of consuming population. It is beyond the scope of this volume to modify the Löschian argument in order to eliminate this inconsistency. However, it is clear that the Löschian diagram would need to exhibit for each commodity greater concentrations of market areas and producers about the central city (the common production center) in order to square with the central city's high level of industrial activity and large laboring population. We construct Fig. 52 merely to suggest such greater concentrations. In Fig. 52 at the lower right we have indicated a second, though less important center, at which production activity is concentrated. Also, below and to the right of this second center is a set of zones which is to be ignored for the present.

Because Lösch's construction implies a relatively high density of laborers and thus population at the core, the size of a market area in square kilometers necessary to generate sufficient demand for a commodity to justify production is much smaller at the core than at a great distance from the core. Further, at a great distance from the core, market areas must be much larger because not only are production sites and industrial population fewer in number but also, as a logical consequence of differential industrial population, agricultural activity is less intensive and agricultural population more sparse than in the immediate hinterland of the central city. Thus, we obtain a pattern of distorted hexagons (if we insist on maintaining the hexagonal form) which in general decrease in size as we approach the central city from

[13] Specifically, the figure covers only four sizes of market areas, the four smallest of the theoretical ones derived by Lösch.

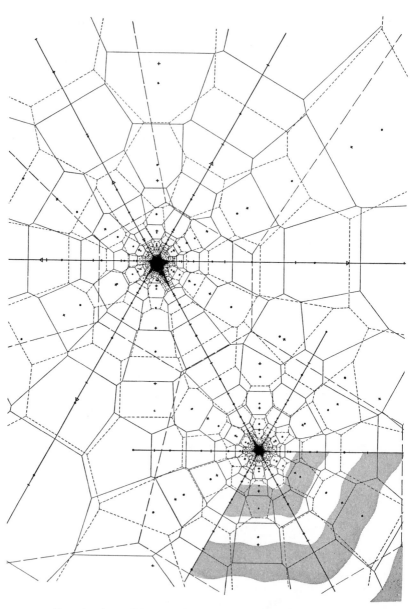

Fig. 52. A modified Lösch system consistent with resulting
population distribution.

any direction. In fact at the central city the hexagonal market areas are so small for certain commodities that they reduce to points when we attempt to depict them on a small scale figure. On Fig. 52 we portray this reduction to points for two sets of commodities, where each set would have a market area of different size in Lösch's scheme.[14] (To avoid confusion we present in Fig. 52 hypothetical market areas for only three sets of commodities. The reader may superimpose others.)

In Fig. 52 we have indicated a secondary center at which production sites and thus industrial population are concentrated. Once again, the hexagonal market areas decrease in size as we approach the core. Moreover, as Lösch recognized, economic forces lead to the development around each core of sectors alternately rich and poor in number of production sites. This is depicted with respect to both centers. Further, the number of production sites tends to be greater in any sector as the concentrations of production sites (cities) which the transport route coursing through the sector interconnects grow larger in magnitude.[15] This relation is shown in Fig. 52 by the heavier concentrations of production sites, and generally smaller hexagonal market areas, along the transport route which interconnects the two centers indicated. Actually, we should have presented in Fig. 52 secondary centers (smaller in size than the first) along each transport route and a hierarchical array of satellite centers, as is a logical consequence of the Löschian argument and as occurs in reality. In order to avoid a complicated and visually meaningless diagram, we have not done so.[16]

Thus Fig. 52 *suggests* the impact of urbanization economies upon the spatial pattern of production sites when the Lösch uniformity

[14] With reference to these two sets of commodities we attempted to adhere to the second and fourth smallest of Lösch's theoretical market areas. Because of specifications for constructing Fig. 52 which are cited below, we were not able to do so in any satisfactory manner.

[15] Unlike Lösch, we locate major transport routes through the heart of city-rich and city-poor sectors rather than at their boundaries in order to catch more fully the significant scale (urbanization) economies in the use of modern transport media.

[16] For examples of patterns of secondary and satellite centers which we have in mind, the reader is referred to the map: *United States, Population Distribution, Urban and Rural, 1950*, U.S. Bureau of Census, Washington, D.C., 1953; to population dot and land use maps for the area around such cities as Indianapolis; to Robert E. Dickinson, *City, Region and Regionalism*, Kegan Paul, London, 1947, especially Figs. 2, 5, 24, 32, and 48; and an expansion of a figure by M. J. Proudfoot in Amos H. Hawley, *Human Ecology*, Ronald Press, New York, 1950, p. 271. In addition, the reader may gain some impression of hierarchical arrangement from Fig. 53 below.

assumptions are admitted, except for modification with respect to population distribution. *The resulting pattern is at best only one of many which can be evolved.*[17] Moreover, because of the underlying uniformity assumptions, this pattern incorporates unrealities in many important characteristics.

A second basic limitation of the Löschian argument is that it pertains to situations where raw materials are not required (as in service activities) or are ubiquitous and everywhere available at the same costs. The argument therefore excludes that production (whether market- or material-oriented) where material sources exert significant locational pulls. Yet this is the very type of production which Weber has treated extensively and for which the Launhardt-Palander construction was designed. It therefore seems generally more valid to envisage an urban economy as consisting of a concentration of firms using localized raw materials[18] (such as the concentration at the lower left of Fig. 50) upon which concentration is superimposed a modified Löschian diagram similar to Fig. 52 to account for industrial, commercial, and service activities utilizing ubiquitous raw materials or none at all. Henceforth, we have in mind this type of structure when we speak generally of urban economies.[19] We shall outline it in some detail in connection

[17] In planning the construction of Fig. 52, I instructed my draftsman, Mr. Gerald A. P. Carrothers, to (1) retain the Löschian deduction that each producer of any given commodity operates at approximately the same cost so that the boundary separating the markets of any pair of neighboring producers is a perpendicular bisector of the line connecting the two; (2) adhere to hexagonal market areas in so far as possible in order to deviate as little as possible from the distinguishing characteristic of the Löschian derivation; (3) depict hexagonal market areas which increase in size with distance from the core in any direction; and (4) construct the hexagonal market areas so that, along any circle drawn with the core as center, the size of the market areas in general tends to decrease as we approach the transport axis of a city-rich sector and increase as we approach the transport axis of a city-poor sector. In the time made available, Mr. Carrothers was not able to adhere strictly to hexagonal forms. The extreme difficulty met in working with hexagonal forms only and, as a consequence, the need to reshuffle constantly the sites of production in order to meet this specification (for this reason the contrast between the size of market areas in the city-poor and city-rich sectors is not as sharp as we initially planned), strongly suggest that the hexagon is a pure concept much as is perfect competition. The hexagon loses much of its significance as a spatial form once agglomeration forces are admitted and, as a logical outcome, inequalities in population distribution recognized. In general, non-hexagonal forms are more consistent with the full interplay of location forces.

[18] Raw materials are conceived broadly so as to include semifabricated and fabricated products which are subject to further processing as well as minerals and other substances in their crude form.

[19] This is not to deny that urban areas may have as their basic activities functions and services and even industries which do not utilize localized raw materials.

with Fig. 54. But first let us proceed with our summary discussion of Chap. 8.

Hitherto, the discussion and figures of this chapter have referred to location factors as they govern interregional and intraregional distribution of basic industry and service activities and the urbanization process. We must now introduce those location forces determining the pattern of agricultural land use.

In Sect. 4 of Chap. 8 the interaction of these latter forces was discussed. The various adjustments of the agricultural farm enterprise were examined in detail. At any given location, the farm enterprise must select the correct proportion of factor inputs and scale of operations for the production of any given crop or commodity mix; this involves, in addition to others, the basic substitution point between land inputs and other inputs, between rent outlays and outlays on inputs other than land. In selecting a particular site for farming, the enterprise again substitutes between rent outlays and all other outlays combined. However, this latter substitution decomposes into a subset of substitutions: one between rent outlays and transport outlays as the farm enterprise considers locations at different distances from the market; and another between rent outlays and the sum of other outlays (excluding transport) since the price of a land input decreases with distance from the market and therefore leads to different factor proportions at sites at different distances from the market.

With respect to these types of substitutions, the general location analysis for the individual farm enterprise is identical with the general location analysis for the industrial firm. The farm enterprise intensively uses land inputs; therefore, to it, cost differentials among sites on land inputs are critical. The industrial firm which is labor-oriented or power-oriented uses labor or power inputs intensively; therefore, to it, cost differentials among sites on labor inputs or power inputs are critical. This firm confronts the same types of substitution relations as identified for the farm enterprise in the previous paragraph, save that labor outlays or power outlays take the place of rent outlays.

In this regard the traditional dualism of an industrial location theory and an agricultural location theory, separate and for the most part unrelated, loses most of its significance. Both the location of the industrial firm and that of the farm enterprise can be treated in the same general analytic framework.

When we view the location problem of the farm enterprise still more

For example, medical, educational, and governmental activities oriented to national markets can serve as basic activities.

comprehensively within a setting where market prices are given, or income and demand functions specified, and when we confront the enterprise with the problem of choosing a crop (commodity-mix) to be produced, we are able to derive a set of rent functions. We can do this by noting the substitution adjustments of the enterprise at all locations with respect to each crop. These rent functions, as they intersect, permit the identification of the familiar Thünen rings, distorted of course by any restraints we may wish to impose which relate to resource content of land, physical barriers, legal, political, and social institutions, etc. When we formulate mathematically the substitution relations governing agricultural land use, as in Sect. 5 of Chap. 10, we are able to harbor a still more embracive set of situations. This set can involve the use of many raw materials, each furnished from a single source or supply area, and a framework of many markets.

A general graphic representation of equilibrium agricultural land-use patterns, as yielded by the analysis, is attempted in Fig. 53. Here we consider a hierarchy of several urban areas and their agricultural hinterlands. A considerable distance intervenes between each pair of cities. Once again to avoid a confusing diagram, we ignore satellite type centers which may exist between any pair and which the reader should bear in mind.

About each city we have drawn Thünen rings. These rings are not concentric circles. Rather they are distorted bands. In part they reflect the impact of lower transport rates along major transport routes, which routes comprise the net suggested by Lösch and indicated in Fig. 51.[20] This net embodies those urbanization economies which stem from scale economies in transportation.

Many other forces distort the symmetry of the Thünen pattern about each city and of the boundary lines which separate the agricultural hinterlands tributary to each city.[21] To the right in Fig. 53 we have indicated an area of marshland which precludes any agricultural activity. To the left we have indicated an area containing soil particularly suited, and therefore devoted, to the production of a crop which ordinarily would not be cultivated so close to a city.

Because we have depicted the impact of only a few disturbing forces, Fig. 53 greatly exaggerates the symmetry of agricultural land-use pat-

---

[20] Again, we revolve the net so that the transport routes course through the middle of city-rich and city-poor sectors.

[21] The boundary lines are yielded by supply area analysis wherein any one commodity (or combination) of many possible ones may be yielded by a given unit of land. Note that one city's agricultural hinterland is entirely enclosed.

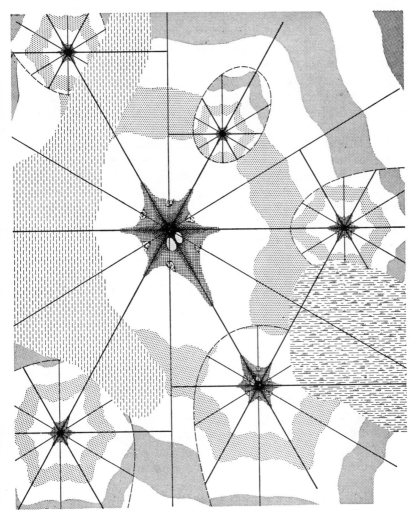

FIG. 53. An agricultural land-use pattern.

terns.[22] The pattern of reality is much more complex. Yet whether we consider the complex pattern of reality or the oversimplified pattern of Fig. 53, the relevant substitution framework reflecting the interplay of competitive forces is the same.

It should be borne in mind that the grid of agricultural bands of Fig. 53 does not conflict with the modified Löschian market areas of

[22] For this reason, we have not attempted to construct Fig. 53 to be rigorously consistent with our theoretical framework. This figure was designed to be visually suggestive.

Fig. 52. Within a city the market areas cover urban residents. As distance from the city increases, the market areas cover increasingly farming populations. The isolated dots at considerable distances from the city indicate small centers of retail and service activities oriented to farming population. To portray this consonance in the use of land we have superimposed upon the market areas at the lower right of Fig. 52 a set of bands indicating an hypothetical agricultural land-use pattern.

We are now in a position to probe somewhat more deeply into the impact of urbanization economies and to examine the pattern of urban land use which results from superimposing upon a concentration of heavy, localized raw material using industries (such as depicted at the lower left of Fig. 50) a modified Löschian system of nets of market areas (such as depicted in Fig. 52). For the more customary situation, the logic of this procedure has been stated.

As one of many suggestive patterns of urban land use, we present Fig. 54 from which boundary lines separating market areas of producers are omitted. Figure 54 is constructed on a larger scale than is Fig. 52. The central city is outlined in greater detail. Apart from the apparent effect upon size resulting from the use of a larger scale, the dimensions of the central city (when compared with those of Fig. 52) are significantly greater because of the city's expanded industrial base. The city's total economy now comprises those activities using localized raw materials as well as those using ubiquitous raw materials or none at all. Because of the addition of operations utilizing localized raw materials, the population and the income stream of the city have mounted, and in turn these have stimulated the expansion within the city of those activities using ubiquitous raw materials or none at all. These latter are for the most part commercial and service type activities. The locations of firms engaging in commercial and service type activities are represented by small dots.[23] The density of these firms is so great at and around the core of the city that the core and its immediate environs appear as almost a solid black mass.

Figure 54 portrays four industrial districts (light grey shading) greatly differing in size. Apart from those firms which manufacture miscellaneous items or use ubiquitous raw materials and which are indicated by a double dagger sign (‡), we have concentrated in one of

[23] The specific spatial pattern as well as the magnitude of these activities is clearly a function of, among other variables, the amount of manufacture which is based on localized raw materials.

It should also be noted that in Fig. 54 dots are no longer used to represent in addition the industrial firms utilizing ubiquitous raw materials, as was the case in Fig. 52.

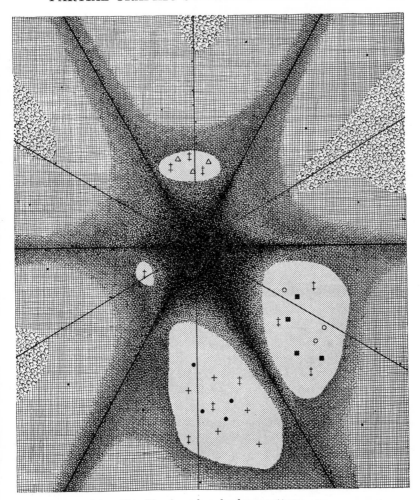

Fig. 54. An urban land-use pattern.

the several industrial districts all producers of any given commodity. By so doing, we retain a pattern consistent with the localization economies hypothesized in connection with Figs. 49 and 50. Thus the four firms in the lower left agglomeration of Fig. 50, which produce the first commodity associated with Fig. 50 and which are represented by a black circle (●), are placed together in the industrial district at the lower center of Fig. 54. The five firms producing the fourth commodity represented by cross signs (+) are located in the same industrial district. The four firms producing the third commodity represented by black squares (■) and the three producing the second commodity represented by white circles (○) are put together in a second industrial district. Lastly, the three producing the fifth commodity and represented by white triangles (△) are concentrated in a third industrial district. Together with the firms which manufacture miscellaneous items or use ubiquitous raw materials and which are present in all four industrial districts, these firms compose the industrial sector of the city.

In addition to designating areas of industrial activity and of commercial and service activity, Fig. 54 identifies a third set of areas allocated to residential use (shown by crosshatched shading, where varying density of shading indicates varying intensity of use), and a fourth set of areas devoted to parks and recreational activities (shrub-like shading).[24]

The land-use design of Fig. 54 represents one of many possible brews of (1) intuition, (2) logic and analytic principles relating to the interaction of general forces governing land use, and (3) facts. It is not a rigorous theoretical derivation. The development of a body of abstract thought on urban land use has not proceeded sufficiently far to allow a firmer statement on optimum urban land-use patterns. One important avenue along which such development might proceed would involve a comprehensive investigation of the interconnections of urban land-use theory and agricultural location theory. As indicated in the Appendix of Chap. 8, there are basic similarities between these two. As in agricultural location theory, urban land-use analysis must place central emphasis upon rent outlays (land values). Further, along the methodological lines of agricultural location theory, rent functions can be derived and used as allocators of urban land. To both the urban land user and the farmer, transport relations are critical. To the former these relations are in terms of effective distance from the core and accessibility to potential customers, although the user of any particular urban site does not customarily incur the major part of the transport outlays (both real and implicit) connected with the sale of product or service. As in the rural setting, we observe that in an urban economy complementary and competitive relations in terms of configuration of uses spatially juxtaposed critically affect unit production costs and accessibility. Moreover, technology, physical and cultural environment, legal institutions, and other factors serve to impose restraints as well as distortions upon otherwise rational land-use patterns.

---

[24] In Fig. 54 we do not purport to indicate all types of land use. Only four major categories are presented. As a consequence, we must define these categories very broadly so that they embrace other types of uses. For example, we include within the land area assigned to commercial and service activities that land required for governmental and institutional functions of a similar character; and within the land for residential purposes that land set aside for elementary school functions.

Despite these basic similarities, there are important forces influencing the array of urban land uses which do not have a correspondingly strong counterpart in the rural setting. As examples, we refer to those shaping journey-to-work phenomena, the pattern of shopping trips and social contact, advertising outlays, and quality competition. Nonetheless, we find a general substitution framework of relevance in approaching urban land-use problems, let alone in attacking the entire range of land-use problems wherein the competition between agricultural uses and industrial, commercial, and residential uses is encompassed as well.

To complete the graphic presentation of this chapter we should depict the flows of commodities and people connected with the various locations, land uses, and cities which have been examined. For the most part our graphic conceptions have referred to static structural situations. They have not underscored the kinetic characteristics: the constant stream of raw material and commodity shipments, interregional and intraregional; the journey-to-work patterns; trips to shopping centers and points of social·contact; intercity movement of people; various interconnections via communications media; etc. To illustrate all these diverse flow phenomena is beyond the scope of this summary chapter. We shall have reference to only one type, namely, that associated with the movement of selected raw materials and finished product. We leave to the reader the task of superimposing upon the patterns already depicted the kaleidoscopic variety of realistic flows.[25]

In Chap. 9, we partially analyze the interrelations of trade (commodity flows) and industrial location. Our particular concern is with the possibility of improving by reformulation both international trade doctrine and location theory, and thereby to obtain a superior set of analytical tools.

With examples of simple sets of conditions, we demonstrate how the distance variable, and thus industries locationally sensitive to transport cost differentials, can be incorporated into trade doctrine. This step involves the explicit consideration of transport inputs and consequently meets certain harsh criticisms levelled at traditional trade theory. Concomitantly, we achieve an extension of location theory,

---

[25] For illustrative materials on flows, the reader is referred to: E. L. Ullman, "Die wirtschaftliche Verflechtung verschiedener Regionen der USA betrachtet am Güteraustausch Connecticuts, Iowas und Washingtons mit den anderen Staaten," *Die Erde*, 1955, Heft 2; "Interregional Highways," *House Document* 379, 78th Congress, 2nd Session, Washington, 1944; and Gerald W. Breese, *The Daytime Population of the Central Business District of Chicago,* University of Chicago Press, Chicago, 1949.

namely, the restatement of transport orientation doctrine in terms of opportunity cost. We find, for example, that traditional Weberian doctrine might suggest in an international trade setting complete transport-orientation when an optimum solution would involve only partial transport-orientation. These reformulations of both long-run

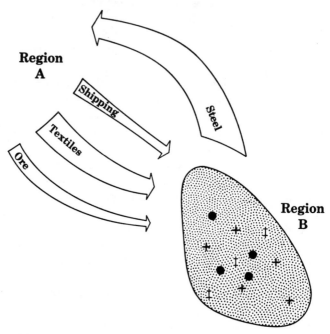

Fig. 55. A commodity flow pattern: intranational trade.

opportunity cost doctrine and transport-orientation dogma are in essence one and the same. They lead to a partial fusion of trade and location theories and pave the way for a more comprehensive integration.

Our examples clearly demonstrate how a change in the distance variable can completely revamp the geographic flow of commodities and the composition of trade and influence in a major way the industrial structure of nations and international location patterns. When graphically presented, these examples also point up basic interrelations with urban economic structure and land-use patterns.

To begin, we assume within a nation three regions A, B, and C with their central cities as terminating and originating points of commodity flows. We take the central city and surrounding area of Fig. 54 to be our region B. Of region B we reproduce in Fig. 55 and subsequent figures only its lower central industrial district. Except for relative position regions A and C are not indicated in Fig. 55. As with nations A, B, and C of Table II of Chap. 9, regions A and C together with region B are geographically situated as the corners of an equilateral triangle. We also postulate initially the same resource endowments, demand conditions, and production functions as are assumed for nations A, B, and C in Chap. 9.

Since it is clear from Table I of Chap. 9 that region C has an absolute disadvantage in the production of each commodity and since among regions within a nation long-run mobility of productive factors, especially labor and capital, may be posited, long-run equilibrium may be assumed to entail the shift of productive factors from C to A.[26] Trade between A and C would be non-existent. Trade between A and B would be approximately as depicted in Fig. 55 with B producing all steel and coal, and A all ore, textiles, and shipping. The producers of steel may be taken to be represented by the black circular marks ($\bullet$).[27] B's imports from and exports to A are indicated by arrows whose widths approximately represent values.

We now introduce national boundaries, in essence change the parametric value of the political variable. We assume regions A, B, and C are three nations as in Chap. 9. Since long-run immobility of factors is characteristic of the international setting, we can no longer postulate that factors will shift from A to C. Rather, the productive units remain at C, and C engages in those activities in which she has least comparative disadvantage. The tables and discussion of Chap. 9 spell out the long-run equilibrium position.

Figure 56 depicts this second situation as it bears upon region B. The change from an intranational to an international setting alters the magnitudes of the flows between B and A and introduces new flows between B and C. Also, we observe that the industrial structure of B changes somewhat. B engages in a new activity, namely, textiles. The firm producing textiles is indicated by a star sign ($\star$).

In Chap. 9 a change in another basic variable, namely, the distance

---

[26] This assumption oversimplifies any real situation. C may possess other resources and be in an advantageous position to produce other commodities not considered in this simple example. Furthermore, short-run immobility may lead to the establishment of industry at C which, once established, becomes economic to operate at C because of relocation costs and other socio-economic factors. Nonetheless, the validity of the general points we wish to make with this and the two succeeding figures is not impaired.

[27] To be consistent, we assume that: (1) the four firms in region B indicated by the cross sign ($+$) obtain raw materials from areas not indicated and produce products wholly consumed within the region; and (2) the three firms indicated by the double dagger sign ($\ddagger$) use ubiquitous raw materials and produce for the local market only.

variable is considered. The relative position of the three nations (regions) *A*, *B*, and *C* is altered. They are assumed to be situated along a straight line with *C* in the middle. Trade flows are completely revamped as indicated in Table IV of Chap. 9. In Fig. 57 we portray these new flows as they relate to region *B*. It should be noted that the industrial structure of *B* undergoes major change. Steel production

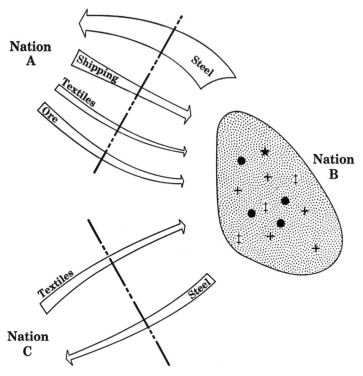

Fig. 56. A commodity flow pattern: international trade.

falls to approximately one-third its former level. Textile output roughly triples in size. These changes are roughly indicated by the numbers of firms producing steel (•) and textiles (★) in the industrial district. If we were to probe more deeply, we should unearth other changes. For example, steel and textiles have different input requirements. This fact implies change in the structure of subsidiary industries in region *B* which feed their outputs into steel and textiles. Further, steel and textiles generate different levels of income and, in general, have different internal multiplier effects, whether we consider industry, employment, or population. As a consequence, the total pattern of land use, as well as the pattern of each type of land use—commercial, industrial, residential, etc.—is altered. This is so not only because steel and textiles have different land requirements and different competitive potentials in bidding for land but, more important, because the structures of industry erected upon steel and textiles are significantly different and require different quantities and qualities of land inputs. Thus we see the basic interconnections among urban land-use patterns (and hence agricultural land-use patterns), commodity flows, and interregional (international) position.

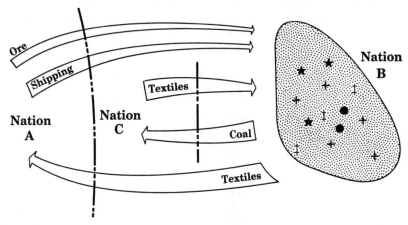

Fig. 57. A commodity flow pattern with modified geographic position of trading nations.

With Fig. 57 we bring to a close the graphic presentation of this chapter. This presentation, in particular Figs. 52–57, reflects the impact upon land-use patterns and commodity flows of the interaction of the various location forces. To the extent that a limited number of diagrams permits, there are embodied in these figures the several kinds of related forces: (1) those tending to transport-orientation and to labor and similar forms of orientation; (2) those stemming from technological change and from economies of scale, localization economies, and urbanization economies; (3) those leading to the formation of the standard types as well as the Lösch type of market and supply areas, of modified Thünen patterns of agricultural land use, and of the intricate patterns of urban land use; and (4) those, such as are generated by political boundary lines, which emerge from the broad social and institutional setting. Together with other similar diagrams which may be constructed, these figures can embrace different kinds of general situations—situations which may involve many regions and cities, where each pair is interconnected by diverse commodity and communication flows and where the population of each consumes many commodities, in the production of each of which many firms may be engaged, where each firm may utilize many raw materials of which each may be available from many sources.

As already intimated, the above diagrams may be taken to represent one path of integration, namely, visual integration. In Chap. 10 we attempt a second contrasting path of integration, one that follows mathematical lines. There we develop a pervasive and basic location principle. The marginal rate of substitution between any two transport inputs or groups of transport inputs, however the transport inputs or groups of transport inputs may be defined, must equal the reciprocal of the ratio of their transport rates, social surplus (however defined) less costs on all other transport inputs being held constant. This principle when supported by appropriate postulates implies various location theories: the transport-orientation dogma of Weber, Fetter-Launhardt market and supply area analysis, Löschian market area schemata, and Thünen agricultural location theory. Thus, this principle demonstrates a basic unity in much of location theory and permits considerable synthesis of location doctrines. Further, with this principle we are able to extend and generalize much of this theory to encompass a much broader range and a more realistic set of situations. Additionally, this principle and the mathematical formulations of Chap. 10 coupled with the notion of a spatial transformation function facilitate the fusing of location theory and production theory.

The above set of summary graphs and discussion bring to a close the analysis of this book. Needless to say, there is a tremendous amount of ground yet to be ploughed. The ways in which production theory and location theory may be interwoven and fused must be spelled out in considerable detail. The logical relations between trade theory and location theory need to be more thoroughly explored and a more explicit synthesis achieved. The transport system and rate structure must be considered as variables rather than as fixed data; to do so would facilitate the merging of the transport problem as conceived by Koopmans and the location problem as developed in this book. The concept of rational behavior must be sharpened via game theory and other conceptual apparatuses; once this concept is defined in concrete and precise (desirably quantitative) terms, its application to the decision making process of the firm will permit a more valid statement on the nature and conditions of locational equilibrium and a deeper understanding of the phenomenon of agglomeration, particularly where pricing policy is a variable and where firms possess considerable geographic mobility.

We need to develop new and superior concepts relating to the spatial structure of society. Spatial interaction phenomena, as manifested for example in the various empirical materials on commodity and communication flows and population movement, must be dissected with tools honed to a much finer sharpness. We especially need to probe deeply into space preferences, i.e., into man's propensity for intricate forms and patterns of herd existence and into the socio-psychological and biological forces which together with economic and other forces govern the spatial patterns of population settlement. These forces have a strong bearing upon urban land-use patterns and the mutual interdependence of the industrial, commercial, and residential sectors.

We must gain further insight into urbanization economies, into the complex interrelations of the sets of net economy curves, and into the structure and functioning of metropolitan regions as socio-economic organisms. How the structure and functioning of any given region are shaped and limited and how the location decisions of its firms are restrained by the region's total resources, income, gross product, and labor productivity, and by the tastes, standards, and expenditure patterns of its populace require thorough investigation. This type of inquiry is very much in the direction of regional science.

We need to pry into the space-economy with welfare considerations in mind, to relate spatial structures to social well-being and to introduce political variables and policy decisions as they reflect attempts to give a concrete basis to values and ideals; and we must study how they in turn influence location decisions and spatial patterns.

Finally, we need to develop, as will be attempted in a future volume, operational models to quantify various interrelations and to provide cutting tools more relevant to policy decisions. Whether we attempt improvement of regional and interregional input-output models, or linear programming techniques, or industrial complex analysis, or projections of gross regional product and its constituents, or gravity models, or other structural schemata involving ordered arrangements of groups and sub-groups and of aggregated and disaggregated sectors, or whether we aim at synthesis of the stronger elements of these models and analytical techniques, we must be able to present and handle more effectively the space-economy as a hierarchy of focal points and transport and communication routes. Substitution in the large must be assigned a much more significant role. Once again such developments would take us along the channels of regional science. It is our hope that these channels will be diligently explored.

Author Index

Subject Index

Abnormal profit, *see* Profits, surplus

Accessibility, as related to transport outlays (time–cost) by consumers, 205, 280
 effect of competitive land uses on, 280
 effect of complementary land uses on, 280
 effect on price of urban land, 200–205
 effect on urban land use, 200–205, 280

Ackley, cases of discontinuous consumer distribution, 165
 competitive behavior as affected by type of market discontinuity, 165
 determinacy of solution with market discontinuity, 165
 lack of generalized solutions because of spatially discrete demand, 165
 stability of solution with market discontinuity, 165

Activity analysis, as an element of regional science, 287
 as appropriate for short-run trade doctrine, 209
 need to synthesize with other techniques, 287
 use of, in simple trade-location case, 214n
  to determine transport rates and commodity flows, 213n
  to study structure of space-economy, 287
  to treat substitution in the large, 287

Advertising outlays, as affecting urban land use, 200–201, 281
 differences in, and overlapping market areas, 264
 effect on cost curves, 203–204
 effect on rent function, 203–204
 neglect of, in Launhardt-Palander construction, 265

Agglomeration, a pattern of, in an urban-metropolitan region, 278–280
 analysis of, as requiring a complex approach, 205n
 as an historical process, 180

Agglomeration—*continued*
 as involving increase in transport outlays, 179, 267
 as not affecting industrial distributions by regions, 172
 as similar to complementarity in land use, 205n
 caused by iron and steel development, 8, 19n
 centers, advantage of existing production points as, 180
 decrease in validity of Weber's assumptions with increase in, 179n
 effect of differential bargaining abilities upon, 180–181, 181n
 exceptions to Weber's conditions for, 178–179, 179n
 forces of, as basic to location analysis, 139–140
 from economies of scale, 173–176, 265–267
 from localization economies, 176–182, 267–268
 from urbanization economies, 182–188, 268–270
 function of economy of, in Weber, 178
 in competitive locational equilibrium along a line, 162, 163n
 industrial, differentials in land outlays as major to, 189
  importance of internal spatial dimensions of, 189
 in early stages of settlement, 2
 labor locations as centers of, 179
 need for critical isodapanes to intersect, 176–178
 of steel fabricating activities, 8
 of urban activities, as determined by rent functions, 204–205
 point of, and substitution between transport outlays and production outlays, 174–175, 179, 179n, 188, 265, 267, 269

293

Isodapanes—*continued*
use in analysis of urbanization, 183, 188
use to determine market area of cheap labor site, 259–260
use to determine market boundary, 259–260
Weber's use of, 130–131, 132, 176–178
decrease of non-circularity of, with distance of deviation, 141
definition of, as an incremental concept, by Weber, 130n
definition of, by Palander, 122
distance between, and likelihood of labor orientation, 141
effect of locational weight upon distance between, 141
effect of transport rate upon distance between, 141
movement from subset to subset of, as involving substitution, 123–124
non-circularity of, 141
subset of, and use by Palander, 123–124
Isolated city-region, *see* Agricultural location theory; City-region
Iso-outlay lines, *see* Price-ratio (iso-outlay) lines
Iso-product curve, definition of, 191n
use of, in agricultural location theory, 191–194
with scale lines, 191–194
with price-ratio lines, 192–194
Iso-revenue lines, use of, in determination of firm's location, 159
Iso-revenue-less-outlay lines, as convex (concave) because of firm's influence on price, 159
construction of, 133–134
for revenue potentials and transport outlays, 133–134
use of, to derive Hotelling's solutions, 170, 170n
to determine equilibrium point, 133–135, 159
to determine orientation to higher-price markets, 133–135
with revenue-outlay substitution line, 134–135, 159, 175
Isotants as market boundary lines, 239
Isotims, as contour lines of transport cost, 122
definition of, 122
use of, by Hoover, 122–123
to construct isodapanes, 122–123
Isovectors, as contour lines of transport cost, 122–123
definition of, 122–123
movement along, as equivalent to substitution between transport inputs, 123–124
use of, by Palander, 122–123
to construct isodapanes, 122–123

Journey to work, pattern of, as basic to analysis of space-economy, 281
effect on urban land use, 281
problem of, increase in with urbanization, 185

Knight, capital theory of, defects of its implications, 83n
distinction between resources and services, 89–90

Knight—*continued*
implications of, for theory of space-economy, 83n
Koopmans transportation problem, *see* Transportation analysis, Koopmans

Labor, aggregate demand in market for, 40–41
as a major location factor, 138–140
attraction of, as Alternativattraktion, 130n
as involving discrete geographic jump, 130n
cheap, as a deviating force, 216–219
as a location factor, 8–9, 10, 31n, 128n, 211–219
and minimum subsistence, 128n
causes of, 8–9, 10, 127n–128n
concept of, 127n–128n
effect on international steel location, 216–219
effect on textile location, 10, 140n, 211–219
efficiency vs money wages, 127n
from cultural factors, 128n
from low transport cost on food, 127n
in surplus food regions, 127n
possible inclusion in transport-orientation, 127n
force, structure of, and decentralization policy, 14–15
geographic distribution of, and economic activity between men, 53n
immobilities of, *see* Immobilities
market for, and nature of capitalism, 40n–41n
and types of migration, 40
productivity, need to study relations with metropolitan structure, 287
secondary, attraction for parasitic industry, 128n
definition of, 128n
generated by basic industry, 128n
immobility of, 128n
skilled, agglomeration economies in the use of, 182, 185
as a location factor, 10
increasing cost of from urban congestion, 185
spatial inelasticity of, 40
structure of market for, 40–41
structure of requirements for, and decentralization policy, 14
see also Factors; Labor costs; Labor orientation
Labor coefficient, as a measure for different industries of potential deviation to labor location, 141
as a technical concept, 36n
as labor cost per locational ton, 141
assumptions in the use of, 141
definition of, 141
general applicability of, 142
power coefficient as a parallel to, 132n, 141–142
pros and cons of ratio of labor cost savings to additional transport outlays, 142
relation to substitution between transport and labor outlays, 141–142
to establish priorities for attraction of industries, 141
use of, to derive ratio of labor cost savings to additional transport outlays, 142